Artificial Intelligence and Instruction
Applications and Methods

Artificial Intelligence and Instruction
Applications and Methods

Edited by
Greg Kearsley
Park Row Software

▲△

ADDISON-WESLEY PUBLISHING COMPANY
Reading, Massachusetts • Menlo Park, California
Don Mills, Ontario • Wokingham, England • Amsterdam
Sydney • Singapore • Tokyo • Madrid • Bogotá
Santiago • San Juan

Library of Congress Cataloging-in-Publication Data

Artificial intelligence and instruction.

Bibliography: p.
Includes index.
1. Artificial intelligence. 2. Computer-assisted
instruction. I. Kearsley, Greg, 1951–
Q335.5.A76   1987   371.3'9445   86-20655
ISBN 0-201-11654-5

ABCDEFGHIJ-AL-8987

Preface

I have been involved in the field of instructional computing for about ten years. During this time, I have designed and developed many computer-assisted instruction (CAI) programs, ranging from arithmetic drills for deaf children to telecommunication simulations for senior managers. Over the years, I have become increasingly disenchanted with the value of CAI programs. The problem is that most of our current attempts to use computers for instruction are too simplistic to have significant effects on learning. We need much more sophisticated instructional software to really help people learn via computers. More specifically, we need to be able to incorporate the kind of teaching strategies and subject matter knowledge possessed by good teachers into our programs.

For many years, I have felt that artificial intelligence holds much promise to improve the effectiveness of CAI programs because it allows us to use computers in more powerful ways. In 1984, I initiated a research program at Courseware Incorporated with the theme of "moving intelligent CAI into the real world." The goal of this program was to catalyze the transition of ICAI research from the lab to the classroom. An important aspect of this program was implementing ICAI programs on commonly available personal computers.

I feel very strongly about the importance of getting ICAI programs to run on machines such as the IBM PC and the Apple Macintosh. Most experts in the field of AI dismiss the current generation of personal computers as uninteresting and not powerful enough for serious AI applications. They work in research labs well equipped with expensive AI machines. They suggest waiting for the next generation of personal computers such as the anticipated "3M" machines (1 megabyte RAM, 1 million instructions per second, 1 million pixel displays). But to me this is unrealistic and out of touch with the reality of the nation's classrooms. The large number of personal computers now available in schools, colleges, and training centers will be there for a number of years. If ICAI is to have any practical impact on the world of education in the next five years, it will involve programs that run on those current machines. The challenge to the ICAI community is to learn how to develop programs starting with this generation of personal computers.

In our research program at Courseware Inc., we were successful in implementing versions of previously developed ICAI programs on IBM personal computers. Two of these programs, PROUST and SEARCH, are described in this volume. We were able to demonstrate that useful ICAI programs could indeed be developed on currently available personal computers. There is absolutely no reason why such ICAI programs could not be used in classrooms immediately.

This book grew out of the Courseware Inc. research program. It documents the attempts of various researchers who share the desire to move ICAI programs into the "real world" of education and training. It contains a collection of articles that describe various aspects of developing ICAI programs. The book is current and comprehensive in its coverage of the topic; however, it is *not* a text on ICAI.

This book should be of interest to many different types of people. It will be useful to computer scientists who want to understand instructional applications of AI. It will be helpful to educators and training professionals who want to understand the kind of instructional strategies possible with ICAI programs. It should also be a valuable resource for software developers who are interested in designing and developing AI programs.

I would like to thank Courseware Inc. for its support of this book and the research program that led up to it. I would also like to acknowledge the help of Robert Seidel and colleagues at the Army Research Institute who provided the opportunity for many of the contributors to share their ideas at a seminal workshop on ICAI. I would also like to thank Peter Gordon of Addison-Wesley for his efforts in bringing this book into existence. Finally, I would like to thank Wendy Ebersberger for her work on the index.

La Jolla, California   G. P. K.

Contributors

John R. Anderson
Department of Psychology, Carnegie-Mellon University, Pittsburgh,
PA 15213

Iain M. Begg
Synaptec, 2140 West Forty-first Street, Vancouver, BC, Canada V6M 1Z4

William J. Clancey
Knowledge Systems Laboratory, Department of Computer Science,
Stanford University, 701 Welch Road, Palo Alto, CA 94304

Paul Harmon
Harmon Associates, 151 Collingwood, San Francisco, CA 94114

Ian Hogg
Burroughs Canada, 6555 Metropolitan Blvd. East, St. Leonard, Quebec,
Canada H1P 3H3

James D. Hollan
Navy Personnel Research and Development Center, San Diego, CA 95152

Edwin L. Hutchins
Navy Personnel Research and Development Center, San Diego, CA 95152

W. Lewis Johnson
Information Sciences Institute, University of Southern California,
4676 Admiralty Way, Marina Del Rey, CA 90292

Greg Kearsley
Park Row Software, 1418 Park Row, La Jolla, CA 92037

Matthew W. Lewis
Department of Psychology, Carnegie-Mellon University, Pittsburgh,
PA 15213

Robert Milson
Department of Psychology, Carnegie-Mellon University, Pittsburgh,
PA 15213

Leon H. Nawrocki
Xerox Corporation, Box 2000, Leesburg, VA 22075

Ok-choon Park
U.S. Army Research Institute for the Behavioral and Social Sciences, 5001 Eisenhower Ave., Alexandria, VA 22314

Ray S. Perez
U.S. Army Research Institute for the Behavioral and Social Sciences, 5001 Eisenhower Ave., Alexandria, VA 22314

Robert J. Seidel
U.S. Army Research Institute for the Behavioral and Social Sciences, 5001 Eisenhower Ave., Alexandria, VA 22314

Derek Sleeman
Computer Science Department, King's College, Old Aberdeen, Scotland, U.K. AB9 2UV

Elliot Soloway
Computer Science Department, Yale University, Yale Station, Box 2158, New Haven, CT 06520

Patrick W. Thompson
Department of Mathematics, Illinois State University, Normal, IL 61761

Bret Wallach
Advanced Processing Laboratories, Inc., 4411 Morena Blvd., Suite 150, San Diego, CA 92117

Louis M. Weitzman
Navy Personnel Research and Development Center, San Diego, CA 95152

Beverly P. Woolf
Department of Computer and Information Science, University of Massachusetts, Amherst, MA 01003

Contents

Part 3 Artificial Intelligence in Training   111

6/STEAMER: An Interactive, Inspectable, Simulation-Based Training System

JAMES D. HOLLAN, EDWIN L. HUTCHINS, AND
LOUIS M. WEITZMAN   **113**

7/Artificial Intelligence Applications to Maintenance Training

LEON H. NAWROCKI   **135**

8/Intelligent Job Aids: How AI Will Change Training in the Next Five Years

Part 4 Building Intelligent Tutors

9/Methodology for Building an Intelligent Tutoring System

10/Theoretical Frontiers in Building a Machine Tutor

11/The TEACHER'S APPRENTICE: Designing an Intelligent Authoring System for High School Mathematics

Part 5 Implementing ICAI Systems

12/Development Strategies for ICAI on Small Computers

13/Authoring Systems for ICAI

IAIN M. BEGG AND IAN HOGG   **323**

Index   **347**

Part 1 Introduction

The two chapters in Part 1 provide an introduction to the book and the field of intelligent computer-assisted instruction (ICAI). Chapter 1 describes the major paradigms of ICAI research and outlines each of the chapters. Chapter 2 surveys past research in ICAI and compares the characteristics of traditional computer-based instruction programs with the features of ICAI systems. These two chapters should help the reader understand the basic issues and concepts of artificial intelligence as they apply to the instructional domain.

A number of points should be apparent after reading Part 1. First, ICAI is an emerging field that is ill-defined at present. The distinction between intelligent CAI systems and traditional computer-based instruction programs cannot be sharply drawn. ICAI programs use AI programming techniques and are implemented in languages such as LISP and Prolog. Developers of ICAI systems focus on problems of knowledge representation, student misconceptions, and inferencing. By and large, they have ignored instructional theory and past research findings in computer-based instruction.

Clearly, this book is provocative. Parts of it might disturb both advocates and critics of traditional computer-based instruction. AI researchers and cognitive scientists might dispute some definitions. Educators might question the instructional value of ICAI programs. Computer scientists might scoff at the lack of structure in ICAI systems. Training specialists might dismiss the whole thing as pie-in-the-sky.

Perhaps there is something important happening here?

1 / Overview

GREG KEARSLEY

Introduction

Computer programs that use artificial intelligence (AI) techniques to help a person learn are called intelligent computer-assisted instruction (ICAI) or intelligent tutoring systems. The design and development of such programs lie at the intersection of computer science, cognitive psychology, and educational research. This field is often referred to as *cognitive science* (see Fig. 1.1), although many cognitive scientists would not include educational research within its domain. The fact that ICAI research spans three different disciplines has important implications. It means that there are major differences in research goals, terminology, theoretical frameworks, and emphasis among ICAI researchers. ICAI research also requires a mutual understanding of the three disciplines involved, a very difficult demand given the problems of keeping up with even a single discipline today.

Luckily, some researchers have been willing to tackle such a challenge. In fact, ICAI research has been going on for more than fifteen years. A great deal has been learned about how to design and implement intelligent tutoring systems in this period. A number of impressive ICAI programs have been built and demonstrated. The chapters in this volume describe the nature and results of some of these projects.

Yet few ICAI programs are currently in regular use in classrooms. Why is this so? There are three major reasons why ICAI has not had practical benefits so far. First, ICAI programs are computationally demanding. Historically, they have required large dedicated mainframes to run on, and even then they have produced very slow response times. Suitable computers for running ICAI programs were available only in university and government research labs.

Second, the problems of understanding how people learn are extraordinarily complex. Almost every cognitive scientist would quickly acknowledge that our current theories of learning are woefully inadequate to explain or predict how people learn. Thus, the research basis needed to build intelligent tutors is mostly lacking.

Third, the number of scientists involved in the ICAI field is quite small. The intersection of computer science, psychology, and education shown in Fig. 1.1

3

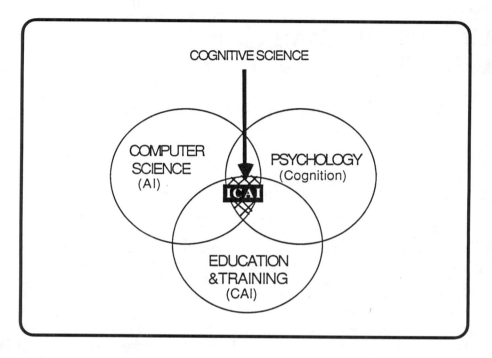

Figure 1.1 ICAI Domains

has not produced a very large set of individuals. Indeed, the total number of researchers active in ICAI during the first ten years of the field probably did not exceed 100 worldwide! This paucity of ICAI researchers has contributed to the slow growth of the field.

Transition Stage

All three of these factors are beginning to change dramatically. The current generation of 16- and 32-bit personal computers with half a megabyte or more of RAM have sufficient power and memory to run ICAI programs with acceptable response times. Thousands of such machines are now installed in schools, colleges, and training centers. In addition, AI languages such as LISP and Prolog, as well as expert system builders, are available for these machines. The implementation of ICAI programs on personal computers means that the programs can be made accessible to students and instructors as well as being portable across systems and locations.

The small core of ICAI researchers is growing quickly. Graduate classes in ICAI have begun to appear at many universities and colleges. Such classes are essential to creating a "pipeline" of future ICAI researchers. More ICAI research is being funded by government, military, and commercial organizations. Training and human factors specialists are becoming interested and involved in the development of ICAI programs.

Progress in understanding how people learn is slow, but a great deal of attention is now focused on this domain. Cognitive science is a major academic discipline and many volumes of research findings are being published. Much of this research is oriented to AI. Furthermore, a number of instructional scientists are attempting to relate current and past learning theory to ICAI.

In short, the field of ICAI is undergoing a transformation from a pure research stage to a developmental phase where it may start to have practical significance. The current volume documents this transition. It contains articles that describe the structure and function of ICAI programs as well as how they are designed and developed. This book is written for computer scientists, educators, and psychologists who want to know what makes ICAI programs "tick."

Readers interested in earlier descriptions of ICAI research and programs may want to consult Barr and Feigenbaum (1982) or Sleeman and Brown (1982).

ICAI Paradigms

The chapters in this book describe different types of AI applications, including tutors for mathematics, a diagnostic tutor for Pascal, mathematical microworlds, intelligent simulations, and expert systems for training. These contributions were carefully chosen to reflect the diversity of ICAI perspectives. Because the ICAI field is still in a formative stage, there is relatively little homogeneity.

Figure 1.2 depicts the five major paradigms that currently make up the ICAI domain. Mixed-initiative dialogues represent the original ICAI paradigm. In this type of ICAI, the program engages the student in a two-way conversation and attempts to teach the student via the Socratic method of guided discovery. The paradigm best fits conceptual or procedural learning tasks. The earliest ICAI programs, such as SCHOLAR and SOPHIE, exemplified this paradigm.

A second important ICAI paradigm is coaches. A coach observes the student's performance and provides advice that will help the student to perform better. Coaches are best suited to problem-solving types of programs (e.g., simulations and games). Examples of coaches are WEST, TRIP, and the Wumpus Advisor.

A third paradigm is diagnostic tutors that "debug" a student's work. These programs are driven by a "bug catalog" that identifies the misconceptions that students may have in solving a problem. Diagnostic tutors are appropriate for almost any type of problem-solving situation, although they are easiest to implement for problems with closed solutions. Examples of such programs are BUGGY and PROUST.

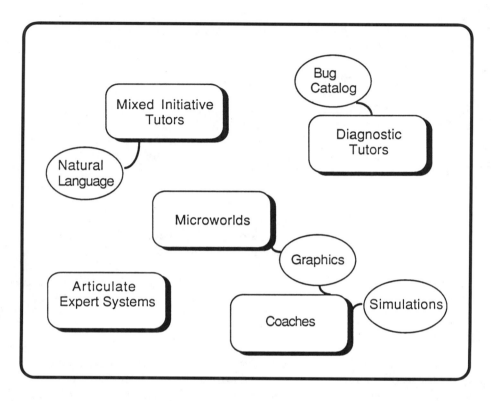

Figure 1.2 ICAI Paradigms

A fourth ICAI paradigm is the microworld concept. This involves developing a computational tool that allows a student to explore a problem domain such as geometry, physics, or music. Papert's work with LOGO is the best known example of this paradigm (e.g., Papert, 1980). Microworlds (and coaches in intelligent simulations) have tended to involve graphics more than the other ICAI paradigms. Microworlds are also the closest paradigm to traditional computer-based instruction (particularly simulations and game software).

The fifth ICAI paradigm is *articulate* expert systems (i.e., expert systems that can explain their decisions). Expert systems can be used as job aids and to provide practice in problem-solving and decision-making skills. They clearly have many potential applications in the training domain. However, there has been no widespread use of expert systems to date in either training or education.

When studying ICAI programs from different paradigms, it is important to keep in mind that each paradigm deals with a certain set of cognitive science issues and ignores others. No paradigm covers all ICAI concerns, nor does any existing ICAI program span more than one paradigm. As the field progresses, ICAI programs are likely to broaden in scope. Furthermore, new ICAI paradigms will undoubtedly emerge.

Despite their outward differences, most ICAI programs deal with a similar set of issues and contain similar components. For example, the most important issue in developing an ICAI program is choosing an appropriate way of representing the knowledge to be taught. Another major concern is how to model the student's current understanding of a topic or problem. All ICAI programs involve inferencing mechanisms capable of reasoning from one item of knowledge to another. Some of the techniques used to implement inferencing (such as forward or backward chaining and tree search heuristics) are standard AI methodology. The shared concepts and methodology provide ICAI with a common focus and a theoretical foundation.

To summarize, ICAI programs representing different paradigms often bear little surface resemblance to each other. However, the underlying research issues and AI techniques used in these programs are quite likely to be similar. This book attempts to present both the paradigmatic differences and the conceptual commonalities.

Chapter 2, by Park, Perez, and Seidel, discusses many of the ICAI programs mentioned above in more detail and compares the characteristics of traditional computer-based instruction with ICAI programs. A careful examination of past research in computer-based instruction is a good starting place for a book on ICAI. There are a legacy of lessons learned and unanswered questions that ICAI should address. The situation is analogous to the period in aviation when jet aircraft replaced propeller-driven planes. Much of the old knowledge of flying was still relevant but needed to be recast in new terms of jet-age technology. ICAI is the jet age for computer-based instruction.

Applications

Parts 2 and 3 of the book describe a number of different ICAI applications in education and training. Chapter 3, by Johnson and Soloway, describes the PROUST program. PROUST (Program Understander for Students) is a knowledge-based system that identifies bugs in Pascal programs and suggests how to correct the bug. The eventual goal of the PROUST project is to build an instructional system around PROUST that assigns programming problems to students, reads their work, and provides feedback. A complete discussion of the theoretical base of the program is given in Johnson (1986).

Programming tutors such as PROUST represent an important research area in ICAI. Earlier efforts in this area include the BASIC Instructional Program (Barr, Beard, & Atkinson, 1975), SPADE (Miller, 1979), and FLOW (Gentner,

1979). Although the version of PROUST described in the chapter runs on a mainframe computer, a version of PROUST (Micro-PROUST) has been implemented on an IBM PC.

Micro-SEARCH is described by Sleeman in Chapter 4. Micro-SEARCH is a diagnostic tutor for problems that involve nondeterministic search, such as algebra, trigonometry, or geometry transformations. The program constructs the search tree for a problem and helps the student work through the solution path. A prototype of Micro-SEARCH has been implemented on an IBM PC.

Chapter 5, by Thompson, describes the concept of microworlds for mathematics learning and teaching. A microworld allows the student to explore the objects and operations that characterize a particular domain of mathematics. The chapter describes the MOTIONS microworld: a program for exploring the Cartesian coordinate system that runs on Apple and Commodore computers. Thompson's work with microworlds continues an important line of ICAI research that includes LOGO (Papert, 1980), Smalltalk (Goldberg & Ross, 1981), and ALGEBRALAND (Brown, 1983).

The three chapters in Part 3 describe intelligent tutoring systems in the context of technical training. In Chapter 6, Hollan, Hutchins, and Weitzman describe the STEAMER system. STEAMER is an *inspectable* simulation designed to assist in propulsion engineering instruction. The program allows students to examine and manipulate the parameters of a steam propulsion unit via interactive graphics. Emphasis is placed on understanding the mental models that people use to reason about complex physical systems and devices.

Maintenance training is a significant problem area in military and industrial training and hence has drawn the attention of ICAI researchers. In Chapter 7, Nawrocki describes the application of ICAI to maintenance training at Xerox. Specifically, a simulation model of a complex photocopy machine was constructed to be used as an ICAI test bed. The model focuses on the electronic troubleshooting and diagnostic skills that must be acquired by technicians to service the copier properly. Of particular interest in this chapter is the realistic description of how an ICAI project evolves over time. Another major project involving ICAI and maintenance training is being conducted by the Behavioral Technology Lab at the University of Southern California (Towne, 1986).

At the present time, intelligent training simulations such as STEAMER and those developed by Nawrocki and the Behavioral Technology Lab run on dedicated AI machines. However, as the computational power and graphics capabilities of personal computers increase rapidly, there is little doubt that these programs will be implemented on inexpensive hardware that can be fielded in training centers.

The relationship between work in ICAI and expert systems is especially important for the training world. Chapter 8, by Harmon, describes how articulate expert systems can be used as intelligent job aids. Traditional job aids in the form of checklists and manuals significantly reduce the amount of training required for a particular job. Intelligent job aids, in the form of expert systems on personal computers, can serve a similar function for certain types of decision-making and problem-solving tasks.

Methodology

Parts 4 and 5 of the book focus on the methodology associated with designing and implementing ICAI programs. In Chapter 9, Clancey describes the theoretical work underlying the development of NEOMYCIN, a tutor for the MYCIN medical expert system. Clancey describes the general methodology for building a tutor. Of particular interest in this chapter is the discussion of how a tutoring program differs from an expert system. A more complete discussion of this issue is provided in Clancey (1987).

In Chapter 10, Woolf outlines some of the theoretical issues involved in building an intelligent tutoring system. This includes the representation of domain knowledge, teaching strategies, and discourse knowledge. Development of authoring tools for ICAI is also discussed. The chapter is illustrated with an example for teaching the physics principles associated with crane booms.

Chapter 11, by Lewis, Milson, and Anderson, describes the TEACHER'S APPRENTICE project. The project has two main goals: (1) development of well-designed and cost-efficient ICAI programs and (2) research into effective tutoring strategies. The subject domain is high school algebra. This system is based on John Anderson's ACT* model of learning, in which skills are represented as sets of productions. A prototype of an algebra tutor has been implemented on an IBM PC.

The two chapters in Part 5 deal with implementation of ICAI programs. In Chapter 12, Wallach discusses development strategies for ICAI on personal computers. AI and non-AI programming languages for ICAI are compared in terms of transportability, licensing, performance, and development costs. All of these factors present important practical considerations in making ICAI programs available on personal computers.

In Chapter 13, the final chapter, Begg and Hogg discuss the development of authoring systems for ICAI. Authoring systems are automatic programming systems that reduce the amount of programming and debugging needed. The availability of authoring systems for ICAI programs on personal computers may encourage the development of more ICAI programs. Freedman and Rosenking (1986) describe additional work on authoring systems for ICAI.

In the midst of all this discussion about ICAI methodology, it is easy to lose sight of the end goal, namely, to develop computer programs that significantly improve learning (or job performance in the case of training). To date, computers have not had the kind of dramatic impact on education they have had on other aspects of society (e.g., transportation, finance, manufacturing, and entertainment). Perhaps ICAI will change this situation.

I hope that this volume will make ICAI design and development techniques more widely known and will promote the creation of more ICAI programs. To the extent that such programs tackle difficult learning problems, ICAI may also make important contributions to educational practice.

References

Barr, A., & Feigenbaum, E. A. (1982). *The handbook of artificial intelligence* (Vol. 2). Los Altos, CA: William Kaufman, Inc.

Barr, A., Beard, M., & Atkinson, R. C. (1975). A rationale and description of a CAI program to teach the BASIC programming language. *Instructional Science, 4,* 1–31.

Brown, J. S. (1983). Idea amplifiers—New kinds of electronic learning environments. *Educational Horizons,* 108–112.

Clancey, W. (1987). *Knowledge-based tutoring: The GUIDON program.* Cambridge, MA: MIT Press.

Freedman, R. S., & Rosenking, J. P. (1986). Designing computer-based training systems: OBIE-1:KNOBE. *IEEE Expert, 1*(2), 31–40.

Gentner, D. (1979). Toward an intelligent tutor. In H. F. O'Neil (Ed.), *Procedures for instructional systems development.* New York: Academic Press.

Goldberg, A., & Ross, J. (1981). Is the SMALLTALK-80 system for children? *Byte, 6*(8), 348–368.

Johnson, W. L. (1986). *Intention-based diagnosis of errors in novice programs.* Los Altos, CA: Morgan Kaufmann Publishers.

Miller, M. L. (1979). A structural planning and debugging environment for elementary programming. *International Journal of Man-Machine Studies, 1,* 79–95.

Papert, S. (1980). *Mindstorms.* New York: Basic Books.

Sleeman, D., & Brown, J. S. (1982). *Intelligent tutoring systems.* New York: Academic Press.

Towne, D. (1986). *Summary of intelligent maintenance training at BTL.* Los Angeles: Behavioral Technology Laboratories, University of Southern California.

2 / Intelligent CAI: Old Wine in New Bottles, or a New Vintage?

OK-CHOON PARK, RAY S. PEREZ,
and ROBERT J. SEIDEL

Introduction

This chapter has two main purposes. The first is to stimulate combined and cooperative efforts between researchers/developers in AI (including ICAI) and instruction (including CBI). The second purpose is to provide conceptual guidelines for the development of future ICAI systems by providing a model of adaptive instruction. Detailed technical methods required to develop ICAI systems are not the concern of this chapter, nor is an exhaustive review of ICAI or CBI systems intended.

Prior to any discussion of computer-delivered instruction, one must first note the changes that have taken place in the field of CBI versus ICAI in the past ten or fifteen years. These changes have come about in the nature of what we would call CBI or ICAI based on the changes in the psychological theories that may or may not be in vogue at a given point in time. For example, in the 1950s and early 1960s and perhaps even into the early 1970s, the most prevalent theoretical position for the construction of programmed instruction and CBI came from an application of Skinnerian behaviorism or neo-Skinnerian behaviorism in which a linear small-step immediate feedback paradigm was what was advocated. Parallel to the Skinnerian influence on CBI was the historical thread characterizing "the computer as a tool." This strand was fostered in the 1960s and early 1970s by physicists and computer scientists (e.g., Luehrman, Papert, and Dwyer) at Dartmouth, MIT, and Pittsburgh, respectively (see Hunter, in Seidel, Anderson, & Hunter, 1982).

The opinions expressed herein are those of the authors and do not express or imply the views of the U.S. Army, the Army Research Institute, or the Department of Defense.

It was the work of the nonpsychologists that prompted psychologists to look closer at the extant theories of Piaget, Harlow, Bruner, and others for relevance to learning by doing, discovery learning, insight learning, and interactive and reactive environments. Another link to what is called ICAI came from the work of Brown and his associates at Bolt, Beranek & Newman and Xerox in studying the development of knowledge structures (like SOPHIE and others). Newell, Simon, and other researchers at Carnegie-Mellon University studied problem solving by building expert chess systems. All of these efforts combined with extreme increases in computing power and the low cost of the microchip to make intelligent CAI a practical research paradigm. The threads have not yet merged, however. Each has its own paradigm focus; for example, on the student model, instructional systems development, and so on, and a different language system, for example, psychology, artificial intelligence (computer science), cognitive science, and so on. This chapter attempts to clarify these issues and show how ICAI can benefit in a practical way by drawing the lines of research together and creating new wine—not just old wine in new bottles.

The use of computer-driven delivery systems for education and training has experienced a dramatic increase over the last decade. This increase in the use of computers as a delivery system can be partly attributed to the development of relatively inexpensive and powerful microcomputers. Additionally, this increase can be explained by the rapidly maturing field of computer-based instruction (CBI) and its demonstrated effectiveness in education and training (Kearsley, 1983; Kearsley, Hunter, & Seidel, 1983; Kulik, Kulik, & Cohen, 1980; Orlansky & String, 1981).

A more recent form of computer-delivered instruction is intelligent computer-assisted instruction (ICAI). ICAI is an example of the application of artificial intelligence technology to instruction. Although ICAI development is limited to laboratory studies, it has been offered as a proven solution to the technical and functional problems in training and educational technology, including CBI. Given the promise of AI technology for education and training, it is necessary to ask how to define ICAI and how it differs from traditional CBI. Is ICAI simply the old wine (instruction) delivered in a new bottle (software and hardware), or is it qualitatively different?

These questions are addressed in this chapter. First, we review the important historical development of CBI from early programmed instruction to ICAI. This review will show that ICAI is an attempt to further advance the current state of instructional technology by the application of AI techniques.

Second, we examine the components of ICAI and technical methods that are used to structure the components in the system in order to introduce the general characteristics of ICAI systems.

Third, we briefly review the development of representative ICAI systems. This review highlights the important characteristics of the system by examining the subject matter area and the technical methods used to develop the system.

Fourth, we discuss important differences between CBI and ICAI, which are mainly attributed to the different theoretical and technical backgrounds of the researchers/developers. It is anticipated that this discussion will be helpful for the researchers/developers of both CBI and ICAI to better understand the respective current state and needs of each computer-delivered instructional system developed by the other scientific community.

Fifth, we identify important terms used by CBI and ICAI researchers/developers and compare the syntactical differences and semantic implications of the terms. We think that the clarification of technical terms not only is important for the understanding of the systems developed in the other scientific field but also is helpful for facilitating communications between the researchers/developers in CBI and ICAI.

Sixth, through our review of existing ICAI systems and comparisons between CBI and ICAI, we have reaffirmed our perception that the next generation of ICAI systems should focus on instructional issues as well as functional and technical issues. Also, we have realized that future ICAI systems should be more complete as instructional systems than existing ones. To provide conceptual guidelines for the development of future ICAI systems, we propose a model of adaptive instruction.

Finally, on the basis of our analytical review of existing ICAI systems and the adaptive instructional model mentioned above, we provide several recommendations that should be considered in the development of future ICAI systems.

Development of CBI: From Programmed Instruction to ICAI

CBI has its roots in teaching machines (Pressey, 1927; Skinner, 1958), which were attempts to build interactive teaching devices. Underlying Skinner's work was a theory of instruction based on operant psychology (Skinner, 1968). This theoretical framework provided the basis for the linear programmed-instruction methodology that was widely used during the 1950s and 1960s. The influx of technology influenced Crowder's (1959) procedure of intrinsic programming, which was based on the nature of the student's response. Programmed instruction was the model for many initial efforts in CBI (Seidel & Kearsley, in press).

One of the most influential efforts in CBI was the work of Suppes and his associates (Suppes, Jerman, & Brian, 1968; Suppes & Morningstar, 1972). One of the major outcomes of Suppes's work was the demonstration that adding brief drill and practice sessions to regular instruction using a computer could significantly improve the student's achievement in basic skill areas. These programs also showed the kind of detailed performance data that could be collected to model the learner and learning process (Suppes, Fletcher, & Zanotti, 1975, 1976). Another important project (SOLO) was conducted at the University of Pittsburg (Dywer, 1974) to let high school students "solo" with computers, that is, learn to use computers as personal tools.

Three CBI system development projects initiated in the sixties have strongly influenced the field of CBI: PLATO, the IBM 1500, and TICCIT. Each of these systems had their own programming languages designed especially for creating instructional programs: Tutor (PLATO), Coursewriter (IBM 1500), and APT (TICCIT). The main goal of both PLATO and TICCIT was to design cost-effective instructional delivery systems, PLATO by means of many terminals sharing the same courseware and TICCIT by virtue of using off-the-shelf hardware components. In addition, TICCIT embraced a unique instructional design framework that influenced the development of courseware (Bunderson, 1974; Merrill, Schneider, & Fletcher, 1980). These systems were field tested at many schools and training institutes. PLATO and TICCIT eventually became commercial systems and are now used in many education and training settings. More important, these systems provided the opportunity for a large number of people to gain practical experience with CBI and resulted in the development of many system design and some instructional principles that were applied to subsequent CBI systems.

Prototypic CBI systems such as PLATO and TICCIT, which featured sophisticated graphics and complex answer-analysis capabilities, opened a new era of CBI. The emergence of easily available microcomputers with similar capabilities at a much lower cost has furthered the growth of CBI.

Although the instructional principles and strategies underlying CBI have not been developed as quickly as computer technology has, the overall quality of CBI has significantly improved by applying a systems approach to the development of the courseware. A systems approach requires several steps of procedural activities, including need analysis, design, development, formative evaluation, implementation, and summative evaluation. This process provides opportunities to incorporate various instructional strategies and computer software techniques in the development process.

The early paradigm of instructional systems development (ISD) was strongly influenced by a behavioral approach to learning. As the concern grew for teaching cognitive tasks such as problem solving, thinking, and language acquisition, however, CBI developers began to incorporate cognitive learning principles and instructional strategies based on cognitive models of learning. Actually, CBI has become an effective means for investigating cognitive learning principles and instructional strategies (Anderson, 1982).

Another important development in CBI was made in the structure of instructional components (i.e., subject content, student information, and instructional strategies). In the early forms of CBI, all the components were combined and stored in the same file. This "combined structure" caused a number of problems when modifying the content or instructional decision rules. For example, if large displays were stored embedded in the instructional decision rules and the displays were extended or modified, the complete lesson would have to be restructured to make room for the additional information or to connect the displays to the appropriate instructional decision rules.

In the early 1970s, Seidel and his associates (Seidel, 1971a; Stelzer & Garneau, 1972) at HumRRO developed a prototype system of computerized training for Army personnel (project IMPACT) in which subject content (e.g., text, graphics, etc.) and instructional decision rules were separated in different data files. Also, this system allowed a variety of activities to occur at the terminals simultaneously (for example, student presentations, course authoring, and background processing for sorting or compiling student records, etc.). This "separated" structure facilitated system maintenance because content or instructional decision rules could be modified without causing reformulations of the whole structure. IMPACT's authoring system made the entire process for retrieving, modifying, and restoring displays easy and simple. IMPACT's authoring system also made it possible for nontechnical personnel to perform most of the authoring chores. Although IMPACT's prototype system had a response-sensitive presentation ability, the instructional process, including presentation formats and the student/computer interactions, had to be specified in the program before instruction. Therefore, the system's capability to adapt instructional processes to the individual student was very limited. Also, the preparation of every display in prespecified formats and procedures was a considerable burden to the developers.

An attempt to overcome limitations inherent in the prespecified and frame-oriented structure was generative CAI (Uttal, Rogers, Hieronymous, & Pasich, 1969). Generative CAI systems had the capability to generate new problems from the combinations of different elements in a large database (for a review of generative CAI programs, see Koffman & Blount, 1975). However, the generative capability was limited to the simple drill-and-practice type of questions in arithmetic and language vocabulary. Also, the adaptive capability to the individual student's learning needs was minimal because the questions were randomly selected within a given range of difficulty level. ICAI is an effort to develop more powerful and accurate adaptive instructional systems by applying AI principles and techniques.

In the following section, we will briefly review the structure of ICAI systems and give some examples of such systems.

Methods for Structuring Instructional Components in ICAI

ICAI systems have taken on many forms, but essentially they have separated the major components of an instructional system in a way that allows both the student and the system a flexibility in the learning environment that closely resembles what actually occurs when student and teacher sit down one-on-one and attempt to teach and learn together (Roberts & Park, 1983). As in any other instructional systems, the components represent content to be taught, the inherent teaching or instructional strategy, and a mechanism for understanding what the student does and does not know. In ICAI systems, these components are referred to as the problem-solving or expertise module, student model, and tutoring module (Clancey, Barnett, & Cohen, 1982).

Expertise Module

An expertise, or problem-solving, module consists of domain knowledge that the system intends to teach the student. Because the expertise module is used to generate instructional content and to evaluate the student's performance, the domain knowledge should be organized within the structure of a computer program for the flexible manipulation of the data in the teaching and learning process. Representative AI methods used to organize the domain knowledge in the expertise module include development of semantic networks, application of production systems, procedural representations, and building of scripts-frames.

Semantic networks incorporate all the factual information necessary to teach the knowledge in a large, static database. A network consists of nodes representing objects, concepts, and situations in the domain knowledge, and links between nodes, representing their relationships. The method is based on psychological models of human associative memory (Norman & Rumelhart, 1975; Quillian, 1968).

Production systems are used to construct modular representations of skills and problem-solving methods. The basic idea of production systems is that the knowledge database consists of rules, called productions, in the form of condition-action pairs: "If ‹this› condition occurs, then do ‹this› action." Production systems were developed by Newell and Simon (1972) for their models of human cognition.

Procedural representations correspond to the subskills that a student must learn to acquire a complete skill being taught in a well-specified situation. Procedural representations act on and transform declarative information, which represents the static aspect of knowledge (i.e., facts) (Winograd, 1975). Procedural representations stress explicit control of the process of using knowledge or problem-solving (e.g., the process of proving theorems).

Scripts-frames are data structures including declarative and procedural information in predefined internal relations. A frame for generic knowledge has specific knowledge slots for facts that are typically known about the generic knowledge as well as attached procedures for determining the specific nature of facts. Script-frame structures have been developed by Schank and Abelson (1977) to represent sequences of events on the basis of Minsky's (1975) work.

Other types of AI knowledge representation methods include logic that is a kind of calculus of the process of making inferences from facts and direct or analogical representations as a way of representing certain aspects of knowledge in more natural forms such as maps, models, diagrams, and so forth. (For a thorough review of AI knowledge representation methods, see Barr & Feigenbaum, 1981, chap. 3.)

Student Model

The student model is used to assess the student's knowledge state and to make hypotheses about his or her conceptions and reasoning strategies employed to achieve the current knowledge state. Because most ICAI systems represent the student's knowledge state as a subset of an expert's knowledge base, the model is constructed by comparing the student's performance to the computer-based expert's behavior on the same task (or problem). Carr and Goldstein (1977) named this technique the "overlay model." Another approach is to represent the student's mislearned subskills, which are not primarily subsets of the expert's knowledge, as variants of the expert's knowledge. This "buggy model," proposed by Brown and Burton (1978b), may represent domain knowledge as rules and potential misconceptions as variants of the rules, referred to as "mal-rules" (Sleeman, 1982). Sleeman attempted to predict models of the student's behavior by using a production rule representation for the rules and mal-rules.

Modeling the student's knowledge and learning behavior uses basically two procedures: (a) charting within the knowledge structure network those areas which the student has mastered or has attempted to learn; and (b) applying pattern recognitions to the student's response history for making inferences about his or her understanding of the skill and the reasoning process used to derive the response. Clancey et al. (1982) listed four major information sources for maintaining the student model: (a) student problem-solving behavior (or performance progress) observed by the system; (b) direct questions asked of the student; (c) assumptions based on the student's learning experience; and (d) assumptions based on some measures of the difficulty of the subject matter material. However, most systems use only the first two information sources to maintain the student model.

Tutorial Module

A tutorial module is a set of specifications of what instructional material the system should present and how and when it should present it. In existing ICAI systems, instructional strategies for specifying the presentation of learning materials are basically represented by two methods: the Socratic method and the coaching method.

The Socratic method provides students with questions guiding them through the process of debugging their own misconceptions (Carbonell, 1970; Stevens, Collins, & Goldin, 1979). In the debugging process, students are assumed to reason about what they know and do not know and thereby to modify their conceptions.

The coaching method provides students with an environment in which to engage in activities such as computer games in order to learn related skills and general problem-solving skills. The goal of the program is to have students enjoy and learn as a consequence of fun (Burton & Brown, 1982; Goldstein, 1982).

As Clancey (1979) pointed out, not all three components are fully developed in every system due to the size and complexity of most ICAI programs. Most systems focus on the development of only a single component of what would constitute a fully usable system. (See Clancey et al., 1982, for a comprehensive description of these three components.)

Development of ICAI Systems

Carbonell's (1970) SCHOLAR system for teaching South American geography served as an impetus for the development of ICAI systems. The database of SCHOLAR is a complex but well-defined structure in the form of a network of facts, concepts, and procedures. The elements of this network are units of information-defining words and events in the form of multilevel trees. In SCHOLAR, the Socratic style of tutoring dialogue is used. The system first attempts to diagnose the student's misconceptions and then presents materials that will force the student to see his or her own errors (Collins, Warnock, & Passafiume, 1975). SCHOLAR's inference strategies for answering student questions and evaluating student answers are independent of the content of the semantic net and applicable in different domain areas.

SCHOLAR is extended by the WHY program (Stevens & Collins, 1977). WHY tutors students about the causes of rainfall, a complex geophysical process that is a function of many unrelated factors. WHY implements Socratic tutorial heuristics to describe the global strategies used by human tutors to guide the tutorial dialogue (Stevens, Collins, & Goldin, 1979, 1982).

O'Shea (1979) developed a system referred to as the self-improving quadratic tutor. This system has two principal components: an adaptive teaching program that is expressed in production rules and a self-improving component that makes experimental changes in the production rules of the teaching program. The system is designed to conduct experiments on the teaching strategy by altering the production rules. Data are collected on the effectiveness of the changes, and those modifications that result in improved student performance are incorporated into the set of production rules. This work is particularly interesting because of its adaptive nature but has not been investigated to any great extent. Another self-improving ICAI system of note is Kimball's (1973, 1982) self-improving tutor for symbolic integration.

Brown, Burton, and Bell (1975) developed the SOPHIE system, which is an attempt to create a "reactive learning environment" in which students acquire problem-solving skills by trying out their own ideas rather than by receiving instruction from the system. SOPHIE incorporates a model of domain knowledge along with heuristic strategies for answering students' questions, providing critiques of their current learning paths, and generating alternative paths (Brown & Burton, 1978a; Brown, Burton, & de Kleer, 1982). SOPHIE allows students to have a one-on-one relationship with a computer-based expert who helps them come up with their own ideas, experiment with these ideas, and debug them when necessary. The principles of SOPHIE have been applied to constructing a diagnostic model, referred to as BUGGY, in learning basic mathematical problem-solving skills (Brown & Burton, 1978b) and for developing a computer coaching model in a discovery learning environment (Burton & Brown, 1979).

The BUGGY program provides a mechanism for explaining why a student is making a mistake, as opposed to simply identifying the mistake. BUGGY allows teachers to practice diagnosing the underlying causes of students' errors by presenting examples of systematic, incorrect behavior.

The coaching model is developed to identify diagnostic strategies required to infer a student's misunderstandings from observed behaviors and to identify various explicit tutoring strategies for directing the tutor to say the right thing at the right time. WEST is a coaching program designed to teach the appropriate manipulation of arithmetic expression in a computer game environment (Burton & Brown, 1979, 1982). Another coaching program is Goldstein and Carr's (1977) WUSOR. WUSOR is designed to foster the student's (game player's) ability to make proper logical and probabilistic inferences from the information given in a game environment called WUMPUS.

Another diagnostic system is the Leeds Modeling System (LMS) (Sleeman, 1982). LMS attempts to infer (predict) models of the student's behavior by using a production rule representation for the rules and mal-rules. However, LMS does not have a capability to do any remedial teaching.

Clancey's (1979, 1982) GUIDON, another program for teaching diagnostic (medical) problem solving, is different from other ICAI programs in terms of the mixed-initiative dialogue by either the system or student. GUIDON uses the prolonged and structured teaching interactions that go beyond responding to the student's last move (as in WEST and WUSOR) and repetitive questioning and answering (as in SCHOLAR and WHY). In GUIDON, the teaching rules are organized into discourse procedures, and the subject materials (medical diagnostic rules) are hierarchically grouped into a separate system, called MYCIN. MYCIN is a computer-based consultation (expert) system for diagnosis and therapy of infectious diseases (Shortliffe, 1976). GUIDON's failure as a teaching system suggested that an expert system's knowledge base is not appropriate to use as the knowledge base of an ICAI system unless supplemented by other levels of the knowledge that help explain and organize the knowledge in the teaching process (see Chapter 9). Thus NEOMYCIN (Clancey & Letsinger, 1981) is designed to represent the subject material that a new version of GUIDON can use to articulate important teaching points.

Matz (1982) has proposed extrapolation techniques that specify ways to bridge the gap between known rules and unfamiliar problems. The extrapolation techniques project what is known, either by figuring out a way to view an unfamiliar problem as a kind of familiar one or by revising a known rule so that it is applicable in the new situation.

Suppes and his associates (Blaine & Smith, 1977; Suppes, 1981) also applied AI techniques to the development of a proof checker (EXCHECK) capable of understanding the validity of a student's proof. EXCHECK has no student model, but its inference procedures in the expertise module allow it to make assumptions about students' reasoning and track their solutions, thus providing a "reactive environment" similar to that of SOPHIE.

Most existing ICAI systems are thoroughly described in two books edited by Barr and Feigenbaum (1982) and Sleeman and Brown (1982), which are the two best sources about ICAI, with the exception of one important line of research based on Anderson's ACT theory (1982). The ACT research apparently was not included in the other books because the primary purpose and methodological approach taken in the development process are radically different from those of most other systems. ACT was the basis for a computerized learning system that simulates a cognitive model of the student's problem-solving behavior. Anderson and his associates (Anderson, Boyle, & Reiser, 1985; Anderson & Reiser, 1985) developed computer tutoring systems for teaching LISP programming and high school geometry on the basis of the cognitive model implemented by the ACT system. The tutoring systems have incorporated a set of cognitive principles that are derived from the cognitive model in ACT (Anderson, Boyle, Farrell, & Reiser, 1985). However, ACT does not represent the general characteristics of ICAI systems that are developed from the application of specific AI techniques (see the description of ICAI components above). Thus we also did not consider ACT in our discussion about ICAI in the remainder of this chapter, although its contribution to the development of ICAI systems is significant.

Another application of AI techniques in CBI is to create a new educational environment through full control of the learning experience by the student. For example, Papert's (1980) LOGO was a programming language developed to help children learn problem-solving strategies by providing opportunities to explore their own ideas in the given situation. The SMALLTALK project conducted at the Xerox Palo Alto Research Center (Kay & Goldberg, 1977) is similar in a number of respects to the LOGO effort. It was an attempt to develop an easy-to-use, high-level programming language (SMALLTALK) within the context of creating a learning environment. Taylor (1980) calls this approach "use of computer as a tutee" to distinguish it from other approaches in which the computer is used as a "tutor." However, this approach is not considered as a type of ICAI in this article because of its different educational perspective and operational procedures.

Fletcher (1984) conducted an extensive review of ICAI systems. The results of his review are presented in Table 2.1. This table compares several systems in terms of the subject matter area and the methods used to represent the functions of the three components of an instructional system: knowledge representation, student model, and tutorial strategy. The table also provides a main reference for each system.

Although Table 2.1 appears to show that every system contains functions representing the three components of instruction, one should not infer that every system has all three modules. Most systems focus on the development of a single module of what would constitute a fully usable system; the functions of representing the three instructional components are integrated into the single-module structure (Clancey et al., 1982). Some systems do not even have the functions for representing one or two instructional components. For example, PROUST (see Chapter 3) and STEAMER (see Chapter 6) do not have functions to provide direct instruction. In our view, a complete ICAI system should have functions for representing all three instructional components (i.e., representation of knowledge, modeling of learning behavior, and providing instruction), regardless of its structure (single module or multiple modules).

Differences between ICAI and CBI

As we discussed in the historical development of CBI, ICAI is an attempt to further advance the current state of CBI by the application of AI techniques. However, ICAI is fundamentally different from traditional CBI in terms of the basic philosophies underlying the structures and development processes of the systems because it has evolved from the field of computer science (particularly AI) and not from instructional psychology or technology. In this section, we attempt to discuss the important differences for researchers/developers of both CBI and ICAI to better understand the respective current state and needs of computer-delivered instructional systems developed by the scientific community.

Development Goals

Traditional CBI has been developed by educational researchers and training developers to solve their practical problems by applying computer technology. In contrast, ICAI has been initiated primarily by computer scientists to explore

System	Subject Matter	Knowledge Base	Student Model	Tutor Model	Reference
SCHOLAR	Geography	Semantic network	Overlay with importance weights	Socratic dialogue management	Carbonell, 1970
WHY	Causes of rainfall	Scripts	Misconception identifier	Socratic dialogue	Stevens et al., 1982
INTEGRATE	Symbolic integration	Self-improving rule–based representation	Overlay	Reactive environment with adviser	Kimball, 1982
SOPHIE	Electronic trouble-shooting	Semantic network with circuit simulator	Overlay	Reactive environment with guided interactions	Brown et al., 1982
WEST	Arithmetic expressions	Rule-based representation	Overlay	Reactive environment with coaching	Burton & Brown, 1979
BUGGY	Subtraction	Procedural network	Misconception identifier	Reactive environment with adviser	Brown & Burton, 1978b
WUSOR	Logical relations	Genetic graph: network	Overlay with familiarity weights	Reactive environment with coaching	Goldstein, 1982
EXCHECK	Logic and set theory	Rule-based representation with logic interpreter	Overlay	Reactive environment with adviser	Suppes, 1981
BIP	Programming in BASIC	Rule-based representation	Overlay	Reactive environment with curriculum net and adviser	Barr et al., 1976

Table 2.1 Some Intelligent Instructional Systems (adapted from Fletcher, 1984, with the author's permission)

System	Subject Matter	Knowledge Base	Student Model	Tutor Model	Reference
SPADE	Programming in LOGO	Rule-based representation	Overlay	Reactive environment with coaching	Miller, 1982
ALGEBRA	Applied algebra	Rule-based representation	Overlay	Reactive environment with coaching	Lantz et al., 1983
LMS	Algebraic procedures	Rule- and mal-rule–based representation	Rule-based diagnostic representation (BUGGY)[a]	Reactive environment (no tutoring function)[a]	Sleeman, 1982
QUADRATIC	Quadratic equations	Self-improving rule–based representation	Overlay	Reactive environment with adviser	O'Shea, 1982
GUIDON	Infectious diseases	Rule-based representation	Overlay with application probability	Reactive environment with structural interactions	Clancey, 1982
PROUST	Programming in Pascal	Semantic network	Misconception identifier	Reactive environment with adviser (no tutoring function)[a]	Soloway et al., 1983
STEAMER	Steamship propulsion	Device model (procedural network)[a]	Overlay onto device model (no student modeling function)[a]	Reactive environment with adviser (no tutoring function)[a]	Williams et al., 1981

[a]Additions in parentheses are ours.

Table 2.1 Some Intelligent Instructional Systems (cont.)

the capability of AI techniques in the process of learning and teaching. Therefore, the focus of ICAI projects has been on the technical aspects of the system
(e.g., knowledge representation techniques, natural language dialogues, inferencing mechanisms, etc.) rather than on instructional or domain features.
The initial interest of ICAI researchers was in the manipulation of specific AI
techniques in order to observe how they work in the instructional process
rather than to improve instructional effectiveness and efficiency of the systems.

Theoretical Bases

Most CBI systems have been criticized as being developed in a theoretical
vacuum (Kearsley & Seidel, 1985). However, most CBI programs have incorporated some principles of learning and instruction in one form or another. For
example, the early forms of CBI were strongly influenced by Skinnerian
behaviorism. Although a programmed-instruction paradigm is still popular
among CBI developers, it has been improved by adopting a "systems approach"
to instructional development. A systems approach allows CBI authors to incorporate various instructional principles and research findings in the design and
development process. However, the application of the systems approach to CBI
development is limited by the developer's knowledge in the field of learning
and instruction and the system's hardware and software capability.

Along with the exploration of AI techniques in the instructional process,
however, many ICAI projects have sought to better understand cognitive processes involved in learning and teaching specific tasks. For example, "overlay"
and "buggy" methods are designed to make inferences about the student's
cognitive structure and the process involved in learning the given task. Some
of the knowledge representation methods (e.g., semantic networks) are also
developed on the basis of cognitive models of human memory and cognition.
Thus many ICAI researchers designed and built their systems on the theoretical
notions of cognitive science that have grown out of information-processing
theory in cognitive psychology.

System Structures and Functions

In most CBI systems, all of the instructional components (i.e., subject content,
student information, and instructional strategy) are stored and implemented in
a single structure. Although some systems have separate modules to store the
instructional components independently, their operational procedures (including instructional presentations) are still determined by preentered specific
pieces of information and by predefined algorithmic processes. This style of CBI
is called "ad-hoc, frame-oriented" CAI (Carbonell, 1970). In the frame-oriented
structure, the student has little or no initiative in the instructional processes.

ICAI, on the other hand, is generative in that it processes knowledge stored in the system to ask questions and respond to the student. Many ICAI systems have abilities to carry on natural language dialogues with the student. The natural language dialogue ability allows "mixed initiatives" between the student and computer, with questions and answers from both sides. That is, ICAI systems use spontaneous inferential processes to diagnose the student's learning needs and prescribe instructional treatments. In contrast, CBI systems use prespecified algorithmic processes; the instructional process is always initiated by the system.

Instructional Principles

Because traditional CBI has been developed as an instructional delivery system, the basic instructional principles used in CBI are not much different from the common approaches practiced in schools and training environments. An exception is the application of the computer's interactive characteristics for individualized instruction. In schools and training environments, teachers and trainers should successfully communicate their knowledge to the students to achieve instructional objectives within given constraints (e.g., time). Thus most instructional methods take a teacher-centered expository form, which requires the student first to understand the teacher's instruction and then to practice given questions to reinforce this understanding. This teacher-centered expository approach was strongly influenced by Skinnerian behaviorism. However, specific methods applied in the expository approach are not limited to behavioristic principles. Actually, many different types of instructional strategies have been applied in CBI, depending on the purpose of the instruction (Hunter, Kastner, Rubin, & Seidel, 1975, chap. 4), the characteristics of students, and the subject matter. Furthermore, as we discussed earlier, many CBI developers are beginning to incorporate cognitive principles and strategies in their development process as the concern for teaching cognitive tasks grows and many instructional psychologists' theoretical perspectives shift from behaviorism to cognitive psychology.

In contrast, ICAI researchers adopted Dewey's philosophy, "learning-by-doing," as the basic instructional approach in the system (Dewey, 1910; Sleeman & Brown, 1982). In this approach, students are required to engage actively in the instructional process to formulate and test their own ideas and to witness the consequences resulting from the system's reactions to their behavior (Brown, Burton, & de Kleer, 1982). Brown, Burton, and Bell (1975) argue that this approach elicits optimal learning and refer to the conditions for this approach as the "reactive learning environment." Thus, in most ICAI systems, instructional methods take a student-centered discovery form, and tutorial dialogues are basically determined by the student's conceptual understandings and learning behaviors. Actually, the provision of a "reactive learning environment" has historically been used in the development of curriculum models by early childhood educators following Piagetian theory (Piaget, 1954; Piaget & Inhelder, 1964).

Methods of Structuring Knowledge

In CBI, task analysis is a common method to identify tasks and subtasks to be taught and content elements required to learn the tasks. Two common methods of task analysis are an algorithmic approach and a hierarchical approach. A combination of the two methods may be used for a complex psychomotor skill or a cognitive problem-solving task.

In ICAI systems, methods for structuring knowledge to be taught are determined from the AI knowledge representation technique, which is selected by the developer to organize the knowledge into a data structure. Whereas task analysis used by CBI developers is a systematic method to identify all necessary subtasks and content elements required to learn the final task, AI knowledge representation methods are techniques to organize knowledge (including the subtasks and content elements) into a data structure for manipulation in the computer system. Although task analysis is not an inherent element of the knowledge representation techniques, few ICAI researchers have applied common task analysis methods or proposed new methods in the development of the knowledge base (or expertise module). The GOMS model proposed by Card, Moran, and Newell (1983) seems to be an indication of some AI researchers' realization of the importance of task analysis in the development of the knowledge base. The GOMS model is a task analysis procedure to identify four components of the learner's cognitive structure: (1) a set of goals, (2) a set of operators, (3) a set of methods for achieving the goals, and (4) a set of selection rules for choosing among competing achievement methods for goals.

Methods of Student Modeling

The early forms of CBI took programmed-instruction paradigms, and most instructional strategies, including sequence, were determined from binary judgments on the student's responses (correct or incorrect). However, following Atkinson's (1972, 1976) mathematical model for selecting optimal instructional presentation of items, a number of quantitative procedures have been applied to model the student's learning and to select instructional treatments on the basis of the quantitative information. For example, Suppes, Fletcher, and Zanotti (1975, 1976) used a regression analysis method for predicting the student's learning achievement and for selecting optimal instructional treatments. Hansen, Ross, and Rakow (1977) also developed a regression model for adaptive instruction in CBI. Tennyson and his associates (Park & Tennyson, 1980; Rothen

& Tennyson, 1978) applied a Bayesian probability theorem for the development of an adaptive CBI system. In the quantitative model, the student learning is characterized in probabilistic terms. (For a review of quantitative models of adaptive instruction, see Park & Tennyson, 1983, and Tennyson & Park, 1984).

Development of a powerful student model has been a main research issue for many ICAI projects (e.g., BUGGY, LMS, and ALGEBRA). The student modeling method used in ICAI is basically qualitative. In a qualitative model, students' learning is assessed from the analysis of their responses (or response patterns); the modeling is a process of making inferences about their conceptions and misconceptions. The qualitative model relies on the developer's subjective judgment, formalized in the system, of the student's response (frequently, a single response more than a response pattern), rather than an objective criterion. However, an effort to combine the two approaches (quantitative and qualitative) in the student modeling process has not yet been proposed.

Instructional Formats

The early CBI programs were developed primarily to supplement the principal instructional process, and the most common CBI format was drill and practice. However, the format has been diversified as CBI has become a main instructional delivery system. Common CBI formats include tutorial, drill and practice, games, and simulations. Games are divided into two types: intrinsic games, in which learning the game rules and skills constitute the main instructional objectives; and extrinsic games, in which the games are used as auxiliary devices for facilitating learning and maintaining motivation (see Malone, 1981).

Most simulations are divided into three types: physical, situational, and process (see Alessi & Trollip, 1985). Although the CBI formats are somewhat arbitrarily classified for practical convenience, the classification indicates the variety of CBI applications. In contrast, most ICAI systems are basically classified into two types of instructional formats: tutorial and games. A tutorial in ICAI is somewhat different from a tutorial in CBI in that an ICAI tutorial is basically a series of question-and-response exchanges, while a CBI tutorial emphasizes the system's expository presentation of instruction. Although some questions may follow the expository presentation in CBI, the questions are to assure or reinforce the student's understanding of the presentation. In ICAI, however, the process of question-and-response exchanges is to make inferences about the student's conceptual understanding of the given problem and to determine the instructional process to be immediately followed.

CBI and ICAI also have different purposes for using games. In CBI, games are used to teach the gaming rules and skills (in intrinsic games) or to maintain the student's motivation (in extrinsic games). In contrast, the primary purpose of using games in ICAI is to provide a "reactive learning environment" in which students explore their own interests (e.g., WEST, WUSOR). ICAI games seem to be similar to extrinsic games in CBI because the subject content to be taught is independent of the gaming structure and rules. However, providing a reactive learning environment is different from using games as simple motivational devices because students are expected to develop a higher level of knowledge (e.g., problem-solving strategies) than that directly required in the given subject content by exploring and testing their own interests and ideas in the gaming process.

Subject Matter Areas

CBI has been widely used in a variety of subject matter areas, from highly structured math and science to relatively unstructured language areas and even the arts. However, most applications of ICAI have been limited to relatively well-structured subject areas such as mathematics (e.g., WEST, WUSOR, BUGGY, LMS), computer programming (e.g., BIP, PROUST, SPADE), medical diagnosis (e.g., GUIDON), and electronics (e.g., SOPHIE). The limited application of ICAI to relatively well-structured subject areas is partially ascribed to the ICAI authors' primary purpose of their projects. As we discussed earlier, their initial goal was to explore the capability of AI technology in the instructional process rather than to develop usable instructional systems. Thus most ICAI researchers seemed to have first chosen AI techniques to explore in the systems and then selected subject matter areas that were most appropriate for the manipulation of the selected AI techniques (Fletcher, 1984).

System Development Process

As we discussed earlier, the development of most CBI programs has taken a kind of systems approach that requires some or all of the following processes: analysis, design, development, formative evaluation, implementation, summative evaluation, and maintenance. Typical members of the development team include an instructional designer, a subject matter expert, and developer(s) with computer-programming skills. When an authoring system is used, roles of the development team members may be different depending on the capability of the authoring system. Most authoring systems provide computer-coding capability without requiring programming from the developers; some systems have built-in facilities to help the developer analytically organize the subject content and select and design instructional strategies.

Because few ICAI projects have been systematically or chronologically documented, the development process of ICAI systems cannot be described in a generalizable procedure. However, the different goal of ICAI researchers from that of CBI developers indicates that their development procedures also vary. For example, GUIDON was simply extended from MYCIN to test the feasibility of a rule-based expert system in teaching; SCHOLAR and WHY focused on tutorial dialogues for handling unanticipated student questions and generating instructional materials for the student; BUGGY, ALGEBRA, and LMS were designed to analyze student errors and to model learning behaviors.

Some ICAI projects required the extensive involvement of domain knowledge experts (e.g., GUIDON). For this case, a main responsibility of ICAI developers was to extract necessary knowledge components from the expert and to codify them into the system. However, most ICAI systems were apparently developed by ICAI researchers alone without much involvement of instructional designers (or psychologists) and subject matter experts. Because instructional issues were not the primary concern of the ICAI researchers, it was obvious why instructional psychologists were not included in the development teams. Furthermore, ICAI researchers apparently chose subject matter areas with which they were familiar; thus they could test their research curiosities with the minimum involvement of other people. Thus the ICAI development process was determined by the individual researcher's goals, his or her instructional development skills, and the characteristics of the domain knowledge selected for the research; as a result, the development process varies among projects.

System Validation

In CBI, the success of the program is determined by the degree of its instructional effectiveness and efficiency. The degree of the program's sophistication or capability to handle special processes is not an important criterion to evaluate the system. To assure the program's effectiveness and efficiency, the CBI development process is monitored with different evaluation methods, such as subject matter expert review, one-on-one tryout, pilot test, and so forth. In contrast, the success of an ICAI program is primarily determined from its capability to handle specific features or processes involved in instruction (e.g., inferencing mechanism, bug analysis procedure, and natural language dialogue capability). Apparently, no systematic evaluation procedures (formative or summative) have been used in ICAI to assure the quality of the program during the development process or to validate its success after development. Because of the unique interest and purpose of ICAI researchers, a program seems to be considered "successful" only if it runs as it was designed to run.

Hardware and Software

During the 1960s and 1970s, special computer systems such as PLATO, IBM 1500, and TICCIT, and recently WICAT and IVIS of Digital Equipment, were developed mainly for CBI. These systems have their own CBI authoring languages: TUTOR (PLATO), Coursewriter (IBM 1500), APT/TAL (TICCIT), WISE (WICAT), and PRODUCER (IVIS). Although the special systems, except the IBM 1500, are still widely used, most of the current CBI programs are developed and implemented using microcomputers. Most microcomputers have been developed for general uses, including education. Thus the principal hardware for CBI consists of a few special kinds of mainframe-based systems (e.g., PLATO and TICCIT) and recently developed microcomputers. Software used for the development of CBI programs consists of four different levels: general-purpose computer languages (BASIC, Pascal, C, FORTRAN, etc.), system-specific authoring languages (TUTOR, COURSEWRITER, TAL, etc.), system-independent CBI authoring languages (PILOT, PLANIT, etc.), and authoring systems (or aids) that provide facilities to develop CBI lessons without programming skills (e.g., Hazeltine's ADAPT) (see Kearsley, 1983, chap. 6). A well-developed authoring system may provide the author with additional capabilities to design instructional strategies and to organize subject contents into structured formats.

In contrast, most ICAI programs have been developed and delivered by using special hardware systems designed for AI research, such as Symbolics, Xerox D machines, TI Explorer, Lamda, and so on. Software, as well, has been limited to a few specific languages such as LISP and Prolog because of the unique capabilities of the languages to handle complex processes involved in AI tasks (e.g., computing with symbolic expressions rather than numbers and representing data as linked-list structures in the machine and as multilevel lists on paper). Versions of LISP and Prolog have recently become available for microcomputers. Also, efforts to develop ICAI authoring programs are currently being undertaken. However, the current use of hardware and software for the development of ICAI programs is still limited to a few specific types.

Table 2.2 presents the summary of our comparisons between traditional CBI and ICAI.

Differences between Terms in CBI and ICAI

The developers of ICAI and CBI agree that their general purpose is to provide quality instruction to the student via computer. Also, components and variables involved in the development of ICAI and CBI systems are basically the same. However, many terms used by CBI and ICAI developers are syntactically and semantically different due to their different theoretical backgrounds and the technical procedures taken in the development process. In this section, we attempt to clarify the syntactical differences and semantic implications of the terms that are frequently used in relation to the three main components of instruction: knowledge or content to be taught, characteristics of the target students, and instructional strategy.

Terms Related to Knowledge

To indicate the "knowledge or content to be taught," most CBI developers use basically the same terms as school educators and trainers. The terms most

Issue	CBI	ICAI
Goals of developers	Development of instructionally effective and efficient systems	Exploration of AI techniques in instruction
Theoretical base	Learning theories and instructional principles	Cognitive science
Structure and process of the system	Frame-oriented static structure; prespecified, system-initiative process	Process-oriented dynamic structure; generative, mixed-initiative process
Instructional principles	Various principles, including expository, discovery, and combined approaches	Mainly discovery approach
Methods of structuring knowledge	Mainly task analysis for identifying subtasks and content elements	AI knowledge representation techniques for organizing knowledge into a data structure
Student modeling	Binary judgment of student responses; prespecified response-sensitive procedures; quantitative methods	Qualitative evaluation of student responses
Instructional formats	Various: tutorial (expository), drill-practice, games, and simulations	Mainly tutorial (inquiry) and games
Subject matter areas	Virtually any area	Limited to well-structured areas
Development process and team	Systems approaches; instructional designer, subject matter expert, and developer (programmer)	Developer's own approach; mainly AI expert (or knowledge engineer) only
Validation methods and criterion	Formative and summative evaluation; instructional effectiveness and efficiency	Mainly technical debugging; functional running of the system
Hardware and software	Mostly general-purpose hardware; general-purpose languages, authoring languages, and authoring systems (aids)	Specific AI-purpose hardware; mainly LISP and Prolog

Table 2.2 A Comparison of CBI and ICAI

commonly used by CBI developers include "curriculum content," "subject matter structure," "content," "knowledge and skill," and "task." In contrast, ICAI developers use terms unique to their development approach, such as "domain knowledge," "problem-solving expertise," and "domain expertise."

Due to the strong influence of behavioristic learning theories on instructional design in the 1960s and early 1970s, the terms used in education and training communities connoted mainly the external structure of the knowledge that provides the observable and measurable learning criterion. As cognitive psychology has emerged as a main area of psychological research since the 1960s (e.g., Hebb's American Psychological Association presidential address, 1960), however, many educators and trainers have taken an eclectic position between the perspectives of behaviorism and cognitive psychology. Consequently, the connoted meanings of many terms used in education and training communities now include cognitive characteristics inherent in the knowledge as well as the external structure. For example, a task analysis is no longer regarded as a simple stepwise method to identify only subtasks; it implies also systematic procedures for analyzing cognitive characteristics and processes involved in the learning of the task.

AI, including ICAI, is theoretically based on cognitive science that has grown out of cognitive psychology and computer science. Thus terms used by ICAI researchers are different from those used in CBI, reflecting the technical procedures applied to analyze and structure the knowledge in the ICAI systems. For example, a task analysis, which is frequently used by CBI developers, involves different procedures from the "knowledge engineering" method used by ICAI developers. "Knowledge engineering" implies a technical process to extract knowledge from experts in the domain area and organize it in a data structure. Consequently, instructional designers/developers in CBI correspond to "knowledge engineers" in ICAI, but they perform different tasks because of the different procedural requirements. Similarly, a content or knowledge base in CBI corresponds to an "expertise module" or "problem-solving knowledge base" in ICAI, but their structural characteristics may be different because of the different technical methods involved in the development process.

Terms Related to Student Characteristics

Students' abilities to acquire various types of knowledge and skills are attributed to many different variables, including aptitudes (e.g., intellectual abilities, cognitive styles), entry behaviors or abilities (e.g., prior knowledge), and on-task performance (e.g., response pattern, motivation status). Each of these variables may provide specific information for diagnosing students' learning needs and for prescribing instructional treatments. Thus the student variables should be used selectively depending on the given situation. Instructional researchers and developers, including CBI developers, use the following terms to describe the different student variables and their characteristics: "learner variables," "student information," "student characteristics," and so forth.

However, student variables used by ICAI developers are mostly limited to the student's on-task performance information (e.g., a single response or a response pattern). Terms such as "student model" and "student diagnostic model" that are commonly used in ICAI systems imply the continuous assessment and updating process of the student's on-task performance information during instruction. Terms such as "student characteristics" or "learner variables," as used by CBI developers, seem to imply the static nature of the information, while terms such as "student model" or "student diagnostic model" emphasize the dynamic nature of the information. However, a real difference between the terms used by CBI and ICAI developers is that the former have more inclusive meanings than the latter. Actually, the student's on-task performance information has been used since early in the teaching-machine era (Crowder, 1959).

Terms Related to Instructional Strategy

In CBI, instructional strategy is generally represented by a set of decision rules and procedures for selecting, designing, and presenting instructional displays and specifying student-computer interaction processes. "Tutorial strategy" or "heuristics rules" in ICAI correspond to "instructional strategy" in CBI. However, they have slightly different implications because of the different emphases of the pedagogical approaches taken in the systems. "Tutorial strategy" in ICAI implies an emphasis of a one-on-one relationship between the computer-tutor and student. "Instructional strategy" (in CBI) includes various methods and formats for organizing and presenting instructional displays. Also, it includes processes for controlling student-computer interactions. By contrast, "tutorial strategy" in ICAI is limited to the process of tutor-student dialogues.

"Instructional strategies," as used in CBI, are theoretically derived from related learning theories and instructional principles. However, "heuristic rules," as used in ICAI, seem to be common-sense–based decision rules for controlling the process of student-computer dialogues.

Table 2.3 compares important terms used by CBI and ICAI developers in terms of their syntactical differences and semantic implications.

A Model of Adaptive Instruction

In our review of the components of the ICAI system, their development, and differences between CBI and ICAI, we observed that most existing ICAI systems have been developed to explore the capability of AI techniques in the instructional process rather than to build an effective instructional system. The next generation of ICAI systems should be concerned, in our view, with instructional issues more than computer science or AI issues such as specific programming

CBI		ICAI	
Terms	**Interpretation**	**Terms**	**Interpretation**
Subject matter, tasks, content, knowledge and skills, etc.	External structure of the knowledge	Expertise, problem-solving knowledge, etc.	Expert's internal knowledge state or problem-solving process
Task analysis, content analysis	Methods to analyze and organize knowledge components	Knowledge representation	AI techniques to organize knowledge components into a data structure
Instructional development	Process of systems approach	Knowledge engineering	Extraction and codification of expert's knowledge
Instructional designer	Expert in instructional design and development	Knowledge engineer	Expert in AI
Content base, knowledge base	Subtasks and content elements structured into a database	Expertise module, knowledge base	A database for representing expert's internal knowledge
Subject matter expert	Person who is familiar with the structure and content components of knowledge	Domain expert, problem-solving expert	Person who demonstrates a high performance on the given task
Student characteristics, learner variables	Include many different variables; descriptive, static, or dynamic nature	Student model, student diagnostic model	Geared to on-task performance information; dynamic and process-oriented nature
Instructional strategy	Rules and procedures for selecting and designing instructional displays and interaction processes; applied to individual and group-based instruction	Tutorial strategy; heuristic rules	Rules for controlling student-teacher dialogues; applied to one-on-one tutorial settings

Table 2.3 A Comparison of Main Terms Used in CBI and in ICAI

techniques, software architecture, and so forth. Thus the first task for the development of CBI or ICAI systems should be to construct a comprehensive model of adaptive instruction in which the contributions of computer science and instructional psychology can be merged.

Although ICAI systems have taken many different forms depending on the individual developer's goals, the characteristics of the domain knowledge, the target students, and the technical methods used, their features and processes can be represented by a typical model.

Figure 2.1 describes a typical process of instruction implemented in most ICAI systems. It indicates that in ICAI a student's performance is evaluated by comparing it with a computer-simulated expert's performance. The difference between the expert's performance and the student's performance is used to infer the causes of the student's problem (or misconception) and his or her learning needs. The interactive process between the computer and student (including the presentation of explanations to correct the student's misconceptions) is determined by tutorial rules.

This typical model of ICAI and our analysis of existing ICAI systems suggest that many current ICAI systems have a number of important shortcomings as complete instructional systems.

First, as Fig. 2.1 shows, the evaluation process of students' performance is solely dependent on the analysis of their response to a given question. This response-specific evaluation is very useful for diagnosing the causes of students' problems and inferring their learning needs. However, it is not appropriate for measuring students' overall performance on the task because the response evaluation is limited to a specific (and frequently very small) aspect of the task. Also, it does not take into account the information available in students' long-term memory because the evaluation is based on the analysis of their immediate response to the given question. That is, existing ICAI systems have diagnostic mechanisms but not appropriate measurement and evaluation components.

Second, existing ICAI systems have ignored many potentially important student variables in the diagnostic and prescriptive process by relying solely on the student's response (or response pattern) to a given question. In most learning situations, a reliable pattern of the student's response is not developed until the student makes significant progress on the given task. Frequently, the system-student interactions required to learn a given task are not long enough to observe the demonstration of the student's response pattern. Thus a powerful ICAI system should include important learner variables in the student modeling process. Significant theoretical discussions and empirical evidence suggest that individual difference variables provide valuable implications for designing adaptive instructional systems.

Third, the capability of generating new instructional displays is limited to the specific set of information units in the knowledge base. Since information units in the knowledge network are very small and at the micro level (e.g., facts

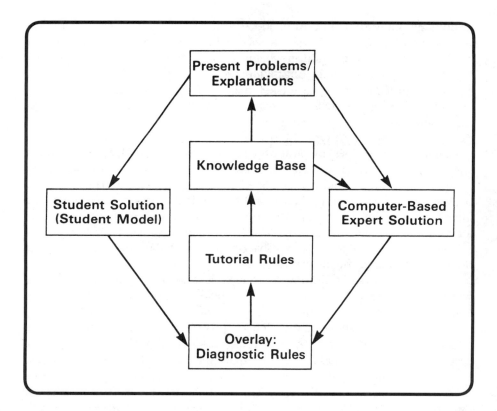

Figure 2.1 A General Model of ICAI

and their relationships), existing ICAI systems do not have the capability to refine or modify the macro level of the knowledge structure (e.g., course or curriculum level).

Fourth, instructional principles and strategies are implicitly represented in the tutorial rules. Although the separation of tutoring expertise from the domain knowledge has been proposed by some ICAI researchers (e.g., Clancey, 1979; Stevens & Collins, 1977), in the implementation, the tutoring strategies are incorporated in the domain-dependent decision rules. There are many different kinds of instructional strategies that can be structured and represented independently of the domain knowledge; the independent structure of instructional strategy in a separate module may facilitate the process of the system development, implementation, and modification.

Fifth, the system's ability for self-improving or updating its diagnostic and tutorial process is mostly limited to the collection and assessment of information in the student model. Few existing systems, if any, have the ability to refine the structure of the knowledge base and diagnostic and tutorial rules.

In order to overcome the above-noted shortcomings of existing systems in the development of future systems, we present a conceptual model of adaptive instruction (Fig. 2.2). This model was originally proposed by Seidel and his associates (Seidel, 1971b) to exemplify their approach to the development of CBI systems in HumRRO at that time. This model does not provide any specific procedures or technical guidelines for designing an ICAI system. However, the cybernetic metasystem approach used in the model is generalizable as a guide for developing more effective and efficient control processes of instructional systems. The model illustrates what components an ICAI or CBI system should have and how those components should be interrelated in the instructional process. Also, the model shows what specific self-improving or updating capabilities the system may need to have.

As Fig. 2.2 shows, this model divides the instructional process into three stages: input, transactions, and output. The input stage basically consists of the analysis of the student's entry characteristics. The student's entry characteristics include not only his or her within-lesson history (e.g., response history) but also pre-lesson characteristics. The pre-lesson characteristics may include information about students' aptitudes (e.g., intellectual ability measures, cognitive/ learning styles, cognitive developmental stages, prior knowledge). The entry characteristics, particularly the within-lesson history, will be updated from the evaluation information of the performance (i.e., output measures).

The transaction stage consists of the interactions between the student and system. On the basis of the student's entry characteristics, the system selects problems or explanations to present; the system then evaluates the student's response (or any other student inputs) to the given problem. The response evaluation provides information for diagnosing the student's learning needs and for measuring overall performance level on the task. The learning needs are inferred according to the diagnostic rules. Finally, the system selects new display presentations and questions for the student according to the tutorial rules.

The output stage mainly consists of performance evaluation. The performance evaluation may include not only the student's overall performance level on a given task but also the analysis of complete learning behaviors recorded in the system. According to the performance evaluation, the instructional components are modified or updated. The instructional components to be updated may include contents in the knowledge base, instructional strategies, diagnostic and tutorial rules, structure of the course or curriculum, and entry characteristics. If the system does not have the capability to modify or update the instructional components automatically, it may allow the human monitor to perform that task.

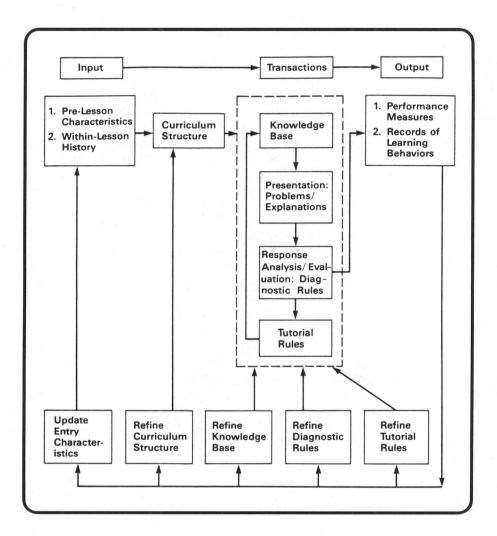

Figure 2.2 A Model of Adaptive Instruction (adapted from Seidel, 1971)

Conclusion

The most important contribution made in the development of ICAI systems is not in the form of an intellectual breakthrough in the field of learning and instruction but rather in the development of powerful computer systems that are able to effectively capture human beings' learning and teaching processes. Thus many ICAI systems have apparently contributed to a better understanding of cognitive processes involved in learning specific skills and knowledge. ICAI systems clearly demonstrate the state-of-the-art levels that CBI could attain in terms of functional capabilities in future development. However, the extent of their practical value as instructional systems is as yet limited, mainly because insufficient attention has been given to important instructional issues in the development process.

The conceptual model that we proposed in the previous section illustrates the kinds of components and functions a powerful adaptive instructional system should have. Although the model was originally developed in the early 1970s, the issues proposed in this model are still relevant and continue to challenge instructional researchers and CBI developers.

It is our view that current application of AI techniques to the development of powerful adaptive instructional systems is an attempt to solve old problems of how to learn and teach with new technology. However, the old problem of "how to teach" still remains, and it is not likely to be solved simply by increasing the functional power of the instructional delivery system (i.e., the computer). AI technology has provided us with a powerful tool for exploring and advancing our knowledge of how to teach. However, the development of effective and efficient instructional systems strongly requires combined and cooperative efforts from researchers and developers in both AI and instructional psychology. Winston (1984) emphasized the importance of this cooperative effort by describing current progress of AI as an "age of partnerships, a period when researchers in AI began to admit that there were other researchers, particularly linguists and psychologists, with whom people in AI can form important liaisons." In order for this cooperation to occur, they must understand and communicate with each other and to that end we can hopefully make significant progress in our knowledge of "how to teach" and can develop powerful adaptive instructional systems.

From the comparative examination of the characteristics of existing ICAI systems to CBI, we are proposing a number of recommendations for the development of future systems.

1. The application of AI techniques to the development of future ICAI systems should focus more on instructional effectiveness and efficiency; AI techniques should be selected (or derived) according to instructional needs.

2. Future systems should increase emphasis on the prescriptive process of the system by integrating various instructional principles and both domain-independent and domain-dependent instructional strategies.

3. Instructional psychologists and subject matter experts should be more involved in the development of future ICAI systems.

4. The application of a task analysis method may facilitate the analysis of the domain knowledge structure and the identification of necessary knowledge

components; AI knowledge representation techniques should then be used to organize the identified knowledge components into a data structure.

5. Various learner variables should be considered in the development of the student model. Also, the process or stages of learning (e.g., requirements to advance from novice to expert) should be considered in modeling the student's learning behavior.

6. Future ICAI systems should have a measurement and evaluation component. Also, the development and implementation of the system should be validated from the application of formative and summative evaluation methods.

7. More ICAI programs should be developed and delivered by using microcomputers to promote the application of AI techniques by various types of users.

In this chapter, we proposed a conceptual model for the development of a relatively complete adaptive instructional system. We also presented a number of suggestions to integrate various instructional issues in the development of ICAI systems. However, to develop a complete ICAI system, as we proposed in Fig. 2.2, may be very difficult at this time because of the complexity of the system and the amount of time and effort required. AI researchers and instructional psychologists are encouraged and expected to work together to build powerful ICAI systems that are instructionally effective and efficient.

In the meantime, we expect that AI researchers and cognitive scientists will further improve the capabilities of current AI technology, such as natural language dialogues and the inferencing process for capturing the human reasoning process. Also, we hope that the rapid development of computer hardware and software (including authoring systems) will significantly reduce the amount of time and effort required to develop ICAI systems.

Finally, the following question presented in the title of our chapter now deserves an answer: "Is it old wine in a new bottle, or is it a new vintage?" An admittedly premature answer is that it is old wine (instructional issues) in a new bottle (delivery techniques); however, the forming of partnerships among computer scientists (particularly, AI researchers), learning and instructional psychologists, and educators and trainers can lead to a new, substantive change in the quality of the wine, and therefore a new vintage.

References

Alessi, S. M., & Trollip, S. R. (1985). *Computer-based instruction: methods and development*. Englewood Cliffs, NJ: Prentice-Hall.

Anderson, J. R. (1982). Acquisition of cognitive skill. *Psychological Review, 89,* 369–406.

Anderson, J. R., Boyle, C. F., Farrell, R., & Reiser, B. J. (1985). *Cognitive principles in the design of computer tutors.* Advanced Computer Tutoring Project, Carnegie-Mellon University.

Anderson, J. R., Boyle, C. F., & Reiser, B. J. (1985). Intelligent tutoring systems. *Science, 288,* 456–462.

Anderson, J. R., & Reiser, B. J. (1985). The LISP tutor. *Byte, 10,* 159–175.

Atkinson, R. C. (1972). Ingredients for a theory of instruction. *American Psychologist, 27,* 921–931.

Atkinson, R. C. (1976). Adaptive instructional systems: Some attempts to optimize the learning process. In D. Klahr (Ed.), *Cognition and instruction.* New York: Wiley.

Barr, A., Beard, M., & Atkinson, R. C. (1976). The computer as a tutorial laboratory: The Stanford BIP project. *International Journal of Man-Machine Studies, 8,* 567–596.

Barr, A., & Feigenbaum, E. A. (1981). *The handbook of artificial intelligence* (Vol. 1). Los Altos, CA: William Kaufmann.

Barr, A., & Feigenbaum, E. A. (1982). *The handbook of artificial intelligence* (Vol. 2). Los Altos, CA: William Kaufmann.

Blaine, L., & Smith, R. L. (1977). Intelligent CAI: The role of the curriculum in suggesting computational models of reasoning. *Proceedings of the Annual Meeting of the Association of Computing Machinery,* Seattle, Washington.

Brown, J. S., & Burton, R. R. (1978a). A paradigmatic example of an artificial intelligent instructional system. *International Journal of Man-Machine Studies, 10,* 323–339.

Brown, J. S., & Burton, R. R. (1978b). Diagnostic models for procedural bugs in basic mathematical skills. *Cognitive Science, 2,* 155–192.

Brown, J. S., Burton, R. R., & Bell, A. G. (1975). SOPHIE. A step towards a reactive learning environment. *International Journal of Man-Machine Studies, 7,* 675–696.

Brown, J. S., Burton, R. R., & de Kleer, J. (1982). Pedagogical, natural language and knowledge engineering in SOPHIE I, II and III. In D. Sleeman & J. S. Brown (Eds.), *Intelligent tutoring systems.* New York: Academic Press.

Bunderson, C. V. (1974). The design and production of learner-controlled courseware for the TICCIT system. *International Journal of Man-Machine Studies, 6,* 479–491.

Burton, R. R., & Brown, J. S. (1979). An investigation of computer coaching for informal learning activities. *International Journal of Man-Machine Studies, 11,* 5–24.

Burton, R. R., & Brown, J. S. (1982). An investigation of computer coaching for informal learning activities. In D. Sleeman & J. S. Brown (Eds.), *Intelligent tutoring systems.* New York: Academic Press.

Carbonell, J. R. (1970). AI in CAI: An artificial intelligence approach to computer assisted instruction. *IEEE Transactions on Man-Machine Systems, 11,* 190–202.

Card, S. K., Moran, T. P., & Newell, A. (1983). *The psychology of human-computer interaction.* Hillsdale, NJ: Lawrence Erlbaum Associates.

Carr, B., & Goldstein, I. P. (1977). Overlays: A theory of modeling for computer aided instruction. *Artificial Intelligence Laboratory Memo 406 (Logo Memo 40)*. Massachusetts Institute of Technology.

Clancey, W. J. (1979). Tutoring rules for guiding a case method dialogue. *International Journal of Man-Machine Studies, 11,* 25–49.

Clancey, W. J. (1982). Tutoring rules for guiding a case method dialogue. In D. Sleeman & J. S. Brown (Eds.), *Intelligent tutoring systems,* New York: Academic Press.

Clancey, W. J., Barnett, J. J., & Cohen, P. R. (1982). Applications-oriented AI research: Education. In A. Barr & E. A. Feigenbaum (Eds.), *The handbook of artificial intelligence* (Vol. 2). Los Altos, CA: William Kaufmann.

Clancey, W. J., & Letsinger, R. (1981). NEOMYCIN: Reconfiguring a rule-based expert system for application to teaching. *Proceedings of the Seventh IJCAI.*

Collins, A., Warnock, E. H., & Passafiume, J. J. (1975). Analysis and synthesis of tutorial dialogues. *Psychology of Learning and Motivation, 9,* 48–87.

Crowder, N. W. (1959). Automatic tutoring by means of intrinsic programming. In E. H. Galanter (Ed.), *Automatic teaching: The state of art.* New York: Wiley.

Dewey, J. (1910). *How we think.* Boston: Heath.

Dywer, T. A. (1974). Heuristic strategies for using computers to enrich education. *International Journal of Man-Machine Studies, 6,* 137–154.

Fletcher, J. D. (1984). Intelligent instructional systems in training. In S. A. Andriole (Ed.), *Applications in artificial intelligence.* Princeton, NJ: Petrocelli.

Goldstein, I. P. (1982). The genetic graph: A representation for the evolution of procedural knowledge. In D. Sleeman & J. S. Brown (Eds.), *Intelligent tutoring systems.* New York: Academic Press.

Goldstein, I. P., & Carr, B. (1977). The computer as coach: An athletic paradigm for intellectual education. *Proceedings of the Annual Meeting of the Association for Computing Machinery,* Seattle, Washington.

Hansen, D. N., Ross, S. M., & Rakow, E. (1977). Adaptive models for computer-based training systems. *Annual Report to Navy Personnel Research and Development Center.* Memphis, TN: Memphis State University.

Hebb, D. O. (1960). The American revolution. *Presidential Address at the Annual Conference of the American Psychological Association,* Chicago, Illinois.

Hunter, B., Kastner, C. S., Rubin, M. L., & Seidel, R. J. (1975). *Learning alternatives in U.S. education: Where student and computer meet.* Englewood Cliffs, NJ: Educational Technology.

Kay, A., & Goldberg, A. (1977, March). Personal dynamic media. *IEEE Computer,* 31–41.

Kearsley, G. P. (1983). *Computer-based training: A guide to selection and implementation.* Reading, MA: Addison-Wesley.

Kearsley, G. P., Hunter, B., Seidel, R. J. (1983). Two decades of computer based instruction projects: What have we learned? *T. H. E. Journal, 10*(3), 90–94; *10*(4), 90–96.

Kearsley, G. P., & Seidel, R. J. (1985). Automation in training and education. *Human Factors, 27,* 61–74.

Kimball, R. (1973). Self-optimizing computer-assisted tutoring: Theory and practice. *Institute of Mathematical Studies in the Social Sciences, Psychology and Education Series, Technical Report No. 206,* Stanford, CA: Stanford University.

Kimball, R. (1982). A self-improving tutor for symbolic integration. In D. Sleeman & J. S. Brown (Eds.), *Intelligent tutoring systems.* New York: Academic Press.

Koffman, E. B., & Blount, S. E. (1975). Artificial intelligence and automatic programming in CAI. *Artificial Intelligence, 6,* 215–234.

Kulik, J. A., Kulik, C. C., & Cohen, P. A. (1980). Effectiveness of computer-based college teaching: A meta-analysis of findings. *Review of Educational Research, 50,* 525–544.

Lantz, B. S., Bregar, W. S., & Farley, A. M. (1983). An intelligent CAI system for teaching equation solving. *Journal of Computer-Based Instruction, 10,* 35–42.

Malone, T. W. (1981). Toward a theory of intrinsically motivating instruction. *Cognitive Science, 5,* 130–145.

Matz, M. (1982). Towards a process model for high school algebra errors. In D. Sleeman & J. S. Brown (Eds.), *Intelligent tutoring systems.* New York: Academic Press.

Merrill, M. D., Schneider, E. W., & Fletcher, K. A. (1980). *TICCIT.* Englewood Cliffs, NJ: Educational Technology.

Miller, M. L. (1982). A structural planning and debugging environment for elementary programming. In D. Sleeman & J. S. Brown (Eds.), *Intelligent tutoring systems.* New York: Academic Press.

Minsky, M. (1975). A framework for representing knowledge. In P. H. Winston (Ed.), *The psychology of computer vision.* New York: McGraw-Hill.

Newell, A., & Simon, H. A. (1972). *Human problem solving.* Englewood Cliffs, NJ: Prentice-Hall.

Norman, D. A., & Rumelhart, D. E. (1975). *Explorations in Cognition.* San Francisco: Freeman.

Orlansky, J., & String, J. (1981). Computer-based instruction for military training. *Defense Management Journal, 18*(2) 46–54.

O'Shea, T. (1979). A self-improving quadratic tutor. *International Journal of Man-Machine Studies, 11,* 97–124.

O'Shea, T. (1982). A self-improving quadratic tutor. In D. Sleeman & J. S. Brown (Eds.), *Intelligent tutoring systems.* New York: Academic Press.

Papert, S. (1980). *Mindstorms.* New York: Basic Books.

Park, O., & Tennyson, R. D. (1980). Adaptive design strategies for selecting number and presentation order of examples in coordinate concept acquisition. *Journal of Educational Psychology, 72,* 362–370.

Park, O., & Tennyson, R. D. (1983). Computer-based instructional systems for adaptive education: A review. *Contemporary Education Review, 2,* 121–135.

Piaget, J. (1954). *The construction of reality in the child.* New York: Basic Books.

Piaget, J., & Inhelder, B. (1964). *The early growth of logic in the child.* New York: Harper & Row.

Pressey, S. L. (1927). A machine for automatic teaching of drill material. *School and Society, 25,* 1–14.

Quillian, M. R. (1968). Semantic memory. In M. Minsky (Ed.), *Semantic information processing.* Cambridge, MA: MIT Press.

Roberts, F. C., & Park, O. (1983). Intelligent computer-assisted instruction: An explanation and overview. *Educational Technology, 23,* 7–12.

Rothen, W., & Tennyson, R. D. (1978). Application of Bayes' theory in designing computer-based adaptive instructional strategies. *Educational Psychologist, 12,* 317–323.

Schank, R. C., & Abelson, R. P. (1977). *Scripts, plans, goals, and understanding: An inquiry into human knowledge structures.* Hillsdale, NJ: Lawrence Erlbaum Associates.

Seidel, R. J. (1971a). *Current status of computer-administered instruction work under project IMPACT.* Professional Paper 18-72, Alexandria, VA: Human Resources Research Organization.

Seidel, R. J. (1971b). *Theories and strategies related to measurement in individualized instruction.* Professional Paper 2-71, Alexandria, VA: Human Resources Research Organization. (Also published in *Educational Technology,* 1971, *11,* 40–46.)

Seidel, R. J., Anderson, R., & Hunter, B. (1982). *Computer literacy.* New York: Academic Press.

Seidel, R. J., & Kearsley, G. (in press). The impact of computers on human learning. In J. Zeidner (Ed.), *Human productivity enhancement.* New York: Praeger.

Shortliffe, E. H. (1976). *Computer-based medical consultations: MYCIN.* New York: Elsevier.

Skinner, B. F. (1958). Teaching machine. *Science, 128,* 969–977.

Skinner, B. F. (1968). *The technology of teaching.* New York: Appleton-Century Crofts.

Sleeman, D. (1982). Assessing aspects of competence in basic algebra. In D. Sleeman & J. S. Brown (Eds.), *Intelligent tutoring systems.* New York: Academic Press.

Sleeman, D. H. (1983). Inferring student models for intelligent computer-aided instruction. In R. S. Michalski, J. G. Carbonell, & T. M. Mitchell (Eds.), *Machine learning: An artificial intelligence approach.* Palo Alto, CA: Tioga.

Sleeman, D., & Brown, J. S. (1982). *Intelligent tutoring systems.* New York: Academic Press.

Stelzer, J., & Garneau, J. (1972). *Project IMPACT software documentation: Overview of the computer-administered instruction subsystem.* Technical Report 72-21, Alexandria, VA: Human Resources Research Organization.

Stevens, A. L., & Collins, A. (1977). The goal structure of a Socratic tutor. *Proceedings of the Annual Meeting of the Association for Computing Machinery,* Seattle, Washington.

Stevens, A. L., Collins, A., & Goldin, S. (1979). Misconceptions in student's understanding. *International Journal of Man-Machine Studies, 11,* 145–156.

Stevens, A. L., Collins, A., & Goldin, S. (1982). Misconceptions in student's understanding. In D. Sleeman & J. S. Brown (Eds.), *Intelligent tutoring systems.* New York: Academic Press.

Suppes, P. (1981). *University-level computer-assisted instruction at Stanford: 1968–1980*. Stanford, CA: Institute for Mathematical Studies in the Social Sciences, Stanford University.

Suppes, P., Fletcher, J. D., & Zanotti, M. (1975). Performance models of American Indian students on computer-assisted instruction in elementary mathematics. *Instructional Science, 4*, 303–313.

Suppes, P., Fletcher, J. D., & Zanotti, M. (1976). Models of individual trajectories in computer-assisted instruction for deaf students. *Journal of Educational Psychology, 68*, 117–127.

Suppes, P., Jerman, M., & Brian, D. (1968). *Computer-assisted instruction: The 1965–66 Stanford arithmetic program*. New York: Academic Press.

Suppes, P., & Morningstar, M. (1972). *Computer-assisted instruction at Stanford: 1966–68: Data, models and evaluation of arithmetic program*. New York: Academic Press.

Taylor, R. P. (1980). *The computer in the school: Tutor, tool, tutee*. New York: Teachers College Press, Columbia University.

Tennyson, R. D., & Park, O. (1984). Computer-based adaptive instructional systems: A review of empirically based models. *Machine-Mediated Learning, 1*, 129–153.

Uttal, W. R., Rogers, M., Hieronymous, R., & Pasich, T. (1969). *Generative computer-assisted instruction in analytic geometry*. Newburyport, MA: Entelek, Inc.

Winograd, T. (1975). Frame representation and the declarative-procedural controversy. In D. G. Borow & A. Collins (Eds.), *Representation and understanding: Studies in cognitive science*. New York: Academic Press.

Winston, P. H. (1984). Perspective. In P. H. Winston & K. A. Prendergast (Eds.), *The AI business: Commercial uses of artificial intelligence*. Cambridge, MA: MIT Press.

Part 2 Artificial Intelligence in Education

To understand ICAI, it is necessary to study specific examples of ICAI programs and the particular instructional problems they address. The structure of an ICAI program emerges from the problem it is designed around. While general AI techniques are involved, they are embedded in the specifics of the problem domain.

The chapters in Part 2 describe three different types of ICAI projects in the realm of education. PROUST is a system designed to help novice programmers find and *understand* bugs in Pascal programs. Micro-SEARCH is a diagnostic system intended to help students solve and *understand* nondeterministic problems in chemistry and mathematics. The MOTIONS microworld is a program that helps students *understand* mathematical concepts and problem solving.

Although the three systems represent quite different types of ICAI, they all share a common goal of improving student understanding. These programs do not teach in any direct fashion—instead they make it easier for students to formulate ideas, see relationships, draw conclusions, and discover their own misconceptions. Other ICAI programs may be more directive in nature, but they still focus on student understanding.

All three systems represent work in progress. PROUST, described by Johnson and Soloway in Chapter 3, is capable of discovering 70% of all bugs in a small set of moderately complex Pascal programs. Johnson and Soloway would like the program to be more accurate and more generalized. They also point out that PROUST is the basis for a full instructional system that would give students remedial help based on their errors.

Micro-SEARCH, described by Sleeman in Chapter 4, is the third incarnation of a problem-solving monitor system. Each version of SEARCH has introduced new design and performance considerations. The different versions have also demonstrated the generality of the system across different instructional domains and types of students. SEARCH illustrates that AI principles could have relatively wide applicability across a number of curriculum areas.

The MOTIONS microworld described by Thompson in Chapter 5 is in the process of acquiring "intelligent" features such as WHY?, PREDICT, EXPLORE, GENERALIZE, and CHALLENGE-ME. The original version of the program did not provide students with a rich enough set of options to help them formulate concepts or test hypotheses as effectively as desired. Thompson discusses the anticipated value of these intelligent features.

All three ICAI systems described in this section have been implemented on personal computers and used experimentally in classrooms. This makes these systems particularly worthy of examination since they represent ICAI programs that could be used in schools in the near future.

3/ PROUST: An Automatic Debugger for Pascal Programs

W. LEWIS JOHNSON and
ELLIOT SOLOWAY

Introduction

PROUST is a knowledge-based system which finds non-syntactic bugs in Pascal programs written by beginning programmers. Whenever students attempt to compile a program, and the program compiles successfully, PROUST is automatically invoked to analyze the program. Any bugs that are present in the program are reported by PROUST to the student.

When we say that PROUST finds bugs in programs, we do not mean that it is a tool which helps programmers find bugs. Furthermore, PROUST is not confined to some narrow class of bugs, such as uninitialized variables. Instead, PROUST is designed to find *every* bug in most novice programs. When we assign moderately complex programming problems to students, PROUST is currently capable of identifying correctly all of the bugs in over 70% of the programs that students write. When PROUST finds a bug, it does not simply point to the lines of code which are wrong; instead, it determines how the bug could be corrected, and even suggests why the bug arose in the program in the first place. Our ultimate aim is to build an entire instructional system around PROUST, which assigns programming assignments to the students, reads over their work, and gives them helpful suggestions.

Reprinted with permission from the April 1985 issue of BYTE magazine. Copyright © 1985 by McGraw-Hill, Inc., New York 10012. All rights reserved.

This work was co-sponsored by the Personnel and Training Research Groups, Psychological Sciences Division, Office of Naval Research and the Army Research Institute for the Behavioral and Social Sciences, under Contract No. N00014-82-K-0714, Contract Authority Identification Number, Nr 154-492.

Additional papers dealing with bug classification, automatic debugging, and the cognitive underpinnings of programming can be obtained by writing to the following address: Cognition and Programming Project, Department of Computer Science, Yale University, P.O. Box 2158 Yale Station, New Haven, Ct. 06520.

49

In designing PROUST it was necessary to deal directly with the variability of bugs in novice programs. If a programming problem is assigned to a class of 200 students, the students will write 200 different programs, assuming that they do not cheat. There is variability both in the students' designs and in their bugs. Some bugs, such as missing variable initializations, are accidental omissions, which are easily recognized and corrected. Other bugs result from failures to reason through the interactions between components. Each piece of the program in isolation may appear correct, but when combined the program does not work. Still other bugs result from misconceptions about programming. The code may appear correct to the programmer, but it doesn't do what he/she expects, for reasons he/she does not understand. Bugs resulting from misconceptions are the most serious; students stand to benefit the most from having such problems pointed out to them.

We make the following claim: if a debugging system is to cope with the various types of errors that programmers make, it must understand what the programmer is trying to do. This may be an obvious point; after all, any programmer knows that a large part of debugging somebody else's program is trying to figure out how it is supposed to work. Still, debugging systems usually do not concern themselves with what the program is supposed to do, they only analyze what the program actually does [1, 2, 6]. Figuring out how a program is supposed to work is not easy; it requires information about the programming problem and knowledge about how to write programs. Nevertheless identifying the programmer's intentions is worth the effort, because knowledge of intentions makes it possible to identify more bugs, as well as to understand their causes.

In what follows we present two examples of buggy programs, to show how knowledge of the programmer's intentions assists debugging. We then discuss why alternative approaches to automatic debugging fail to identify such bugs. After this comes a description of how PROUST goes about analyzing such programs. Finally, we present some statistics showing PROUST's performance on large numbers of novice programs, to show that PROUST's approach is adequate for the vast majority of novice programs.

Examples of Program Bugs

Figure 3.1 shows a simple programming problem, which we will call the Averaging Problem. The student's program must compute the average of a series of positive numbers. It must ensure that the input to the program is in fact positive. The input terminates when a specific value, 99999, is read. We call values such as this, which signal the end of input, sentinel values.

Figure 3.2 shows an example solution to the Averaging Problem. This program works correctly, except for the following bug: if the user types 99999 immediately after typing a nonpositive value, the program will continue to prompt for data after the 99999 is read. When the program finally does termi-

Write a program which reads in a sequence of positive numbers,
stopping when 99999 is read. Compute the average of these numbers. Do not include the 99999 in the average. Be sure to reject any
input which is not positive.

Figure 3.1 The Averaging Problem

nate, the average will be incorrect. For example, suppose that the user inputs
5, −5, 99999. Instead of terminating when the 99999 is read, the program
requests another input. If the user then entered another 99999, the average
which the program would print would not be 5, but instead would be (5
+99999)/2, or 50002.

The reason why this program interprets 99999 as data when the sequence
5, −5, 99999 is read is as follows. When the program reads the −5, it enters
the input validation loop which starts with line 11, **WHILE Val <= 0 DO**. This
loop is intended to iterate until a positive value is typed in. 99999 is positive,
so when the 99999 is read control leaves the input validation loop. However,
the program was written with the assumption that when the input validation
loop is exited the current value of **Val** is a valid input datum. In this case **Val** is
not a valid datum; it is 99999, the sentinel value. The loop nevertheless processes
99999 as if it were data. There should be a test for the sentinel after the input
validation loop, to guard against this case.

Figure 3.2 includes PROUST's output describing the missing-sentinel-test
bug. The error is described in two different ways: first, the bug is described in
English, then an example of data which cause the program to fail is generated.

Now look at the program in Fig. 3.3. This is also a solution to the Averaging
Problem, similar to the previous solution. The bug in this program is also fairly
obscure. If the user types a positive value followed by a negative value, the
negative value will be included in the average. Thus if the user types −2, 2,
99999, the average will be 2, but if the user types 2, −2, 99999, the average will
be 0.

Unlike the example in Fig. 3.2, this program is not missing a test for the
sentinel. However, the test which the programmer has written is in the form of
a **WHILE** statement instead of an **IF** statement. The student most likely has a
misconception about the distinction between **WHILE** statements and **IF** statements. Students with this misconception do not understand how the control
flow in a **WHILE** loop works. As long as the body of loop is straight-line code
the students have no difficulty. If the body of the loop contains tests, however,
the students think that the tests should be written as **WHILE** statements, to
ensure that they repeat when the body of the loop does. We will refer to this

```
1   PROGRAM Average( Input, Output );
2     CONST Stop = 99999;
3     VAR Sum, Count, Val, Avg: REAL;
4     BEGIN
5       Sum := 0;
6       Count := 0;
7       Writeln( 'Enter value:' );
8       Read( Val );
9       WHILE Val<>99999 DO
10        BEGIN
11          WHILE Val<= 0 DO
12            BEGIN
13              Writeln( 'Invalid entry, reenter' );
14              Read( Val );
15            END;
16          Sum := Sum + Val;
17          Count := Count + 1;
18          Writeln( 'Enter value:' );
19          Read( Val );
20        END;
21      IF Count = 0 THEN Writeln( 'No data entered' )
21        ELSE BEGIN
23            Avg := Sum/Count;
24            Writeln( 'The average is ', Avg );
25        END;
26      END.
```

PROUST's output:

You're missing a sentinel test. If a sentinel value is input immediately following a nonpositive value, your program will treat it as valid data.

Try the following data in your program to see this:
    5 −5 99999

Figure 3.2 Example Buggy Program

```
 1   PROGRAM Average( Input, Output );
 2     CONST Stop = 99999;
 3     VAR Sum, Count, Val, Avg: REAL;
 4     BEGIN
 5       Sum := 0;
 6       Count := 0;
 7       Writeln( 'Enter value:' );
 8       Read( Val );
 9       WHILE Val<>99999 DO
10         BEGIN
11           WHILE Val< = 0 DO
12             BEGIN
13               Writeln( 'Invalid entry, reenter' );
14               Read( Val );
15             END;
16           WHILE Val<>99999 DO
17             BEGIN
18               Sum := Sum + Val;
19               Count := Count + 1;
20               Writeln( 'Enter value:' );
21               Read( Val );
22             END;
23         END;
24     IF Count>0 THEN
25         BEGIN
26           Avg := Sum/Count;
27           Writeln( 'The average is ', Avg );
28         END;
29     END.
```

PROUST's output:

You are using a WHILE statement at line 16 where you should have used an IF statement. You probably want the code starting at line 16 to execute once each time through the loop; your code will make it execute many times.

The statement in question is:
    WHILE Val<>99999 DO . . .

Figure 3.3 Example Buggy Program

misconception henceforth as the **WHILE**-for-**IF** misconception. PROUST must be prepared for misconceptions such as these, and be able to explain the misconceptions to the student. PROUST's output for this example, which takes the misconception into account, is shown in the figure.

The bugs in Figs. 3.2 and 3.3 illustrate the following points. First, bugs frequently cannot be detected without knowledge of what the program is supposed to do. Both of the programs shown run no matter what input is read; in order to determine that there is a bug one must recognize that the programs output different results from what they should. Bugs such as these are not unusual; the missing-sentinel-test bug alone occurs in 18% of novice programmers' solutions to the Averaging Problem. The second point is that novice programmers need help in identifying such bugs. These bugs cause the programs to fail only after unusual inputs, ones which novice programmers are unlikely to test. In the case of the **WHILE**-for-**IF** misconception, even if programmers test the case in question they will probably not understand why the program fails, since they expect the **WHILE** statement to perform a different function from what it actually does.

Debugging Requires Reasoning about Intentions

In order to support the claim that debugging requires knowledge of programmers' intentions, we will examine the principal alternatives to intention-based debugging, and show why they fall short. The methods which we will consider will be analysis of I/O behavior, analysis of data flow, and recognition of patterns of buggy code.

Debugging by analysis of I/O behavior involves determining when the output of the program is incorrect, and suggesting bugs which might cause the faulty behavior [2]. This approach treats debugging as similar to medical diagnosis. The faulty behavior can be thought of as the symptoms of the program, and the bugs as the diseases. Debugging systems which adopt this approach consequently operate in a similar way to automatic medical diagnosis systems [5]. There are two problems with this approach: a program's symptoms cannot always be determined, and these symptoms cannot always be related to the bugs. The bugs in the programs in Figs. 3.2 and 3.3 only affect the output of the program occasionally, and recognizing when this happens requires knowledge about what the output should look like. Since the **WHILE**-for-**IF** example fails to test the input for validity after the first positive value is read, it would appear that this program is missing an input validation test. It is only after inspecting the code that it becomes clear that the bug is not in the input validation, but in the sentinel test.

Another approach which we might try for identifying bugs is data-flow analysis [1]. This is the approach that many error-checking compilers use for identifying bugs. Data-flow analysis checks for clear anomalies in the pattern of data definition and use in a program. It can identify when a variable is defined and never used, or when a variable is never defined. However, as long as there are no anomalies in data flow, data-flow analysis will not detect any bugs. Neither example in the preceding section has data-flow anomalies, so no bug would be detected.

Since I/O behavior and dataflow analysis do not provide what we need, we might try analyzing the structure of the program itself and see whether or not this suggests the presence of bugs. We could build up a library of templates for common bugs, such as missing sentinel tests, or **WHILE** statements in place of **IF** statements. We would then match these templates against the program in order to identify the bugs. The problem with this approach is this: there is no way of knowing where to match the bug templates in the program. For example, the **WHILE**-for-**IF** example has three different **WHILE** loops. How could we tell which **WHILE** loop really should be an **IF** statement, or if any of them should be an **IF** statement? We could try to make the bug template more specific, by making it apply only when there are two loops with the same exit test, one inside the other. That would make the template too specific; it would not apply to other cases where **WHILE** statements appear instead of **IF** statements.

The problem with all of these approaches to debugging is that they attempt to identify bugs without any understanding of what the program is supposed to do. Any such approach does little more than to make guesses as to what bug is involved. To do better, a debugging system has to be able to infer the programmer's intentions and relate them to the code.

PROUST's Approach

PROUST is a program written in T, a dialect of Lisp. The full system contains roughly 15000 lines of Lisp, and runs on a VAX 750. A stripped-down version, called Micro-PROUST, has been developed in conjunction with Courseware, Inc., San Diego, Ca.* Micro-PROUST was written in Gold Hill Common Lisp, and runs on an IBM PC. Micro-PROUST is capable of recognizing the kinds of bugs that are described in this article. Nevertheless, there is a variety of tricky bugs which PROUST can identify but Micro-PROUST cannot. Those who are interested in PROUST's full diagnostic capabilities should consult [3].

PROUST's analysis of programs is based upon knowledge about the programming problem that the students are working on. The students may solve the programming problem in a variety of ways, and their programs may have a variety of bugs, but there is one thing which does not vary: the students are

---

* The authors would like to thank Greg Kearsley, Leszek Izdebski, and Bret Wallach for their efforts in developing Micro-PROUST.

all trying to solve the same problem. Knowledge of the programming problem makes the variability of novice solutions more manageable. It also provides important information about the programmers' intentions.

In order to provide PROUST with descriptions of the programming problems, we devised a problem description language. We describe each problem in this language, and provide PROUST with a library of the descriptions. Each problem description is a paraphrase in PROUST's problem description language of the English-language problem statement that we hand out to the students.

Knowledge of the problem that the students are working on helps to provide an understanding of the students' programs, but it is not enough. It is a description of what the program should do, but not of how it should do it. Solutions to a given programming problem may be implemented in a variety of different ways. PROUST therefore needs knowledge about programming so that it can understand how each student designed and implemented his/her solution. Once it understands the programmer's intentions, it can then use knowledge about common bugs in order to identify the bugs in the student's program.

To see why knowledge of the programming problem alone is insufficient for identifying bugs, consider the following. Suppose that there were only one possible way for testing input for validity in a Pascal program, namely to insert a **WHILE** loop at the top of the main loop, such as in Figs. 3.2 and 3.3. Once PROUST knew that a program must validate input, it would know to look for such a loop, as well as the sentinel test which must follow. However, there are in fact several ways of validating input. Figure 3.4 shows a loop which tests input in a very different way. Instead of there being one input validation loop, there are two; one is at the bottom of the loop and the other precedes the loop. No additional sentinel test is required when this method is used, because as soon as input is validated control flows to the main exit test of the **WHILE** loop. Therefore, without knowing what method the programmer is using for validating input, PROUST cannot tell whether or not to look for a sentinel test within the body of the loop. In Fig. 3.2 it is an error not to have such a sentinel test, but in Fig. 3.4 it is not an error.

The method which PROUST uses for analyzing programs is analysis by synthesis. When PROUST examines a program, it looks up the corresponding problem description in its problem description library. Using its knowledge about how to write programs, it makes hypotheses about the methods which the programmer may use for satisfying each requirement in the problem description. Each hypothesis is a possible correct implementation of the corresponding requirement. If one of these hypotheses fits the student's code, then PROUST infers that the requirement is implemented correctly. If PROUST's hypotheses do not quite fit the program, then PROUST checks its database of common bugs, to see if they can explain the discrepancies.

```
Read ( Val );
WHILE Val < = 0 DO
  BEGIN
    Writeln ( 'Invalid entry, reenter' );
    Read ( Val );
  END;
WHILE VAL<>99999 DO
  BEGIN
    Sum : = Sum + Val;
    Count : = Count + 1;
    Writeln( 'Enter value:' );
    Read( Val );
    WHILE VAL < = 0 DO
      BEGIN
        Writeln ( 'Invalid entry, reenter' );
        Read ( Val );
      END;
  END;
```

Figure 3.4 An Alternative Method for Validation Input

PROUST's Problem Descriptions

Problem descriptions in PROUST describe the principal requirements which must be satisfied. We call such requirements *programming goals*. Problem descriptions also describe the data which the program must manipulate. We call individual sets of data *objects*.

We will introduce problem descriptions by showing how the Averaging Problem is translated into PROUST's problem description language. The first step in translating an English-language problem statement into PROUST's problem description language is to make explicit the various goals which were mentioned in the problem statement. Recall that the text of the Averaging Problem statement is the following:

Write a program which reads in a sequence of positive numbers, stopping when 99999 is read. Compute the average of these numbers. Do not include the 99999 in the average. Be sure to reject any input which is not positive.

Solutions to this problem operate on a sequence of input data; let us call this sequence *New*. The following goals can be extracted from the problem statement:

- Read successive values of *New*, stopping when a sentinel value, 99999, is read.
- Make sure that the condition *New* <= 0 is never true.
- Compute the average of *New*.
- Output the average of *New*.

We must now take these goals and use them to generate a problem description for PROUST. Each data object that the goals refer to is named and declared. Each goal extracted from the problem statement is recorded in the problem description. The resulting problem description is shown in Fig. 3.5.

Like all data structures which we will discuss in this article, problem descriptions are in list notation, where every statement and expression is enclosed in parentheses. The name of the program is indicated with a **Define-Program** statement. Objects are named using **Define-Object** statements. Goals are indicated using **Define-Goal** statements.

Object names are preceded by question marks. There are two objects defined in the Averaging Problem description, **?Sentinel** and **?New**. The question mark notation is used frequently in AI programs; it indicates that the variable is not a literal value, but is a parameter which must be substituted when the data structure is used. For example, the input data object **?New** will be substituted with the name of the Pascal variable that the student uses for storing the input data. The object **?Sentinel** has the value 99999; wherever **?Sentinel** appears in the problem description it can be substituted by 99999.

Objects can be either constant-valued or variable-valued. In this example, **?Sentinel** is a constant, with value 99999, and **?New** is a variable. In the general problem description language of PROUST objects can have a variety of properties associated with them; we will not need any such properties in this simple example, however.

Goal statements consist of a name of a type of goal, followed by a list of arguments. In the form (**Average ?New**), for example, **Average** is a type of goal, to compute an average, and **?New** is the argument of the goal. This form requires that the program compute the average of **?New**.

Arguments to goal expressions can take a variety of different forms. They can be objects, predicates, or even other goal expressions. In the expression (**Input-Validation ?New** (<= **?New** 0)), one argument is an object, and the other is a predicate **?New** <= 0. In Lisp function names and operators precede their arguments, which is why the <= precedes the **?New** and 0 in the expression (<= **?New** 0). If goals are nested, as in (**Output** (**Average ?New**)), the outer goal

```
((Define-Program Average)
 (Define-Object ?New)
 (Define-Object ?Sentinel Value 99999)
 (Define-Goal (Sentinel-Controlled-Input ?New ?Sentinel))
 (Define-Goal (Input-Validation ?New (<= ?New 0)))
 (Define-Goal (Output (Average ?New))))
```

Figure 3.5 Problem Description for the Averaging Problem

refers to the value computed by the inner goal. Thus this goal requires that the program output the average of **?New**.

We see in this example that PROUST's problem descriptions are a reasonable approximation of the content of the original English-language problem statements. These problem descriptions describe what the programs must do, but not how they are supposed to do it. PROUST must analyze each individual program and determine how it is intended to satisfy the problem requirements.

Programming Knowledge

As indicated earlier, PROUST analyzes programs using an analysis-by-synthesis approach. PROUST examines the program requirements listed in the problem description, suggests methods for implementing these requirements, and then compares each possible method against the method that the programmer actually uses. In order to suggest what the possible methods are, PROUST requires programming knowledge.

Programming knowledge in PROUST is frame-based [4]. The two kinds of programming knowledge which we will consider here are goals and plans.* Goals are problem requirements, such as appear in problem descriptions. Plans are stereotypic methods for implementing goals. We assume that a large part of the process of writing programs consists of identifying goals which must be satisfied, and selecting plans which implement these goals. In a similar fashion, PROUST retrieves plans from its knowledge base for each goal referred to in the problem description. It compares these plans against the student's program to determine which fits the program best.

Figure 3.6 shows PROUST's definition for the **Sentinel-Controlled-Input** goal. The goal definition contains a series of slots, **InstanceOf, Form, Main-Segment:**, etc., together with fillers for each of these slots, **Read&Process,**

---

* Other types of programming knowledge are described in [3].

```
(Goal-Definition Sentinel-Controlled-Input
        InstanceOf              Read&Process
        Form                    (Sentinel-Controlled-Input ?New ?STOP)
        MainSegment             MainLoop:
        MainVariable            New
        NamePhrase              "sentinel-controlled loop"
        OuterControlPlan        T
        Instances               (Sentinel-Process-Read-While
                                 Sentinel-Read-Process-While
                                 Sentinel-Read-Process-Repeat
                                 Sentinel-Process-Read-Repeat
                                 Bogus-Counter-Controlled-Loop))
```

Figure 3.6 A Goal

MainLoop:, **New,** etc. These slots serve various functions, only some of which will be discussed here. The most important slots are the **Instances** slot and the **InstanceOf** slot. The **Instances** slot lists the various plans in PROUST's knowledge base for implementing this goal. The filler of this slot is a list of five items, each of which is the name of a plan. The **InstanceOf** slot indicates the class to which this goal belongs. The goal class in this case is **Read&Process,** which is the class of all goals which involve reading a sequence of values and processing them.

Figure 3.7 shows a plan, the SENTINEL PROCESS-READ WHILE PLAN. This is one of the instances of the **Sentinel-Controlled-Input** goal. This plan is a simplified version of the plan which PROUST actually uses. Plans are also defined in terms of slots and fillers. The most important slot is the **Template** slot, which describes the form that Pascal code implementing this plan should take. Plan templates consist of Pascal statements, subgoals, and labels. The Pascal statements are written in list notation, rather than ordinary Pascal syntax; for example, the form **(WHILE ($\diamond$?New Stop)...)**, in Pascal syntax, would appear as **WHILE ?New $\diamond$?Stop DO** ... Symbols which are preceded by question marks are pattern variables; these are substituted when the plan is used. **?New** is substituted by a Pascal variable containing the input data, and **?Stop** is substituted by a constant, the sentinel value. **?*** is a "wild-card" pattern which can be substituted by an arbitrary sequence of Pascal statements; this is just a place holder in the plan. Subgoals are indicated by **(SUBGOAL ...)** forms in the template; these are goals which must in turn be implemented using other plans.

```
(Plan-Definition Sentinel-Process-Read-While
        Constants          (Stop)
        Variables          (New)
        Template           ((SUBGOAL (Input ?New))
                           (WHILE (<> ?New ?Stop)
                               (BEGIN
                               ?*
                               (SUBGOAL (Input ?New))))))
```

Figure 3.7 A Plan for Implementing **Sentinel-Controlled-Input**

Matching Plans

Let's now look at how plans and goals are used in order to understand a program. We will start by looking at a plan which has been implemented correctly in the programs in Fig. 3.2. We show how PROUST hypothesizes a plan that the program might use, and then matches this plan against the program. In this case the match succeeds, because the plan is implemented correctly. In the next section we will examine what happens when plans fail to match, because the student's code has bugs.

The first step, before any analysis of goals and plans takes place, is to parse the student's Pascal program. This results in a parse tree. All subsequent analysis of the program is performed on the parse tree, rather than on the original program text.

When PROUST analyzes a program it selects goals from the problem description, one at a time. Let us suppose that the goal which is selected first is (**Sentinel-Controlled-Input** ?**New** ?**Sentinel**). PROUST substitutes into the goal expression any objects whose values are already known. At this point the only information available about ?**New** and ?**Sentinel** is what appears in the problem description. There the value of ?**Sentinel** is listed as 99999, but the value of ?**New** is not listed. Therefore the value of ?**Sentinel** is substituted into the goal expression, but ?**New** is left unchanged. The resulting goal expression is (**Sentinel-Controlled-Input** ?**New** 99999).

PROUST must now retrieve from its programming knowledge base plans which could be used to implement the goal **Sentinel-Controlled-Input**. It retrieves the filler of the **Instances** slot of the definition of **Sentinel-Controlled-Input** shown in Fig. 3.6. This filler is a list of five items: **Sentinel-Process-Read-While**, **Sentinel-Read-Process-While**, **Sentinel-Read-Process-Repeat**, **Sentinel-Process-Read-Repeat**, and **Bogus-Counter-Controlled-Loop**. Each of these is the name of a plan. PROUST selects the first plan from the list, **Sentinel-Process-Read-While**. This will be PROUST's initial hypothesis of how the program implements the goal **Sentinel-Controlled-Loop**.

Just as known values of objects were substituted into the goal expression (**Sentinel-Controlled-Input ?New ?Sentinel**), these same substitutions must now be performed on the selected plan. **?Stop** is replaced by 99999, and **?New** is left unchanged. Because **?New** is unchanged, PROUST assumes that the process of matching the plan against the program will determine what the value of **?New** is.

Figure 3.8 shows how the SENTINEL PROCESS-READ WHILE PLAN is matched against the program example in Fig. 3.2. Matching starts with the **WHILE** loop. The pattern in the plan for the **WHILE** loop is (**WHILE** ($\diamondsuit$ **?New** 99999) ...). There are two **WHILE** loops in this program: **WHILE Val** $\diamondsuit$ 99999 **DO** ... and **WHILE Val** $\leq$ 0 **DO** ... PROUST tries to match each pattern against each of these statements. (**WHILE** ($\diamondsuit$ **?New** 99999) ...) matches **WHILE Val** $\diamondsuit$ 99999 **DO** ..., provided that **Val** is substituted for **?New**. (**WHILE** ($\diamondsuit$ **?New** 99999) ...) does not match **WHILE Val** $\leq$ 0 **DO** ..., because the statement has a $\leq$ test instead of a $\diamondsuit$ test, and because it tests against 0 instead of 99999. Therefore PROUST selects **WHILE Val** $\diamondsuit$ 99999 **DO** ... as the match for the plan pattern. Since **Val** must be substituted for **?New** in order for the pattern to match, **Val** is recorded as the binding for **?New**. Afterwards any component of the plan which has **?New** in it will have **Val** substituted for **?New**.

The plan component that PROUST matches against the program is (**BEGIN** ...). There are several different **BEGIN** statements in the program which could be matched against this pattern. However, in the plan template the (**BEGIN** ...) pattern appears inside of the **WHILE** pattern that was just matched. This means that the **BEGIN** statement that this pattern matches must be located inside of the **WHILE Val** $\diamondsuit$ 99999 **DO** ... statement. There is therefore only one **BEGIN** statement which is an appropriate match.

When PROUST tries to match the (**SUBGOAL** (**Input ?New**)) components, a different type of processing is required. These plan components are goals; in order to match them against the program, PROUST must go through the same plan selection process that it went through in selecting the SENTINEL PROCESS-READ WHILE PLAN. It first substitutes all pattern variables in the goal expression which have bindings. Since **?New** has **Val** as a binding, the subgoal expression becomes (**Input Val**). PROUST then retrieves plans from the plan database which implement **Input**. One such plan is the READ PLAN, which employs a Pascal **Read** statement to input the value. This plan matches the **Read** statements in the program.

This example shows how PROUST analyzes programs, by predicting the plans which might be used, and then testing these predictions. By selecting from a range of different plans and subplans for each goal, PROUST is able to generate a variety of different ways of implementing each goal. Since PROUST

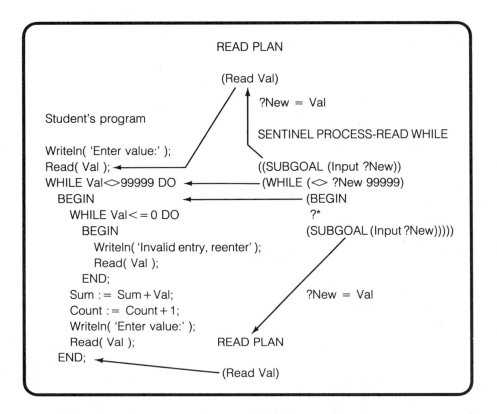

Figure 3.8 Matching a Plan against a Program

first generates a possible implementation and then matches it against the program, it is performing analysis by synthesis. In general, generating plan hypotheses and matching them against programs is rather more complex than the scenario presented here; for further information, see [3].

Identifying Bugs

When the SENTINEL PROCESS-READ WHILE PLAN was matched against the program in Fig. 3.8, the plan matched exactly. Since there were no match errors, there must not have been any bugs in that particular plan. It is frequently the case, however, that none of the plans which PROUST predicts matches the program. When this happens PROUST must look for bugs which account for the mismatches in one of the plans. In this section we will discuss one of these mismatches in connection with the **WHILE**-for-**IF** example in Fig. 3.3, and show how it leads to the discovery of a bug.

The bug in the **WHILE**-for-**IF** example is discovered in processing the **Input-Validation** goal. One of the plans which PROUST suggests for implementing this goal is the so-called BAD INPUT LOOP TEST PLAN. This plan consists of the following components:

1. a **WHILE** statement which tests the input to see if it is out of range,

2. an error message inside the **WHILE** loop,

3. an **Input** subgoal which re-reads the input if it is out of range, and

4. a test to see if the exit condition for the main loop has been satisfied.

In solutions to the Averaging Problem a correct implementation of this plan would be the following:

```
WHILE Val <= 0 DO
   BEGIN
      Writeln( 'Invalid data, please re-enter' );
      Read( Val );
   END;
IF Val <> 99999 THEN
   . . .
```

The BAD INPUT LOOP TEST PLAN matches the **WHILE**-for-**IF** example in all respects save one: there is no test for the exit condition of the main loop, such as **IF Val** <> **99999 THEN** . . . Where an **IF** statement is expected, a **WHILE** statement appears instead. PROUST has thus encountered a *plan difference*, i.e., a difference between the expected plan and the code. When PROUST encounters plan differences it does not give up on the plan; instead, it tries to find a way of interpreting the plan differences as bugs.

In most cases plan differences are explained by means of *bug rules*. Each bug rule has a test part, which examines the plan differences to see whether or not the rule is applicable, and an action part, which explains the plan differences. Figure 3.9 shows the bug rule which is invoked to explain the plan difference in the **WHILE**-for-**IF** example. The rule is written in slot-filler notation; one set of slots constitutes the test part of the rule, and another set constitutes the action part. In the **WHILE**-for-**IF** rule the test part consists of a **Statement-Type** slot and an **Error-Pattern** slot. The **Statement-Type** slot indicates that the plan component which failed to match the program must be an **IF** statement. The **Error-Pattern** slot has the value (**IF** . **WHILE**); this indicates that a **WHILE** statement was found when an **IF** statement was expected. These test conditions are both met in the **WHILE**-for-**IF** example, so the action part of the rule is activated. The action part of this rule consists of a **Bug** slot; the filler of this slot is a description of the bug associated with the plan difference. The bug in this case is a **WHILE**-for-**IF** confusion. PROUST's bug analyses of student programs consist of bug descriptions such as this. When PROUST presents its

```
(Define-Rule WHILE-for-IF
      Statement-Type      IF
      Error-Pattern       (IF . WHILE)
      Bug                 (WHILE-for-IF-Confusion (FoundStmt ,*MRet*)
                                                  (HistInst , *HistoryNode*)))
```

Figure 3.9 The WHILE-for-IF Bug Rule

findings to the student, it takes each bug description and generates an English-language translation for it, and if appropriate generates data illustrating the presence of the bug.

Test Results

PROUST has been tested on large numbers of novice programs. The following are the results of one such test. We assigned a class of novice programmers the Rainfall Problem, shown in Fig. 3.10. This is an elaboration of the Averaging Problem discussed earlier.

Write a Pascal program that will prompt the user to input numbers from the terminal; each input stands for the amount of rainfall in New Haven for a day. Note: since rainfall cannot be negative, the program should reject negative input. Your program should compute the following statistics from this data:

1. the average rainfall per day;
2. the number of rainy days;
3. the number of valid inputs (excluding any invalid data that might have been read in);
4. the maximum amount of rain that fell on any one day.

The program should read data until the user types 99999; this is a sentinel value signaling the end of input. Do not include the 99999 in the calculations. Assume that if the input value is non-negative, and not equal to 99999, then it is valid input data.

Figure 3.10 The Rainfall Problem

We tested PROUST as follows. We modified the Pascal compiler that our students were using so that it would save copies of every syntactically correct program that they compiled. This allowed us to examine not only the final solution which the students handed in, but also every intermediate version of their programs. We then ran PROUST off line on the first syntactically correct versions of each program. Since the first versions are likely to be the buggiest versions, this enabled us to test PROUST under the most difficult conditions possible.

Figure 3.11 shows the result of testing PROUST. There were 206 different programs in the test set. Of these, PROUST was able to derive a complete understanding of 75% of the programs. When it did so, it identified 95% of the bugs, a percentage far higher than people are able to achieve. The chart also indicates that 5% of the bugs were not recognized, and 46 bugs were false alarms. Bugs are counted as not recognized either if they are misdiagnosed or if they are missed entirely. Bugs are counted as false alarms either if they are not present in the program or if the bugs are present but misdiagnosed. Consequently misdiagnosed bugs are counted both as false alarms and as not recognized, thus inflating the total number of diagnosis errors.

When PROUST fails to understand a program completely, its ability to recognize bugs deteriorates. Twenty percent of the programs were analyzed partially. In such cases PROUST deleted from its bug descriptions those bug analyses which were questionable, given that the program was only partially understood. The bug descriptions that remained were frequently wrong, but at least PROUST was able to warn the student to take the analysis with a grain of salt. The remaining 5% of the programs deviated from PROUST's expectations so drastically that it could not analyze them at all. In these cases no bug report was generated.

We are not yet sufficiently satisfied with PROUST's accuracy to make it generally available to students. The false alarm rate should be lower, and the fraction of programs which PROUST analyzes completely should be higher. When part of a program cannot be analyzed, PROUST should try to determine why it is that part of the program cannot be analyzed, and try to account for the unanalyzed code. Once this is done we expect PROUST to succeed on 80% to 85% of the programs that it analyzes. At that stage we will make it available to students on line.

Concluding Remarks

PROUST is capable of high-quality analysis of bugs in novice programs. It is verging on the level where it could be incorporated into a programming curriculum and provide significant benefit to students. This paper gives a simplified view of how bugs are found by PROUST, but one which accurately reflects most of the bugs PROUST has to diagnose.

Total number of programs:	206	
Number of programs with bugs:	183	(89%)
Number of programs receiving full analyses:	155	(75%)
Total number of bugs:	531	
Bugs recognized correctly:	502	(95%)
Bugs not recognized:	29	(5%)
False alarms:	46	
Number of programs receiving partial analyses:	40	(20%)
Total number of bugs:	220	
Bugs recognized correctly:	79	(36%)
Bugs deleted from analysis:	80	(36%)
Bugs not recognized:	61	(28%)
False alarms:	36	
Number of programs PROUST did not analyze:	11	(5%)

Figure 3.11 Results of Running PROUST on the Rainfall Problem

The logical next step is to build an automated programming course around PROUST. Such a system would not only correct the students' mistakes, but also suggest additional problems for the students to solve, in order to give the student practice where needed. This would be an important milestone in applying artificial intelligence to teaching programming.

References

1. Fosdick, L. D., and Osterweil, L. J. (1976). Data flow analysis in software reliability. *Computing Surveys 8,* 3, 305–330.

2. Harandi, M. T. (1983). Knowledge-based program debugging: A heuristic model. *Proceedings of the 1983 SOFTFAIR,* SoftFair.

3. Johnson, W. L. (1985). Intention-based diagnosis of programming errors. Report No. 395, Yale University Department of Computer Science.

4. Minsky, M. (1975). A framework for representing knowledge. In P. Winston (Ed.), *The psychology of computer vision.* New York: McGraw-Hill.

5. Shortliffe, E. H. (1976). *Computer-based medical consultations: MYCIN.* New York: Elsevier.

6. Wertz, H. (1982). Stereotyped program debugging: An aid for novice programmers. *International Journal of Man-Machine Studies, 16,* 379–392.

4 / Micro-SEARCH: A "Shell" for Building Systems to Help Students Solve Non-deterministic Tasks

DEREK SLEEMAN

Overview

Students of science and mathematics react poorly to tasks that involve the use of nondeterministic algorithms, that is, algorithms in which they are required to make *arbitrary* choices. There appear to be several reasons for this. Students' "world views" of subjects appear to be too small; they *expect* all tasks to be solvable by well-defined algorithms. Moreover, their teaching does not prepare them for this class of algorithms, as it seldom discusses search as a necessary strategy for solving a whole range of tasks (Anderson, 1981). Because many tasks in high school mathematics involve nondeterministic search (such as the transformation of algebraic and trigonometric forms and proofs in geometry), this type of problem solving is important.

The first section of this chapter seeks to explain the nature of nondeterministic tasks first by means of several examples drawn from mathematics and then more abstractly. The second section discusses in outline how such tasks are currently taught—and how they might be taught if the inherent *search* process was made more explicit. The remainder of the chapter discusses three systems, called problem-solving monitors (PSMs), which have been implemented on different computers to help students "explore" search spaces. The emphasis in these sections is on describing the functionality of the programs. The systems described here draw some characteristics from the work on microworlds (diSessa, 1982; Lawler, 1981; Thompson, Chapter 5) and intelligent tutoring systems (ITSs) (Sleeman & Brown, 1982), in that they allow the student to "explore" a closed world and yet provide (tutorial) support when it is requested. Indeed, they appear to be good examples of (intelligent) Socratic systems (Sleeman & Hartley, 1969).

What Is a Nondeterministic Algorithm?

Figure 4.1 shows a search tree for transforming a trigonometric expression $\tan x/(1 + \tan^2 x)$ into two alternative forms. Similarly, Fig. 4.2 shows the paths by which an algebraic expression is transformed into two alternative forms. The important point to note is that there is no one "correct" transformation to be applied at any stage. This can be seen from inspection of these figures. Computer scientists call such diagrams search trees and talk about the search procedure as being nondeterministic, because at any one stage it may not be possible to decide uniquely on a single operator to apply. In such cases, the algorithm makes an *arbitrary* choice of operator, and only after exploring the path is it clear whether the earlier choice was correct. Exploring such trees frequently entails *backtracking*—retreating from states that are themselves clearly "cul de sacs."

Figure 4.3 illustrates this process more abstractly. Typically the user is given the initial state (I), the goal (G), and explicitly or implicitly a set of pertinent transformations. The figure shows that node 1 can be transformed in three ways,

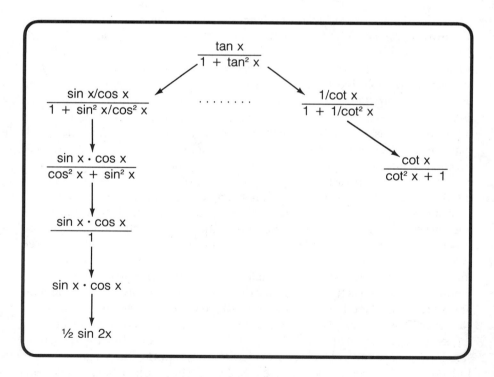

Figure 4.1 Transformation of $\tan x/(1 + \tan^2 x)$ into both $\frac{1}{2} \sin 2x$ and $\cot x/(\cot^2 x + 1)$

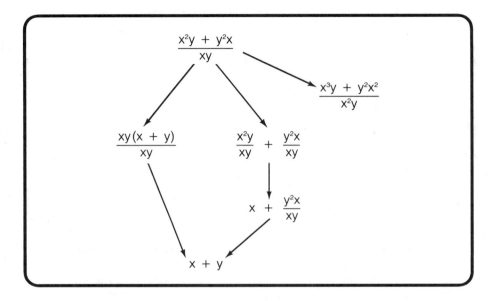

Figure 4.2 Transformation of $(x^2y + y^2x)/xy$ into $x + y$ and $(x^3y + y^2x^2)/x^2y$

yielding nodes 2, 3, and 4; similarly, node 2 can be expanded to yield nodes 5 and 6, and so on. The square boxes around nodes 11, 12, and 13 indicate that they are failure nodes, and the circle around node 14 indicates that it is the goal, G.

Thus, at node 1 the person solving the task can know that three out of the complete set of transformations are applicable, but would not know which, if any, would lead to the goal, G. So a strategy to "solve" such tasks is to apply each of the transformations in turn and after each node has been expanded check to see if the goal has been achieved. If the goal has *not* been achieved the tree is expanded further. There are several ways of creating—or traversing—a possible solution tree; the one noted above corresponds to the breadth-first search algorithm (Nilsson, 1971). When a node results in a failure, no further expansion is made on that branch, and the next node on the node-list is expanded. If there are no more nodes to expand, then the search fails; that is, the algorithm concludes that the goal is not attainable.

An alternative algorithm for searching trees is the depth-first search algorithm (Nilsson, 1971), which explores "one avenue of investigation" exhaustively before considering another. If the tree in Fig. 4.3 had been searched by a depth-first algorithm, the nodes would have been expanded in the order 1, 2, 5, 11 (backtrack to 5), 12 (backtrack to 5, then to 2), 6, 13 (backtrack to 6), and 14 (stop as the goal, G, is attained, unless the algorithm was asked to find

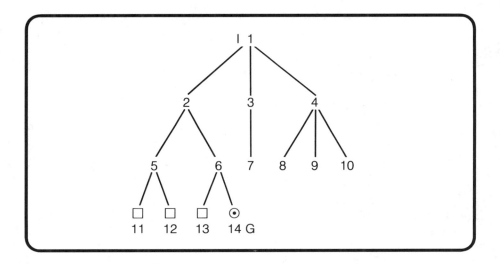

Figure 4.3 I designates the *initial* node and G the *goal* node. The figure
shows a space being searched systematically.

all possible solutions). With this algorithm nodes 3, 4, 7, 8, 9, and 10 would not
be explored. Because of the nature of the depth-first search algorithm, it is
necessary to truncate the algorithm's search at a prespecified depth; indeed,
nodes 11, 12, and 13, labeled earlier as failure nodes, are where the search has
been truncated.

The Teaching of Nondeterministic Algorithms

As mentioned earlier, nondeterministic algorithms are currently taught poorly.
Students are not taught that search is a legitimate strategy. When tasks like those
in Figs. 4.1 and 4.2 are discussed, the teacher frequently states the next transformation to be applied without explaining why this is so, thus giving students
little guidance as to how to solve such tasks. We suggest that students should
be explicitly asked (1) to state all the transformations they consider to be appropriate to the task and (2) to systematically explore the complete solution space,
that is, to draw trees analogous to Figs. 4.1 and 4.2. The major disadvantage of
this approach is the potential size of the search space. (Davis, 1984, discusses
search as appropriate for solving equations of the form: SEND + MORE =
MONEY, but does not advocate it as a more general approach.) In the regular
classroom situation this can be dealt with by limiting the number of transformations to be considered for any task and by telling the student the length of the

shortest known solution path. This latter information would suggest a cutoff point for the search. Alternatively, it is possible to implement a computer-based system that will support students when they explore such spaces. These systems can ensure that the space is explored systematically, and can provide certain support facilities.

Problem-Solving Monitors (PSMs)

We have called systems that provide this type of support either problem-solving monitors or coaches. Sleeman (1975) implemented the first such system to assist students with the interpretation of (simple) nuclear magnetic resonance spectra. Students were provided with a molecular formula and a spectrum, and were required to produce the molecular *structure*. This system could handle three types of inputs:

1. *An assertion,* that is, a solution to the next step of the task. Assertions in this domain basically stated the composition of the next chemical group and the corresponding peak in the spectrum.
2. *A request for HELP.* Possible assertions would then be listed.
3. *A request for an explanation.* Explanations were available only after an incorrect assertion.

These inputs were processed as follows:

1. The system checked to see that the assertion was syntactically correct and used only resources still remaining. For example, an assertion that tried to "use" a peak not remaining in the spectrum would be rejected. Transformations that passed these tests corresponded to feasible transformations.
2. The *first* request for HELP would list all the transformations possible at a particular node. The *second* request for HELP indicated what the algorithm believed was the best next move, or pointed out that the goal could not be achieved in a "reasonable" number of moves. Solution paths greater then N times the length of the best solution path were rejected; N was a variable set by the investigator.
3. The EXPLAIN request—available only after an incorrect assertion—demonstrated that the goal would not be accessible if the rejected goal was accepted. That is, the algorithm reports the whole of the tree below the "rejected" node.

Note that this PSM supported a depth-first search of the problem space; this seemed to be most "natural" for relatively naive users. (Certainly the "housekeeping" is less complex than with the breadth-first algorithm, as with the latter algorithm one appears to "abandon" nodes only to return to them sub-sequently.)

A Generalized Version of the PSM: TSEARCH

As it was realized that there was a whole class of tasks that involved a nondeter-ministic search, France and Sleeman (1979) implemented a more general "do-main independent" PSM, called TSEARCH. Earlier, Shortliffe (1976) had demonstrated that one could separate an inference engine from its knowledge base. TSEARCH was built to solve tasks that involved nondeterministic searches, and it provided a variety of support facilities for its users. In a very real sense, TSEARCH was a shell for building a class of intelligent tutoring systems. Figure 4.4 lists the user commands available in TSEARCH and provides a brief explana-tion of each command. Note that TSEARCH did not allow a student to type in the transformed expression but merely the *number* of the transformation to be applied. Thus TSEARCH would work only in a domain in which the set of operators could be specified in advance—that is, a closed world was assumed. We decided to provide this facility as we believed that students would make a considerable number of errors typing the complex expressions involved in these domains. Effectively, this system *assumed* that the student knew the do-main operators and how to apply them, but that the student might have difficulty in deciding *when* the operators should be applied; that is, students had difficulty in deciding on a solution *strategy*. (However, we know that the assumption that students are able to apply operators correctly is not always true, Sleeman, 1982.)

One command given in Fig. 4.4 should be highlighted. REVIEW juxtaposed the user's and TSEARCH's solution path for the current task—once it had been solved. We noted earlier that the nature of the goal strongly influences which transformation will be the best to apply at any stage. It appears that the expert in such domains has inferred a whole range of *heuristics*—that is, useful rules of thumb which suggest *likely* rules to be used in given situations. The REVIEW command was intended to enable users to see gross inefficiencies in their solution path (such as $x \rightarrow 1 * x \rightarrow x$) and additionally that studying, or reflecting on, the differences between the two traces would enable the user to build up a set of good heuristics. Further, it was hoped that this information would encourage students to reflect on their solution process—and hence refine their problem-solving strategies. The study of this introspection process has become an important area in psychology known as metacognition (A. L. Brown, 1975).

To demonstrate TSEARCH's potential as an ITS shell, databases were im-plemented for trigonometry, algebra, and Boolean algebra.

TSEARCH had two other facilities of note. First, a command NEW-PROBLEM allowed the user—usually the database implementor—to specify a new task. Second, TSEARCH kept a "transformation matrix" for each user on *each* task.

COMMAND	Prints a list of commands.
PROBLEM	Selects next task.
PRINTRULES	Prints a list of all rules in the database.
PRINTRULE R	Prints rule R.
USERULE N	If possible, apply rule N to current expression —if there are many possible matches ask user which is applicable.
HELP	First use on each task gives: all the rules which could apply. Subsequent uses for each task give: either the rule TSEARCH would apply or advice that the goal is not reachable in a "reasonable" number of steps.
FORGET	Backtracks one step.
REMEMBER	Forgets the FORGET command; reapplies the previously undone transformation.
REVIEW	Juxtaposes the user's and TSEARCH's solution paths. (Only available once the task has been solved.)
BYE	Allows the user to leave the system.

Figure 4.4 User Facilities Provided by TSEARCH

This data structure recorded, for each step in the task, the transformation chosen by the student and that chosen by TSEARCH. Thus entries on the diagonal of the matrix indicated that the student and TSEARCH chose the same transformation. Nondiagonal terms indicated a different choice. Each off-diagonal entry indicated that the student selected what the algorithm thought was a nonoptimal move. Similarly, TSEARCH also kept a cumulative matrix, that is, a matrix that recorded for a single student the transformations that he or she had applied across all the tasks worked.

These transformation matrices can be viewed as student models. Indeed, one simple way of using the information would be to associate remedial comment strings or remedial procedures with the off-diagonal cells. For example, if the student suggested operator A in a particular situation and the algorithm suggested operator B, then the algorithm might suggest that when in analogous situations the student might consider using operator B—explaining its superiority to A in the current context. (Clearly, more sophisticated uses of the "models" could be made in which actions would be contingent on the conditions of several cells.)

Critique of TSEARCH

TSEARCH had four shortcomings:

1. The major disadvantage of TSEARCH was its speed for any nontrivial task. In particular, the system took a long time to respond to HELP requests, because they involved expanding a sizable number of nodes.

2. TSEARCH allowed students to be very passive in learning because they could use the HELP facility for a prompt at each stage. A more sophisticated system would keep a record of the user's requests and would make the HELP facility *unavailable* under certain circumstances.

3. The task selection algorithm should make use of the information in the transformation matrix to select (appropriate) tasks for the user.

4. The transformation matrix provides valuable information for the type of issue-based coach implemented in the WEST system (Burton & Brown, 1982). Such a coach would occasionally point out better solution paths than those chosen by the user.

The Design of Micro-SEARCH

Micro-SEARCH represents the latest evolution (or condensation) of this PSM. Micro-SEARCH is a version of TSEARCH implemented on an IBM PC using an interpreted LISP system (see discussion by Wallach in Chapter 12). Of the issues raised in the last section the only one addressed to date by Micro-SEARCH has been that of speed. It was realized that the efficiency of the algorithm could be critical. (TSEARCH had been implemented in Rutgers LISP on the DEC-10.) The following design changes were made between the TSEARCH and Micro-SEARCH versions:

1. Instead of using *all* the rules for each type of task, we used only those that are known to be relevant. That is, we *segmented* the rule set.

2. The system now has two phases: an off-line phase that creates the "complete" solution space ("complete" up to some predefined cutoff point), and an on-line phase that accesses the solution and interacts with the student. As noted earlier, this separation is possible because the set of possible transformations is predefined (cf. the design of LMS/PIXIE, Sleeman, 1983).

As noted earlier, speed is of particular importance with the HELP facility. The on-line system could have been improved further had we used a data structure for the nodes in the solution tree that allow both forward and backward searches to be done rapidly. (In TSEARCH the complete solution tree was an embedded list.) The data structure suggested for the nodes in Micro-SEARCH had three "fields": the names of parent nodes (may be more than one), the expression, and the names of its offspring. Still further improvement could be achieved by adding an additional "field" to the data structure for the node, namely, the list of all the applicable transformations. Each node would be given a *symbolic* name, and the data structure corresponding to the node would be stored on a property list; this would ensure a uniform and rapid access to all the nodes in the solution tree.

Micro-SEARCH, as TSEARCH, encourages students to do a depth-first search of the task space. Figure 4.5 gives the complete layout of the screen at the beginning of a trigonometric transformation task and shows the first transformation—note that at each stage the screen displays the list of possible transformations together with initial, goal, and current states. Figure 4.6 shows an intermediate step in solving a Boolean algebra task. Although not available for this version of Micro-SEARCH, the REVIEW facility described in the last section will be available in the next version of the system.

Pedagogical Possibilities with Micro-SEARCH

Although the experience we have of using PSMs is limited to date, we have been very encouraged by students' reactions. Even without a graphical interface, the students seemed to appreciate the idea of a search space and were soon able to use the system to solve tasks from their regular classwork. To date, only limited informal studies have been carried out with chemistry undergraduates (PSM-NMR), and high school mathematics students (TSEARCH and Micro-SEARCH).

Micro-SEARCH would also be valuable for both teachers and teacher trainees. One would hope it would help them appreciate the nature of the search space underlying nondeterministic algorithms, and that they would then teach many topics, including algebraic and trigonometric transformations, in a radically different way; preferably, they would teach the inherent search explicitly.

Further Work

Given the existence of Micro-SEARCH on a relatively inexpensive computer, it would be very desirable to carry out the following studies:

- Run a controlled experiment in several classrooms to determine the relative effectiveness of teaching, say, trigonometric transformations conventionally versus making the search explicit.

Problem: 1   Current Step: 0   Maximum Steps: 7

Transformations:
1: TAN X $\longrightarrow$ 1 / (COT X)
2: A / (COS X) $\longrightarrow$ A * (SEC X)
3: COT X $\longrightarrow$ (COS X) / (SIN X)
4: TAN X $\longrightarrow$ (SIN X) / (COS X)
5: A + A $\longrightarrow$ 2 * A
6: 1 * A $\longrightarrow$ A
7: A / 1 $\longrightarrow$ A
8: A / (B / C) $\longrightarrow$ (A * C) / B

Initial State: TAN X + 1 / (COT X)
Goal State: 2 * ((SIN X) * (SEC X))
Current State: TAN X + 1 / (COT X)

      HELP — prints this out
      NEXT — goes to next problem
      QUIT — exits . . .
OK> 1

Apply transformation to
      TAN X + 1 / (COT X)

Answer Y or N — Y

Problem : 1   Current Step: 1   Maximum Steps: 7

Transformations:
1: TAN X $\longrightarrow$ 1 / (COT X)
2: A / (COS X) $\longrightarrow$ A * (SEC X)
3: COT X $\longrightarrow$ (COS X) / (SIN X)
4: TAN X $\longrightarrow$ (SIN X) / (COS X)
5: A + A $\longrightarrow$ 2 * A
6: 1 * A $\longrightarrow$ A
7: A / 1 $\longrightarrow$ A
8: A / (B / C) $\longrightarrow$ (A * C) / B

Initial State: TAN X + 1 / (COT X)
Goal State: 2 * ((SIN X) * (SEC X))
Current State: 1 / (COT X) + 1 / (COT X)

OK>

Figure 4.5 Layout of the screen at the beginning of a trigonometric transformation

Problem: 2   Current Step: 3   Maximum Steps: 6

Transformations:
1: T AND P → P   9: P AND (NOT P) → F
2: T OR P → T   10: P OR (NOT P) → T
3: F AND P → F   11: P AND P → P
4: F OR P → P   12: P OR P → P
5: NOT (NOT P) → P
6: P OR (Q AND R) → (P OR Q) and (P OR R)
7: NOT (P AND Q) → (NOT P) OR (NOT Q)
8: NOT (P OR Q) → (NOT P) and (NOT Q)

Initial State: A OR (NOT (A OR (NOT B)))
Goal State: A OR B
Current State: (A OR (NOT A)) and (A OR B)
OK> 10

Apply transformation to
        (A OR (NOT A)) AND (A OR B)

Answer Y or N — Y

Problem: 2   Current Step: 4   Maximum Steps: 6

Transformations:
1: T AND P → P   9: P AND (NOT P) → F
2: T OR P → T   10: P OR (NOT P) → T
3: F AND P → F   11: P AND P → P
4: F OR P → P   12: P OR P → P
5: NOT (NOT P) → P
6: P OR (Q AND R) → (P OR Q) and (P OR R)
7: NOT (P AND Q) → (NOT P) OR (NOT Q)
8: NOT (P OR Q) → (NOT P) and (NOT Q)

Initial State: A OR (NOT (A OR (NOT B)))
Goal State: A OR B
Current State: T AND (A OR B)

Figure 4.6 Layout of screen at intermediate step in solving a
            Boolean algebra task

- Repeat the above experiment but with the experimental group using Micro-SEARCH as a classroom demonstration aid.

- Determine the effectiveness of Micro-SEARCH with individuals; probe students' procedural and conceptual understanding by means of individual clinical interviews.

- Use Micro-SEARCH as a test-bed for seeing how a more individualized set of tasks, individualized discussion of issues (in the WEST sense), and control over the availability of HELP would affect student performance. (The enhanced system would use the inferred student "models"—the transformation matrices—extensively.)

- Probe the extent to which students have acquired a notion of search as a general technique for solving a certain class of tasks. Specifically, one could attempt to show that students taught trigonometric transformations where search was taught explicitly would do better on algebraic transformations than students taught trigonometric transformations conventionally. It is envisioned that both traditional experimental design and clinical interviews would be used to investigate these issues.

Related Activities

Suppes and his group at Stanford have implemented several computer-based instructional systems for whole courses in college-level set theory and logic. These programs allow the student to solve tasks in a supportive environment (Suppes & Sheehan, 1981; Blaine, 1981).

Anderson and his group at Carnegie-Mellon University have implemented a system that helps students explore geometry problems (Anderson, 1981). Brown and colleagues at XEROX PARC have implemented a system, ALGEBRA-LAND, which allows users to transform algebra equations (Brown, 1983). The latter group has stressed the potential importance of such systems in helping students reflect on their solution processes.

Acknowledgments

Stuart France contributed significantly to the design of TSEARCH and was largely responsible for that implementation. More recently Bret Wallach has done an excellent job of implementing Micro-SEARCH in a very short period. Leszek Izdebski has played a valuable supporting role in this implementation.

References

Anderson, J. R. (1981). Tuning of search of the problem space for geometry proofs. In *Proceedings of IJCAI-81* (pp. 165–170).

Blaine, L. (1981). Programs for structured proof. In P. Suppes (Ed.), *University level computer-assisted instruction at Stanford: 1968–1980* (pp. 81–119). Stanford, CA: Stanford University Press.

Brown, A. L. (1975). The development of memory: Knowing, knowing about knowing, and knowing how to know. In H. W. Reese (Ed.), *Advances in child development and behavior* (Vol. 10). New York: Academic Press.

Brown, J. S. (1983). Idea amplifiers—New kinds of electronic learning environments. *Educational Horizons* (pp. 108–112).

Burton, R. R., & Brown, J. S. (1982). An investigation of computer coaching for informal learning activities. In D. Sleeman & J. S. Brown (Eds.), *Intelligent tutoring systems* (pp. 79–88). New York: Academic Press.

Davis, R. B. (1984). *Learning mathematics: The cognitive science approach to mathematics education* (pp. 238–258). New Jersey: Ablex.

diSessa, A. A. (1982). Unlearning Aristotelian physics: A study of knowledge-based learning. *Cognitive Science, 6,* 37–75.

France, S. A., & Sleeman, D. H. (1979). TSEARCH: A data-driven system to help students solve non-deterministic algorithms. Technical Report, Dept. of Computer Studies, University of Leeds.

Lawler, R. W. (1981). The progressive construction of mind. *Cognitive Science, 5,* 1–30.

Nilsson, N. (1971). *Problem solving methods in artificial intelligence.* New York: McGraw-Hill.

Shortliffe, E. H. (1976). *Computer based medical consultations: MYCIN.* New York: Elsevier.

Sleeman, D. H. (1975). A Problem Solving Monitor for a deductive reasoning task. *International Journal of Man-Machine Studies, 7*(2), 183–211.

Sleeman, D. H. (1982). Assessing aspects of competence in basic algebra. In D. Sleeman & J. S. Brown (Eds.), *Intelligent tutoring systems* (pp. 185–199). New York: Academic Press.

Sleeman, D. H. (1983). Inferring student models for intelligent CAI. In R. S. Michalski, J. G. Carbonell, & T. M. Mitchell (Eds.), *Machine learning* (pp. 483–510).

Sleeman, D., & Brown, J. S. (1982). *Intelligent tutoring systems.* New York: Academic Press.

Sleeman, D. H., & Hartley, J. R. (1969). Instructional models in a computer based learning system. *International Journal of Man-Machine Studies, 1*(2), 177–188.

Suppes, P., & Sheehan, J. (1981). CAI course in axiomatic set-theory. In P. Suppes (Ed.), *University level computer-assisted instruction at Stanford: 1968–1980* (pp. 1–80). Stanford, CA: Stanford University Press.

5/ Mathematical Microworlds and Intelligent Computer-Assisted Instruction

PATRICK W. THOMPSON

My work with microworlds has been to design computerized environments that allow two foci: conceptual development and mathematical problem solving. The theory behind that approach has been elaborated elsewhere (Thompson, 1985a). In this chapter I will only briefly touch upon theoretical motivations, devoting the majority of the discussion to what I mean by a mathematical microworld, how one works, and to issues of designing microworld environments.

The discussion in this chapter is framed by the research program in which I have been engaged over the past four years. Figure 5.1 outlines the principal components of that program. It shows that remarks given here about the design of software to be used in mathematics teaching and learning are not given in isolation. Rather, they are informed by results, conceptions, and metaphors from investigations of cognitive processes of mathematical comprehension and problem solving, prescriptions for cognitive objectives of instruction, and analyses of mathematical content (Dreyfus & Thompson, 1985; Thompson, 1985a). Each of these, in turn, is informed by knowledge gained through research and development of software for teaching and learning mathematics (Thompson, 1985b, 1985c; Thompson & Dreyfus, in press). I do not mean to say that one must accept the research program outlined in Fig. 5.1 to design mathematical microworlds. Rather, I mean only to say that issues of design are at heart theoretical, and as an aid to communication it helps to make explicit one's theoretical perspective from the outset.

Revised version of a paper presented at the Invitational Workshop on Intelligent Computer-Assisted Instruction and Personal Computers, San Diego, CA, February 1985. The author wishes to thank Matthew Lewis for his helpful and insightful reactions to a draft of this chapter.

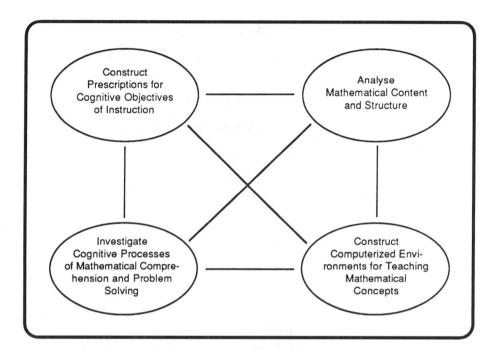

Figure 5.1 The four components of a research program on understanding and improving mathematics teaching and learning.

Before characterizing mathematical microworlds, it will be instructive to discuss the educational problem they address. It is this: far too many students do not understand that mathematical symbol systems are fundamentally representational; they are contrived by individuals or communities to provide economic ways to think about complex ideas. Instead, students typically perceive that mathematics is concerned primarily with making marks on paper, and that the aim of mathematics instruction is to teach them how to make correct marks at correct positions on the paper. The goal that mathematical microworlds serve is to provide students with opportunities to create mental models that reflect the structure and composition of the formal systems our culture has deemed important to learn. Once in place, a mental model serves as a stepping-stone for students in their reconstruction of their qualitative knowledge into a formal system. In short, a mathematical microworld provides a dynamic semantics for a formal system.

I should also make clear an underlying philosophy of mathematical microworlds. It is that they act as objective systems, in the sense of physical systems studied by scientists. A consequence of this philosophy is that microworlds do not teach; they do not provide instruction. The reason is that when a scientist performs an experiment upon a physical system, the system does not comment on the quality of the experiment. Rather, it merely behaves. A scientist attempts to hypothesize the principles by which a system operates by observing the system's behavior under experimental conditions. The scientist does not get advice from the system.*

This chapter has five sections. The first discusses general characteristics of microworlds and gives an in-depth example of one—a microworld for isometric transformations of the plane. The second and third sections discuss issues and principles in designing mathematical microworlds. The fourth section discusses shortcomings that have been found and enhancements that make use of artificial intelligence. The fifth section discusses possibilities for intelligent microworlds in schools.

Mathematical Microworlds

I will use "mathematical microworld" to mean a system composed of objects, relationships among objects, and operations that transform objects and relationships. This characterization is meant to capture the idea of a mathematical system as constructed from primitive terms and propositions, where the full system initially exists only potentially but includes features that allow students to expand that potential.

It is unfortunate that the generic term "microworld" has been used so many different ways. Papert's (1980) use of "microworld" includes a procedure to create spiral polygons and a program to simulate Newton's third principle of thermodynamics (diSessa, 1982). Lawler (1982) uses "microworld" to describe mental constructs that are often called schemata in cognitive psychology; in Lawler (1984), "microworld" describes any program that provides "inherently interesting phenomena." Rather than attempt to create a new name, I use the qualifier "mathematical" to distinguish the systems described here from what have been called microworlds by others.

In practice, a mathematical microworld incorporates a graphical display that depicts a visualization of the microworld's initial objects. The display in conjunction with operations upon the microworld's objects constitutes a model of the concept or concepts being proposed to the students. In a very real sense, the microworld embodies the structure of the concept. The students' task is to internalize that structure and make it their own.

The last criterion listed—that the system contain operations by which new objects can be made—is essential. This is what makes a mathematical micro-

---

* My favorite analogy is one concocted by a graduate student: If you want to become an expert archer, you practice archery. Suppose you shoot an arrow at a target and the arrow is wide to the left. The target doesn't yell "Hey, more to the right." Rather, you judge the efficacy of your procedures by their results and modify them accordingly.

world mathematical. In a sense, it forces the system to be a mathematical programming language. However, the result of programming is not a "program." The result is a new mathematical object. That is, a mathematical microworld constitutes the core of an intuitive axiom system, where students can define new objects and operations and interactively investigate their properties.

Examples of Mathematical Microworlds

Fuller, Prusinkiewicz, and Rambally (1985) have developed a microworld called LEGO for creating geometric illustrations. Though their intention was that LEGO be used only by a teacher for demonstrations, it contains all the ingredients listed above for being a mathematical microworld. Each command in LEGO is a function that happens to create a geometric object. New functions (objects) are defined by composing existing ones and giving the composition a name. New operations on objects (such as intersection and union) are also defined by composition. Greenleaf (1984) reports a similar system, called EUCLID. EUCLID not only gives the capability of composing functions, but also includes a programming language. Neither LEGO nor EUCLID runs on microcomputers. LEGO runs on a VAX-730, under Franz LISP, while EUCLID requires specially developed hardware.

Rocky's Boots, by the Learning Company, is almost a mathematical microworld for Boolean algebra. One constructs "selection mechanisms" (logic circuits) that cause Rocky the Raccoon to kick objects that possess certain attributes. One feature it lacks is that it does not contain a formalism that allows a student to represent the effect of one's mechanisms. The need to include a formalism in a mathematical microworld is addressed in a later section on design issues.

Other examples of mathematical microworlds are the Geometric Supposer by Judah Schwartz, published by Sunburst, and a Marble Bag microworld being developed by Wally Fuerzeig (1986) under the sponsorship of the National Science Foundation.

MOTIONS is a microworld for isometric transformations of the plane (mappings of the plane that preserve distances between points) that I developed several years ago to run on Apple II's and Commodore 64's. It is designed to be used at a number of grade levels, ranging from junior high school to university teacher education courses. At the teacher education level, it typically is used for a total of 10 weeks (sometimes spanning two courses).

MOTIONS was designed with a set of cognitive goals in mind. These, briefly, are that students understand motion geometry as a *mathematical system,* and that they develop concepts of multivariate mappings, invariances under mappings, and of composition as an operation upon mappings. Thompson (1985a) gives a detailed treatment of MOTION's cognitive goals.

The MOTIONS microworld shows a pennant within a Cartesian coordinate system. The pennant has three properties: a position, a heading, and an orientation. Each property is defined by convention. The pennant's *position* is the position of the bottom tip of its staff. The pennant's *heading* is the direction of the ray emanating from its position and passing through its staff, as measured from the right horizontal. Its *orientation* is the direction one would turn (right or left) were one traversing the pennant from the tip of its base.

The pennant's position and heading are given in a status line, along with the measure of the angle formed by the horizontal *x*-axis, the origin, and the pennant's position (Fig. 5.2). The pennant's orientation is not listed since it is visually apparent.

The operations allowed by MOTIONS are translations, rotations, and reflections (flips). The format for executing each is given below.

COMMAND	MEANING
T *heading distance*	Translate the plane in a direction of *heading* through a distance of *distance* units.
R *degrees*	Rotate the plane about the origin through an angle of measure *degrees*.
F *heading*	Flip (reflect) the plane through the line passing through the origin in the direction of *heading*.

Figure 5.3 shows a succession of displays as commands are entered. Each command operates upon the last-drawn pennant. Hence, effects upon the

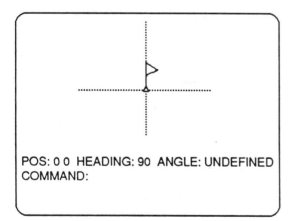

POS: 0 0 HEADING: 90 ANGLE: UNDEFINED
COMMAND:

Figure 5.2 The initial display of MOTIONS. POS gives the pennant's position. HEADING gives its direction as measured counter-clockwise in degrees from the right-horizontal. ANGLE gives the measure in degrees of the angle formed by the pennant's position, the origin, and the positive x-axis.

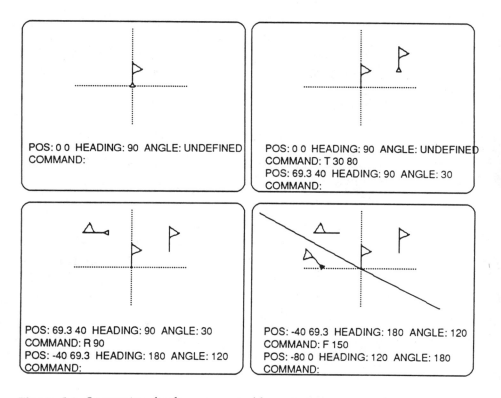

Figure 5.3 Successive displays generated by entering commands to MOTIONS. From top-left to right-bottom: (1) The initial display. (2) T 30 80 moved the plane containing the current pennant 80 units in a heading of 30°. (3) R 90 rotated the plane containing the current pennant 90° about the origin. (4) F 150 flipped (reflected) the plane through the line passing through the origin at a heading of 150°.

plane are cumulative. The end state of a pennant under one command is the beginning state of the pennant for the next.

One composes transformations in several ways. The most intuitive is simply to enter them all on the same line. Each command is executed as if entered separately, and each intermediate pennant is drawn (Fig. 5.4). A second way, which more closely represents the mathematical idea of composition, is to enter the commands surrounded by brackets. When a set of commands is entered in brackets, the *composition* is performed (Fig. 5.5). A third way to compose transformations is to define a new transformation that is made of a

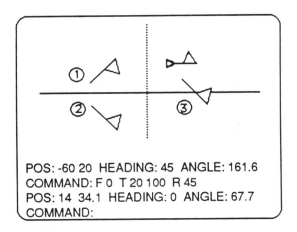

POS: -60 20 HEADING: 45 ANGLE: 161.6
COMMAND: F 0 T 20 100 R 45
POS: 14 34.1 HEADING: 0 ANGLE: 67.7
COMMAND:

Figure 5.4 Entering commands on one line causes each command to be executed in turn. F 0 executed while the pennant was in state 1, causing it to take on state 2. T 20 100 executed while the pennant was in state 2, causing it to take on state 3. R 45 caused the pennant to change from state 3 to its ending state.

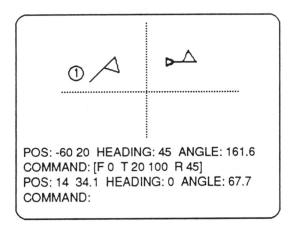

POS: -60 20 HEADING: 45 ANGLE: 161.6
COMMAND: [F 0 T 20 100 R 45]
POS: 14 34.1 HEADING: 0 ANGLE: 67.7
COMMAND:

Figure 5.5 The display after the composition [F 0   T 20 100   R 45] is entered. The pennant began in state 1. The composition caused the pennant to take on its final state. Compare the initial and final states here to those in Fig. 5.4.

composition of existing ones. To define a new transformation, one enters DEF (for DEFine), the new transformation's name, and the composition that defines it (Fig. 5.6). If one wishes a new transformation to be defined so as to take variable arguments, then the composition defining it is preceded by the list of variable names used in the composition. Variable names are preceded by colons in the defining part of the composition (Fig. 5.7). The list of variable names preceding a composition has the purpose of distinguishing names that stand for arguments from names that are automatically supplied by the microworld (e.g., XCOR and YCOR for the *x*- and *y*-coordinates of the pennant's position, and HEADING for its heading).

The last feature of MOTIONS to be discussed is not a feature of the program. Rather, it is the problem sets that accompany the program. Without problems to structure students' investigations, they would be limited for the most part to undirected exploration of the program per se, and would most likely avoid coming to grips with the intricacies of the subject matter itself.

The problems are divided into three groups, each group emphasizing different levels of abstraction and generalization. The first group assumes that students will consider the pennant to be the object operated upon and focuses their attention on invariances under various transformations (heading and orientation are invariant under translation, while position varies; orientation and center of rotation are invariant under rotation, while position and heading vary; line of reflection is invariant under reflection, while position, heading, and

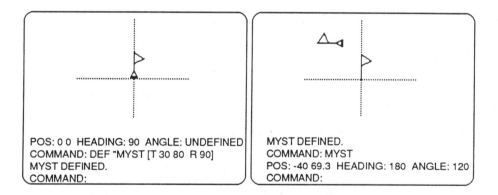

POS: 0 0 HEADING: 90 ANGLE: UNDEFINED
COMMAND: DEF "MYST [T 30 80 R 90]
MYST DEFINED.
COMMAND:

MYST DEFINED.
COMMAND: MYST
POS: -40 69.3 HEADING: 180 ANGLE: 120
COMMAND:

Figure 5.6 Defining a composition by name. The name MYST means to do the composition of T 30 80 and R 90. The display on the right shows the effect of entering MYST. The composition is, in fact, a rotation about the point (-14.65, 54.65) through an angle of 90°.

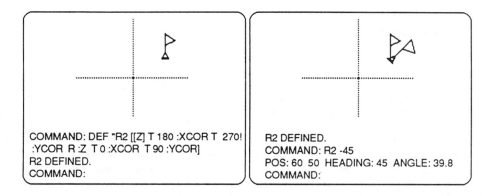

COMMAND: DEF "R2 [[Z] T 180 :XCOR T 270!
:YCOR R :Z T 0 :XCOR T 90 :YCOR]
R2 DEFINED.
COMMAND:

R2 DEFINED.
COMMAND: R2 -45
POS: 60 50 HEADING: 45 ANGLE: 39.8
COMMAND:

Figure 5.7 Defining a motion that takes variable arguments. Variable names
in the defining composition are preceded by a colon to distinguish them from names of operations. The name Z is in a list to
distinguish it from names supplied by MOTIONS (XCOR and
YCOR). The effect of R2 is to rotate the pennant :Z degrees about
its current position, as shown in the display on the right. The
exclamation mark (!) indicates that the user's command is continued on the next screen line.

orientation vary). The first group also emphasizes that students should become
skilled at visualizing the effects of the transformations.

The second group of problems focuses on transformations of the plane
as multivariate mappings. Students are asked to develop generalizations about
the effect upon each of the three properties of the pennant (position, heading, and orientation) under the various transformations. An example of this
type of problem:

> While doing his homework, John entered F 70 while the pennant was at
> position (30,20) with orientation RIGHT. By how much did the pennant's
> initial heading change?*

The third group of problems emphasizes operations *upon* transformations.
The primary operation of concern is composition. The problems address the
intricacies of composition in a number of ways. One is negation, as in:

* Initial heading is unstated, so students must determine the general relationship between initial
and resulting heading of a pennant under a reflection.

> Mary entered T 30 80 R 70. Tell her *one* transformation that will take the pennant back to its original state.

and:

> Frank entered F 70 F 90 when he intended to enter F 70 R 90. What *one* transformation could Frank use to put the pennant in the state it would have attained had he entered his command correctly?

Another approach to composition is seen in problems that ask students to determine the *net effect* of entering two or more transformations at once. "Net effect" is defined as the single transformation that one could enter to achieve the same result as that of the combined transformations. Still another approach asks students to form "addition tables" of transformations that are closed under composition. This takes them into the realm of algebras of transformations.

Differences between Mathematical Microworlds and CAI

There are five primary differences between mathematical microworlds and traditional CAI. The first centers around the idea of information transmittal. In the past, most CAI has been designed with the idea that some body of information is to be transmitted from the program to the student, or that the program will guide the student to a point of "discovery." A CAI program that is tutorial in nature poses questions, gives examples and illustrations, and generally "talks" to students. The idea of information transmittal has no relevance to the design of a microworld, except to the extent that its design makes it easier or harder for students to *infer* information.

The second difference between tutorial CAI and mathematical microworlds is that the focus of a mathematical microworld is on the construction of meaning and relationships, while CAI tends to focus on facts and skills. Kearsley (1985) pointed out that my comments here do not apply to simulations, and I agree. However, I would not want to classify simulations and mathematical microworlds together. A simulation simulates *something*. But what does a mathematical microworld simulate? At most, it "simulates" an axiom system, in the sense that it is an instantiation of a formal system and embodies its structure. I would think a microworld to be more of a model of a formal system than a simulation of a prototype (cf. Kleene, 1952; Kneebone, 1963).*

A microworld's focus upon relationships leads directly to an emphasis on transformations, at least within mathematics. Two mathematical objects are related when there is some way to transform one or more attributes of one into attributes of the other.

---

* My remarks here apply only to *mathematical* microworlds. Microworlds as described by Papert (1980) and by Lawler (1984) typically do have a "real world" sense to them, and are more like simulations.

The third difference between CAI and mathematical microworlds is in the layered approach to structure in microworlds. To learn mathematics, students must construct mathematical objects, construct relationships among them, and then take those relationships as new objects to be operated upon. Mathematical microworlds are designed to facilitate that process, whereas mathematical structure in CAI has typically been ignored.

The fourth difference is the assumed role of the teacher. My impression of CAI, both traditional and intelligent, is that designers envision their programs as being temporary substitutes for the teacher—that a teacher would send students off to use the program with the confidence that it will do a good job in his or her stead. My vision of a teacher using a microworld is as a tool to provoke classroom discussions. A teacher might have one computer with a large-screen monitor at the front of the classroom and use it to challenge the class to think about what will happen when a particular command is entered and about what is generally true under various circumstances. That is, a microworld's design is predicated upon the assumption that a teacher will be integrally involved in the students' explorations. A teacher will certainly have students work individually with microworlds, but will do so only with the aim that they investigate some particular feature of the mathematics embodied within it.

Fifth, in traditional CAI, the program and the curriculum are inextricably intertwined. In a mathematical microworld there is a strong distinction between the curriculum and the environment upon which students act. The software presents the environment and metaphor and incorporates the mathematical structure within a model. Instructions, explanations, and questions for students are given in printed materials. This allows teachers to adapt the curriculum to the purposes of instruction as well as to the levels of the students. Continued use of a model under these circumstances is apt to contribute to the integration, in students' minds, of the various levels at which the concept can be examined.*

Issues of Design

In this section I will recount the dialectic between designing MOTIONS and assessing its impact on preservice elementary teachers who were using it. Throughout the design and evaluation processes, the aim was to uncover fundamental features of their cognitions that were retarding their understanding of fundamental concepts, and to modify the microworld to address those difficulties directly. After discussing the evolution of MOTIONS, I will summarize principles of designing mathematical microworlds that have evolved from the implementation of it and five others.†

* For example, one microworld (for teaching and learning integers) has been used in grade 1 to teach addition, in grade 6 to teach negation, and in college in teaching commutative groups.

† The five others cover integers and introductory algebra, probability, number theory, equivalence relations, and elementary arithmetic.

The Pedagogical Problem

The program was first conceived as an alternative to teaching transformation geometry through straightedge and compass constructions. In that approach, the aim was to have students develop procedures for various constructions (e.g., copying an angle, bisecting a line segment, etc.) and apply those procedures to problems of mapping points in the plane under isometric (length-preserving) transformations. That approach was singularly unsuccessful, for two reasons. First, students would become absorbed in a construction's details and lose sight of the mathematics that they were supposed to learn. Second, they considered each application of a procedure to be a unique transformation, even if it was applied as a subprocedure. For example: they were asked to find the image of triangle ABC under the translation defined by directed line segment β (Fig. 5.8a). They would construct the images of A, B, and C (by copying angles and segments), connect them, and be done. However, in their thinking they performed three translations: one that took A to A', one that took B to B', and one that took C to C' (Fig. 5.8b). They did not understand that the entire set of points in the plane was mapped by the translation and that we merely located the images of three of them. This might not appear to be a serious problem. However, when we began to cover compositions of transformations they were bewildered by my asking them to find the image of a triangle, for example, under the composition of two translations when in their view the problem involved nine translations: six to do two translations of a triangle and three to link the original points with their final images. Moreover, they could not understand how one could equate the entire process of translating a triangle with a single translation, since (in their view) any translation moves only a single point.

The Design of the Interface

The initial idea behind MOTIONS was to remove the drudgery of straightedge and compass constructions so that students could focus upon the mathematics of the transformations. The first issue to address was the design of the screen and the manner in which students would interact with the program. The design of the screen was relatively easy, as transformation geometry is commonly taught analytically, where the transformations are represented by matrices and points of the plane are represented as vectors. Thus, the screen needed to show a Cartesian coordinate system. The decision to have a flag as an object was made for two reasons: first, it is much easier to understand a transformation's effect upon the plane by observing preimage-image correspondences between sets of points than by observing the effect upon individual points. Second, whatever figure was to be displayed needed to be such that changes in orientation are apparent.

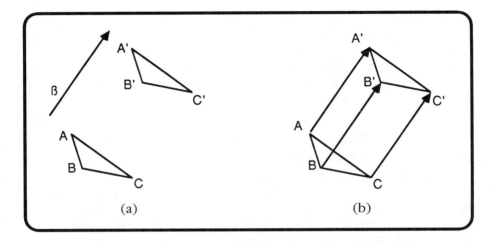

Figure 5.8 (a) Translate the plane in the direction and distance defined by
the directed line segment β. (b) A student's conception of the
translation depicted in (a): translate A to A′ (one translation);
translate B to B′ (two translations); translate C to C′ (three
translations).

The decision about how to have students interact with the program was
also relatively easy to make. Since the aim was to teach transformation geometry
as a mathematical system, and since the objects in that system are functions, the
program needed to allow students to type common representations of those
functions in order to "see" their meaning.

Translations   To do a translation they would enter T, along with some measure of the distance and direction in which to translate. An alternative would
have been to define T as taking two arguments that denote horizontal and
vertical displacement. The two definitions of translation are equivalent. Since
the former definition is easier to visualize (as a vector connecting initial and
final position), I settled on the former and included activities and problems that
focused on having students uncover the equivalence of the two representations.

Rotations   To do a rotation they would enter R, along with the measure of the
angle about which to rotate. Since the center of a rotation could also vary, it
would have been sensible to have a rotation's center be variable. However, I
chose to let students investigate how one *could* do an arbitrary rotation by
composing existing transformations (as in Fig. 5.7) instead of providing them
with a command that would trivialize the problem.

Reflections   To do a reflection (flip) they would enter F (since R is already used to denote rotation) along with some defining characteristic(s) of the line through which the flip was to be performed. Again, I chose conservatively. The default class of lines were those through the origin, and their defining characteristic was their heading (direction). This was decided in anticipation of providing students with the problem of how to define an arbitrary flip.

Instructional Design

It became apparent early on that the preservice teachers who were using MO-TIONS would need guidance in their investigations if they were to cover anything resembling a curriculum. I decided to provide that guidance through the form of a handout containing nothing but an introduction to the program (how to start it, the commands, etc.) and a list of questions. The students did not like that approach. Their major complaints were (1) that they would work on a question and not know whether or not they had answered it "correctly" and (2) that they did not understand what they were supposed to learn. I rephrase their complaints this way: their first complaint arose because they did not understand that the aim of a question was that they "play" with a problem—varying parameters, varying conditions, and so on. It was not that the questions were ill-defined. They were well-defined. Rather, the questions were unlike those they were used to. The second complaint, about not knowing what they were supposed to learn, again arose because of the novelty of the approach. In their previous experiences in math courses they were told what they were supposed to learn—how to perform some procedure. They had little conception of solving a problem with the aim of forming a generalization from their solution methods.

Intricacies of the Content and Students' Difficulties with MOTIONS

A number of small matters (in my initially naive view) about the design of MOTIONS became significant obstacles to students' understanding of the content. Aside from making the program more effective, addressing these issues opened a host of research questions on mathematical thinking. I became aware of them largely as a result of my practice of listening to students talk among themselves while working on MOTIONS problems in the computer laboratory.

Reference Systems   A pennant exists within three reference systems—Cartesian, polar, and clock (orientation). It is important to understand that a transformation affects the pennant's properties relative to all three. Students had a horrible time coordinating the three, and had particular difficulty with the idea of a system of headings that "moved" with the pennant. For example, when thinking of translating the plane when a pennant was off the origin many would imagine the heading from the origin instead of from the pennant's position, and would become hopelessly confused about how such a thing could be accomplished.

My awareness of this difficulty resulted in the addition of DOT and LINE commands so that students could experiment with position and heading independently of each other. DOT takes two inputs (an x- and a y-coordinate) and places a dot at that position. LINE takes three inputs (two coordinates and a heading) and draws a line through the given point with the given heading. Then I added activities to the handout that focused on the independence of position and heading.

Command Formats   When first writing MOTIONS, it seemed natural to structure the command for performing a translation so that the user specified first a distance and second a direction. The image I relate to this format is that you first delineate a set of possible image points (the circle of radius *distance* from the pennant's position) and then restrict those to a single point—the intersection of the circle and the line having direction *heading* and passing through the pennant's position. However, students could not conjure up this image. They insisted that they needed to know the direction first and the distance second in order to imagine a translation. Apparently, when the distance was given first they would wait for the direction, switch the arguments, and then consider what translation that command represented. They found switching arguments bothersome and distracting. After changing the command format for translations I have yet to hear a similar complaint.

Specifying an Initial State   Occasionally, one wishes to have a pennant start from a particular initial state. It might be that the pennant is too close to the screen's edge to see the result of the next command, or that one wishes to perform two motions from the same starting state. The command originally included in MOTIONS to put the pennant in a given state was GOTO. GOTO took a position, a heading, and an orientation as inputs, and placed a pennant in that state.

The problem with GOTO was that students thought of it as a transformation—on a par with T, R, and F. Apparently, the common-sense meaning of *go to* made them think of the pennant going from "here" to "there." It appeared to them as a state-change operator.* I changed GOTO to START.AT, and the problem disappeared.

Comparing Transformations   It is essential that students understand that a transformation is applied to the entire plane, and that we merely "highlight" its

---

* The reason that GOTO cannot be a state-change operator is that it acts only upon the state of a pennant, and not upon the entire plane. GOTO 20 30 40 RIGHT (go to the state of position (20,30), heading 40, and orientation RIGHT) would affect the plane one way were a pennant at the origin and a different way were a pennant at position (50,70).

effect on a particular subset of it. For example, T 30 80 has the same effect regardless of the initial state of the pennant. However, students tended to think that T 30 80 applied to the plane with the pennant in two different states resulted in two different motions, since they "looked" different. The solution to this problem was not another feature added to the program. Rather, it was a new set of activities that focused upon the independence of state and effect. Or, put another way, the activities focused upon invariant relationships between initial and final states under classes of transformations.

The Concept of Net Effect   The original treatment of composition consisted of having students enter two or more commands on a line. Each motion was performed separately; the composition was the motion that related the pennant's initial and final states (see Fig. 5.4).

The approach was logically sound. All one must do is ignore intermediate states of the pennant. However, few students could ignore the intermediate pennants. The presence of intermediate pennants "dominated" their conception of a command-set's net result. An analogy would be someone's absolute insistence that a trip from San Diego to New York via Denver and Chicago cannot be equated with a trip from San Diego directly to New York. Students felt that the two are different transformations since they involve different itineraries. This conception of equivalence is acceptable as common sense, but it completely blocks a student's access to the mathematical idea of composition.*

The solution to the problem of representing composition within a microworld was to allow the student to compose transformations in two ways. The first, as already described, is by entering a sequence of motions and having MOTIONS carry them out individually. The second is to allow students to group a sequence of motions within brackets—make a unit of the sequence, so to speak. Whenever a sequence of commands is grouped in brackets, only the composition is performed (see Fig. 5.5). Thus a student can examine a composition at two levels: intuitively, as the consecutive execution of individual commands where the pennant's end state under one motion is the beginning state for the next, and more formally, where only the initial and final states of the pennant are shown. The idea of composition did not become "easy" as a result of this change, but it did become accessible.

Composition as a Mathematical Operation   One of the most difficult ideas for students is the idea that some object can be represented in a number of different ways. In the context of MOTIONS, this difficulty first appeared in problems requiring that students understand that a translation can be both that

---

* An example of a student who understands that they are the same in terms of their composition is one who would say that a direct flight from New York to San Diego negates either trip, so they must be equivalent in their net effect.

translation and a composition of others. For example, T 0 5 is also represented by the composition [T 45 3 T − 45 4]. Students fall victim to the same misconception about composing functions that young children have about computing sums, which is that a sum is the answer you get from adding. It is not a number satisfying a logical relationship with two other numbers. The parallel with MOTIONS is in problems such as "Mary entered two translations. The first was T 45 3. The net effect was T 0 5. What was the second motion?" Unless students understand that T 45 3 bears a logical relationship to T 0 5 they will not think to "subtract" the effect of T 45 3 from T 0 5 (by entering [T 0 5 T 45 −3]) to see what translation remains.* For this difficulty, I did not put anything into the microworld. Rather, I forced the issue by having students work problems that emphasize logical relationships among compositions.

Defining New Transformations   It was surprising to find that students did not think of compositions denoted by the use of brackets (e.g., [R 70 F 10]) as being on a par with the primitive motions denoted by T, R, and F. Students thought of them much as many LISP students think of lambda-expressions: as "temporary" functions having no ontological status. In the thinking of students of transformation geometry, if a motion does not have a name, then it is not a bona fide transformation and cannot be equated to one that does have a name. To counter this misconception I added a feature whereby they could name a composition, and moreover, could specify variable parameters (whence the DEF command; see Figs. 5.6 and 5.7).

Principles of Designing Microworlds

Several design principles have emerged from the continuing use and evaluation of MOTIONS and from the implementation of several other microworlds. These are discussed below.

Orientation toward Functions

One of the first requirements in designing a mathematical microworld is to describe the system one aims at modeling. In mathematics, a system *is* a system because it is closed under some set of transformations and operations, or more generally, functions. Idiosyncracies of any system are a result of the functions that define it, and are independent of the objects upon which the functions are evaluated.† Thus, since mathematical microworlds are meant to focus upon

---

* The translation T 45 −3 is the inverse of T 45 3.

† Changing the objects produces a system that is isomorphic to the original system (*iso*—"same"; *morphic*—"structure").

mathematical systems, they automatically have a bias toward being function oriented. This means that a user commands a microworld to do something, and the "something" it does has an effect on the state of the system.

Command Formalism

Since the aim of a mathematical microworld is to provide students an entry into a mathematical system, and since mathematical microworlds are by nature function oriented, they are also command oriented. Two issues must be addressed in deciding upon the formalism students will use to interact with the microworld: the presentation of commands and the format in which students will use them.

Presentation   One could present a list of commands in a menu and have students choose from the list. This is disadvantageous for a number of reasons. First, it is distracting, since the menu must disturb the display, and it is the current state of the display that will be affected by the student's next command. Second, choosing from a written list is antithetical to what one does when *doing* mathematics. I have found that menus detract from students establishing a correspondence between a formalism and its semantics. It is much more effective simply to give students a written glossary of commands as part of the printed material that contains problems and activities. Third, when students enter individual commands, their attention is focused on *that* command and its effect on the system's state. Thus, they have a much more explicit set of experiences from which to generalize (e.g., F x does *this*) than when choosing commands and parameters from a menu.

Command Format   The command format must be concise, and must at least resemble conventional mathematical formalism. In MOTIONS, T x y corresponds to the mathematically conventional $T_{x,y}$; R x corresponds to R_x. In a microworld for probability, P[A B C] corresponds to the conventional P[A and B and C]; P[[A B] [C D]] corresponds to P[(A and B) *or* (C and D)].* A microworld for integers and algebra uses prefix notation instead of infix, but represents functions and composition as one would in tenth-grade algebra [e.g., as either $f(g(x))$ or $(f \circ g)(x)$]. In short, one is somewhat constrained in choosing a command format by the conventions already established in mathematics.

Graphics Display   Decisions about the design of the graphics display are important, but are not among the most crucial decisions one makes in designing a mathematical microworld. The only strong constraint is that there is a clear

---

* This microworld focuses upon representing the sample spaces of experiments as trees. [A B C] represents the path in the experiment tree containing those outcomes. Thus, it would be nonsensical to represent P[[A B] *and* [C D]] if [A B] and [C D] are of different paths. *A priori,* the probability is 0.

correspondence between the *change* in the display effected by a command and the mathematical meaning of the command.

The Problem Sets   The creation of problems for students is not part of designing a mathematical microworld per se, but the problems exert a strong influence upon a microworld's design. This point was illustrated in the section on the evolution of MOTIONS. In order to pose problems and activities that focused on the independence of position and direction, the microworld needed to include DOT and LINE commands. Also, to pose problems that focused upon composition of transformations on several levels of conceptual complexity, the microworld needed to allow several ways to represent composition. That is, the designer of a mathematical microworld must have an idea of the kinds of problems one wishes to pose so that the microworld allows the problems to be posed meaningfully.

A consensus is building that the problems one commonly asks students to solve has a dramatic influence on students' cognitive structures in scientific domains (Heller & Hungate, 1985; Larkin, 1981a, 1981b; Reif & Heller, 1982; Thompson, 1985a). As such, careful consideration must be given to the content and organization of the problems one asks students to solve in the context of a mathematical microworld. One crucial feature of the problem sets is that they address the subject matter at several levels of abstractness, and the microworld needs to allow a student to use it at any of those levels at any time.

"Levels of abstractness" in the problems means that initial objects are related by functions, and classes of functions are related by operations. This is reflected in Fig. 5.9. Entry-level problems focus on states, as depicted in the graphics display, with functions serving to connect states (Level 0). Problems for Level 0 can be of two kinds. The first kind is problems that focus students upon states and their defining characteristics (e.g., the state of a pennant in MOTIONS); the second kind provide any two of

[*State 1, State 2, function*]

and asks the students to provide the third. Problems at Level 1 focus on functions, with states serving as a background for describing a function's general effect. Level 2 problems focus on unary and binary operations upon functions, such as negation (inverse under some binary operation), composition, and (generalized) arithmetic operations. The process of dividing problems into levels is discussed in Dreyfus and Thompson (1985), and Thompson (1985a).

Microworlds Are Sometimes Not Enough

Mathematical microworlds can effect significant improvements in students' mathematical understandings and abilities (Thompson, 1985c: Thompson & Dreyfus, in press). Most students benefit from the use of mathematical micro-

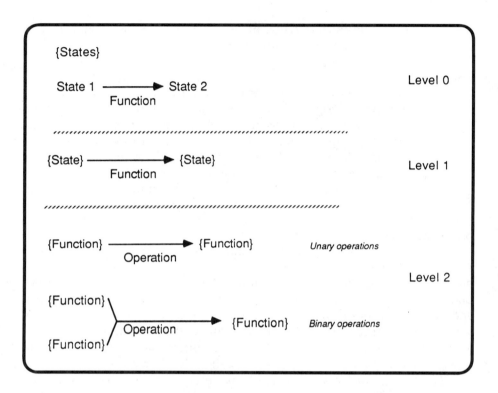

Figure 5.9 A framework for organizing problems. Level 0 problems focus on
states and functions as relationships among states. Level 1 problems focus on the general effect of classes of functions on states.
Level 2 problems focus on unary and binary operations on
classes of functions.

worlds by exploring them somewhat scientifically, such as by controlling variables while manipulating others, and by using visual feedback to "debug" faulty
understandings of the subject matter whenever they lead to unexpected results.
However, a significant minority of students using microworlds are effectively
blocked from taking advantage of their semantically rich environments. These
are students who fail to understand the initial concepts depicted by a microworld, who do not know how to explore ideas, and/or who do not know how
to generalize from examples. For these students, microworlds are not enough.
They need assistance in coming to terms with the *raison d'etre* of microworlds.
The following is a discussion of a current research project at Illinois State

University that emphasizes concepts of exploration and generalization in micro-world environments for students who have difficulty with them.*

We are immediately in a conundrum when redesigning mathematical microworlds to address misconceptions. The nonjudgmental, passive nature of microworlds is a strong positive feature that serves the goal of long-term mathematical development. But to assist students who have misconceptions, those misconceptions must be diagnosed and remediated. The ability to diagnose and remediate means that a microworld must pose problems, judge responses, and give appropriate feedback—features that are antithetical to the design of mathematical microworlds. The resolution to this conundrum was this: rather than have a tutor decide when to intervene and how to structure the lesson, we allow *students* to decide when to invoke the tutor. This allows us, and students, to maintain a strong separation between a microworld and its tutor.

A second design issue was how students would interact with a microworld so as to allow it to make inferences of *qualitative* misconceptions, as distinct from misconceptions about formal rules and their application (such as those investigated by Matz, 1982, and by Sleeman, 1982). Our solution is to allow students to have qualitative interactions with a microworld, such as by pointing to screen positions or sketching predictions on the screen. These latter features demand input facilities equivalent to a mouse.†

A third design issue was how to represent qualitative knowledge of mathematical content to allow automatized inferences about a student's concepts. Current tests suggest that semantic networks, augmented by bug catalogs, provide at least a viable solution to this problem.‡

What Does an Intelligent Microworld Look Like?

The major extensions to MOTIONS are designed to address misconceptions of basic concepts and misconceptions of exploration and generalization. To address misconceptions of basic concepts, we incorporate two new commands: a WHY? command, which will cause the computer to explain why it did what it did in response to the previous command, and a PREDICT command, which allows a student to predict the outcome of a command and have the computer comment on the prediction. WHY? and PREDICT are discussed in the next section.

---

* As of this writing, only pieces of the programs described herein are actually running. However, since the major issues discussed concern design, I will speak as if the programs are complete.

† Intelligent microworlds are being implemented for the Apple Macintosh™.

‡ I should point out that the link between mathematical microworlds and ICAI has not arisen because of a penchant for finding applications of artificial intelligence in education. Rather, the nature of the pedagogical problem and the design issues noted above have led to a natural marriage.

We plan to address misconceptions of exploration and generalization by incorporating another three commands: EXPLORE, GENERALIZE, and CHALLENGE-ME. The commands EXPLORE and GENERALIZE will work together to emphasize that exploring, hypothesizing, generalizing, and then exploring again is a natural and powerful method for understanding mathematics. CHALLENGE-ME will provide a context for a microworld to interact with students about problem-solving strategies. EXPLORE, GENERALIZE, and CHALLENGE-ME are discussed in a succeeding section.

WHY? and PREDICT

The WHY? command provides students with explanations. Whenever a student enters a command in the context of attempting to solve a problem and the command leads to an unanticipated result, often the source of the error is a misconception of some basic concept. If the student cannot understand why the microworld acted differently than expected he or she can enter WHY? and have the microworld explain its actions.

The level of an explanation is a function of the microworld's current model of the student in regard to the concepts involved in the explanation. A student model with high values on the component concepts receives explanations in terms of theorems (supposedly) already known to that student. A student model with neutral values on the component concepts leads to an explanation in terms of basic definitions and relationships. A student model with low, negative values on the component concepts leads to detailed explanations in terms of basic definitions and relationships accompanied by graphical illustrations.

The more detailed explanations are available to students with high and neutral values in their respective student models by their entering WHY? again, until the microworld has given the most basic explanation of which it is capable. Afterward, the student is referred to the instructor.

The inclusion of a PREDICT command serves two purposes. First, estimating the effect of an operation helps students understand mathematical definitions, relationships, and principles. Second, by having a student register his or her prediction of a command, the microworld then has information from which to infer misconceptions. For example, a very common misconception in transformation geometry is that the direction in which a pennant will move is always determined from the origin (intersection of x- and y-axes) when the plane is moved by a translation. In fact, the direction a pennant is moved is determined from its position. Students with this misconception cannot understand the idea of composition of translations, for the pennant never ends up where they expect it (see Fig. 5.10). This misconception is easily uncovered once a student predicts the end state of a pennant prior to performing two translations.

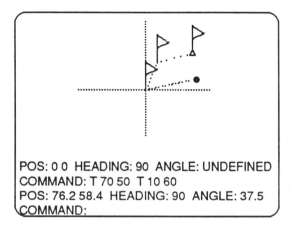

POS: 0 0 HEADING: 90 ANGLE: UNDEFINED
COMMAND: T 70 50 T 10 60
POS: 76.2 58.4 HEADING: 90 ANGLE: 37.5
COMMAND:

Figure 5.10 The difference between the actual result of entering T 70 50
T 10 60 and a student's estimate of the result (marked as ●).
This student thought that all directions are measured with lines
passing through the origin, not realizing that directions can be
measured relative to any position in the plane.

EXPLORE, GENERALIZE, and CHALLENGE-ME

We address misconceptions of exploring and generalizing in two ways. The first
is to incorporate an EXPLORE command. When a student enters EXPLORE, the
microworld begins to record the student's commands in the anticipation that
at some time he or she will enter GENERALIZE. In response to GENERALIZE,
the microworld computes a number of generalizations from the student's commands, some, none, or all of which may be valid; nevertheless, they fit the data.
The student then chooses one for further exploration and continues to enter
commands. The microworld estimates the relevancy of the commands to the
chosen generalization, and communicates its estimations when the student enters the command COMMENTS?. The student can also enter YOUR OPINION?,
which causes the microworld to give what it considers to be a viable set of
commands to test the chosen generalization. The student can enter WHY? to
have the microworld explain its choice of commands.

A second way that we address misconceptions of exploring and generalizing
is to incorporate a CHALLENGE-ME option. The student can select the type of
problems on which to be challenged by referring to a section in the booklet
that accompanies the microworld. For example, in the MOTIONS microworld,
CHALLENGE-ME 3.4 means that the student wishes to be challenged by a
problem dealing with the composition of rotations and reflections (chapter 3,

section 4). The microworld's knowledge of problems is stored as schemata that describe the types of displays, transformations, problems that can be posed, and legitimate plans for solving those problems. It judges students' problem-solving strategies by attempting to fit the commands they enter into one of its lists of legitimate plans.

The GENERALIZE and CHALLENGE-ME commands provide occasions for a microworld to comment on specific problem-solving strategies. These are the only two commands that provide the microworld with definite information about the problem a student is solving. In the case of CHALLENGE-ME, we can constrain the types of problems to those we think are particularly illustrative of important concepts and methods. With prior knowledge of the types of problems upon which a student will work, we can anticipate specific misconceptions, errors, and strategies.

Intelligent Microworlds in Schools

Mathematics education in the nation's schools is ripe for intelligent microworlds. Many states report a critical shortage in qualified mathematics teachers while at the same time they are raising minimum mathematics requirements for graduation. A short-term measure adopted by many states is the practice of allowing teachers to "cross over" from nonscientific disciplines to become mathematics teachers—without requiring further training in mathematics. Shortages and crossovers are occurring at the same time that government and professional reports point out the necessity for an increased emphasis on problem solving in the K–12 mathematics curriculum.

Clearly, schools need assistance in their mathematics classrooms. Microworlds can provide one form of assistance, in that teachers need not be burdened with the task of creating models through which the students can explore and understand mathematical concepts. Moreover, pedagogically sound and mathematically valid intelligent microworlds can put a cognitive scientist, a mathematician, and a diagnostician within calling distance of any student using them. More than a few teachers could benefit from such assistance.

Even with today's critical problems, prospects for the introduction of intelligent microworlds, or ICAI in general, into the nation's mathematics classrooms are not good. By and large, schools are still purchasing 64K 8-bit computers, and there is no reason to believe that they will significantly change their purchasing habits at any time soon (Mazer Corp., 1983; Strategic, Inc., 1984).

An even greater obstacle than the lack of suitable ICAI hardware is the problem of overcoming teachers' conceptions of how one should learn mathematics. Too often, their conception is that one learns mathematics by memorizing fixed, inflexible algorithms for answering stereotypical problems. I have comments written by classroom teachers who have participated in microworld-based demonstration lessons wherein they state that though they found microworlds to be interesting, what they witnessed was irrelevant to the topics as they teach them. Microworlds "do not teach rules well enough.".

Another obstacle to large-scale implementation of ICAI is the small number of computers available to any one teacher. Presentations on how to use one computer with 30 students are generally among the best attended at mathematics education conferences.

The present structure of the mathematics curriculum and the various bureaucratic systems for changing it present another obstacle to realizing mathematics ICAI in the schools. Large-scale implementation of ICAI will require restructuring the curriculum, if only to allow time for students to interact with computers. Such changes are likely to be within the purview of textbook adoption committees, and innovations in general have not fared well at that level. We would do well to recall the pitfalls encountered by large-scale curriculum projects of the 1960s and 1970s (Conference Board of the Mathematical Sciences, 1976; Vogeli, 1967).

Finally, the greatest obstacle to realizing ICAI in the schools is the need for teachers to rethink their management of time and resources and the need for them to rethink their role in students' learning processes. Subject matter, classroom management, and student-teacher interactions all change when a microworld is integrated with instruction. The subject matter must be rethought so as to be presented within the model embodied in the microworld. Also, when using a computer as a teaching tool teachers are no longer in complete control of the situation; they are no longer the center of attention in the classroom. Their role becomes more that of a choreographer than a manager. They ensure that all the people and props are in the right place at the right time, provide the motivation for the "piece," and then hope for the best.

The potential benefits of intelligent mathematical microworlds, and ICAI in general, are great enough to warrant our best efforts to realize their application to classroom teaching and learning. But we should not think that their value will be apparent to potential consumers. Nor should we think that their value will be easily demonstrated.

References

Collis, K. F., & Biggs, J. B. (1982). *Evaluating the quality of learning: The SOLO taxonomy (Structure of Learned Outcomes)*. New York: Academic Press.

Conference Board of the Mathematical Sciences, National Advisory Committee on Mathematical Education. (1976). *Overview and analysis of school mathematics: Grades K–12*. Washington, DC: CBMS.

diSessa, A. (1982). Unlearning Aristotelian physics: A study of knowledge-based learning. *Cognitive Science, 6*, 37–76.

Dreyfus, T., & Thompson, P. W. (1985). Microworlds and Van Hiele levels. *Proceedings of the Tenth Annual Conference of the International Group for the Psychology of Mathematics Education.* Utrecht, The Netherlands: IGPME.

Fuerzeig, W. (1986). Algebra slaves and agents. Manuscript to appear in *Artificial Intelligence,* Special Issue, Winter 1986.

Fuller, N., Prusinkiewicz, P., & Rambally, G. (1985). L.E.G.O.—An interactive computer graphics system for teaching geometry. *Proceedings of the World Conference on Computers in Education,* Norfolk, VA.

Greenleaf, N. (1984). EUCLID: A graphics language for plane geometry. In V. Hansen (Ed.), *Computers in mathematics education.* Yearbook of the National Council of Teachers of Mathematics. Reston, VA: NCTM.

Heller, J. I., & Hungate, H. N. (1985). Implications for mathematics instruction of research on scientific problem solving. In E. A. Silver (Ed.), *Teaching and learning mathematical problem solving: Multiple research perspectives.* Hillsdale, NJ: Lawrence Erlbaum.

Kearsley, G. (1985). Personal communication.

Kleene, S. (1952). *Introduction to metamathematics.* New York: D. Van Nostrand.

Kneebone, G. (1963). *Mathematical logic and the foundations of mathematics.* New York: D. Van Nostrand.

Larkin, J. H. (1981a). Cognition of learning physics. *American Journal of Physics, 49,* 534–541.

Larkin, J. H. (1981b). Enriching Formal Knowledge: A model for learning to solve textbook physics problems. In J. Anderson (Ed.), *Cognitive skills and their acquisition.* Hillsdale, NJ: Lawrence Erlbaum.

Lawler, W. (1982). The progressive construction of mind. *Cognitive Science, 5,* 1–30.

Lawler, W. (1984). Designing computer-based microworlds. In M. Yazdani (Ed.), *New horizons in educational computing.* London: Ellis Horwood.

Matz, M. (1982). Toward a process model for high school algebra errors. In D. H. Sleeman & J. S. Brown (Eds.), *Intelligent tutoring systems.* New York: Academic Press.

Mazer Corporation (1984). *Trends '83: The school microcomputer market.*

Papert, S. (1980). *Mindstorms.* New York: Basic Books.

Piaget, J. (1951). *The psychology of intelligence.* London: Routledge and Kegan Paul.

Reif, F., & Heller, J. I. (1982). Knowledge structure and problem solving in physics. *Educational Psychologist, 17,* 102–127.

Rumelhart, D., & Ortony, F. (1977). The representation of knowledge in memory. In J. Anderson, S. Spiro, & W. Montague (Eds.), *Schooling and the acquisition of knowledge.* Hillsdale, NJ: Lawrence Erlbaum.

Skemp, R. R. (1979). *Intelligence, learning, and action.* London: Wiley.

Sleeman, D. (1982). Assessing competence in basic algebra. In D. H. Sleeman & J. S. Brown (Eds.), *Intelligent tutoring systems.* New York: Academic Press.

Strategic, Inc. (1984). *Educational software: The next boost to the microcomputer market.* San Jose, CA.

Thompson, P. W. (1985a). Experience, problem solving and learning mathematics: Considerations in developing mathematics curricula. In E. A. Silver (Ed.), *Learning and teaching mathematical problem solving: Multiple research perspectives.* Hillsdale, NJ: Lawrence Erlbaum.

Thompson, P. W. (1985b). Computers in research on mathematical problem solving. In E. A. Silver (Ed.), *Learning and teaching mathematical problem solving: Multiple research perspectives.* Hillsdale, NJ: Lawrence Erlbaum.

Thompson, P. W. (1985c). A Piagetian approach to transformation geometry via microworlds. *Mathematics Teacher, 78,* 465–471.

Thompson, P. W., & Dreyfus, T. (In press). Integers and algebra: Parallels in operations of thought. *Journal for Research in Mathematics Education.*

Vogeli, B. (1967). The rise and fall of the "new math." *Inaugural lecture as Clifford Brewster Upton Professor of Mathematical Education.* New York: Columbia University, Teachers' College.

Part 3 Artificial Intelligence in Training

Although in theory the domains of education and training should be concerned with similar issues and problems, in reality they are quite different. Applications of computers in training tend to differ from educational applications not only in content but also in teaching strategies and underlying pedagogy. Higher education stands at the crossroads between education and training and can take on the characteristics of either domain.

This dichotomy is reflected in AI applications to training. ICAI programs developed for training applications tend to focus on the use of intelligent simulations and the teaching of procedural skills. Expert systems play a much more important role in the training domain than in education (at least for the present).

Chapter 6, by Hollan, Hutchins, and Weitzman, describes STEAMER, a steam plant simulation developed for use in propulsion engineering courses. The focus of the STEAMER project has been on the design of intelligent graphics interfaces that can help students understand the dynamics of a complex system (a steam plant). As described in the chapter, STEAMER is not yet an instructional system; nonetheless, it has a useful role to play in training in its current form.

Chapter 7, by Nawrocki, describes the use of ICAI for maintenance training. Again, an intelligent simulation is involved. The use of knowledge engineering tools is also discussed. Nawrocki describes the organizational factors that shaped the evolution of the ICAI program. In the training domain, these "real-world" considerations can be as important in defining the nature of the program as the instructional problem involved.

In Chapter 8, Harmon discusses the role of expert systems as intelligent job aids. He elaborates on the distinction between education and training in order to explain the important role of job aids in training (and their relative unimportance in educational settings). In Harmon's view, expert systems will have a significant impact on how future training is conducted. There also is an important role for expert systems in teaching problem-solving and decision-making skills in both the training and educational domains.

ICAI applications in training are fundamentally concerned with helping the student/employee achieve a better understanding of a specific process or procedure. In this respect, they share the same primary goals as most educational applications of AI. In some cases, AI systems (particularly expert systems) may simply be used as tools to help people do their jobs more effectively, and the training task involves teaching how to use the tool. Teaching how to use AI tools is a perfectly legitimate training application of AI, although it is not strictly ICAI.

6/ STEAMER: An Interactive, Inspectable, Simulation-Based Training System

JAMES D. HOLLAN,
EDWIN L. HUTCHINS, and
LOUIS M. WEITZMAN

Introduction

Since we are firmly convinced that ideas, like people, have histories and can only be fully understood in the context of those histories, we will begin by discussing the underlying ideas that motivated us to initiate the STEAMER effort. They include the following:

- *Mental models.* We were and still are caught up in the notion of mental models and of how important it is to better understand the models people use to think and reason about complex dynamic physical systems and devices. Without richer and more detailed understandings of the nature of these models instructional applications are going to be severely limited.

- *Graphical interfaces for interactive inspectable simulations.* We believe that graphical interfaces to simulations of physical systems deserve extensive exploration. They make possible new types of instructional interactions by allowing one to control, manipulate, and monitor simulations of dynamic systems at many different hierarchical levels. The key idea in STEAMER is the conception of *an interactive inspectable simulation.* We have consistently sought to make the system inspectable. This includes not only providing graphical views of the system but also allowing one to inspect various

Reprinted with permission from *The AI Magazine* (Summer, 1984), published by the American Association for Artificial Intelligence.

aspects of the procedures for operating the system. Interactive inspectable simulations have the potential of being major mechanisms for supporting the development of understandings of *process*.

■ *Conceptual fidelity*. We are very much concerned with graphically depicting models that attempt in a fundamental sense to approximate those that experts employ to reason about a physical system. We want to focus on the conceptual rather than physical fidelity of the system to gain a deeper appreciation for how one might support and encourage the development of the mental models people need to understand and reason about dynamic physical systems.

■ *Implementation philosophy*. From the first we wanted to build a non-toy system and to keep the tools we constructed as generic as possible. We felt very strongly that in order to establish the credibility of these ideas in the training community, we needed a usable system which addressed a real training problem in a complex training domain. It had to be more than a demonstration of the technology's potential and it had to cover that domain. Also, we have tried to keep the focus beyond just implementing STEAMER but on the more general questions associated with teaching people to understand complex dynamic systems.

We hope these underlying ideas are still evident after the many design, pragmatic, and political decisions that comprise the making of a system like STEAMER.

An Overview of STEAMER

The Choice of Domain

The fundamental research goal of the STEAMER project is to evaluate the potential of new AI hardware and software technology for supporting the construction of computer-based training systems. Just as Papert (1980) holds that one cannot think about thinking without thinking about thinking about something, one cannot evaluate technology in the abstract. We choose to work in the area of propulsion engineering for a number of pragmatic and scientific reasons.

1. There is a critical need for improvement in training in this area in the Navy. Thus, it has wide visibility, and we saw the potential for adequate research funding.

2. Alternative forms of training are quite expensive. A high-fidelity simulator costs about 7 million dollars. This has allowed us to explore hardware alternatives that currently are expensive, but which we anticipate will be much less expensive in the near future.

3. We had access to a detailed mathematical simulation model of a common (1200 psi) steam propulsion system. This permitted us to focus on the interface, tutorial, and explanation issues which are our major interest.

4. We wanted to work in a nontactical area for both personal and pragmatic reasons.

5. We wanted to focus on the use of graphical interfaces to support the development of useful mental models.

6. It seemed engineering domains provided the most instructional leverage from the use of these techniques. Since engineering is an area concerned with designed systems and physical mechanisms, it appeared to be promising for exploring the nature of mental models.

A steam propulsion system is an exceedingly complex physical system. The propulsion spaces account for about one third of the space in most Navy ships. There are thousands of components interconnected by miles of pipes. The operation of the plant is supervised by an engineering officer of the watch and controlled by a team of 16 to 25 individuals who operate in the most trying of circumstances. They often work long hours in a hot, dirty, and quite dangerous environment. Frequently, an individual must cover more than one watch station in a seemingly unending sequence of watches (6 hours on/6 hours off). The status of the plant is primarily revealed by observing gauges depicting important operational parameters, although operators also make use of other forms of evidence as indicators of plant status, particularly how the plant *sounds* and *feels*. It takes years of instruction and experience to be able to understand and competently operate a propulsion plant. In addition, rich robust mental models of the plant are needed to be able to respond to the myriad casualty conditions that can and do arise.

The STEAMER Graphical Interface

A principal intuition behind STEAMER is that it could be quite valuable to be able to provide a color graphics interface to a simulation of a propulsion plant so one could view and manipulate the plant at a number of different hierarchical levels. Overall control of the system is accomplished by means of the multi-paned window interface, depicted in Fig. 6.1. This interface provides a view of the overall status of the plant, the ability to make major transitions of plant state, controls for running the mathematical simulation, the ability to impose casualties, and access to a large number of diagrams of the plant.

In the current system we have one hundred color views available and have devised a quite powerful object-based graphics editor for modifying and expanding this set of views. The views range from high-level fairly abstract rep-

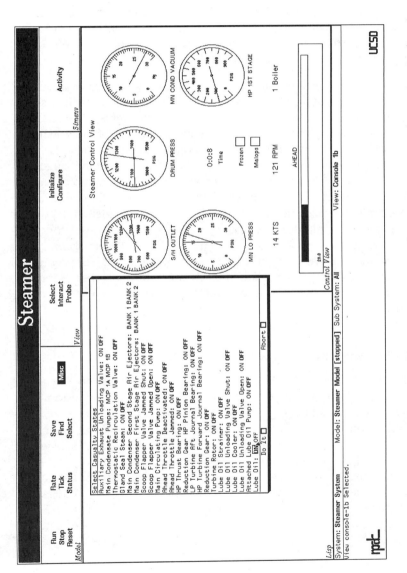

Figure 6.1   Steamer Interface. This interface is used to select views of the plant to be displayed on the color screen, to control the mathematical model, and to impose casualties. It also provides basic plan status information and the ability to control the throttle. Most control of the plant is accomplished by "touching" icons of the color screen with the mouse.

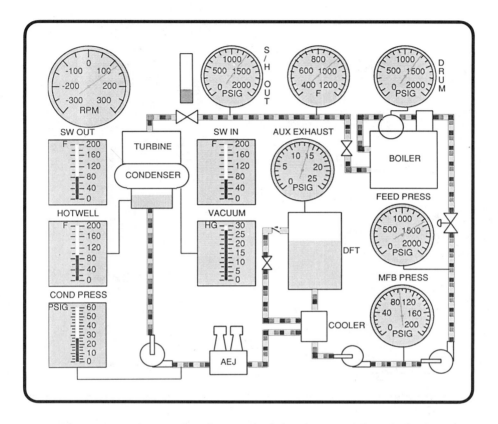

Figure 6.2 Basic Steam Cycle. This is a high-level view of the whole steam
plant. One of the important aspects of STEAMER is the ability to
depict the propulsion system at many different levels.

resentations of the plant like the *Basic Steam Cycle* depicted in Fig. 6.2, to views
of subsystems such as *Make-Up and Excess Feed* shown in Fig. 6.3. Other views
show gauge panels which depict sets of gauges quite like actual gauge panels
in a ship, as in Fig. 6.4, and diagrams specifically constructed to reveal aspects
of the system not normally available in a real plant but which might be beneficial
for understanding some particular aspect of plant operation.

It is important to understand that this graphical interface functions in two
ways. First, it reflects the state of components in the simulation. Thus, it reveals
that a particular component is operating or not by means of changes in color
or other graphical features of the iconic representation on the color screen. For
example, a pump's state is depicted as green if it is operating and red if it is
off. The interface also allows one to view many aspects of the plant that one

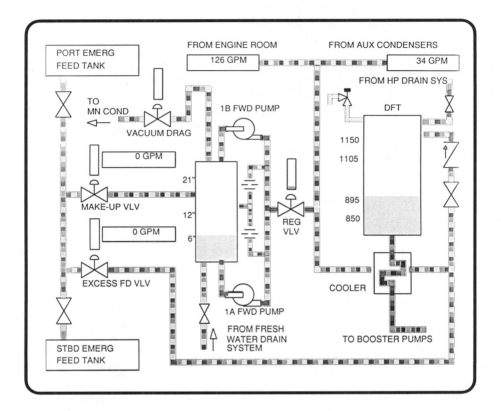

Figure 6.3 Make-Up and Excess Feed. This diagram provides a more detailed view of a subsystem. Adequate coverage of the plant has required approximately 100 diagrams.

cannot normally witness in a real plant. One can, for example, see flow rates in pipes. This information provides more than just state information. It can make much of the causal topology of the system more directly apparent. We think the ability to depict such characteristics of the plant is quite important for assisting an individual attempting to build a mental model of the operation of the plant. The second function of the graphical interface is to permit control of the components within the simulation. This control is provided by pointing to components with a mouse pointing device and clicking on them.

As an example, consider the Make-Up and Excess Feed Diagram depicted in Fig. 6.3. If one were to increase the level of the deaerating feed tank (DFT)*

---

* The deaerating feed tank is a storage tank intended to accommodate fluctuations in demand for water above.

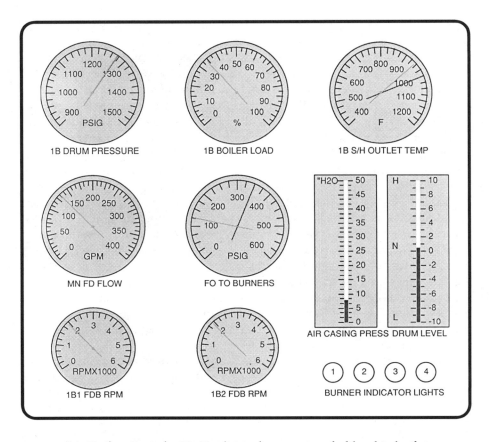

Figure 6.4 Boiler Console 1B. Traditional gauge panels like this boiler
console panel can also be depicted.

(by pointing to a high position in the tank and clicking), the DFT's level would
rise to the position indicated. As a result of this change in tank level, the Excess-
feed Valve would go fully open and flows would increase through that portion
of the system. Thus, the graphical interface allows both the monitoring of the
state of the plant and also its manipulation. It is important to note the potential
instructional significance of allowing students not only to interact with things
that exist in the real plant (e.g., valves), but also of allowing students to manipulate things which one could not directly manipulate, e.g., DFT levels, which
potentially can be of import to supporting the development of an understanding
of the operation of a system.

One aspect of the graphical interface arising from our concern with mental
models and conceptual fidelity is the ability to provide the user with depictions
which approximate the models experts seem to use in reasoning about the

system and which have the potential of supporting the development of useful reasoning models. The ability to provide dynamic interactive graphical interfaces is one of the real virtues and powers of the new *display engines.* Their high-resolution bit-mapped displays make possible a very different form of explanation which one might term *dynamic graphical explanations.*

These forms of graphical explanation can be of considerable benefit in revealing important aspects of normally opaque systems. For example, one portion of a steam propulsion system that is quite difficult to understand is the automatic boiler control system. This part of a propulsion plant is a complex system of negative feedback circuits that senses variables such as steam pressure, steam flow, and supply of combustion air and fuel in order to control the rate of firing of a boiler. The internal behavior of the system is characterized by the propagation of pneumatic signals in a world of multiple dynamic equilibria. Normally in a propulsion plant, this system would be viewed by means of a set of gauges like those depicted in Fig. 6.4. The flow of casualty and the nature of the responses of the system to various perturbations is very difficult to see in the readings of the gauges. Furthermore, in this system the first derivative of the signal is more important than the absolute value of the signal. Thus, what matters is not the actual level of the signal but whether the signal is, in any particular instant, rising, falling, or steady. We created a *signal* or *derivative icon* to depict this information explicitly.

Figure 6.5 shows how this icon would appear at various points in time if it were reflecting the variable whose values are shown on the associated graph. This icon can be used to depict graphically the rate of change of a variable.

We have used the signal icon to create a series of diagrams to assist in explaining the behavior of an automatic boiler control system. Dynamic systems are particularly difficult to explain in language, in part, because of the serial nature of language. However, relationships that are difficult to describe unambiguously in words are often easily depicted graphically. Putting a layer of interface computation between a user and a quantitative model provides a graphical qualitative view of the underlying model. Such a qualitative graphical interface can operate as a *continuous explanation* of the behavior of the system being modeled by allowing a user to more directly apprehend the relationships that are typically described by experts. In a number of views we have instrumented the control air lines with signal icons to reveal the pneumatic signals that are being transmitted. A typical use of these views is to make some throttle change and then single-step the model and watch the transmission of signals. What evolves is a graphical description of the plant's behavior which closely resembles an expert's qualitative explanation of the same perturbation.

It should be clear that these various graphical depictions are appropriate for use by people with very different levels of knowledge about the automatic combustion control system.

The gauge panel is appropriate for an expert who has a rich understanding of the system and needs very little support for his model. A series of signal icons

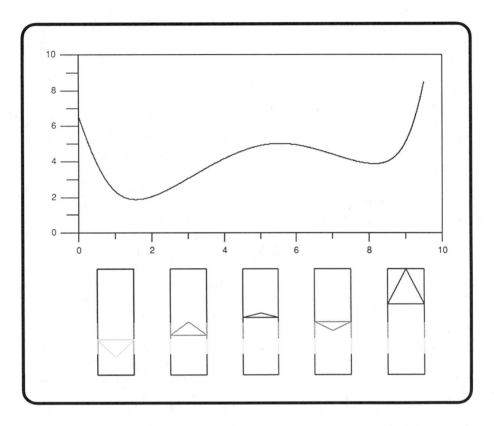

Figure 6.5 Signal Icon. These signal icons depict rate of change of the variable shown in the graph. We have used them to make visible aspects of automatic control systems which are difficult to see with traditional gauges.

arrayed in an order to fit a causal explanation is more appropriate for someone just developing an understanding of the system. An integrated view with both signal icons and normal gauges provides information to support a bridging from the causal depiction to operational gauge panel displays.

The STEAMER Graphics Editor:
A Flavor Is Worth a Thousand Pictures

In order to build and modify the large number of views required to adequately cover the complex propulsion domain, we have implemented an object-based graphics editor.

Figure 6.6 depicts the user interface to the editor. A user interacts primarily by choosing options from this display and positioning and critiquing graphical icons on the color display.

In order to give you a bit of feel for the graphics editor, we will go through some events in a scenario of constructing a diagram. We choose the icons from a menu of available icons (see Fig. 6.6). The available icons consist of basic graphical primitives (lines, circles, etc.), various indicators (dials, columns, graphs, etc.), and a large set of icons specifically designed to depict objects in the propulsion domain (a variety of pumps, valves, pipes, and electrical components).

A sampler of icons is provided in Fig. 6.7. The user interacts by choosing items from menus and positioning the icons on the color screen. His major actions are *pointing* and *selecting*. When he selects an object and points to a position for it, he immediately gets a specific instantiation of the object with many characteristics defaulted (e.g., the color of a dial, its minimum and maximum values, the number of divisions on its scale, etc.). Then through a process of incremental refinement, he critiques the display, reformulates it, and eventually makes it into what he wants. We think this form of interchange is very important. It seems quite natural and allows both the machine and the person to do what each does best. The critique is facilitated by requiring only the choice of different values for parameters which have not defaulted to the required values. What is created as a result of this interaction is not just the color graphic depiction of a diagram, but a program which contains a number of dynamic entities capable of responding to messages and of providing graphical support to an interactive instructional system. The editor then is a facility which makes it possible for a nonprogrammer to create some fairly complex pieces of LISP code.

For purposes of demonstration, consider creating a "dial" for use in a STEAMER diagram. You would click on dial on the black and white screen. The cursor would then be taken to the color screen where you would position and size the dial. You immediately would get a default dial on the screen. Then, you would critique that dial by changing its parameters (position, size, scale, font, color, label, etc.) to match those required.

Figure 6.8 shows some characteristics of a dial that would get created by this simple interaction. Not only are all of the specific details of the dial created, but also, as a particular type of object, it inherits a large collection of messages from the objects out of which it is composed.

A dial, like the other graphical icons, is thus a dynamic object created out of a mixture of more basic elements which can be instantiated to meet the needs of particular applications. It is capable of responding to a variety of commands (messages) to perform specific actions. These messages make possible a very powerful generic interface ability which has been exceedingly useful in building STEAMER.

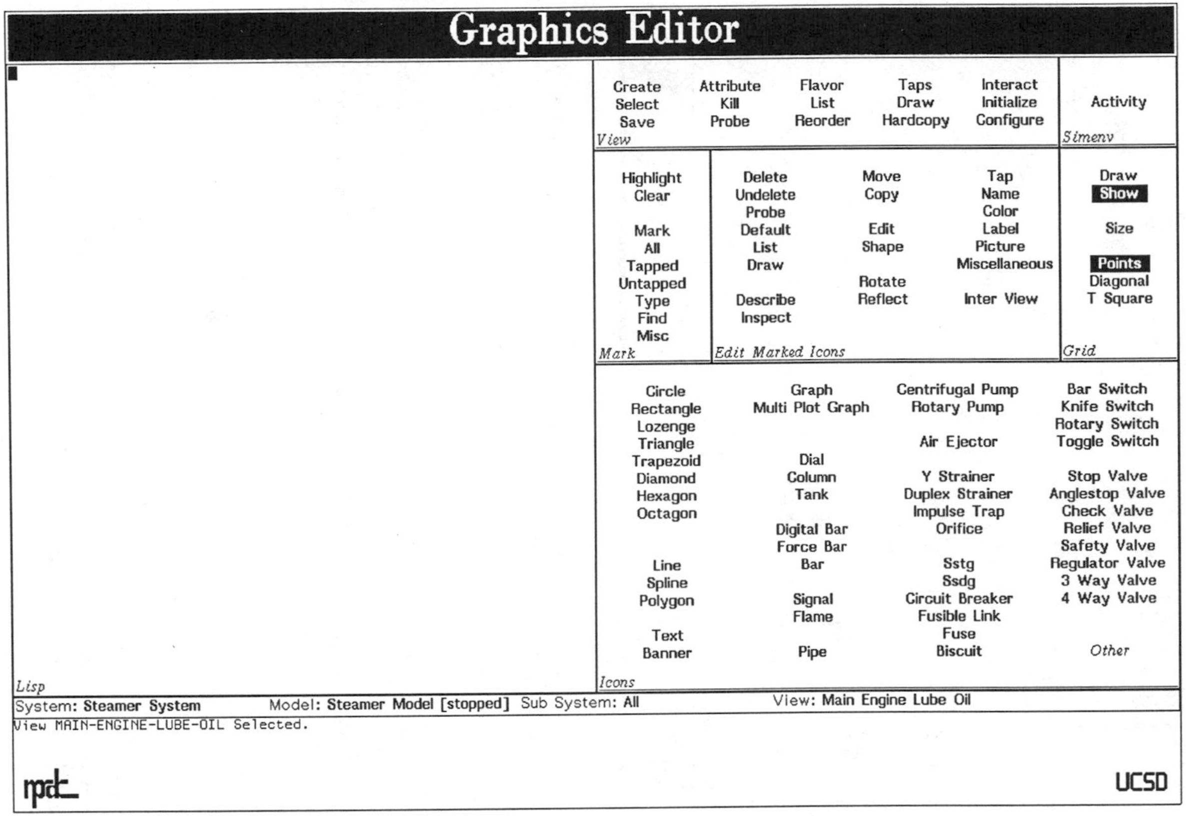

Figure 6.6 Graphics Editor Interface. The editor is a powerful facility for creating graphical interfaces to control the underlying simulation and to reflect the state of its components.

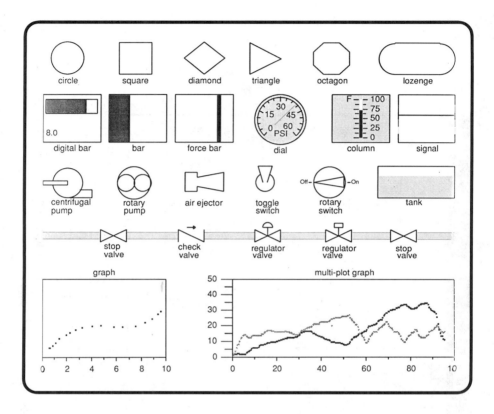

Figure 6.7 Sample Icons. Icons are implemented using the object-oriented flavors system of ZetaLISP.

Once satisfied with the visual characteristics of a diagram, the user then must tie the components to an underlying simulation or real-time interface. We refer to this process as *tapping*. By selecting an object and clicking on the "tap" in the graphics editor display, you would be provided with a pop-up menu to facilitate the association of the icon to variables in the mathematical simulation. Here you can specify not only the variable(s) whose value(s) will be reflected by the icon, but also the variable(s) in the math model which can be changed as a result of clicking on the icon. The editor provides a variety of mapping options to simplify translation from an underlying variable type (say logical) to appropriate messages to the object (say "ON" or "OFF"). In addition to associating icons with the mathematical simulation, one can also associate diagrams and the icons which compose them with what we term *model augments*. An aug-

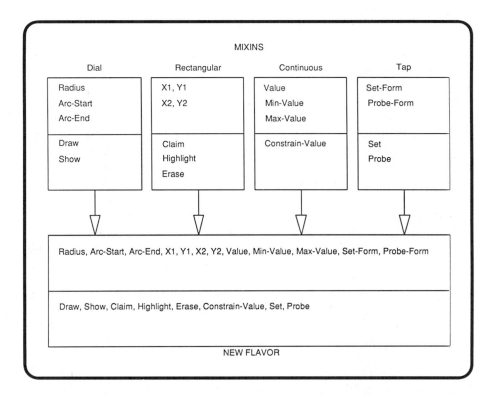

Figure 6.8 Internal Structure of the Dial Icon. Each icon is a message-receiving object composed by mixing together flavors. A subset of the 8 flavors used in a dial icon and the 40 instance variables and 122 messages that the flavors contribute is represented in this figure.

ment allows additions to correct inadequacies of the simulation model, it supports the writing of more complex tapping code, and it provides stand-alone simulations for diagrams.

An example of the first augment is depicting flows. Flows are not represented in the STEAMER math model. It is quite easy though to tie a section of pipe to a function in the augment which computes flow rate based on things which are represented. Typically one would check to see if there is a flow path through the section of pipe and then flow the pipe in proportion to the speed of the appropriate pump. We have also found augments valuable as a mechanism for implementing various mini-labs within STEAMER to demonstrate important physical principles involved in the propulsion domain. In many cases the model augment provides the total mathematical model for a mini-lab and runs independent of the large simulation model.

The editor then is a complete system for constructing diagrams and interfacing them to an underlying mathematical model. It has gone through a long period of evolution and refinement. In its present state, it is very usable by computer-naive individuals. In fact, most of the diagrams in STEAMER have been originated or refined by a retired boiler technician with more than 20 years of propulsion plant experience, but with no previous computer experience. In a number of tryouts of STEAMER in Navy schools, we have found that a short period of training is all that is required for instructors to begin to be able to use the editor productively. The only problematic thing is tapping diagrams into the math model. Our subject matter expert now has no problem if an appropriate variable representing a component is available. However, for more complicated tappings like those involved in pipes, where one must write a bit of LISP code or where a stand-alone model is required, we must provide programming support.

The graphics editor is an extremely general and powerful tool with potential applications ranging far beyond STEAMER. In designing and implementing the graphics editor we have capitalized on the very flexible object-oriented *Flavors System* of ZetaLISP. This editor has been used to create all of the STEAMER diagrams. We have also used it in some quite different domains to explore its generality. For example, in collaboration with one of our colleagues at the University of California at San Diego, Dave Rumelhart, the editor has been used to build a graphical interface to a number of parallel distributed models of cognition. In many ways the problems facing a researcher when implementing such models are much the same that we face in STEAMER. When there is a complex dynamic system which needs to be understood, researchers can benefit from graphical views of that system at various hierarchical levels. Having a powerful tool like the editor available when actively developing a simulation model can be incredibly valuable. In addition, there are a wide variety of other potential applications of the graphics editor. For example, it would be very valuable for process control applications where one might tie icons to a real-time interface rather than an underlying simulation.

Where Is the AI in STEAMER?

One might view STEAMER as being fundamentally a cognitive science rather than an AI research enterprise since we are primarily concerned with how people understand and reason about complex dynamic systems and how interactive graphical interfaces might support the development of useful mental models. On the other hand, we think STEAMER is a most important AI application because it called for a very careful look at what aspects of AI technology are ready for application to the design and implementation of computer-based instructional systems. One of the most important AI technologies is the programming environment within which we work. The support provided by this *exploratory programming environment* has made it possible to successfully pursue the construction of a system like STEAMER. The system could not have been constructed without the powerful programming tools which AI programming environments make available. Our work has been accomplished within the ZetaLISP environment (Weinreb & Moon, 1981). For an excellent description of a similar exploratory programming environment see Sheil's (1983) recent article.

Of course, using AI tools, either those associated with programming environments or even our use of a truth-maintenance system (McAllester, 1982) for maintaining the consistency of a database of assertions about plant state and student knowledge, doesn't make a project into an AI venture. Most of the genuine AI aspects of STEAMER derive from our interest in knowledge representation. We have been very concerned with how one might represent the knowledge involved in the propulsion domain. Much of this has involved efforts to elicit and represent the types of models that human experts use in reasoning about propulsion plant components and procedures (Williams, Hollan, & Stevens, 1982). Considerable effort, thought, and code have gone into issues of representation. We have been concerned with representing the information required to adopt various perspectives on the plant and to maintain a flexible model of the state of the plant and of the student. This is very much the current focus of our efforts. What might be perceived as slowness in getting to this portion of the development is a necessary result of not building a toy system. It would have been easy not to fully complete the earlier graphical phases of the project or to settle for something less than good coverage of the complete propulsion plant or a less general graphics editor.

We would like to give you some examples of the knowledge representation aspects of the project that involve nongraphical aspects of our domain. When you spend from 50 million to a few billion dollars for a Navy ship, you also get an extensive users manual. One form of this manual contains a list of procedures, called the Engineering Operational Sequencing System (EOSS), for operating the plant. This set of manuals, which would fill a good sized book case, contains all of the procedures needed to run the ship's propulsion system. We have been attempting to represent these procedures in a form such that they can be executed and explained at different hierarchical levels. In some sense we face similar problems when creating the views needed to adequately cover the graphical representation of the propulsion domain. We have come to a similar solution: the creation of an editor. This editor, a *Procedures Editor,* makes available sets of generic components, generic procedures, and engineering principles. It allows for the composition of procedures not by writing down their steps, but by performing mappings from abstract generic components and procedures to particular instances.

Figure 6.9 depicts an example of the types of information that might be involved in the composition of a procedure. The identification of abstract devices and generic components is very much a research activity. That activity requires a deep knowledge of the domain, an appreciation for the generic models that experts use, and the ability to iteratively refine, extend, and reformulate those models which sufficiently cover the EOSS procedures. This is complicated because no such principled process was followed in constructing the existing EOSS procedures. They are a mixture of engineering constraints, rules of thumb, and historical accidents. We are attempting to identify the types of generic components which range from very abstract and general objects (e.g., two-port devices) to less general components (e.g., positive displacement pumps). The editor permits the user to instantiate particular instances of generic procedures and associate the steps that are derived with various underlying engineering principles. The editor provides considerable support for this process. For example, it detects collisions in orderings of steps and allows their resolution. Currently we are discussing what would be the most convenient form of interface to provide for the editor. In some ways a graphical interface seems appealing. In fact, some of the information could be gathered with and support the process of using the graphics editor. For example, knowledge about abstract pumps with suction and discharge valves could be represented. When the user places a pump into a diagram with the graphics editor, the system could assist in making an identification of the associated suction and discharge valves.

An initial version of the procedures editor has recently come to life and is starting to meet our needs for putting procedures into the system. It will make it possible to represent procedures in such a way that intelligent use can be made of them by providing the necessary representations to permit the system to adopt different viewpoints on portions of the propulsion system. One might, for example, view a particular pump as an instance of a *positive displacement pump* or as a component of a *pumping station.* We are developing a frame-based representation system that supports multiple perspectives and permits integration of the vast amount of structural, functional, topological, and graphical information contained within STEAMER.

We have also been experimenting with a growing number of interpreters, which we call *presenters,* for allowing STEAMER to talk about the propulsion system. Thus, a presenter might take an object and discuss how it is connected to other objects in the system in terms of its physical connections, energy connections, or information connections. Procedures also are objects in the representational system and can be talked about from a variety of perspectives. For example, the system can discuss the components of a procedure, salient procedural fragments which occur in many other procedures (e.g., the securing of an isolation valve or the establishment of a flow path), or the engineering principles which jointly conspire to constrain the ordering of the steps within

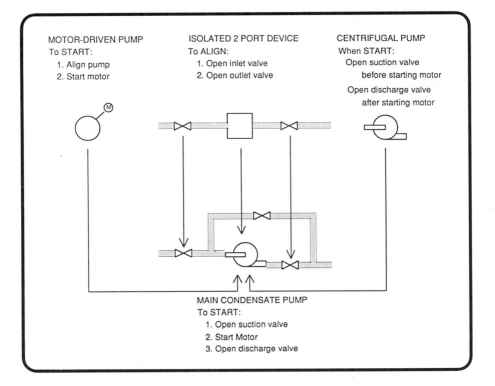

Figure 6.9 Composition of a Procedure from Generic Components. We are exploring techniques for composing procedures from generic components and for providing principled explanations.

a given procedure. Considerable work remains to be accomplished in this area, but currently, we think the procedures editor may turn out to be as valuable and powerful as our graphics editor.

In summary, we think there are a number of factors which distinguish STEAMER from traditional AI efforts. Most derive from our fundamental cognitive science perspective on creating a training system that will help students come to understand and reason about a complex dynamic system. The effort, at this point, has been dominated not by attempting to build an expert system to replace a person, but rather by a deep commitment to graphics, to interactive graphical forms of support for understanding, to a concern with how to make more and more of the propulsion domain inspectable, and with the creation of generic tools (like the graphics editor) that allow nonprogrammers to create a significant portion of interactive inspectable training systems. These efforts have forced us to be very concerned with explanation as a primary goal rather than something that might be tacked onto the end of an expert system to help it recruit faith in its inferences. The types of principled explanations that we need can only derive from a rich and powerful representation of the generic components and procedures that seem to allow a human expert to parse and understand the tremendous complexity of the propulsion domain.

Directions for the Future

We are moving in essentially five directions in the future:

- We plan to continue the development of an integrated representation system to tie together the many different types of knowledge currently represented.

- We will work on providing STEAMER with a consistent interface to create a central point of view and a consistent means of controlling the growing variety of things the system can do and that can be done to it. In short, we want to provide STEAMER with a *style* and *consistent personality*.

- We will pursue the extension of generative and reactive aspects of STEAMER. In particular, we will be providing the diagrams with a form of instructional augmentation containing the information needed to support mixed-initiative interactions with the diagrams. We need to be able to represent consistently the important things that a diagram might reveal to a student, to provide a mechanism for posing questions to the student which might be answered not by typing but by doing things to the diagram, and to provide mechanisms for monitoring a student's behavior while attempting to answer questions. For example, in the *Make-Up and Excess Feed diagram* (Fig. 6.3) there are important control relationships between when and how far valves open, based on the levels of the tanks in the system. The system might, for example, ask the student to manipulate the diagram to get the Excess-Feed Valve fully open. In our initial evaluation of the system, we have found that having a student put forth hypotheses in this way results in the crossing of an important instructional and motivational threshold.

- We plan to pursue the implementation of an expanded student model. Presently we have only explored a very limited differential model which notates a student's knowledge of engineering principles. There is much that remains to be done here.

- Finally, in a related project, NPRDC's group plans to pursue a generalization of the graphics editor to include the ability to construct a simulation model interactively. The general notion here is to provide default behaviors for objects analogous to the current provision of default visual characteristics.

This *Behavior Editor* will allow the user to critique the behavior associated with an object in much the same way he or she can currently critique graphical characteristics. We would like to see the extent to which a non-programmer can construct a simulation program by means of the same sorts of interactions that currently allow a user of our graphics editor to construct a graphical interface.

Conclusions, Concerns, and Counsel

We have tried to provide a brief overview of our current and projected efforts with STEAMER. More importantly, we have attempted to point out what we see as the underlying ideas in the project:

- Mental models;
- Graphical interfaces to interactive inspectable simulations;
- Conceptual fidelity; and
- Implementation philosophy.

We think we are just now seeing the introduction of the requisite hardware, software, and cognitive theory to permit principled instructional applications. We are quite convinced that the major constraints on progress currently are our knowledge of cognition and the methods with which to represent the vast amount and myriad types of domain knowledge needed to support instruction. We are also convinced that we will see more and more STEAMER-like systems in the future. They provide the opportunity for a qualitatively different and superior form of training which focuses on providing the interactions needed to build up useful mental models and understandings of complex dynamic physical systems. Such systems can also increase the amount of supervised practice available to students by orders of magnitude.

The great promise of the application of artificial intelligence software and hardware technologies to the solution of problems in a variety of domains is a refrain heard often these days. We are both encouraged and fearful of the attention AI is currently receiving. We are encouraged because we too see tremendous promise in the technology and in the types of explicit computational accounts of cognition emerging from AI and the other cognitive sciences. There is a danger that real developments, substantive though they may be, will fall far short of inflated expectations. Such a turn of events could result in a backlash against AI similar to that suffered by computer-based instruction in the past decade.

It does not require an intellectual historian to see the parallels between the current interest in AI and early interest in computer-based instruction. It was some two decades ago that people first began to advocate the potential of computer technology to provide and improve instruction. Unfortunately, most actual instructional applications of the technology have fallen far short of its promise. We have argued elsewhere that one primary reason is that it is perhaps too easy to see the potential of the technology for instructional applications. It seems to require very little exposure to computation before most people are aware of its instructional potential. Without an appreciation for how much tacit knowledge underlies good instruction performed by human instructors, how difficult it is to make that tacit knowledge explicit, and what kinds of software and hardware are required to support its delivery, it is easy to visualize the potential without really knowing what might be required to make it a reality. As we mentioned earlier, within computer-based instruction we think we are just now beginning to see the kinds of hardware, software, and most importantly, the explicit computational formulations of cognitive theory essential to principled instructional applications. Without these requisite tools and theories, the types of instructional applications have and will continue to fall far short of the technology's potential. We also are particularly fearful that important research breakthroughs will be used inappropriately to sell aspects of the technology which, while still ripe for further research progress, are not yet ready for application. This could result in a slowing down of important research and development at a time when it should be accelerated.

We also would like to give some counsel on the application of AI to other instructional domains based on our experience with STEAMER. In addition to warning about overzealous and uninformed advocates, we would like to put forth the following observations and recommendations:

1. We think it is tremendously important not to rush into applications. Premature application of a fragile technology will instill the same kinds of negative attitudes that premature applications of computer-based instruction did.

2. It is exceedingly important to provide sufficient basic research funding to make possible the development of a strong technological base to support future applications. Here we commend a recent letter to the editor in *Science* to your attention. Lindamood (1983) puts forth the novel thesis that the primary impact of the Japanese Fifth Generation Project may be *managerial* rather than *technological*. In particular he focuses on the nature of funding of that research endeavor and points out what may be the primary fault of U.S. research funding: *overspecifying and overmanaging the research endeavor*. This is typically done in the hopes of obtaining early application results but seems more likely to result not in early application but only poor science.

3. There is a real need for additional centers of excellence for providing a strong scientific and technological base. It is vital that mechanisms for transitioning the more promising results also be established as part of these

centers. Interdisciplinary centers with ties to academia, industry, and the military are particularly important.

4. Very careful consideration should be given to the choice of a few well-funded initial demonstration systems. Such systems are very important for establishing the credibility of the best research ideas and can serve as important guide posts for subsequent efforts. Given the shortage of experienced people in AI and cognitive science, this seems a particularly wise approach.

5. Finally, much thought and research needs to be addressed to methods for evaluating these new AI-based instructional systems. There are some tremendously hard problems involved. Here we want to include not only the traditional view of evaluation but also evaluations of how these systems affect the communities within which they are placed. Powerful technologies sometimes have unanticipated beneficial or detrimental consequences. An evaluation of an application of this technology that considers only effects on the problem the technology is intended to solve may miss important consequences of the use of the technology.

Acknowledgments

The senior author of this paper, James Hollan, initiated the STEAMER effort five years ago in collaboration with Mike Williams (then at NPRDC and now at IntelliGenetics). Al Stevens of Bolt Beranek and Newman (BBN) joined the collaboration shortly thereafter. Since that time, a significant amount of the effort has been conducted under contract to BBN, and a number of people have been involved in the project. At NPRDC, the STEAMER project currently involves the efforts of James Hollan, Edwin Hutchins, and Louis Weitzman. The BBN side of the effort presently includes Bruce Roberts, who in many ways is the principal software architect of STEAMER, Terry Roe (a retired boiler technician chief with 22 years of propulsion operational experience who serves as our subject matter expert and although employed by BBN works with us in San Diego), and the part-time efforts of Albert Boulanger and Glenn Abrett. Also, over the years, we have been most fortunate to have received the capable assistance of Larry Stead (the original implementor of the STEAMER graphics editor and now with Symbolics), Ken Forbus (MIT), and Brian Smith (then at MIT and now at Xerox Parc).

References

Lindamood, G. E. (1983). Japanese Computer Project. *Science, 221,* 1008.

McAllester, D. A. (1982). Reasoning utility package user's manual. AI Memo 667, Massachusetts Institute of Technology.

Papert, S. (1980). *Mindstorms: Children, computers, and powerful ideas.* New York: Basic Books.

Sheil, B. (1983). Power tools for programmers. *Datamation, 29,* 131–144.

Weinreb, D., & Moon, D. (1981). *LISP machine manual.* Cambridge, MA: MIT Artificial Intelligence Laboratory.

Williams, M., Hollan, J., & Stevens, A. (1983). Human reasoning about a simple physical system. In D. Gentner & A. Stevens (Eds.), *Mental models.* Hillsdale, NJ: Erlbaum.

7// Artificial Intelligence Applications to Maintenance Training

LEON H. NAWROCKI

Introduction

This chapter discusses the evolution and results to date of a joint military-industry research project to evaluate the application of artificial intelligence (AI) technology to maintenance training. Specifically, the problem addressed is that of troubleshooting and diagnostic training. It should be made clear at the outset that the current project is ongoing, and that formal evaluation remains to be completed. However, the methodological and research issues already encountered should provide practical guidelines for those who are considering similar efforts. While this chapter is written with the relative newcomer to artificial intelligence in mind, technical terms are introduced if these are likely to be encountered in the general literature. The reader is encouraged to investigate the cited references for further elaboration of technical issues.

We will first review the maintenance training problem from the perspective of the maintenance community. We will next consider the opportunity presented by artificial intelligence. The remainder of the chapter will focus on the approach and results to date of the current project. The project work itself will be presented in chronological order of events within the three major thrusts: (1) knowledge-base development; (2) tutorial strategy; and (3) evaluation of the training program. The historical approach is used to provide the reader with a view not only of the practice of AI but also of the pitfalls.

Maintenance and Diagnostic Training

One result of the increasing technological sophistication of equipment is a corresponding increase in the concern of both the military and industrial com-

A major portion of the research discussed in this paper was funded by the U.S. Army Research Institute under contract MDA 903-84-C-0189. The views and opinions expressed by the author do not imply or reflect those of the Department of Defense or other federal government agencies.

munities for cost-effective maintenance of such equipment. A holistic view of alternative solutions addressing this concern is depicted in Fig. 7.1. At the core, engineering reliability techniques can eliminate the maintenance problem entirely. To the extent this is not effective, self-diagnostic capabilities (another area of application for artificial intelligence technology) and job aids can be introduced to reduce reliance on human expertise. What maintenance requirements remain are then resolved by training human technicians.

The evidence to date strongly suggests that all four solutions are required to ensure adequate maintainability (Nawrocki, 1980) and that what varies from equipment to equipment is the proportion of the maintenance system devoted to each of the solutions. Ironically though, advances in state-of-the-art technologies for the engineering, built-in diagnostic, and job aid approaches have potentially increased the difficulty of providing effective training. That is, the most predictable and quantifiable equipment problems can generally be dealt with by a combination of the first three approaches, reducing the need for large numbers of human technicians. Yet the maintenance problems that remain are often highly complex and unique diagnostic problems such as those due to intermittent or interactive malfunctioning components. Thus fewer but higher-skilled technicians may be needed.

Compounding the need for higher-skilled technicians is the demographically demonstrable reduction in the entry-level labor force projected for the United States; hence there will be increased competition for technicians with the desired skills (Russell, 1982). In addition, although data on aptitudes and trainability are inconclusive, there appears to be a downward trend in the basic skill achievement level of persons entering the labor force. In summary, the training of skilled technicians remains a significant element in the improvement of maintenance system capabilities but the training focus is shifting toward developing a higher level of generic diagnostic skills.

Artificial Intelligence and Training

Traditional training methods, including classroom training and on-the-job training, play a useful role but are often inadequate for teaching complex diagnostic and repair skills. Elements of realism are missing with these traditional methods, even when the instruction includes supporting graphic aids and video sequences. As Kolodner (1984) notes, experts in diverse fields often indicate that appreciation of knowledge obtained in the formal instructional setting often does not occur until the learner is able to combine that knowledge with actual experience and determine how to apply the knowledge.

Computer-based instruction (CBI), which includes the recent introduction of interactive videodisc, offers greater instructional flexibility and trainee interaction than traditional methods. However, current CBI is typically not powerful enough to contain the knowledge needed to perform troubleshooting

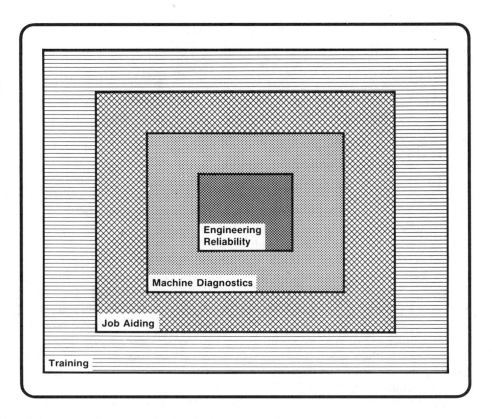

Figure 7.1 Elements of a Total Maintenance Support System

(diagnostic) tasks, model student conceptual strengths/weaknesses, simulate a complete range of malfunctions and symptoms, and engage in a tutorial dialogue with the trainee. The use of AI technology to augment CBI combines the necessary courseware, software, and hardware to construct such complete tutoring systems. Ideally this combination, intelligent computer-assisted instruction (ICAI), provides the opportunity to integrate system functions, subject matter expertise, and learner states to provide individualized, Socraticlike tutorials. Thus ICAI has the potential to provide multiple training functions to include initial knowledge measurement and followup on skill proficiency maintenance. These characteristics suggest that ICAI may be a means for decreasing the time to migrate from novice to expert technician, while increasing the number of trainees successfully reaching an expert level. In addition, the status and potential of AI technology for expert systems appear sufficiently advanced (Winston, 1984) to warrant pursuing related uses such as ICAI.

ICAI Concepts

Possibly the earliest successful ICAI project was a geography tutor called SCHOLAR (Carbonell, 1970). From this beginning, prototypic systems emerged in topics as diverse as meteorology (Stevens, Collins, & Goldin, 1976), medical diagnosis (Clancey, 1979), mathematics (Brown & Burton, 1978; Burton & Brown, 1979; Suppes, 1981), and computer programming (Miller, 1981; Anderson & Reiser, 1984). A system of particular interest for diagnostic ICAI is SOPHIE (Brown, Burton, & de Kleer, 1981), which explored simulation techniques for training electronic troubleshooting.

ICAI systems to date have adopted the orientation of cognitive science, a discipline combining elements of cognitive psychology with computer science (Bregar & Farley, 1980). Early projects were intensive in manpower and computing resources and limited in scope to a narrow range of topics. The U.S. Army fielded a computer-based system with partial ICAI aspects to support training in field radio repair. The system contained some ICAI features, such as adaptive sequencing and problem selection based on analysis of student input, although within a highly limited tutorial capability (Knerr & Nawrocki, 1978; Knerr, 1979). The development of additional supporting tools and the maturation of AI technology (Anderson & Reiser, 1984) have made it even more feasible to consider linking ICAI technology to real training environments.

Figure 7.2 illustrates one conceptual design for an idealized ICAI system. Components in dotted line borders are those which the current project has only recently begun to address. While each of the components is of value, an ICAI approach to training may not require full development of each component or may not find such development feasible, a decision issue in the project to be discussed later in this chapter. However, we will briefly discuss each of these components to provide a context for the later project description.

The Domain Expert component in Fig. 7.2 refers to both the general and domain specific knowledge regarding the subject domain, for example, general knowledge about the principles of electronics and specific knowledge about the function and operation of a component in an electronic circuit. Problem-solving strategies would be included in the domain expert. Often an ICAI system must be able to solve domain problems in several ways to correspond to reasonable alternatives that the learner might employ during different stages of training. The subject matter can be organized in a variety of ways such as semantic nets, decision trees, procedures, and production rules. Ideally the knowledge base should also contain a capability to explain (articulate) how conclusions are derived from the knowledge base.

The Student Model contains a repertoire of the particular learner's skills and misunderstandings (conceptual "bugs"). This component records and maintains an information base on such learner characteristics as preferred learning mode and current skill mastery. A number of model structures have been proposed; the reader is referred elsewhere for elaboration of these (Burton &

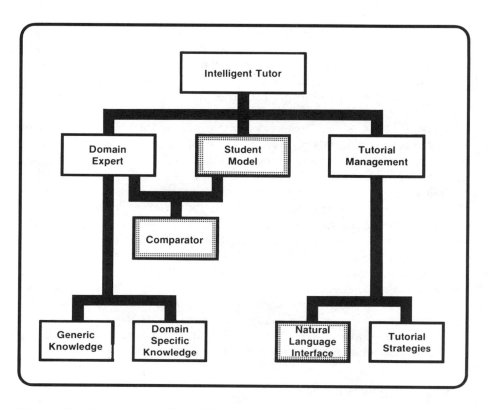

Figure 7.2 Components of an ICAI System

Brown, 1981; Burton, 1981; Goldstein, 1981; Sleeman, 1981). A comparator component permits the integration of the domain and student models to establish a basis for determining feedback or instructional adaptation to individual learner needs.

Finally, a Tutorial Management component provides a mechanism for conducting the tutorial dialogue with the student. Natural language interface is desirable and may be a primary concern if a Socratic tutoring strategy is desired. In a Socratic strategy system a natural language interface is necessary to permit response flexibility. It is important to note that natural language can include mathematical notation, special symbols, and pictures if these are a user-accepted form of communicating information in a task situation.

ICAI and Electronic Troubleshooting

We will now consider the previously described ICAI model in the context (domain) of electronic or electromechanical system diagnosis, as this is the domain selected for the project to be discussed. Contrary to popular impression, electronics is not thoroughly formalized. While some aspects, such as the behavior of individual components in a circuit, are well understood (at least when operating normally) specific circuit characteristics and component behavior under fault conditions are less well specified. The lack of specification creates some difficulties. First, it is difficult to capture and encode the knowledge. Second, the production of generic expert systems to permit ease of transfer to new subject matter is made more difficult. The challenge is to develop methods which can provide the student with generalizable skills and knowledge beyond that which can be supported by automated diagnostics or job aids.

Much of the knowledge involved in troubleshooting is of electronics and the functioning of the specific circuits to be analyzed, with additional skills unique to the troubleshooting activity. It is often advantageous to consider separate, though not independent, knowledge bases: knowledge about the rules and principles regarding the operation of components and their functional relationship in a circuit; and knowledge about troubleshooting strategies and problem-solving techniques. As humans use considerably different strategies than quantifiable algorithms suggested by "optimal" models, it has been suggested that the expert system strategy be articulated to the learner in causal and qualitative terms (Brown, Collins, & Harris, 1978). It is in this context of qualitative reasoning that the current research project was initiated.

ICAI Development Example

The research to be discussed was generated by the U.S. Army and Xerox in recognition of the need to develop a new approach to technician training. Both the military and industry were aware that rote learning of procedures does not enable technicians to readily and efficiently adapt to new or modified equipment. On the other hand, teaching theory is ineffective as scientific or engineering design level of knowledge is considerably different than the knowledge needed to troubleshoot equipment at a functional level. For example, it is not necessary to be knowledgeable about Bernoulli's principle to understand and describe the function of a carburetor. Nor does one have to be a chemist to conceptually relate combustion to the firing of a spark plug. Thus the proposed strategy was to replace theoretical knowledge with conceptual knowledge and to teach technicians a "vocabulary" for organizing and expressing that knowledge. In more formal terms, the hypothesis was that procedural (i.e., troubleshooting) skills can be learned more effectively by providing qualitative, causal models of how a system functions, and by enabling the learner to rationalize procedural knowledge via semantic descriptions of the system, task, and context.

To demonstrate the potential utility of the preceding approach for real-world problems, the research was directed toward (1) selecting a task domain representative of a significant problem area; (2) applying cognitive techniques to produce an appropriate instructional model; (3) providing a computer-based instructional system to support the model; and (4) evaluating the system in an operational training environment. The first phase would focus on a target sub-system of a copier and construction of a knowledge representation for the operation of the subsystem at a causal level. The second phase would emphasize construction of the supporting instructional interface to include the computer support environment. The third and last phase would be directed toward evaluating the instructional system and refining the system based on results. It was assumed that the phases would overlap and that the total development process would be iterative.

Beyond advances in expert systems modeling, two additional factors influenced the initiation of the project: advances in AI software development tools and computers with sufficient power at an acceptable cost. In this project, the software development environment was Interlisp-D, a substantially enhanced version of LISP that consisted of an integrated set of system, programming, and interface design aids.* This software environment provided the capability for rapid prototyping, that is, a process which permits continuous, real-time revisions of software. The hardware support was the Xerox 1108, a 3.5 MB machine developed specifically to provide AI computational power in either a stand-alone or networked mode.

Knowledge-Base Development

The initial direction was based on an examination of the job and job training path for Xerox technicians. This examination revealed four major areas of opportunity for testing of ICAI concepts. Figure 7.3 shows a simplified version of this path. New trainees are pretested for basic electronic knowledge and, contingent on the outcome of the test, are provided with an instructional package on the fundamentals of electronics. This package includes information on circuit symbols, fundamental operations of circuit components, basic circuit measurement techniques, and a fixed set of relatively simple troubleshooting problems on a generic circuit. The instruction is supported by two physically constructed circuits, and the module is referred to as Task Aids. It is important to note that the Task Aids instruction includes items not necessarily required for the beginner and is also used as an optional refresher training tool for more advanced technicians. This is indicated by the return paths in Fig. 7.3, the dotted box reflecting the optional nature of the basic knowledge training.

Trainees then advance to a course on generic fundamentals of reprographic devices and the use of troubleshooting tools, manuals, and information sources. All trainees are given an overview of the Xerographic process in the context of seven functional stages and the relationship of these stages to major machine

---

* For a fundamental explanation of the LISP language and its importance to AI, see Hofstadter (1985).

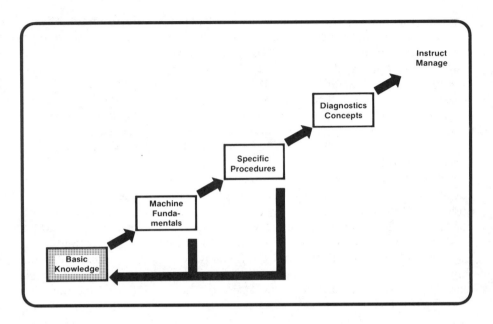

Figure 7.3 Training Path

components. Trainees are then assigned to training on specific machines, and this training emphasizes the use of job aids for troubleshooting. These structured job aids, called Fault Isolation Procedures (FIPs) are step-by-step decision tree–based instructions for diagnosis and repair. Extensive Xerographic instruction is provided to technicians receiving copier training, and is integrated with the specific machine design being taught. Over time, trainees receive additional machine specific training to widen the range of machines, within a similar product class, that they can maintain.

Technicians can advance to a more senior technician level, at which point they are now encouraged to bring to play their own problem-solving strategies to assist lower-level technicians when problems are encountered that go beyond the documented strategies and the job aid support. In time, highly qualified technicians generally migrate to managerial positions or assignments as in-house instructors and instructional developers.

Given the typical job training path, the knowledge base prior to specific procedure training appeared an appropriate target. This knowledge appears to underly the generic and domain specific knowledge required for a novice to transition to expert. A common task domain within this level, and one representing a major portion of expert knowledge, is that of Xerography. Given that task domain, a preliminary simulation was constructed that represented the Xerographic engine of a complex copier (1075). The Xerography engine provides a complex electromechanical ICAI test bed. The underlying Xerographic process represents a central system function with connections to multiple subsystems and is an imprecisely defined domain. The domain permits the representation of hierarchical structures and the decomposition of functions suitable for organizing into causal nets. Of equal importance is that Xerography is a major component of technician training. At the start of the project the 1075 training was conducted at a centralized training site and used technicians with mid-level experience, making it an excellent target for later evaluation.

The level of simulation and complexity represented a best guess at a starting kernel simulation. The kernel notion is to develop a core representation for the task domain and to expand this core by the cumulative addition of subcomponents until the knowledge base can analyze and explain those symptom-fault relationships representative of the target expert. The kernel concept has previously been used to produce instructional manuals. This iterative and cumulative building from a kernel is enabled by rapid prototyping.

Figure 7.4 shows one of the evolutionary prototypes (ARIA) developed in the first phase of the research program. The central rectangle in Fig. 7.4 represents a horizontal view of the photoreceptor (PR) belt with functional components along the outer edge. The process occurs counterclockwise along the belt. At this stage of the development, interviews with experts (instructors) had provided for modifications and simulation capabilities that expert judgment indicated were necessary to analyze significant faults. The symptom set was that of copy quality (smears, lines, spotting, etc., of copy), a major initial symptom output reflecting machine operation status. The simulation initially permitted 13 identifiable copy-quality symptoms and 20 fault sources, drawn primarily from technical documentation. It was also at this stage that the features of the simulation began to include those suggested by the initial tutorial notions. For example, the positive and negative charge indicators visible along the edge of the belt and the ability to check the status of paper copy at process intervals (document samples shown in Fig. 7.4) permitted the learner to construct causal chains and to envision elements within this chain.

A parallel development was undertaken to take advantage of previous work on a microcomputer CAI simulation and to determine the capability of subject matter experts to learn and employ AI technology. This development also served as a test bed for the utility of supporting software tools used in producing the kernel simulation. The second simulation was based on a similar but less complex 1045 copier, and the starting point was at a less sophisticated and FIP-based troubleshooting level, typical of the novice technician capability. Thus this simulation portrayed the external machine indicators used by novice technicians and included on-line access to FIPs and a simulated analog multimeter to perform circuit checks. An interesting feature was the availability of simulated diagnostic codes representing· information from built-in machine diagnostics. Figure 7.5

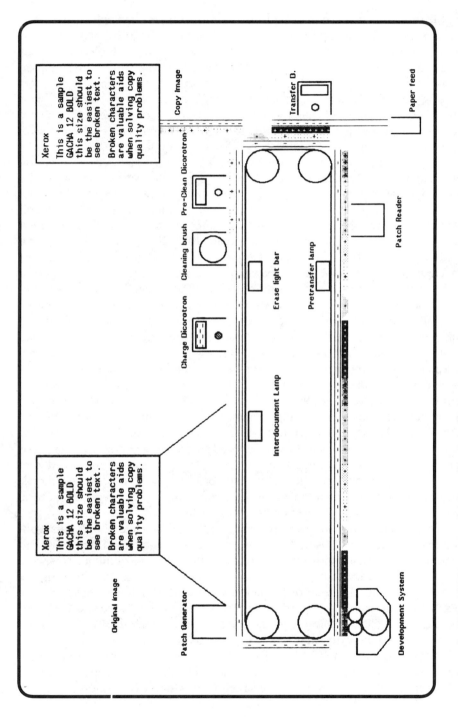

Figure 7.4 ARIA 1075 Xerographic Engine Simulation

shows the features of this simulation, also at an early stage of development. The circuit at the bottom of the figure is from the FIP, and written instructional steps from the FIP were an optional feature. The alphanumeric codes, mid-right of the figure, represent circuit test points coinciding with FIP component indicators. The center left box in the figure is the display on the operator control panel of the copier.

As the parallel developments moved forward, it appeared that at some point in time the simulations could be meshed such that the learner could move from the surface to deep level of the machine, thus relating the procedure following diagnosis to cognitive-based procedural knowledge at a deeper level. It was at about this stage of the development that events made a shift in the project strategy necessary.

The first event that required a project shift was a corporate change in the technician training policy. A substantial portion of the job skills for technicians was moved from diagnosis to the use of diagnostic aids, or increased reliance on FIPs and related documents. This particularly impacted on the ARIA 1075 model as the 1075 training itself was reoriented to decentralized training sites and the documentation modified to emphasize procedure *following* rather than proceduralized *problem solving*. This change in policy made it necessary to reconsider the nature of an instructional module and evaluation milieu.

A second event, or rather set of discoveries, was that the functional documentation provided to technicians, to include the FIPs, was inadequate as a basis for knowledge representation. Existing documentation did not provide the semantic structure that interviews with expert technicians suggested was necessary to relate copy quality to Xerographic causes. Also, the FIPs assumed single faults and often a procedure string terminated in a "dropout" statement requiring knowledge normally gained through troubleshooting experience. A related and interesting input from instructors was that technicians frequently had difficulty in employing the FIPs because they did not comprehend the structure and rationale for the FIP logic. These discoveries suggested that the ICAI content should include a balance of problem-solving strategies and procedural guide comprehension.

Finally, in attempting to enhance ARIA and the 1045 simulation and build instructional modules around the simulators, it became apparent that the original simulations were at an inappropriate kernel level for the development of generic instruction needed by the novice. This was reinforced by feedback from project staff who attended Basic Technician, 1045, and 1075 courses as students. Also, a belated discovery is relevant to future developers of similar ICAI simulations. That is, while the quick selection and construction of a graphic portrayal was initially useful in suggesting additional simulation requirements, the graphic representations had tended to constrain thinking on underlying knowledge representation.

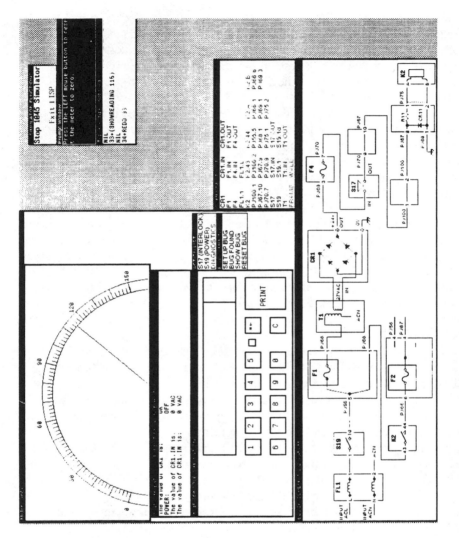

Figure 7.5 FIP-Based 1045 Simulation

It is important to note that tutorial ICAI and job aiding are not mutually exclusive. For example, a tutorial module can be built to familiarize a technician with the effective integration of job aids and task performance. On the other hand, one could construct open-ended (heuristic) job aids that could be used to support diagnostic hypotheses generated by the technician. In fact, the term "traiding" has been used in the literature to emphasize the joint application of training and job aiding. While investigation of these options has recently been initiated, the purpose of the current project is to examine the tutorial potential of AI.

Revised Simulation Concept

In response to the preceding events, the ICAI knowledge base conceptualization was modified by subdividing development activities. A major split was made between the primary Xerographic process model and the model required for the 1045 simulation. The latter was based entirely on imparting electronic circuit troubleshooting knowledge, so was selected as a related but separate task domain. Within the primary ARIA Xerographic simulation, five interrelated software subsystems were defined:

ARIA Core	A qualitative model of the 10 Series Xerographic process
ARIA Circuit	An electronic circuit simulator to serve as a subset of the Xerographic process and as a generic circuit simulator for electronic troubleshooting modules
ARIA Graph	A structure for constructing computer-based graphic elements within the Xerographic engine, to include three-dimensional representations and interface to peripheral graphic delivery vehicles
ARIA Edit	A development interface to modify the other ARIA subsystems
DUET	A spinoff from ARIA Core focusing on a database of copier components, each bounded by input and output conditions

Each of the subsystems is nearly complete and the ARIA cluster will permit the design of knowledge bases for the 10 Series class of copiers. This will provide the flexibility to quickly prototype a copier specific simulation for evaluation in a changing training environment on an opportunistic basis. DUET will provide the capability to be copier design independent and extend the scope of the task domain. The initial software for these subsystems has already been effectively employed to develop the first generic instructional module to be discussed in the Tutorial Model section.

The original 1045 simulation is now focused on electronic circuit diagnosis and redirected to supporting a building block approach to instruction in electronic diagnostic skills. The multimeter portion of the simulation is being developed as a stand-alone module. Basic electronic training is being addressed by simulation support for the Task Aids program and as a test bed for the generality of the ARIA circuit simulation. Finally, these instructional modules will be integrated into an instructional module providing experience in FIP use.

Given the progress on the expert knowledge base, project emphasis has shifted to design of the student model. This development process has reached the requirements determination stage and little can be said at this time regarding the final structure. However, it is clear that the model will contain several key elements. From the standpoint of the student model database the following are planned:

Knowledge status
>   Domain specific (e.g., component definition)
>   Domain independent (e.g., nontechnical vocabulary)

Skills status ·
>   Domain specific (e.g., use of measurement tools)
>   Domain independent (e.g., reading level)

Cognitive capabilities (e.g., memory limitations)

Meta-cognitive skills (e.g., understanding of performance feedback)

Given a student model database there are two primary processes needed: a capability to record student interactions and deduce the student's current knowledge state; and a set of rules for modifying the feedback and instructional material as a function of student knowledge gaps. It is likely that coaching and prompting techniques from earlier ICAI models will be used as a baseline to develop these capabilities. It could be argued that the student model should be developed earlier in the ICAI modeling process, but our experience suggests that the student model is so potentially open-ended that it is more feasible to first develop a stable expert domain to provide a boundary for the student model.

Tutorial Strategy and Instructional Design

The cornerstone of the tutorial model is to enable the student to rationalize the knowledge representation and to assist in this rationalization process by inducing meaningfulness via semantic presentation of the knowledge. In a simplified sense, this semantic rationalization can be likened to a communication problem. The expert contains a body of information (images, associations, rule representations) describing the knowledge base of Xerography. This information base must be encoded, transmitted to, and decoded by the receiver, or student. The basis for communication is the transmission of symbols. In the human case these are sounds, visual images, and other sensory inputs. In terms of our ICAI model, the Interlisp software is a mechanism for symbolically encoding the knowledge. Transmission is by means of the instructional presentation and format. Accurate decoding by the student is addressed by introducing presentation principles derived from instructional and cognitive science. In this analogy, semantic rationalizations are the means for enhancing the accuracy of the transmitted material and reducing noise. Of course, continuing the analogy, the actual process will involve several intermediate encoding and decoding stages, to include the developers as intermediaries between experts and the knowledge base, digital coding of the images and characters, and so on.

Returning to the semantic rationalization notion, there are four general derivations or sources for the semantics of our ICAI system (Brown, 1982): tasks/goals; system/machine; human capabilities; and general context. The task-based semantics are those which enable the learner to comprehend, organize, and sequence goals and activities necessary to accomplish the task(s). Other aspects include relating the task(s) to the structure of the machine and explicating boundaries or limitations of the machine functions.

There are three primary system/machine semantic sources. The first is qualitative descriptions of component behaviors and their causal relationships. The second is the functional description of the system in terms of each of its parts, where functions may not be isomorphic to actual components (either a carburetor or fuel injection system might underly the function of fuel/air mixing). Third, there are often constraints in which rules can describe the actions of a component (any two of voltage, current, and resistance predetermine the third).

Semantics can also be based on human processing capabilities. These would include cognitive load capacity, mnemonic organization, and the ability to associate previous and new events. Finally, at a more global level, semantics may be used to reflect peripheral concerns and contexts related to the task, such as safety and work efficiency goals. For example, in procedure learning, error-checking procedures are frequently part of the knowledge to be acquired.

ARIA-7 ICAI Simulation and Tutorial

The revised ARIA subsystems were used to build a Xerography simulation (ARIA-7) which demonstrates the semantic rationalization approach and several other key concepts referred to previously. The overall simulation strategy was to teach three concepts subsumed within Xerography and necessary as precursors to induce a knowledge base for troubleshooting: process steps (causal network), functional decomposition, and enabling technologies. Figure 7.6 depicts the basic process flow in the Xerographic process.

A photoreceptor (PR) receives a charge (+), and the original image is processed and exposed to the PR. Toner is attracted to the charged PR via the development process. The toner is then attracted to the paper in the transfer process. The paper is further processed by fusing the toner to the paper, and the toner remaining on the PR is removed so the PR is ready for reiteration of

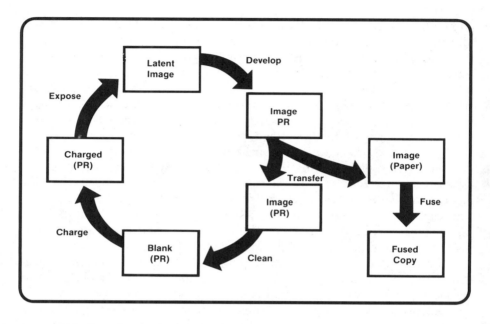

Figure 7.6 Causal Net of Xerographic Process

the sequence. The semantic rationalization of this process consists of linking the process terms in a causal net and portraying this both verbally and via a visual simulation. Figure 7.7 shows the visual simulation of the process with the original entering from the upper right.

In addition to the overall causal net, the instructional approach is aimed at providing semantic links to the underlying machine through use of functional decompositions of the process, which can in turn be semantically linked to the physical components and eventually instruction on the operating functions of components. Figure 7.8 demonstrates a partial functional decomposition description of the Xerography process. The understanding of subprocesses at the functional level can then be supported by additional graphic simulations such as the graphic (in reality animated) depicting the process of charging the PR (Fig. 7.9). The functional level of the knowledge required is determined by that found to be known by the expert technician rather than that of the physicist or engineer. In fact, it is the expert that defines the border between basic theory and functional knowledge, that is, a top-down determination of knowledge needs.

Once the fundamental knowledge of machine functioning is in the student's knowledge base, we can begin to relate this to problem-solving strategies. In the Xerography process the project focus is on developing means for assisting

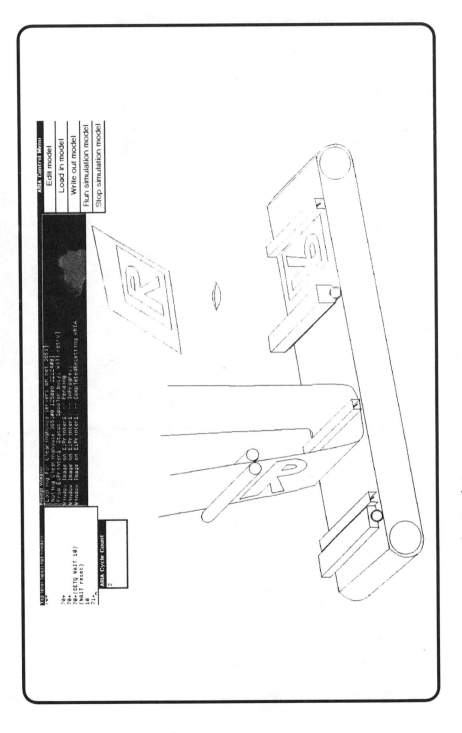

Figure 7.7 ARIA-7 Xerography Simulation

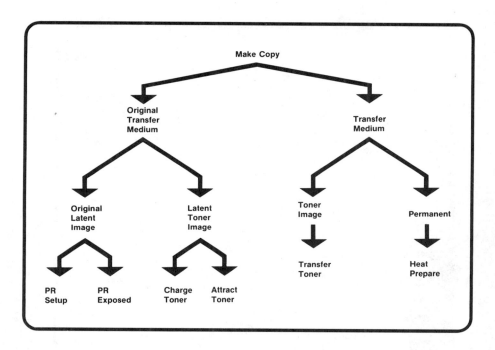

Figure 7.8 Functional Decomposition of the Xerographic Process

Figure 7.9 Putting a Charge on the Photoreceptor ... the Hard Way ...

the student in developing causal reasoning skills. For the most part these consist of the concept of chaining functions, identifying equivalent states (status of a function), and identifying equivalent processes. Each of these skills starts with a focus on general causal knowledge, in terms of component functions, and then provides an environment for the student to relate this knowledge to specific machine components and measures. For example, the specific version of a sequence of causal steps and a parallel generic form might appear as follows:

SPECIFIC FORM	GENERIC FORM
Charge PR = 400V	Charge PR = X
Flash 1/100 sec at 1K lumens	Exposure
Charge PR = 250V	Charge PR = Y, X > Y

Note that the generic form takes advantage of qualitative descriptors and values, that is, "exposure" and "greater than." This type of instructional capability is not yet fully integrated into an instructional module, but will be the next phase of project development. The ARIA-7 module not only has proved useful as a test bed for the preceding notions, but also has led to the development of an instructional design environment (IDE) to assist in the rapid prototyping of other modules.

Instructional Design Environment (IDE)

A major supporting software implementation that is still in process is the IDE. Briefly, the IDE began with the use of NoteCards™, a software tool that is available in the programming environment for creating and manipulating a database. This tool is similar to having an actual set of file cards, interlinked. Initially the software was extended to include the capability to create "cards" with pictures, animations, text, instructional scripts, sequencing of material, and so on. More recently, the production extension capabilities have been enhanced to include design strategies using cognitive and instructional concepts to provide for the orderly and integrated embedding of ICAI simulations into complete instructional modules. Most important, the process emphasizes providing a rationale for instructional decisions and relating these to the learning objectives. Figure 7.10 gives an overview of the design portion of the IDE.

Each of the items on a card can be called up in a hierarchy of information (note the relationships of the card headings). Figure 7.11 shows one chain leading from Learning Principles to an end note (top-down order) stating the nature of the principle. The IDE takes advantage of the Interlisp environment such that cards act as windows on the display screen. They may be opened, closed, rearranged, and reshaped. As the hierarchical architecture can sometimes create difficulty in determining links and locations, a "browsing" function is available to give a tree structure overview of the file organization (Fig. 7.12).

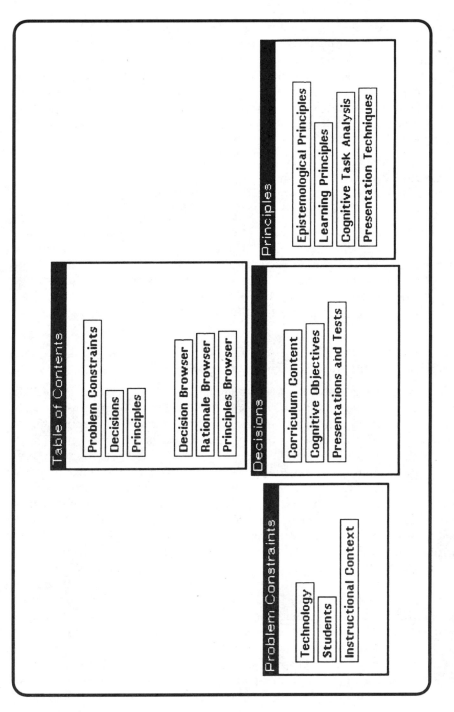

Figure 7.10 Overview of IDE Contents

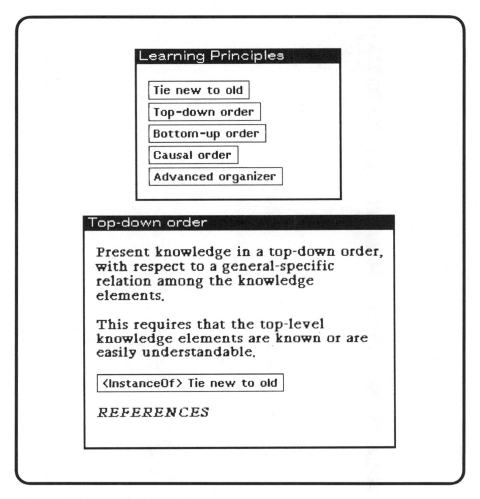

Figure 7.11 Example of IDE Chain

The browser can be scanned by moving the window vertically or horizontally, and nodes in the tree can be expanded at any point to examine the contents. As the IDE is being developed dynamically, operational definitions of elements and final structural relations are not yet complete, but the IDE is already a major tool in support of the project.

Since the IDE is a blank structure (albeit with recommended input categories), the design principles and rationale adopted by the developer become the tutorial strategy. That is, IDE is both a potential general instructional tool and, if used, a documented tutorial strategy.

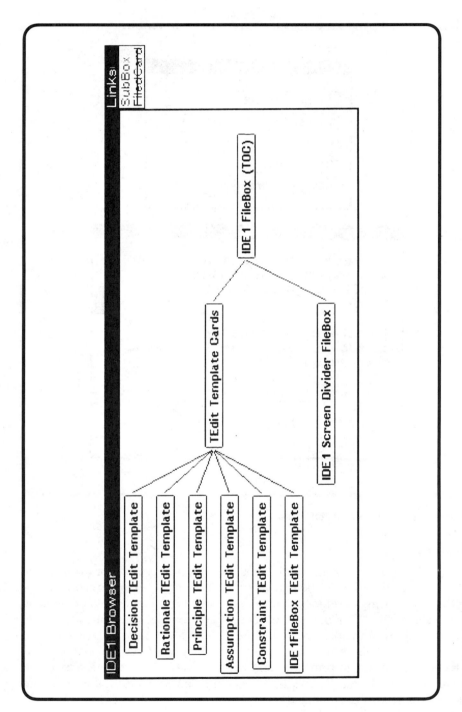

Figure 7.12 IDE Browser Example

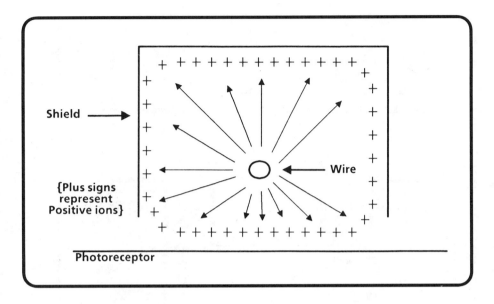

Figure 7.13 Cross-Section of a Corotron

In addition to the preceding Xerographic tutorial developments, DUET, the component level model, will provide means for instructing the student in enabling technologies. Figure 7.13 shows a simulation graphic for one critical component of the Xerographic process, the Corotron. The student will be able to examine the operation and function of components in an isolated case, and thus use both a top-down and a bottom-up approach to developing a rationalization of the system.

Electronics Tutorial

As was noted earlier, the 1045 FIP-based simulation is now a set of electronic related instructional simulations still under development. The instructional context and implementation are described more fully in the evaluation section of this chapter. The graphic design and basic circuit structure for a multimeter module, and a Task Aids module are in preparation. Figure 7.14 shows a simple circuit such as is used in Task Aids.

Symbology has been slightly modified from standard symbols to be more available to novices. Elements can be edited using the window features to the right, and this graphic circuit construction tool is being expanded. A key feature will be the use of the ARIA Circuit model to drive the simulations so that a variety of scenarios can be readily constructed. The ARIA Circuit is a more

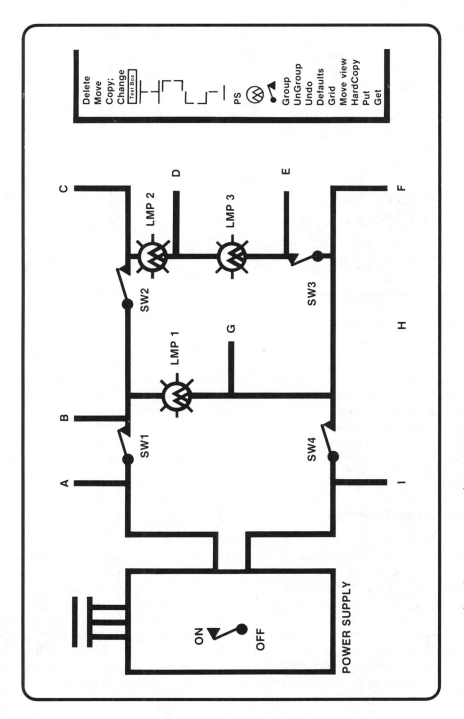

Figure 7.14 Task Aids Circuit Example

quantitatively structured model and appears appropriate to the electronic circuit feedback required for providing a basic electronic troubleshooting instructional package. However, the ARIA Circuit will permit the instructor or course designer to modify circuit behavior through use of a qualitative circuit editor. An early version of the editor function, called "Q-Type," is shown in Figure 7.15.

Figure 7.15 shows the entry level of the editor and a sequence of call-ups in the edit hierarchy (the order indicated by the numbers 1–7). The object (component) selected for editing is the PowerSwitch (4), and windows (5–7) that allow the user to modify values or states of the component are depicted. The eventual circuit editor may be organized somewhat differently based on user feedback. Finally, it is anticipated that experience gained from the development of DUET, the Xerographic component modeling tool, will provide a basis for a similar approach to circuit construction.

ICAI Project Evaluation

There is little empirical evidence to support the ICAI potential at this stage of the project. The ARIA-7 has been introduced in a field training site, but primarily as a pilot to obtain instructor and student feedback. The simulation was presented via an AI machine as an interactive, exploratory portion of the standard instructional module, normally a lecture and slide presentation. Parts of the standard presentation were modified to ensure consistent terminology with the simulation and to support the qualitative, causal approach. Informal responses have been highly positive with regard to the perceived information value and the simulation has been found to be interesting and motivating by both students and instructors. Project staff have participated in the role of instructor, which has proven very useful in recognizing modification needs.

The change in training policy noted previously, with an emphasis on specific procedure following and decentralization of training, required substantial revision of the original evaluation. Initially, a single, comprehensive Xerography module was to replace the central ("school") module in the 1075 course. This is no longer possible. There are four general evaluation situations available, summarized in Table 7.1. The first two represent decentralized, regional training centers focusing on novice or mid-level ("apprentice") technicians. The Xerography fundamentals, multimeter instruction, and Task Aids simulations will be evaluated at these sites. Pilot evaluations will be conducted as an open evaluation, that is, an informal test bed with observational and informal evaluative feedback—as the ARIA-7 pilot has been done. Modules that have been stabilized will be placed in similar sites under more controlled circumstances in which the modules replace existing segments, and student achievement will be compared with the standard training. All technician training is currently based on criterion-referenced testing, so in addition to student time to reach criterion,

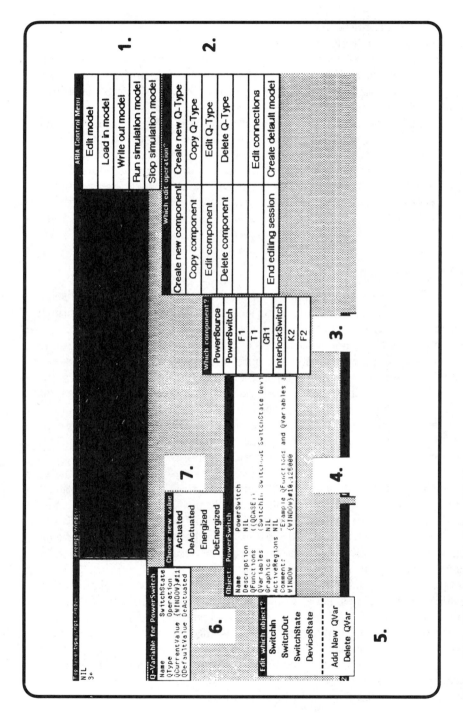

Figure 7.15 Q-Type Circuit Editor Display

Site	Trainee	Modules	Condition
Decentralized	■ Novice ■ Apprentice	Integrated	Field Open
Decentralized	■ Novice ■ Apprentice	Integrated	Field Control
Operational	■ Apprentice ■ Expert	Independent	Field Open
Central	■ Expert	Independent	Experimental Control

Table 7.1 Evaluation Options

special tests are being constructed to measure deeper knowledge. Instructor ratings of student performance will also be obtained.

The third situation represents evaluation at operational, as opposed to training, sites. At such sites one has access to a typical mix of experienced technicians. All simulations will be provided as stand-alone, self-paced instructional modules and be under the control and direction of the site manager. For evaluation purposes all simulation will be presented on AI machines. The integration of the simulation with the remaining instruction will be accomplished by redoing the instruction using IDE. That is, existing curricula will be revised using IDE with maximal use of simulation to provide guided practice. In the case of classroom environments the student will branch to the ICAI portion of the presentation as the module is scheduled and then return to the normal environment to continue instruction. For on-the-job training environments, the simulation will be supported by introductory manuals that include specification of entry-level knowledge required by the student. Scheduling and use will be student controlled.

The basic evaluation scheme here is to record usage by technicians and maintain longitudinal data on job performance. Measures will be both quantitative (mean time to repair, return of functioning parts) and qualitative (manager and peer groups ratings of technical knowledge and skill). While it is likely that other factors such as individual motivation, organizational incentives, and so on, will wash out knowledge gains, the effort is low cost with a potentially high evaluation payoff.

Finally, the possibility of introducing a series of controlled experiments at the formal, central training site is being discussed with the service training management. Should this prove feasible (nondisruptive), more sophisticated measures of problem-solving knowledge can be obtained and used to modify future simulations.

Summary

In this chapter we have presented several basic concepts for ICAI and diagnostic training. The major concepts are those of (1) communicating functional machine component operations and (2) the causal relationships between events. Communication to the learner is based on using interactive simulation to encourage a semantic rationalization process. This general model is being implemented in an ongoing project through the use of hardware and software specifically developed to support AI implementations. The activities and results to date suggest the theory and technology support exists to provide tangible, if somewhat constrained, ICAI tutorials. However, implementation continues to require highly qualified and experienced AI scientists, and the continuing development of ICAI support tools appears to be the most significant means for alleviating this cost. Even with the existence of sophisticated tools, however, project experience suggests that while the dollar cost has become reasonable, the iterative process required to produce an ICAI system will continue to require time.

While ICAI is certainly not the only, or necessarily the best, approach to training, the application of tutorial ICAI can extend the range of options available for enhancing job performance. Finally, tools and concepts developed in pursuit of ICAI are likely to prove beneficial elsewhere. As an example, the IDE is now being extended to serve as an instructional prototyping environment for generating diagnostic instruction that may actually be delivered via interactive videodisc or other computer-based simulation systems.

References

Anderson, J. R., & Reiser, B. J. (1984). The LISP Tutor. *Byte, 10,* 159–175.

Bregar, W. S., & Farley, A. M. (1980). Artificial intelligence approaches to computer-based instruction. *Journal of Computer-Based Instruction, 6,* 106–114.

Brown, J. S. (1982, Dec.). The semantics of procedures. Xerox Electro-Optical Systems Proposal 4393-105.

Brown, J. S., & Burton, R. R. (1978). Diagnostic models for procedural bugs in basic mathematical skills. *Cognitive Science, 2,* 155–192.

Brown, J. S., Burton, R. R., & de Kleer, J. (1981). Pedagogical, natural language and knowledge engineering techniques in SOPHIE I, II and III. In D. Sleeman & J. S. Brown (Eds.), *Intelligent tutoring systems.* New York: Academic Press.

Brown, J. S., Collins, A., & Harris, G. (1978). Artificial intelligence and learning strategies. In H. F. O'Neil, Jr. (Ed.), *Learning strategies.* New York: Academic Press.

Burton, R. R. (1981). Diagnosing bugs in simple procedural skills. In D. Sleeman & J. S. Brown (Eds.), *Intelligent tutoring systems.* New York: Academic Press.

Burton, R. R., & Brown, J. S. (1979). Toward a natural language capability for computer assisted instruction. In H. F. O'Neil, Jr. (Ed.), *Procedures for instructional systems development.* New York: Academic Press.

Burton, R. R., & Brown, J. S. (1981). An investigation of computer coaching for informal learning activities. In D. Sleeman & J. S. Brown (Eds.), *Intelligent tutoring systems.* New York: Academic Press.

Carbonell, J. R. (1970). AI in CAI: An artificial intelligence approach to computer-aided instruction. *IEEE Transactions on Man-Machine Systems, 4,* 190–202.

Clancey, W. J. (1979). *Transfer of rule-based expertise through a tutorial dialogue.* Report No. STAN-CS-769, Computer Science Dept., Stanford University.

Goldstein, I. P. (1981). The genetic graph: A representation for the evolution of procedural knowledge. In D. Sleeman & J. S. Brown (Eds.), *Intelligent tutoring systems.* New York: Academic Press.

Hofstadter, D. R. (1985). *Metamagical themas.* New York: Basic Books.

Knerr, B. W. (1979, April). *Adaptive computerized training system (ACTS): Relationships between utility similarity and strategy similarity.* U.S. Army Research Institute, Research Memorandum 79-5.

Knerr, B. W., & Nawrocki, L. H. (1978, Sept.). *Development and evaluation of an adaptive computerized training system (ACTS).* U.S. Army Research Institute, Utilization Report 78-1.

Kolodner, J. A. (1984). Towards an understanding of the role of experience in the evolution from novice to expert. In M. J. Coombs (Ed.), *Developments in expert systems.* New York: Academic Press.

Miller, M. L. (1981). A structured planning and debugging environment for elementary programming. In D. Sleeman & J. S. Brown (Eds.), *Intelligent tutoring systems.* New York: Academic Press.

Nawrocki, L. H. (1980). Computer-based maintenance training in the military. In J. Rasmussen & W. B. Rouse (Eds.), *Human detection and diagnosis of system failures.* New York: Plenum Press.

Russell, L. B. (1982). *The baby boom generation and the economy.* Washington, DC: The Brookings Institute Press.

Sleeman, D. H. (1981). Assessing aspects of competence in basic algebra. In D. Sleeman and J. S. Brown (Eds.), *Intelligent tutoring systems.* New York: Academic Press.

Stevens, A. L., Collins, A., & Goldin, S. (1976). *Diagnosing student's misconceptions in causal models.* Bolt, Beranek and Newman Inc., Report No. 3786, Cambridge, Massachusetts.

Suppes, P. (1981). *University-level computer assisted instruction at Stanford: 1968–1980.* Institute for Mathematical Studies in the Social Sciences, Stanford, California.

Winston, P. H. (1984). *The AI business.* Cambridge, MA: MIT Press.

8 / Intelligent Job Aids: How AI Will Change Training in the Next Five Years.

PAUL HARMON

Overview

This chapter describes one probable use of small and mid-sized expert systems in business training environments. Most instructional developers working in the area of training have concluded that it is usually more cost-effective to use techniques that prompt an employee in the performance of a task rather than asking the employee to memorize a procedure or learn the theory, or deep structure, underlying a procedure. Techniques for prompting employee performance are collectively called "job aids" (Duncan, 1985; Foley, 1969). This chapter argues that small expert systems can function as job aids and that the availability of expert system development tools will lead to a rapid proliferation of "intelligent job aids" and the simultaneous decline in "memory or theory-oriented" instruction in training environments.

Education and Training

The development of the modern discipline of instructional technology began in the late 1950s, primarily as a result of the work of B. F. Skinner and other behavioral psychologists who popularized teaching machines and developed programmed instruction (Skinner, 1960). For most practical purposes, by the late 1960s, instructional technology had effectively split into two branches: educational technology, which focuses on the problem of designing educational materials, and training technology (or performance engineering), which focuses on solving human performance problems that arise in business, industry, and government (Gilbert, 1978; Harmon, 1982).

This chapter draws on some material that originally appeared in *Expert Systems: Artificial Intelligence in Business* by Paul Harmon and David King (New York, Wiley, 1985).

If one is primarily concerned with training problems, as I have been, one focuses on what the learner is expected to do on the job after completing a training program. Thus the performance on the job becomes the criterion by which one can judge the effectiveness of the instruction. This focus emphasizes immediate, practical outcomes rather than the broader goals usually pursued by educators.

Most of the time, an instructional technologist working in a job setting is concerned with developing instruction that results in a very specific performance. The successful designer is always concerned with minimizing the cost of training and is therefore inclined to use the most cost-effective method available that will result in the desired performance.

A Diversion into Cognitive Psychology

While behavioral psychology provided the initial research base for the development of instructional technology, the emergence of cognitive approaches to the analysis of behavior has led to a new emphasis on the nature, development, and representation of knowledge Predictably, the development of expert systems will do for cognitive psychology what programmed instruction did for behavioral psychology in the 1960s: it will require psychologists to operationalize their theories and subject them to very pragmatic tests.

The development of expert systems has already led businesspeople to consider the possibility that valuable domains of human knowledge and problem-solving skills can be encoded in software programs. In fact, expert systems are only in an early stage of development, and only a few types of human knowledge can be represented in computer formalisms. But the mere possibility has suggested new, practical ways to describe the various types of knowledge that human experts use in problem solving. Figure 8.1 illustrates one classification schema that is currently popular among AI researchers and expert system designers.

The level horizontal arrow in Fig. 8.1 indicates how much knowledge the individual has acquired. Knowledge is not accumulated as one might add pennies to a pile, of course. New pieces must be related to previous pieces to form a pattern. Thus, as an individual moves from left to right along a horizontal continuum, acquiring knowledge, he or she not only accumulates data but simultaneously "compiles" that data into a complex pattern.

"Compiled knowledge" is a metaphor borrowed from computer science. A software program is "compiled" when an original program, typically one written in a higher-level language like Pascal or Fortran, is revised, usually by recoding it into a lower-level language, to make it run more efficiently. Human knowledge is "compiled" when it is organized, indexed, and stored in a way that can be easily accessed and used for problem solving. Put another way, compiling is the

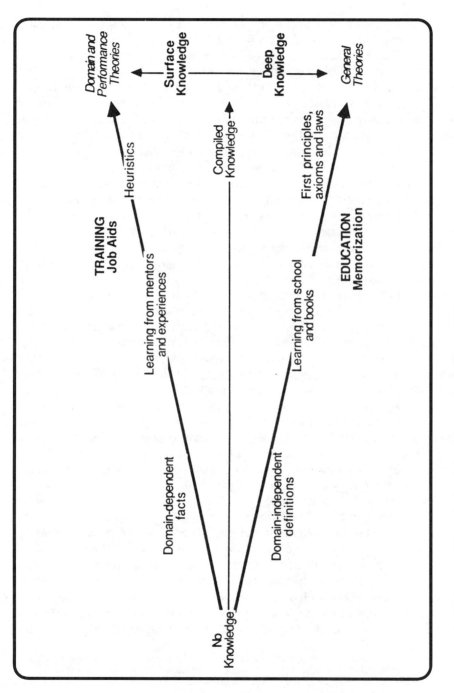

Figure 8.1 Varieties of Knowledge (after Harmon and King, 1985).

process of *chunking*. Meaningful sets of facts and relationships are associated and then stored and retrieved as functional units.

Humans acquire knowledge in two complementary ways. First, topics may be studied formally, as in a school, or when we attend lectures and read textbooks. As a result of such study, knowledge is chunked as definitions, axioms, and laws. Successful students emerge from courses in accounting or physics with a firm grasp on the terms, equations, and laws that constitute the formal theories and accepted principles of their disciplines. Typically, however, even though they can describe the knowledge they have learned, they do not know exactly how to apply that knowledge in any practical way.

Principles, laws, and axioms are useful in describing and explaining events. They can also be used to justify why a solution succeeds or fails. Unfortunately, such formal knowledge is often not very helpful when we are trying to find a solution in the first place. General laws usually fail to indicate exactly how one should proceed when faced with a specific problem. Except in simple cases, formal axioms and general theories tend to generate problem spaces that are too large to search.* Formal knowledge is more descriptive than procedural. This type of knowledge is primarily communicated by means of education.

Knowledge can also be acquired by means of experience or by learning from a mentor. Experiential knowledge is different from formal knowledge. Domain-specific facts are learned first. Experience, or a mentor, usually teaches the student to rely on rules of thumb to analyze tasks or solve problems. Apprentices develop competence quickly by learning domain-specific theories. Thus an individual who learns accounting from a mentor behaves *as if* he or she knows the general theories of accounting, even though he or she may not.

Knowledge compiled from experience results in specific procedures and *heuristics,* or rules of thumb, that allow the user to prune a particular type of problem space to a manageable size. With domain experience, people become competent because they learn to look for the key patterns or important relationships that indicate how to approach the problem.

Compiled heuristic knowledge gives you an edge when you face and solve numerous daily problems. The form of the knowledge is simple while its power is drawn from all the experience that it summarizes. Each of us acquires experiential knowledge as a result of our ordinary activities, but this type of knowledge can also be communicated by means of well-designed training programs.

Different types of knowledge manifest themselves in different types of human problem-solving behavior. One type of problem-solving behavior can be observed when you struggle with a new and relatively unfamiliar problem. With little to go on, you find yourself guessing and experimenting. You use a

---

* A *problem* or *search space* is a collection of all of the possible situations (or *states*) defined by the interaction of problem elements and operators that can manipulate those elements. A problem can be formally defined as an effort to find a path that leads from an initial situation to a goal state. A search space is usually formalized as a network or a decision tree.

different approach when you encounter problems that you know a lot about. In this case you systematically gather relevant information, build prototype solutions, ignore lots of irrelevant details, and revise your hypotheses in the light of constraints.

Experts perform well because they have a large amount of compiled, domain-specific knowledge. It is estimated that a world-class expert, like a grand master in chess or a Nobel laureate in chemistry, has learned from 50,000 to 100,000 chunks of heuristic information about his or her specialty (Newell & Simon, 1972; Simon, 1969).

Each chunk, with all its myriad associations, can be retrieved, examined, and utilized at will. Further, psychologists believe that it takes at least ten years to acquire 50,000 chunks. This estimate is based on the constraints that our mental "hardware" places on our ability to memorize new information. A decade also seems to fit available biographical data—chess grand masters, honored scientists, and respected professionals all seem to require at least ten years of study and practice before they become acknowledged experts (Simon, 1969).

The amount of knowledge an expert requires is such that it is nearly impossible to gain it all from experience. Experience can be too confusing and difficult to organize if one lacks general categories to help classify and index one's experience.

Skilled technicians and master craftspersons sometimes start as apprentices, observe mentors, and become experts within their domain without benefit of formal training. Similarly, some academic specialists, like logicians or theoretical mathematicians, compile general theories without benefit of experience. Most experts, however, begin by studying their specialty in school. They acquire a knowledge of the first principles and general theories that are regarded as basic to their profession. Then they begin to practice their profession. If they are lucky they have a mentor who helps orient them to the specific practices of their profession. In any case, they gain experience, and in the process, they recompile what they know. Thus they move from a descriptive view of the subject matter of their profession to a procedural view of the particular specialty they practice.

By the time individuals have become expert, they have rearranged their knowledge so they can respond to problem situations by using heuristics and specific domain theories. Practicing experts hardly ever explain their recommendations in terms of first principles or general theories. If they encounter unusual or very complex problems, however, they will return to first principles to develop an appropriate strategy.

AI researchers refer to the heuristics and domain theories that experts typically rely on as *surface knowledge,* which is closely related to the knowledge that performance engineers usually work with. Most expert systems include only surface knowledge, and it normally suffices. The first principles and general theories that an expert will fall back on when faced with a really difficult problem are termed *deep knowledge.* The application of deep knowledge, which is derived from *education,* provides a broad view of an area and its interrelationships with other areas, but as previously noted, it tends to result in problem spaces that are too large to search effectively. The use of the heuristics and domain-specific facts that constitute surface knowledge, on the other hand, tends to prune a problem space to a manageable size. All existing expert systems rely on domain-specific surface knowledge for their power.

ICAI and Expert Systems

Recent work in artificial intelligence (AI) offers developers of computer-aided instruction a new set of techniques to use in improving their efforts. One important subset of AI techniques is often clustered together and called *expert systems.* An expert system is a software program designed to solve problems.

In essence, an expert system consists of an inference engine and a knowledge base. The inference engine interfaces with the user and controls the overall operation of the program. The heart of the inference engine is an algorithm designed to manipulate any modules of knowledge contained in the knowledge base. The knowledge base contains facts and statements about known (or probable) relationships between facts. The modules of knowledge can take different forms. In smaller expert systems, the modules of knowledge usually take the form of if-then rules. In a rule-based expert system, the inference engine gathers facts from a user and manipulates those facts with other facts and rules in its knowledge base to determine additional facts, some of which are presented to the user as conclusions or recommendations.

When one thinks of intelligent computer-aided instruction (ICAI), one generally imagines a software architecture similar to the one pictured in Fig. 8.2. One could reasonably describe this as a cluster of four expert systems. The domain system contains information about some domain of knowledge and is prepared to reason about that domain. The tutor system contains information about effective tutorial practices and monitors the status of the student model and recommends what course the dialogue should take next. The student model contains information about what the student knows. The integration system controls the entire process; it asks the student a question and then passes the student's response on to the other systems. The student's response is evaluated by comparing the student model with domain knowledge to determine flaws in the student's knowledge. Based on this evaluation, the domain system generates a new problem which is then presented to the student in the manner suggested by the tutoring system.

When we speak of an expert system or an intelligent job aid, we are speaking of the domain knowledge system. In effect, small expert systems that can be used as job aids contain knowledge of a task domain but lack any sophistica-

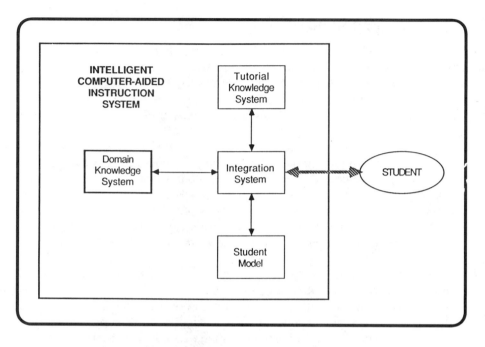

Figure 8.2 Architecture of an ICAI System

tion about how to interact with the student to develop the student's knowledge or understanding of the domain. Instead, an expert system simply asks questions and then makes recommendations.

Although there has been considerable progress, as several of the chapters in this book demonstrate, there are still considerable problems to be overcome in the design of powerful and robust student models, tutorial knowledge systems, and integration systems. The one component of the overall ICAI package that we currently know how to build is the domain knowledge system. We do not know too much about how to build domain knowledge systems that capture deep knowledge—an important goal of many ICAI developers—but we do know how to develop small knowledge systems that contain the procedural knowledge and surface heuristics that most trainer programs focus on.

Instructional technologists can begin developing these systems immediately. When problems associated with the other subsystems are solved, they will then be in a position to integrate domain knowledge with the other components to form ICAI systems. In other words, the development of small expert systems that initially serve as job aids is a practical way to prepare for the more sophisticated ICAI packages that will be developed in the years ahead.

Expert System-Building Tools

An expert system-building tool is an inference engine in search of a knowledge base. A tool allows a developer to develop a knowledge base without worrying about the more complex programming involved in the development of an inference engine and thus expert system-building tools are the key to the rapid development of a large number of expert systems applications. In 1984, with the introduction of expert system (ES) building tools that could operate on personal computers, the commercial market for expert system applications split into two segments. One segment is focused on the need for large expert systems. The other segment is concentrating on the practical applications of small expert systems.

Large expert systems are systems that truly attempt to emulate world-class human experts. The most successful of these systems use AI techniques that allow their designers to construct systems that would be hard to construct using conventional programming techniques.

Small expert systems, on the other hand, do not try to capture true expertise. Instead, they aid a user in the analysis of a small but difficult problem and they usually provide the user with specific advice on how to deal with the problem. They rely on AI techniques, but not to the extent that the larger systems do. Their main advantage over conventional approaches lies in the fact that users with only a minimal knowledge of computers can quickly learn to develop very useful small systems.

Perhaps we should not call these small systems "expert systems" at all. Many AI researchers prefer to call them *knowledge systems.* One British writer calls them *technician systems.* I personally prefer to call them *intelligent job aids.*

Expert Systems as Job Aids

One of the practical insights that instructional technologists bring to the analysis of performance problems is that instructional efforts can be divided into those that are primarily focused on *memorization* and those that are essentially focused on *prompting performance* (Gilbert, 1978).

If an instructor expects memorization, the instructor wants students to respond to some situation without looking up information in a book, using a calculator, or relying on any other sort of external assistance. In other words, the instructor wants the students to be able to recall information from memory. Most education and a considerable amount of training still focuses on having the student memorize information. If you are asked for your home phone number, you probably have it memorized and would simply state the number without thinking about it at all. On the other hand, if you are asked for the phone number of your local civic center, you probably would not know it. You would know, however, that you could look it up in a telephone directory. A telephone directory is a job aid. We have all memorized a little bit of information (i.e., that phone numbers are available in the phone directory and that they are indexed alphabetically). Beyond that, however, we simply depend on a directory to provide us with the information when we need it.

Job aids are devices that prompt performance. An instructional designer develops job aids in order to avoid the time and expense required to develop memorized responses.

Computer-aided instruction (CAI) has taken two forms. Most of it is designed to help the student memorize facts. The best CAI uses simulation to allow the student to explore problems and gain insights into the principles underlying the sets of relationships modeled in the simulation. While in theory CAI can be used in training to teach procedural and heuristic knowledge by means of simulations (e.g., GUIDON) (Clancey, 1984), most CAI to date has aimed at teaching laws and principles that are more appropriate to an educational environment.

Unlike most CAI, which focuses on placing information in the student's memory, job aids only attempt to provide specific information to prompt performance that is in progress. The use of small expert systems as job aids will greatly enhance the instructional designer's ability to provide such assistance to performers and will correspondingly decrease the need for memorized information (see Fig. 8.3).

Job aids have become a key element in the instructional technologist's approach to solving training problems in a cost-effective manner. They reduce training time while simultaneously increasing the quality of the performer's work (see Table 8.1). They minimize memorization and maximize accurate responses. And in many cases they allow a less-trained employee to perform tasks that previously required a more highly trained, and hence more expensive individual (Duncan, 1985; Harmon, 1981).

Job aids have generally consisted of checklists, step-by-step procedures, cookbooks, worksheets, and other paper devices (see Table 8.2). To some extent, computers have already begun to act as job aids. The bank teller who uses a small terminal to determine a customer's balance is using a job aid. And, of course, help screens and menus are examples of job aids that are available within conventional computer programs. Until recently, however, job aids were limited to relatively simple procedural tasks. Complex tasks require that a performer consider a large number of different facts and apply many different heuristics to determine a correct response. A bank officer faces such a task when he or she is considering a loan application. Job aids to help someone perform complex tasks usually become so large that they are difficult to use. Most procedures manuals are attempts at job aids that fail because they are simply too complex to use. The conventional wisdom among training technologists is that a company is better off hiring someone who already knows how to perform such tasks or providing a class to teach individuals how to perform such tasks.

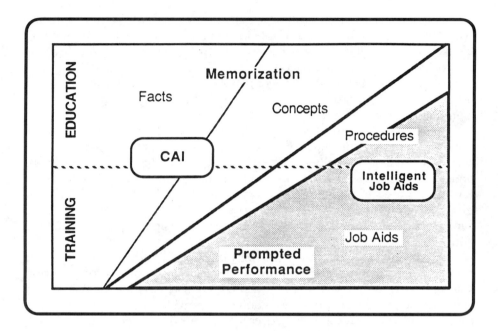

Figure 8.3 The relative importance of procedural and especially prompted performance in solving training problems and the relationships of CAI and intelligent job aids to those techniques.

For this reason, job aids to assist bank loan officers in the evaluation of loan applicants are generally dismissed as impractical.

Intelligent job aids will rapidly change the way performance engineers analyze such problems. The existence of small expert system-building tools will allow skilled performers to record their knowledge in a manner that will provide practical assistance to new employees.

A Training Problem

Given that brief overview of the current state of training technology, let us consider a typical training problem. Campbell's Soup Company puts the final touch on a can of soup by running the can through a hydrostatic sterilizer, commonly called a "cooker." Over the years Campbell has built several of these machines, each slightly different, to reflect changes in technology and construction techniques. The typical cooker is some seven stories tall and has a throughput of some 200 cans per minute. The cooker is normally maintained by site personnel, but when something serious goes wrong, the site mainte-

If	Then
■ Response speed is very important (More important than accuracy) ■ Task is frequently performed ■ Small errors won't have large consequences ■ Reading instructions would interfere with performance, or ■ Job prestige requires a memorized response	Choose MEMORIZATION
■ Response speed is not as important as accuracy (Small errors have large consequences) ■ Tasks are infrequently performed ■ Reading instructions won't interfere with performance ■ Tasks involve many steps or a complex decision-making process	Choose JOB AIDS

Table 8.1 Criteria to Use When Considering Whether to Use a Job Aid or a Memorization Strategy

Information aids	Provide user with names, numbers, codes, etc.
Procedure aids	Provide user with a step-by-step procedure to follow
Algorithmic decision aids	Provide user with a step-by-step procedure to use in making a decision
Heuristic decision aids	Provide user with rules of thumb to use in making a decision

Table 8.2 Types of Job Aids (after Harmon, 1981)

nance manager calls on Aldo Cimino, the engineer at corporate headquarters who originally designed most of the cookers. Depending on the nature of the crisis, Mr. Cimino may talk the site personnel through the problem, or he may hop on a plane and go to the site. It is very expensive to shut a cooker down. It's also expensive to fly Mr. Cimino around and, to make matters worse, he's 63, planning to retire, and he doesn't have a successor who understands the existing plants the way he does (Abatemarco, 1985; Harmon, 1981).

It sounds like a problem for a performance engineer, right? A quick front-end analysis (FEA) to be sure that the problem really is an instructional problem, as it appears, then a good task analysis and . . . a workshop for all of the site maintenance personnel, a good procedures manual, and some job aids.

Two years ago I would have said that, but not today. Today, the first thing I would consider, once I completed the FEA, is the possibility of developing a small expert system.

That is exactly what Campbell did. They hired a knowledge engineer from Texas Instruments to work with Mr. Cimino to develop a system that could capture Mr. Cimino's knowledge about diagnosing and repairing cookers. The knowledge engineer from TI met with Mr. Cimino for the first time on November 5, 1984. They spent four days together discussing cases and techniques. On December 10, the knowledge engineer returned to Campbell with a prototype expert system that contained 32 rules. The prototype convinced Campbell managers, Mr. Cimino, and selected field site maintenance personnel that the approach was viable. In the ensuing four months the system grew from 32 rules to 151 rules. At that point the system was fielded, and it is currently being hailed as a success. Campbell is now working on two additional systems.

I did not mention this case to suggest that instructional technologists are about to be put out of work by knowledge engineers. Rather, I suspect that instructional technologists will incorporate knowledge engineering skills into their repertoire and begin to develop small expert systems whenever they are faced with problems calling for complex job aids. If the development of the "Cooker Maintenance Advisor" had required sophisticated programming skills I would not suggest this. I'm not a programmer and I know that most training technologists lack any programming skills.

The Cooker Maintenance Advisor was developed on Texas Instruments' Personal Consultant, a small expert system-building tool that cost $900. A "tool," as it is used here, is like Lotus 1-2-3. It's a shell that runs a program once the user has put in specific information. In the Campbell case, the knowledge engineer encoded Mr. Cimino's knowledge in the form of rules. A typical rule reads as follows:

IF the cooker's symptom is TEMPERATURE-DEVIATION
AND the problem temperature is T30-INTERMEDIATE-COOLING-SPRAY
AND the input and output air signals for TIC-30 are correct

AND the valve on TCV-30 is not open
THEN the problem with the cooker is that TCV-30 is not working properly
and you should check the instrumentation and the air signal

Once this rule and others like it are loaded in a small expert system, the system knows how to create and conduct a dialogue with subsequent users. Thus, when Campbell site maintenance personnel have problems, they now put a floppy disk into a personal computer and call up the Cooker Maintenance Advisor. The program generates questions from the rules and pursues the appropriate line of questioning until it is able to recommend specific actions to the user. In effect, the Cooker Maintenance Advisor is an "intelligent" procedures manual; it asks questions to determine what the user needs to know and then provides the user with the correct procedure.

Another Example

Consider another example, the problem of helping clerks process insurance applications. The knowledge required for such a task would not normally be compared to the knowledge possessed by a highly specialized physician, yet there is quite a bit that the clerks must know and mistakes can be costly. In a typical insurance company, knowledge of application processing is usually possessed by one or more senior application examiners. New clerks receive a week or two of training and a procedures manual. Once they begin to work at the task they slowly acquire additional knowledge and heuristics by directing questions to the senior examiners whenever they encounter unusual cases.

Now, by using a small expert system-building tool, the senior clerk can develop an intelligent job aid to help new clerks evaluate applications. The new clerks will be able to turn to this small expert system whenever they might otherwise leaf through a procedures manual or ask questions of the senior examiner.

The senior examiner might not get the system right on the first try, but that is one of the virtues of small knowledge systems: they are highly modularized and can be quickly revised. Every time the system fails to help a new clerk and the clerk is forced to ask the senior examiner a question, the senior examiner is prompted to add some new knowledge to the system. Like large expert systems, intelligent job aids do not need to be "finished" to be used. They are used, revised, updated, and maintained by the people who use them. In the case of our example, the Application Evaluation Advisor System would become a responsibility of the senior examiner in the department. In a reasonably short time, of course, the system should save that examiner time that would previously have been used in answering questions and allow everyone in the department to be more productive.

Small Expert System-Building Tools

Obviously an effort like the one I just described could not happen if the senior examiner had to learn how to program in a programming language like LISP or use a mainframe computer. It probably could not even be done if it required the assistance of data-processing personnel, since the task is rather small and not nearly as pressing as the many larger tasks waiting for the attention of the data-processing department. The success of the small effort I described depends on user-friendly small expert system-building tools that are at least as easy to use as the better electronic spreadsheet programs. Moreover, the tools must run on personal computers. Programs of this type first became available in the summer of 1984, and they are rapidly increasing in number and quality, while their prices are declining.

Selecting the Right Problem

Although some of the small expert system-building tools currently available are quite powerful and flexible, they are still very limited when compared with the wide range of tasks that humans routinely confront and solve. Considerable care must be exercised in choosing problems that lend themselves to small tool solutions.

There must be a human expert or senior technician who can currently solve the problem. No expert systems have ever been built that did not initially obtain their knowledge from a human expert. If a human cannot solve the problem, then you cannot build an expert system to solve it. If the expert currently relies on a policy or procedures manual, so much the better.

The solution to an appropriate problem should rely on specific, formal knowledge, not on common sense. More formalized areas like engineering and medicine lend themselves to expert system development because doctors and engineers have already developed precise vocabularies in which to discuss problems. Common sense refers to a vast amount of knowledge that we all acquired experientially in the process of growing up. It's not formalized and is very hard to encode in an expert system. If someone mentioned "garden flowers" and later mentioned "dirt" you would probably not be surprised, since "everyone knows" that gardens contain dirt. We can all imagine exceptions, but we assume that such statements are true in situations in which we anticipate that they apply unless we are told that they are not. Trying to capture and formalize the vast amount of similar knowledge that every speaker assumes every listener has is well beyond the current generation of expert system-building tools.

At the moment the appropriate problems for small expert system-building tools are largely found in one general area: diagnosis/prescription problems. These problems are characterized by a limited set of possible recommendations.

One or more of the possible recommendations are chosen as a result of reasoning about evidence for and against them. A physician employs this approach when diagnosing a disease and deciding what drugs to prescribe. An engineer uses the same general strategy when considering a construction problem and deciding which structural materials to employ. A senior examiner uses this approach in reviewing an application and deciding which of several agencies should review it. An automotive technician uses a diagnostic/prescriptive approach when asking questions and conducting checks to determine the specific cause of an auto malfunction.

In addition to choosing a problem that depends on a diagnostic/prescriptive approach, the task should be narrowly defined. Once you solve a small problem, you can always consider expanding your system.

Most of the systems built with existing small tools rely on typed input, though an increasing number take signal data from some type of sensor or start with data from an external database. *If you are developing a system that will conduct a dialogue with the user, you should choose problems that require minimal physical or sensory examination.* At most, the system will have to ask the user to make an examination and report the results. Thus the problem should be one that a human expert could solve over the telephone by asking questions and suggesting additional things to check before suggesting how to solve the problem.

Finally, the solution to the problem should depend primarily on acquiring facts and then reasoning about them by making logical inferences and applying heuristics. The expert should be drawing on past cases and rules of thumb to help in solving the problem. The problem should not require a large amount of mathematical calculation. Most of the small systems can handle mathematics, but they are optimized for judgmental reasoning, not mathematical calculation.

Developing an Intelligent Job Aid

The process that results in an expert system is often called *knowledge engineering,* and now that expert systems are hot everyone wants to know exactly what it is that knowledge engineers do. Most of the books that have been published to date have confined themselves to generalities, and some have suggested that the entire process is an art. Some, engaged in the development of small expert systems by means of commercial tools, have claimed that it's really not all that hard. Others, engaged in implementing large expert systems in large corporations, have discovered that there is a lot of management and planning that needs to go into the process that doesn't seem to fall under knowledge engineering.

Figure 8.4 provides a broad overview of the small expert system development and implementation process, as it has emerged from interviews with lots of people who have fielded applications in commercial environments.

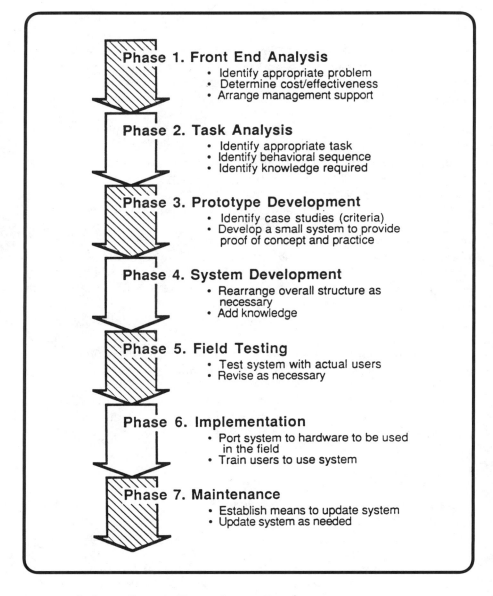

Phase 1. Front End Analysis
- Identify appropriate problem
- Determine cost/effectiveness
- Arrange management support

Phase 2. Task Analysis
- Identify appropriate task
- Identify behavioral sequence
- Identify knowledge required

Phase 3. Prototype Development
- Identify case studies (criteria)
- Develop a small system to provide proof of concept and practice

Phase 4. System Development
- Rearrange overall structure as necessary
- Add knowledge

Phase 5. Field Testing
- Test system with actual users
- Revise as necessary

Phase 6. Implementation
- Port system to hardware to be used in the field
- Train users to use system

Phase 7. Maintenance
- Establish means to update system
- Update system as needed

Figure 8.4 Seven Steps in Expert System Development

Phase 1. Front End Analysis

The first phase involves all of the smart questions one should ask before beginning an expert system project in the first place. During this initial phase one should determine if an expert system is appropriate, would be cost-effective, and so on. One should also identify sponsors, arrange to manage expectations, and do all of the other things one does to make any important development project a success.

Phase 2. Task Analysis

During this phase one studies how the task is currently performed, meets with existing experts, and identifies test items (usually composed of case data) that will allow one to determine if the resulting system is successful. One studies how the new system would best fit in the environment it will be used in. And one studies the exact nature and quantity of knowledge that one hopes to capture in the expert system.

Phase 3. Prototype Development

This phase involves the development of a small version of the expert system to demonstrate feasibility and to experiment with the various problems one will encounter when full-scale development is undertaken.

Phase 4. System Development

During this phase the great majority of the knowledge is added to the system. The core of the expert's knowledge is usually captured rather quickly, and the majority of the time is consumed in adding rules to cover the many exceptional cases. In the process of developing a complete system, the expert often becomes directly involved in writing rules and often learns enough about the process that he or she can later expand or update the system.

Phase 5. Field Testing

This phase involves testing the system in user environments and modifying and polishing the system until it performs as desired.

Phase 6. Implementation

The sixth phase involves actually fielding the system. This may involve porting the system to different hardware, and it certainly involves training user personnel to accept and use the new system.

Phase 7. Maintenance

Maintenance is the final and ongoing phase. It involves arranging to have the system revised and updated as necessary.

Although a knowledge engineer can be involved in any part of this overall effort, *knowledge engineering* usually refers to the activities in phases 2 through 4. In the remainder of this chapter, we will ignore phases 1 and 2 and focus on a systematic procedure for developing a prototype and then an expanded version of a small expert system.

We will discuss a procedure that we have taught to individuals interested in developing small expert systems. These systems typically consist of less than 300 rules and are developed on commercially available tools that are rule-based backward-chaining systems. Hence, the approach and the procedures discussed here must be considered a very limited subset of the approach and procedures that a knowledge engineer working in LISP on a large, hybrid tool like ART, KEE, or Knowledge Craft might employ.

In teaching someone to develop a small expert system, assuming that they have already completed phases 1 and 2, we suggest that they follow a three-step process. First, they should enter "fast and dirty" rules that capture the knowledge to be included in the system. Then they should make changes in the rules to get the overall consultation to ask questions in the proper order. Finally, they should go back and polish the whole knowledge base and add additional display information to get the final user interface to look and act exactly as desired. In other words:

Step 1. Declarative knowledge acquisition. Capture basic information.

Step 2. Procedural arrangement. Rearrange clauses and rule order and add confidence factors, and so on, to get the overall consultation to run smoothly and effectively.

Step 3. Interface development. Reword rules, add text of questions, displays and special text entries, and test and revise with users to assure that the system works with users.

There is nothing sacred about this sequence. It doesn't make sense in some cases and it certainly doesn't apply to nondialogue systems or those developed without a conventional rule-based backward-chaining tool. Even when this approach does apply, the actual system development process is an iterative process and one constantly shifts back and forth. Typically, we work through this process three times, as illustrated in Fig. 8.5.

Phase 3-a. Initial Prototype

This effort may occur during phase 2 or it may be a mini version of phase 3. In either case, it involves developing a very small prototype to provide

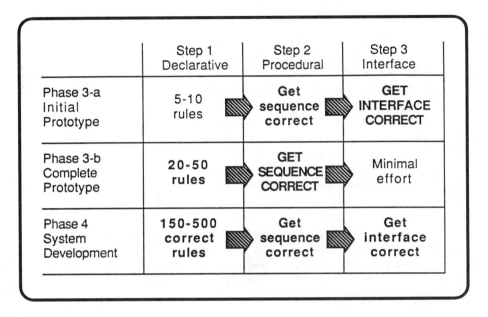

Figure 8.5 Emphasis during Different Steps and Phases

managers, experts, or users with an example of the application you are proposing to develop. In some cases it is a vital step in selling management, an expert, or a sponsor on the project. To develop this mini-prototype, one usually develops a system that consists of five to ten rules. The knowledge embedded in the rules need not be very accurate or detailed. The rules typically serve simply to show how the system might ask questions and divide the task into two or three parts. It is important to get the procedural flow correct. If the system will ask for initial information, that should probably be demonstrated, if only in an abbreviated form. Moreover, the sequence of questions ought to flow naturally. The greatest emphasis during this first trial round is to get the user interface correct. Bend the wording of the rules as necessary to assure that the actual text that appears on the screen makes good sense to those who look at the mini-system. If your tool allows display screens and explanations that can be attached to attributes, develop them. One of the main reasons for limiting this first system to about five rules is to assure that you will have all the time you need to work out a pleasant user interface. Be sure to get a naive outsider to work through the system several times to identify any bugs before you show it to management.

Phase 3-b. Prototype

Once you have sold the concept, you should begin to develop a prototype system in earnest. During this round you should focus on two things in turn. First, capture a significant block of knowledge. If you must choose, go after two deep branches rather than trying to be systematic in covering the breadth of your knowledge domain. You are looking for problems that will indicate how you should structure the objects and overall rule patterns in your final version, and you want to be sure you have a good idea of all of the various kinds of problems the task will present you with. Second, once you think you have a good sample of the knowledge, you need to play with the control aspects of your system to get the procedural aspects of your system to flow smoothly. Do not worry very much about the user interface during this round.

The prototype is used to demonstrate how the final system will work. If it is to be demonstrated to senior management, more effort must go into the user interface, but normally the primary function of the prototype is (1) to convince the expert(s) and other technical managers that the system will be able to actually help them perform the task (i.e., solve some problem) and (2) to allow the knowledge engineer to determine how to structure the knowledge base.

"Algorithmic" vs. "Heuristic"-Based Expert Systems

Broadly speaking, there are two general types of problems that small expert systems are being built to solve. On the one hand, small expert system-building tools are being used to capture knowledge that is already well defined. In other words, one is simply using the tool to make it easy to transfer information that already exists in procedures manuals or on checklists into a format that can be presented to a user on a computer. Our Restaurant Advisor falls in this category; we could easily obtain most of the information from an existing restaurant guidebook. We refer to such problems as "algorithmic" since they could easily be solved using conventional programming techniques. An expert system tool is used because the developer does not wish to develop a procedural algorithm in a conventional language. In addition, the use of a tool often leads to a shorter development time, and it certainly facilitates future modifications of the knowledge base. When one is working with such well-defined knowledge, the real emphasis is necessarily on the procedural aspects of the system since the actual terms and relationships can be easily entered once you know exactly what rule templates you will be using.

On the other hand, some people are developing small expert systems to solve problems that involve knowledge that is not well defined. In this latter case, one uses techniques analogous to those used in the development of large expert systems. One must extract information from an expert. The expert may or may not be very precise about how he or she actually solves problems. The knowledge engineer must work with the expert to specify typical cases. In many situations, the expert can quickly obtain case data from his or her files and then it is just a matter of the expert and the knowledge engineer working together to annotate each case. Then the knowledge engineer writes a set of rules that would solve each case. The prototype, in this situation, is a small version of the final system that can effectively solve a set of typical cases. When one begins to move from the prototype to the final system, one develops several additional cases and the knowledge engineer and the expert work through the cases adding new rules, using the resulting system to try to solve the cases, adding more rules, and so forth. The development of a truly heuristic system puts much more emphasis on identifying the basic terms and relationships that are important if one is to analyze and solve problems in the particular task domain.

Phase 4. System Development

Once the prototype is done, you are ready to begin to develop the final system. If you developed a reasonable prototype, you now have a pretty good idea of the type of problems you will run into in developing the complete knowledge base. You will probably want to start creating the knowledge base from scratch. Rules that made sense during the development of the prototype will, in retrospect, seem unnecessarily restrictive, and so on. During this phase you will go through the three steps one after another. First you will want to enter as much of the task knowledge as you can. Then you will want to polish the procedural sequence, and finally, you will want to get the user interface in order. If you skimp on anything at this point you will probably spend a little less time on the user interface than you should since you know that the next phase will involve user testing and that will force you to focus on cleaning up any problems that remain in the user interface.

When the knowledge engineer begins to develop the final system, he or she must think about how the final system will work in considerable detail. The rules in the prototype system should be rearranged and experimented with until the knowledge is arranged in a form that will support a smooth consultation. Then the knowledge that was contained in the prototype system should be reformatted and reentered. After that you add additional rules to complete the declarative specification of the system.

The reconceptualization of a system usually involves identifying attributes that can be grouped to form new rules. In structured rule-based systems that support objects or contexts, reconceptualization often involves adding or changing the objects or contexts. Either way, all the rules that were written during the prototype phase are usually heavily edited or reentered. This occurs primarily because of what was learned in round 2 when you tried to polish the procedural flow of your initial knowledge. You normally discover that the declarative knowledge is correct, but that a different rule format will make it easier to control the procedural flow.

Consider a simple example. We are working with a committee to develop a Restaurant Selection Guide for an upcoming convention. At our first meeting we discussed the sorts of things that convention attendees would want to consider in selecting a place to eat. We developed a "rule template" that captured all of the information. One rule looked like this:

> IF the establishment you want advice about IS a restaurant
> AND you would prefer a restaurant that IS a five-minute walk
> AND the food served IS seafood
> AND the atmosphere you desire IS pleasant but crowded
> AND the comfort level IS businesslike
> AND the view you desire IS not important
> AND the clients ARE mostly businesspeople and tourists
> AND the price of a typical entrée IS $8 to $18
> AND standard credit cards ARE accepted
> AND reservations ARE not accepted
> AND the number in your party IS eight or less
> THEN a restaurant to consider IS Scotts
> AND DISPLAY Scotts

The information could just as well have been conceptualized as a matrix with the criteria along the vertical axis and a list of restaurants along the horizontal axis. In fact, after developing the "template," we developed a worksheet that local chapter members could use to rate restaurants. I went ahead and developed a four-rule knowledge base and loaded it into a small tool just to demonstrate how the final system might look. The committee was suitably impressed and everyone left eager to gather information on restaurants to be included in our Restaurant Advisor. Since there were only four rules in the system and since the committee didn't really think about it, the initial system impressed them. The minute you think about it a little longer, however, you can see that if the final system is made up of rules like this it will not be very useful. The effect of having all of the information about each restaurant in one rule is that one makes an all-or-none decision out of it. In other words, if one liked everything about Scotts and Scotts had a spectacular view besides, you would not want to eliminate Scotts from consideration. In the final system we will need many "shorter" rules. Some will identify the price range, the number in the party, and the type of food—the true all-or-none aspects of the decision that will need to be associated with each particular restaurant. Others will consider things like view or atmosphere and add or subtract confidence to specific recommendations. The rule above captures the basic information, but it doesn't facilitate the correct consultation flow. Figure

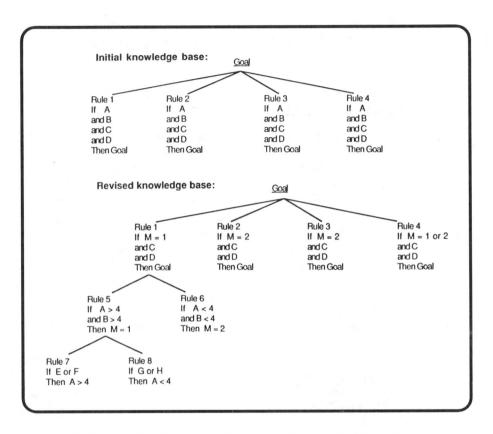

Figure 8.6 An Initial or Prototype Knowledge Base and a Revised
Knowledge Base

8.6 illustrates how we might group attributes and add "screening" rules to
facilitate a better consultation.

By the same token, after developing the prototype, you may decide that it
would make sense to incorporate a conventional database in your system or
you may decide you need to use some sort of control cycling or limited forward
chaining. In most cases you can avoid worrying about these things during the
prototype and "fake it" with rules and backward chaining, but once the number
of rules starts to become large, you need to deal explicitly with these matters.

Obviously this development process as described is a little too neat. Each
actual development effort has its own unique twists. Still, if you are just beginning to develop a small expert system this approach has much to recommend
it. It stresses knowledge acquisition first, followed by polishing to improve the
flow of the consultation and then to improve the user interface. It minimizes

the number of details one needs to master at any one point while providing a systematic approach that assures that all of the important steps are covered. Moreover, in its general outline, it seems to reflect what a lot of successful developers say they do.

Expert Systems as a Medium

Small expert systems are really just a new medium to use when you seek to develop complex job aids. Moreover, as the Campbell example illustrates, they can be a very effective medium. The critical information was gathered in a short amount of time, the solution was complete and ready to go as soon as the rules (i.e., the task analysis) were completed, and the program asked the user questions, gradually narrowed its search, and finally made specific action recommendations. The Campbell system is now in place and has effectively solved the problem. A workshop and documentation would have been much more expensive to develop and would not have worked as well. A paper job aid would not have been able to capture the same information in nearly as convenient a form, nor could a paper job aid conduct a dialogue with the user that would eventually identify the specific action to recommend. In other words, a small expert system was the ideal medium to use, in this instance, to communicate information to the performer.

In the near future any instructional designer who is faced with a task that involves complex problem solving that admits to the use of a computer will want to consider acquiring and using a small expert system-building tool to develop an intelligent job aid.

Expert Systems and the Analysis of Knowledge

Although this chapter has stressed the use of expert systems for the development of job aids, an interesting side effect should be noted. When you try to develop an expert system, you quickly learn about the knowledge in a particular domain. More broadly, you learn about how evidence is accumulated and weighed and how inference is used. Most experts and all developers learn a great deal in the process of developing an expert system. Thus the process of developing an expert system is an important tool to use to analyze the knowledge necessary for expert performance. In effect, even if one does not field an expert system, the process of creating it serves as a highly effective approach to cognitive task analysis.

Educators could utilize small expert system-building tools to teach students to think more logically, to help them to study problem solving, and to introduce them to new subject matter domains. Thus, for example, sixth graders may soon be taught to develop expert systems to classify common types of animals, while anthropology students may study a demographic theory by building a small expert system that will apply the theory to a set of cases. Rather than use expert systems to develop ICAI that will teach students, it may be more effective in many cases to give the students a small expert system-building tool and allow the students to learn by constructing a system for themselves.

Future Developments and Potential Problems

The current crop of expert system-building tools will rapidly be succeeded by much better tools. The next generation of tools will be much easier to use and much more powerful. Some of the tools will be domain specific tools designed to assist developers construct very specialized job aids. For example, Tektronix is currently experimenting with Detektr, a tool especially designed to allow engineers to develop intelligent troubleshooting aids to accompany new electronic hardware. Similarly, Texas Instruments has fielded a small system that uses a spoken interface so that users can consult with the program without taking their hands off their work. In the very near future, instructional developers are going to be able to choose from a wide variety of specialized tools that are each designed to be particularly efficient and effective with a particular subset of instructional problems.

On the other hand, it is perhaps worth mentioning that the extensive use of intelligent job aids may lead to some potential problems. To the degree that we develop intelligent job aids that ask questions and then recommend solutions, we "deprive" users of the experience of "messing" with a problem until they figure it out. In other words, we deny the users the rich period of experimentation that normally leads to the development of an expert. By automating troubleshooting and problem solving we will undoubtedly increase the quality and consistency of human performance in the near term. In the long run, however, we may find that we will need more sophisticated simulation programs (more education rather than training) to create the experts who will ultimately create and update the intelligent job aids that most employees will increasingly depend on.

Expert Systems and the Future of Training

I've been engaged in analyzing human performance problems and developing solutions for the last 15 years. I've worked on a wide range of problems at major corporations, including management education programs, sales training programs, programmer training programs, accounting programs, and a wide variety of programs to provide instruction for all kinds of operational and clerical personnel. About half of the problems I've encountered involved attitude problems, motivational and incentive problems, and related management issues, all problems that require noninstructional solutions. The remaining half required the development of materials to provide people with information they needed to perform some part of their jobs. Of this latter half, at least half called primarily for job aids. In other words, one-fourth of all problems I have encountered have been amenable to job aid solutions.

Since the media available for the development of complex job aids were limited, I've often developed workshops and provided general theory (education) or procedures manuals rather than try to package all of the necessary information as a job aid. Now, with the advent of small expert system-building tools, I expect to be much more effective in solving a wide variety of the human performance problems. Moreover, I think my approach will soon be typical of most instructional technologists. In fact, I expect that despite any potential problems, the number of workshops and manuals developed will steadily decline, while intelligent job aids will gradually become the primary media used by those who develop training for business, industry, and government.

References

Abatemarco, F. (1985, Nov.). An expert whose brain was drained. *Personal Computing, 98.*

Campbell Soup puts expert system to work in their kitchens (1985, Nov.). *Artificial Intelligence Letter, 1*(5), 1–4. Austin, TX: Texas Instruments Data Systems Group.

Clancey, W. J. (1984). The use of MYCIN's rules for tutoring. In B. G. Buchanan & E. H. Shortliffe (Eds.), *Rule-based expert systems: The MYCIN experiments of the Stanford Heuristic Programming Project* (pp. 464–493). Reading, MA: Addison-Wesley.

Duncan, C. S. (1985, May). Job performance aids. *Performance and Instruction Journal, 24*(4), 1–4.

Foley, J. P., Jr. (1969, April). *Job performance aids research, summary and recommendations.* Air Force Human Resources Laboratory, Air Force System Command, Wright Patterson Air Force Base, Ohio.

Gilbert, T. F. (1978). *Human competence: Engineering worthy performance.* New York: McGraw-Hill.

Harmon, P. (1981, Aug. 31). Simplifying training with job aids. *Computerworld, 15*(35), 2–8.

Harmon, P. (1982, Fall). The design of instructional materials: A top-down approach. *Journal of Instructional Development, 6*(1), 7–14.

Harmon, P., & King, D. (1985). *Expert systems: Artificial intelligence in business.* New York: John Wiley & Sons.

Newell, A., & Simon, H. (1972). *Human problem solving.* Englewood Cliffs, NJ: Prentice-Hall.

Simon, H. (1969). *The sciences of the artificial* (2nd ed.). Cambridge, MA.: MIT Press. See especially chap. 4, pp. 101–128.

Skinner, B. F. (1960). The science of learning and the art of teaching. In A. A. Lumsdaine & R. Glaser (Eds.), *Teaching machines and programmed learning: A source book* (pp. 99–113). Washington, DC: National Education Association of the U.S.

Part 4 Building Intelligent Tutors

The chapters in the previous two sections have described a variety of different ICAI systems and applications. The three chapters in this section focus on the methodology of building intelligent tutors. Many of the basic concepts and components of ICAI (e.g., knowledge representation, student models, inference mechanisms) that have been referred to in previous chapters are discussed at length in this section.

In Chapter 9, Clancey discusses the design considerations associated with the development of the NEOMYCIN tutor, which was based on the medical expert system MYCIN. What is especially interesting about this effort is the differences between the structure of an expert system and a tutoring system—two different classes of AI programs.

In his chapter, Clancey emphasizes the importance of collaboration in the development of ICAI systems. The most critical collaboration is between the system developers and the subject matter experts. A second important collaboration is between system developers and cognitive scientists who may be able to help with the design decisions based on principles of human cognition.

In Chapter 10, Woolf discusses three major classes of knowledge needed to build an intelligent tutor: domain, teaching, and discourse. The process of specifying domain knowledge is illustrated by the formulation of a tutor to teach the physics of crane booms. To discuss the specification of teaching and discourse knowledge, the Meno tutor system is described.

The last part of Chapter 10 discusses the development and use of authoring tools to create ICAI programs. Authoring tools are a critical issue for ICAI because the enormous time investment and very specialized background required to build tutoring systems present a major obstacle to their wider development. As Woolf points out, the development of viable authoring tools is closely intertwined with the knowledge representation issues discussed in her chapter.

Chapter 11, by Lewis, Milson, and Anderson, continues the discussion of design methods in the context of the TEACHER'S APPRENTICE—an intelligent tutoring system for high school mathematics. The chapter describes the detailed design decisions made at each step of the development process. The importance of authoring tools is also discussed in this chapter. The authors address some of the practical classroom considerations that influenced the design of the system.

Both Chapters 10 and 11 make allusions to the more powerful machines needed to move ICAI into the classroom. Ironically, it is clear from these chapters that the major limitations in bringing ICAI into the classroom are not more powerful machines but a better understanding of how people learn and teach and ways to represent these processes in computer programs. Our computers are already powerful enough; our design knowledge and tools are still very weak.

9/ Methodology for Building an Intelligent Tutoring System

WILLIAM J. CLANCEY

Introduction

Over the past five years my colleagues and I have been developing a computer program to teach medical diagnosis. Our research synthesizes and extends results in artificial intelligence (AI), medicine, and cognitive psychology. This chapter describes the progression of the research, and explains how theories from these fields are combined in a computational model. The general problem has been to develop an "intelligent tutoring system" by adapting the MYCIN "expert system."* This conversion requires a deeper understanding of the nature of expertise and explanation than originally required for developing MYCIN, and a concomitant shift in perspective from simple performance goals to attaining psychological validity in the program's reasoning process.

Others have written extensively about the relation of AI to cognitive science (e.g., Boden, 1977; Lehnert, 1984; Pylyshyn, 1978). Our purpose here is not to repeat those arguments, but to present a case study that will provide a common point for further discussion. To this end, to help evaluate the state of cognitive science, we outline our methodology and survey what resources and viewpoints have helped our research. We also discuss pitfalls that other AI-oriented cognitive scientists may encounter. Finally, we present some questions coming out of our work that might suggest possible collaboration with other fields of research.

Goals: Intelligent Tutoring Systems

An *intelligent tutoring system* is a computer program that uses AI techniques for representing knowledge and carrying on an interaction with a student

---

This paper first appeared as Chapter 3 in *Methods and Tactics in Cognitive Science,* edited by Kintsch, Miller, and Polson, Hillsdale, N.J.: Lawrence Erlbaum Associates, 1984.
* A glossary appears at the end of the chapter.

(Sleeman & Brown, 1981). Among the most well-known systems are WHY (Collins, 1976, uses Socratic principles for teaching causal reasoning in domains like meteorology), SOPHIE (Brown, Burton, & Bell, 1974, provides a "simulated workbench" in which a student can test electronics troubleshooting skills), and WEST (Burton & Brown, 1979, coaches a game-player on methods and strategies for exploiting game rules). This work derives from earlier efforts in computer-aided instruction, but differs in its attempt to use a principled or theoretical approach. First and foremost, this entails separating subject material from teaching method, as opposed to combining them in ad-hoc programs. By stating teaching methods explicitly, one gains the advantages of economical representation (the methods can be applied flexibly in many situations and even multiple problem domains) and the discipline of having to lay out subject material in a systematic, structured way, independently of how it is to be presented to the student. So the primary application of AI to these instructional systems is in the representation of teaching methods and domain knowledge. Ideally, this enterprise involves having a theory of teaching and the nature of the knowledge to be taught.

When we separate domain knowledge from the procedures that will use it, we say that we are representing knowledge "declaratively" (Winograd, 1975) (with respect to those procedures). For example, in a medical domain, we would represent links between data and diagnoses so they could be accessed and used for solving any given problem. A strong advantage of this approach is that the tutoring system can cope with arbitrary student behavior: no matter what order the student chooses to collect data (or troubleshoot a circuit, or make moves in a game), the program can evaluate partial solutions, and use its teaching knowledge to respond. Typically, the declaratively stated knowledge base of diagnostic rules, causal relations, and the like is used during a tutorial to generate an "expert's solution," which, when compared to the student's behavior, provides a basis for advising the student.* The combination of a knowledge base of this kind and an interpreter for applying it to particular problems constitutes an *expert system,* with an intelligent tutoring system having an expert system inside it (Fig. 9.1).

In general, an *expert system* is a kind of AI program that is designed to provide advice about real world problems that require specialized training to master. Some examples are MYCIN (Shortliffe, 1976), which provides advice about antibiotics for infectious diseases; SU/X (Nii & Feigenbaum, 1978), which analyzes sonar signals; and R1 (McDermott, 1980), which configures the components of computer systems. These systems are built by interviewing experts in

---

* In such a "first order" system, the model of the student's knowledge, as built by the program, is a subset of the internal, idealized knowledge base. This kind of model does not take into account student misconceptions or "bugs," an important area of research (see, for example, [Stevens, Collins, & Goldin, 1978] and [Brown & Burton, 1978]). The research described in this chapter focuses on the (as yet unsolved) problem of constructing the expert knowledge base, the material to be taught.

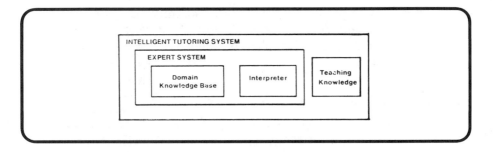

Figure 9.1 Components of an Intelligent Tutoring System

the given domain, and representing their knowledge in the form of heuristics, or "rules of thumb." For example, in an expert system for field biologists, one might find the rule, "if there are many buttercups and goldfield flowers, then the kind of underlying rock is probably serpentine." We call this kind of conditional statement, consisting of a premise and conclusion, a *production rule.*

In expert systems, there is no attempt to *simulate* how human experts think, for example, to model the order in which they typically attack a problem. Instead, these programs are intended to capture the efficient leaps an expert makes from a problem description to an interpretation. This is what a production rule does. Expert systems differ in the nature of the task they solve (constructive, diagnostic, interpretative, etc.) and in their formalism for representing knowledge ("frames," "semantic nets"), but they all use rule-like associations.

The interpreter of an expert system is a program that controls the order in which the rules are considered. Common control strategies are *backward chaining* (working backwards from a goal) and *forward inferencing* (applying those rules whose conditions are satisfied by the problem description). These strategies correspond to two common ways of structuring the rule base, namely by the goal mentioned in the conclusion and by the problem description mentioned in the premise. By this structuring, the interpreter can index the rules and apply them. By the same token, the structure of a given rule base constrains how it can be used, the possible kinds of strategies the interpreter can use to access it.

The particular tutoring system we will be considering is built upon the knowledge of the MYCIN expert system. MYCIN's rules have to be restructured in order to be applied to teaching; the new system is called NEOMYCIN (Clancey & Letsinger, 1981). Our methodology for building NEOMYCIN is the subject of this chapter. The key idea is that using an expert system for teaching requires a shift in orientation from simply trying to output good solutions, to simulating in some degree of detail the reasoning process itself. The production rules that are used by MYCIN to provide good advice are inadequate for use as teaching material because certain kinds of reasoning steps, whose rationale needs to be conveyed to a student, are implicit in the rules. We need a more explicit, psychologically valid model of problem solving—one that can be understood and remembered by a student and incorporated in his behavior.

From MYCIN to GUIDON (an AI Enterprise)

MYCIN is an expert system that was developed by a team of physicians and AI specialists. The program was designed to advise non-experts in the selection of antibiotic therapy for infectious diseases. The domain knowledge base (refer to Fig. 9.1) contains approximately 450 rules, which deal with diagnosis of bacteremia, meningitis, and cystitis infections. The interpreter uses backward chaining, working from high-order goals, such as "determine whether the patient requires treatment" down to more specific subgoals, such as "determine whether the patient has high risk for Tuberculosis." A typical rule is (roughly stated) "if the patient has been receiving steroids, then his risk for Tuberculosis meningitis is increased." Most rules are modified by a "certainty factor" indicating the rule author's degree of belief, on a scale from -10 to 10, that the conclusion holds when the premise is known to be true. Figure 9.2 shows excerpts from the diagnostic portion of a MYCIN consultation. Rules are chained together, working downwards from the high order goals; the program asks a question when it needs data to apply a rule. After the diagnosis is complete, a therapy program selects the most optimal therapy for the organisms most likely to be causing the infection. Additional tests might also be ordered.

The success of MYCIN as a problem-solver, as measured in several formal evaluations (Yu, Buchanan, Shortliffe, Wraith, Davis, Scott, & Cohen, 1979; Yu, Fagan, Wraith, Clancey, Scott, Hannigan, Blum, Buchanan, & Cohen, 1979), encouraged us to explore its application for teaching. The program's good performance, coupled with an ability to explain its line of reasoning, made it seem particularly suitable as teaching material. The rules had been acquired from physicians over many hours of discussion, comparing the program's behavior to their judgment, modifying rules to improve the program and testing the program on new problems. The rules pertaining to infectious meningitis were especially carefully constructed from experience with over 100 cases from local hospitals and medical journal articles. Therefore, we decided to focus on using the meningitis rules for teaching.

In order to understand what is good about MYCIN's rules and how they fall short for use in teaching, one must understand something about their construction, and what kind of explanation a tutorial program can provide by using them. Rules are not written independently of the whole rule base: a rule author must think about how a given rule will fit. Any given rule must make a conclusion about some goal that appears in at least one other rule premise, otherwise the rule would never be used (recall the mechanism of backward chaining).

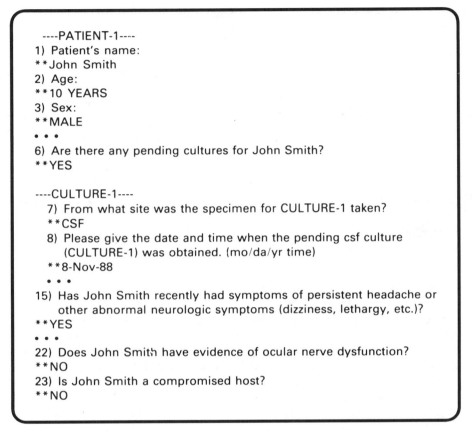

```
    ----PATIENT-1----
1) Patient's name:
**John Smith
2) Age:
**10 YEARS
3) Sex:
**MALE
• • •
6) Are there any pending cultures for John Smith?
**YES

    ----CULTURE-1----
   7) From what site was the specimen for CULTURE-1 taken?
   **CSF
   8) Please give the date and time when the pending csf culture
      (CULTURE-1) was obtained. (mo/da/yr time)
   **8-Nov-88
   • • •
15) Has John Smith recently had symptoms of persistent headache or
    other abnormal neurologic symptoms (dizziness, lethargy, etc.)?
**YES
• • •
22) Does John Smith have evidence of ocular nerve dysfunction?
**NO
23) Is John Smith a compromised host?
**NO
```

Figure 9.2 Excerpt from MYCIN Consultation

Moreover, some means must be provided to evaluate the subgoals mentioned in the premise, by writing other rules to make the appropriate conclusions and/or by making it possible for the system to gain the information from the user. So, in effect, a rule author is writing a kind of program in which goals are chained together by rules.

The author's choice of goals in the program constitutes a decomposition of the problem into reasoning steps. Figure 9.3 shows part of this internal goal structure in MYCIN. One method for determining the type of the infection brings into consideration whether the infection is meningitis and whether the patient has leukemia. To determine if the patient has leukemia, the program checks to see if the patient is immunosuppressed, and so on.

The explanation capability of MYCIN (Scott, Clancey, Davis, & Shortliffe, 1977) is based upon the assumption that these steps, provided by a human

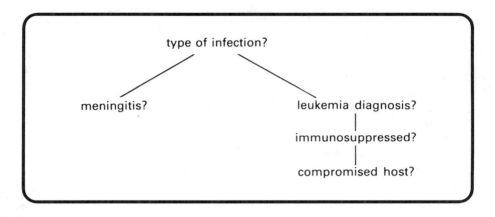

Figure 9.3 Portion of MYCIN's Goal Structure

expert, will make sense to the consultation program user. Figure 9.4 shows how the steps factor into an explanation of why MYCIN is requesting a datum. After the rule currently being considered is printed, repeated "Why" questions are answered by moving up the inference stack. Thus, the goals of Fig. 9.3 are mentioned in the context of the particular rules now being considered that tie them together. This constitutes the program's "line of reasoning."

In the "question-answer" interaction after MYCIN has given its advice, the user can inquire in more detail about how data was used and how conclusions were made (see Fig. 9.5). Again, all explanations are based on the rules and goals of the system.*

There are two important kinds of explanations that MYCIN cannot give: *it cannot explain why a particular rule is correct, and it cannot explain the strategy behind the design of its goal structure.* These deficiencies only became important to us in the course of developing GUIDON. In effect, we were forced to reconsider our conception of "transfer the expertise," the model by which we viewed the process of representing expertise and using it in an AI program (see Fig. 9.6).

Instead of thinking of expertise transfer as a process of moving knowledge down a pipeline from an expert (via Davis' Teiresias system [Davis, 1979]) to a client or student, we were forced to be more precise about the different kinds and purposes of knowledge. At a certain level, MYCIN is aphasic—able to perform, but unable to talk about what it knows. Teaching and explanation, we came to recognize, place different demands on an expert than simply solving problems. A teacher can provide analogies, multiple views, and levels of expla-

---

* The AI technology that makes this possible—giving the program knowledge about its representation so that it can dissect its rules—is not of prime concern to us here. The interested reader can find details in Davis (1976).

23) Is John Smith a compromised host?
**WHY
[i.e. WHY is it important to determine whether PATIENT-1 is a compromised host?]
[3.0] This will aid in determining whether PATIENT-1 is
immunosuppressed.
  If
    [3.1] *John Smith is not a compromised host*
  then
    It is definite (1.0) that John Smith is not immunosuppressed
  [RULE343]
[back to question 23 . . .]
**WHY
[i.e. WHY is it important to determine whether PATIENT-1 is
      immunosuppressed?]
[4.0] . . . in order to determine the diagnoses of PATIENT-1.
  If
    [4.1] *John Smith is not immunosuppressed*
  then
    *it is definite (1.0) that leukemia is not one of the diagnoses of
      John Smith*
    *it is definite (1.0) that lymphoma is not one of the diagnoses of
      John Smith*
  [RULE395]
[back to question 23 . . .]
**WHY
[i.e. WHY is it important to determine the diagnoses of PATIENT-1?]
[5.0] . . . in order to determine the type of the infection.
    it has already been established that
      [5.1] *the infection which requires therapy is meningitis, and*
      [5.2] *only circumstantial evidence is available for this case, and*
      [5.3] *John Smith does not have a tb risk factor*
    Therefore, if
      [5.4] *1) Leukemia is one of the diagnoses of John Smith, or*
            2) Lymphoma is one of the diagnoses of John Smith
    then
      *there is weakly suggestive evidence (.3) that the type of the
        infection is not tb*
[RULE056]
[back to question 23 . . .]
**NO

Figure 9.4 Excerpt of MYCIN Consultation Showing Explanation Capability
           (User input follows **)

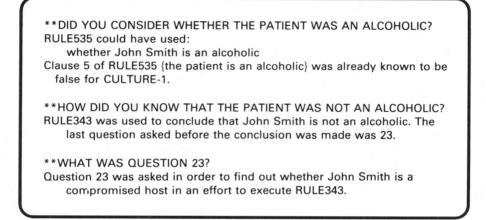

**DID YOU CONSIDER WHETHER THE PATIENT WAS AN ALCOHOLIC?
RULE535 could have used:
   whether John Smith is an alcoholic
Clause 5 of RULE535 {the patient is an alcoholic} was already known to be
   false for CULTURE-1.

**HOW DID YOU KNOW THAT THE PATIENT WAS NOT AN ALCOHOLIC?
RULE343 was used to conclude that John Smith is not an alcoholic. The
   last question asked before the conclusion was made was 23.

**WHAT WAS QUESTION 23?
Question 23 was asked in order to find out whether John Smith is a
   compromised host in an effort to execute RULE343.

Figure 9.5 Excerpt of Question/Answer Interaction after a Consultation

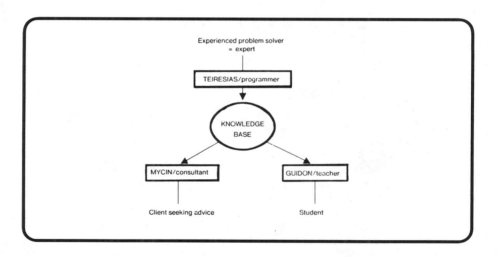

Figure 9.6 Transfer of Expertise: Learning, Advising, and Teaching

nation which are unknown to MYCIN. In building MYCIN, we did not make
explicit *how an expert organizes his knowledge, how he remembers it, and
strategies he uses for approaching problems.*

    These shortcomings became clear in the course of developing GUIDON, a
project undertaken in a typical AI way as a "constructive experiment." GUIDON
was a test of the assumption that the rule base could be used for purposes other

than problem solving, so in designing the system we held the rules fixed. Moreover, to test the idea that teaching knowledge could be represented wholly separate from domain expertise, the system was designed to work with any rule base written in MYCIN's language (see van Melle, 1980). Therefore, the rules are treated syntactically: GUIDON's teaching procedures are designed to discuss how a goal is achieved in terms of the data appearing in rule premises and to evaluate a student's hypotheses in terms of conclusions made by the rules. Figure 9.7 shows an excerpt from a dialogue with GUIDON.*

GUIDON was improved over time by annotating the rules to separate the "key factors" of the rule from contextual and "screening" clauses that determine applicability of the rule (so complex rules with 5 clauses and a table of conclusions can be summarized by saying "the CSF protein is evidence for viral infection"). Clause distinctions of this kind are part of the implicit design knowledge that is unknown to MYCIN because it lies outside of the rule syntax.

But simple annotations were insufficient; the knowledge base also lacked medical knowledge necessary for teaching. We found that students were unable to remember the rules, even after discussing a single problem with GUIDON many times. Students who apparently knew what data to collect were unsure of the order in which to collect it, and consequently had no confidence that their investigations were complete. This experience suggested that the program needed to teach a problem solving strategy that a student could follow, as well as some underlying mnemonic structure for understanding and remembering the rules. No formal experimentation was necessary, the program plainly lacked the necessary medical knowledge.

From GUIDON to NEOMYCIN (a Cognitive Science Enterprise)

In the course of studying the teaching problem, we learned that the expertise and explanations of MYCIN are narrowly conceived. On the one hand, we have not captured all that an expert knows, for example, his causal models of disease processes by which he understands rules and can use as a basis for violating them. On the other hand, some of what we have captured is *implicit* in the rules, namely the taxonomic structure of diseases and the search strategy (top-down refinement). This knowledge is procedurally embedded in the choice of subgoals and their ordering in a rule. This is illustrated by the alcoholic rule (see Fig. 9.8).

Clauses 1–3 specify that this rule about particular bacteria will only be applied after bacterial meningitis infection is established (three levels of the taxonomic hierarchy). Clause 4 is based on the fact that children are usually not alcoholics, illustrating that the rules are based on implicit knowledge about the world, too. Finally, the rationale for associating alcoholics with the listed bacteria

---

*The teaching procedures are not our main concern here. (See Clancey, 1979a,b for details.)

```
**FACTORS
The following factors will be useful to determine the type of the infection:
      3a.  whether the meningitis is partially treated
      3b.  whether a lumbar puncture has been performed on John Smith
      3c.  the duration of the neurological signs
      3d.  the CSF protein
 (*) 3e.  whether John Smith has symptoms of Herpes Zoster virus

                        {Section omitted}

  Factors marked with '*' have already been stated. Based on what we
  have already mentioned, you should be able to conclude about: 3b.

**USE 3C
The duration of the neurological signs is 7.2 hours.
Using other information available to you now, the duration of the neu-
rological signs enables you to conclude that the type of the infection is
bacterial (.2) viral (.2) [RULE524].

**IKNOW 3B
Good. MYCIN has also made a decision.
The site of CULTURE-1 is evidence that a lumbar puncture has been
performed on John Smith [RULE112].
Back to our discussion of the type of the infection. . . .

**3D
The CSF protein is 40.

**HYPOTHESIS VIRAL
You're right, there's strong evidence that the type of the infection is viral,
given the CSF protein, the duration of neurological signs, and the fact that
the patient has symptoms of Herpes Zoster virus.
What other facts about this case tell you that the type of the infection is
viral?
(Enter one factor per line.)
>>
```

Figure 9.7 Excerpt of GUIDON Interaction

is not represented. Figure 9.9 illustrates the different kinds of knowledge that the human expert relied upon to construct this rule, which we did not represent explicitly in the program. The kinds of knowledge are labeled as strategic, structural, and support knowledge.

The MYCIN program shows us clearly that the task orientation to develop a program with a high level of performance alone does not lead to a process model of human problem solving. MYCIN does subgoaling, as people some-

RULE535

If: 1) The infection which requires therapy is meningitis,
    2) Only circumstantial evidence is available for this case,
    3) The type of the infection is bacterial,
    4) The age of the patient is greater than 17 years,
    5) The patient is an alcoholic,

Then: There is evidence that the organisms which might be causing the
      infection are diplococcus-pneumoniae (.3) and e.coli (.2).

Figure 9.8 The Alcoholic Rule

times do, but it doesn't do diagnosis like people. For one reason, subgoaling is not the key element of diagnostic rule application; focused forward-inferencing is. For teaching purposes, we need to model how an expert uses and remembers his knowledge—not just capturing the associations he makes, but capturing also why these associations come to mind. It is the task orientation of tutoring that makes these considerations relevant and that will be the measure of adequacy for the models we construct.

To recap, in building an intelligent tutoring system, we are forced to move beyond the constraints of performance and consider the psychological constraints of teaching. We need to be able to articulate how the rules fit together, how they are constructed. We have studied MYCIN's rules and developed an epistemology of the kinds of knowledge that relate to the teaching of heuristics (see Fig. 9.9 and Clancey, 1983). Following the theory, a new representation was developed in which the original MYCIN rule set is reconfigured to make these kinds of knowledge explicit (Clancey & Letsinger, 1981). Figure 9.10 illustrates the main components of this new system, NEOMYCIN. With its theoretical, epistemological underpinning, NEOMYCIN is designed to represent the subject material that a new version of GUIDON can use to articulate important teaching points.

Figure 9.10 shows that the key feature of NEOMYCIN is separation of domain-specific disease knowledge from general procedures for doing diagnosis. The strategical knowledge "gets a handle on" the disease knowledge by way of alternate "views" or structural organizations of the disease knowledge. It is through these general indexing relationships, such as the hierarchical relationships of "sibling" and "father," that a general procedure can examine and select specific problem-solving knowledge to apply it to a given problem. The causal view indexes the disease hierarchy through causal abstractions. (For example, "double vision" might be caused by "increased pressure in the brain," which

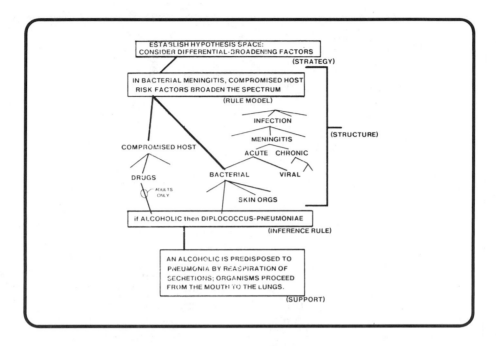

Figure 9.9 Strategic, Structural, and Supporting Knowledge for a Heuristic

might be caused by "a brain tumor," "a brain hemorrhage," and so on.) The process view pertains to general features of any disease, which describe its location, progression of symptoms, degree of spread, and so on—general concepts by which the problem solver can index his knowledge about diseases to compare and contrast competing hypotheses. Figure 9.10 shows the working memory which will be described later.

So far we have been considering how NEOMYCIN, as a representation, adheres to an epistemological theory of knowledge, that is, how it separates out expertise by the divisions suggested in Fig. 9.9. The "content" of NEOMYCIN is a psychological theory for gathering and interpreting new data, in part, the content of the meta-strategy box in Fig. 9.10. NEOMYCIN embodies a psychological theory of medical diagnostic reasoning for the purpose of monitoring a student's problem solving and providing assistance that a student can follow. For example, we will be teaching forward-directed inferences—leaps from data to hypotheses—that we represent in NEOMYCIN's *trigger rules*. With this additional knowledge of how people think, GUIDON Version 2 will have leverage for interrupting the student to test his knowledge, as well as having a better basis for understanding a student's partial solutions.

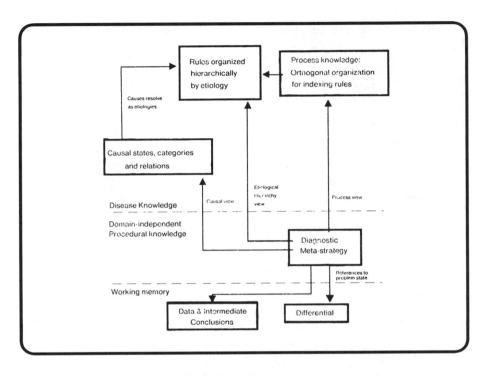

Figure 9.10 Components of the NEOMYCIN Expert System

Although this chapter is not primarily about teaching strategy, we hasten to clarify that we do not propose to directly teach students a model of what experts do. Indeed, the epistemological separation of knowledge in NEOMYCIN brings out individual steps of reasoning that we believe are "compiled" in experienced problem solvers, just as in MYCIN's original rules. The point of the decomposition is to provide a rationale for surface expert behavior so a student can understand it. Thus, on the surface NEOMYCIN is designed to behave like an expert in its focusing, data collection, and hypothesis formation. Moreover, the types and organization of knowledge are those of an expert. But the process itself is drawn out here into "diagnostic tasks" (the meta-strategy) that we believe an expert follows when stuck, but generally does not consciously consider, knowing what to do in each situation from years of practice.

Furthermore, we have not specified how this material will be presented to a student. The sequencing of material and various support stories for understanding and memory are part of the theory of teaching which we do not address here.

The Relation of Theory, AI Formalism, and Program

NEOMYCIN is more than an ordinary AI system built to simply do some task. It is not an ad hoc system built to get performance—it is an implementation of a theory of diagnosis and certain principles for representing knowledge. Our tutoring goals require that the program combine both: a theoretical model of medical diagnosis, so that the student's problem solving can be interpreted and advice offered; and an epistemological theory of knowledge, so that this model of diagnosis can be articulated to the student. These theories are instantiated in a program by way of AI formalisms for representing and controlling knowledge, some of which are novel and grew out of the theoretical goals. Figure 9.11 shows how theory and model are related in NEOMYCIN. This section describes in more detail how the theories factor into the AI formalisms and the actual code of the system.

The Psychological Theory of Medical Diagnosis

The questions addressed by the theory of medical diagnosis we are developing are: how does a physician use problem data and disease knowledge to formulate hypotheses; to request additional data; and to reach a diagnosis? Issues pertaining to the processing of new information, the structure of disease knowledge, the nature of procedural knowledge, and its relation to disease knowledge, among others, are appropriate. The theory is general, both in its application to multiple problems in a given domain and its potential applicability to other domains, thus the problem of arbitrariness in process models (van Lehn, Brown, & Greeno, 1984) is partially ameliorated. Underlying regularities become manifest through this constant consideration of multiple tasks and multiple domains (Kosslyn, 1980).*

The theoretical features described here do not literally appear anywhere in the program. These are descriptions of behavior that were written down clearly and explicitly before any coding began. They were not extracted from the program; they were designed into it.

In writing down the principles of the theory, we were almost always thinking about their implementation in the program, often requiring that we return to be more precise about the theory. For example, we could not simply write down that, "data are used immediately in a forward-directed way." Should every rule that uses new information be allowed to fire? This did not fit our observations. For example, when thinking about "steroids" in the context of a possible meningitis case, inferences are obviously focused by the problem at hand; tuber-

---

* This is on top of the principled character of representation deriving from our epistemological framework. Generality stemmed, first of all, from our need for teaching general principles to students. Ultimately, the enterprise has engineering value: we can lift the representation framework as well as the domain-independent diagnostic strategy into another problem domain and develop a new consultation system with this as a starting point.

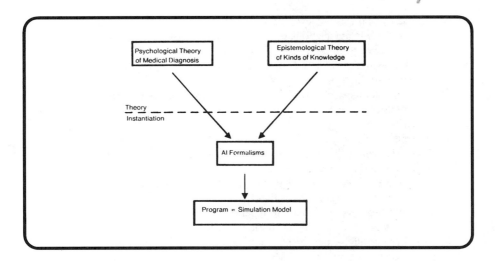

Figure 9.11 Relation of Theory to AI Formalisms and the Model

culosis might come to mind, not the possibility of a law suit in college athletics. In turn, our evolving knowledge representation (also on paper) suggested that this focusing might be modeled by only firing rules that appear in subtrees of the etiological hierarchy below hypotheses currently being entertained (so "tuberculosis" would come to mind because it is below "meningitis").*

The following is a brief presentation of the key theoretical features of NEOMYCIN, fairly similar to how they appeared before we wrote any code:

A. Incoming data are immediately applied by forward-directed reasoning leading to more abstract descriptions of the problem and support for specific diagnostic hypotheses:
  1. trigger rules place hypotheses on the differential (working memory of hypotheses) directly as data is received. The differential is maintained so more specific causes replace general hypotheses;
  2. data are abstracted immediately, for example, "diplopia" is thought of as an "abnormal neurological finding";
  3. process-oriented questions are immediately asked, relevant to the domain, but not directed to any particular hypothesis, for example, asking when a symptom began and how it has changed over time;
  4. data suggest causal state-categories, possibly jumping over a chain of causal links to conjecture some generic problem whose subtypes are later considered (as "brain pressure" suggests "space-occupying substance in the brain" rather than the specific causes of "brain pressure");

---

* This idea bears some obvious relation to frame theory; an elaboration is beyond the purpose of this chapter.

    5. data/hypothesis associations are applied in the context of the current differential. Only associations that appear in subtrees below the current hypotheses come to mind;

  B. The following knowledge sources are represented separately and explicitly, in accord with the epistemological theory:
    1. a problem-space hierarchy to which data/hypothesis rules are attached, "etiological taxonomy" (previously implicit as the "context clauses" of rules);
    2. causal rules that ultimately tie into this hierarchy (see Fig. 9.10);
    3. world relations that constrain the relevance of data (previously implemented as "screening clauses");
    4. disease process knowledge that cuts across the etiological distinctions, useful for initial program formulation.

  C. A hierarchical set of domain-independent meta-rules constitutes a diagnostic meta-strategy. These rules examine the knowledge sources listed above and the current differential to select a hypothesis to focus on and the next datum to request.

Turning now to the content of the strategic rules, we determined that the key strategic idea to teach students is that the purpose of collecting circumstantial evidence, in preparation for making physical measurements, is to "establish the hypothesis space," to determine the *range of possibilities* that might be causing the problem. Strategies for achieving this involve looking for evidence that will broaden the space of possibilities by considering common and unusual causes.

There are two orientations when establishing the hypothesis space: (1) "group and differentiate"—upward-looking, initial problem formulation in which one tries to cluster the data under some generic process (cause); and (2) "explore and refine"—attempting to confirm successively more specific causes. The trigger associations mentioned here bring the problem solver "into the middle" of his problem space hierarchy. These strategies together establish a path to a diagnosis.

The initial problem formulation we want to teach goes beyond MYCIN's expertise, requiring both the strategy of "group and differentiate" as well as additional medical knowledge. Essentially, we want to teach a student not just how to confirm that meningitis is present, MYCIN's task, but when one should think about meningitis, and what it might be confused with. One normally associates these questions with the "primary care" physician, as opposed to a consultant like MYCIN. These perspectives, stemming from our tutorial goals, led us to adopt a more theoretical understanding of the task of diagnosis itself.

The AI Formalisms of NEOMYCIN

A tacit principle of AI is that an AI program must be describable in terms of theoretical formalisms of knowledge representation and control. Thus, in a real sense we might move the "theory/instantiation" line of Fig. 9.11 to below the "AI formalisms" box. For just as what we write down about trigger rules in our psychological theory is separable from its implementation as code, the mathematical, logical, and AI concepts of "antecedent rule," "hierarchy," and the like are abstractions for entities and processes in our FORTRAN or INTERLISP programs. However, they are apparently "closer" to our code than is the psychological theory, often even designated by procedure and variable names that make the correspondence explicit to the programmer.

A good example of the use of AI technology in NEOMYCIN are the diagnostic strategies, which are represented as meta-rules, an adaptation of a pre-existing formalism (Davis, 1976). These rules are applied as a *pure-production system* for each subtask (e.g., "find a new focus" is a subtask). *Abort conditions* are inherited to simulate shifting of focus (and return to higher goals) as data broadens the differential or exploration suggests that a conjecture is unlikely.

We mention these examples of AI formalisms in NEOMYCIN to illustrate the point that a cognitive scientist doesn't simply sit down and write any program whatsoever as a model of his theory. As in mathematics and logic, there are certain notations that have been developed for couching theoretical relations, and the notations evolve as the theories become more complex. The work of writing AI programs is made much easier by previous efforts to abstract representational devices such as "meta-rules." These devices become like a bag of tools for expressing theories. In order to communicate the NEOMYCIN model to other AI programmers, it was essential to adapt whatever tools were already in common use, rather than inventing new terms or arbitrarily combining old formalisms. So in describing NEOMYCIN, indeed in *thinking about it,* we say that the meta-rules are applied as in a pure production system; the disease process knowledge is represented as a frame associated with each disease; and so on. Furthermore, AI's bag of tools provided a ready-at-hand, suggestive set of organizational and processing concepts for expressing the psychological theory. Finally, in this special case AI provided the data (MYCIN's rules) that enabled us to study human knowledge in a new way.

When Is a Program Ad Hoc?

The scheme shown in Fig. 9.11 provides an interesting handle on the question of ad hocness in computational models. It shows that there are multiple perspectives from which the model can be said to be ad hoc. From the AI perspective, code is ad hoc if it is loosely put together without regard for unified, simple, and elegant formalisms. If NEOMYCIN's diagnostic meta-strategy had been implemented in INTERLISP procedures directly, instead of a hierarchy of meta-rules applied cyclically with abort conditions, etc., the implementation would be said to be ad hoc. Here ad hocness would have interfered with our teaching goals as well as program maintenance.

Moving up a level, if we had used MYCIN's rule language, an AI formalism, instead of the NEOMYCIN scheme of an etiological hierarchy combined with meta-rules, our implementation would have been said to be atheoretic from the epistemological perspective. That is, we would have represented different kinds of knowledge in a uniform way, losing distinctions—in some sense the essence of an ad hoc implementation.* Indeed, it was the ad hoc representation of strategies and taxonomic concepts in MYCIN rules that limited its usefulness for teaching.

Finally, looking at the left theoretical arm of Fig. 9.11, an implementation can be ad hoc from the psychological perspective. If we had persisted in using exhaustive, top-down refinement, as in MYCIN, and several other medical AI systems, we would have constructed a program that does medical reasoning, but in an ad hoc way, limiting the usefulness of the program for interpreting student behavior. Note that exhaustive top-down refinement is not an ad hoc implementation from the AI formalism perspective, but it is a psychologically implausible model of search.

Observe that from all three perspectives, it is the task orientation that determined what aspects of the implementation were relevant, those which should not be done in an ad hoc way. In general, the question of where we should "draw the line between implementation detail and relevant model content" (Miller, Polson, & Kintsch, 1984) depends on what we want to model, what we want the program to do. The attempt to apply the model to a real world task will provide the empirical feedback that reveals what was ad hoc and now needs to be implemented in a theoretical way. But note again, we do not *extract* the theoretical principles from the program (contrast with Pylyshyn, 1978), we write them down, then build them in. By default all other coding decisions will be ad hoc, and we won't know whether that matters until we do more testing.

Summary of NEOMYCIN as a Model

To summarize, NEOMYCIN is an information-processing model that uses AI formalisms to instantiate psychological and epistemological theories of knowledge and processing:

1. The epistemological theory specifies how different kinds of knowledge interact, specifically how organizational knowledge interacts with strategies.

2. What the expert does is not simply listed: the strategies are domain-independent, they specify how different kinds of knowledge sources are called into play to massage a guess that is being constructed and refined (domain-

---

* Notice the tension between the epistemological and AI formalism levels: without uniformity there is no formalism, but the uniformity chosen may not allow important distinctions to be expressed.

independence makes the process model more psychologically plausible and extensible [van Lehn, Brown, & Greeno, 1984]).

3. Associations of data with hypotheses are described in terms of the working memory and a structured representation of the problem space (following from the diagnostic theory).

4. The model of strategies specifies hierarchical organization of knowledge in the form of rules for achieving tasks; the problem solver is said to be oriented to "what he is trying to do" (diagnostic theory).

5. Different kinds of follow-up questions are not simply listed: The model specifies how subgoals can be set up by associations that trigger when data is received, and how immediate follow-up questions are associated with data abstractions (diagnostic theory).

In short, NEOMYCIN specifies organization of different kinds of knowledge and processes by which this knowledge is called into play. It is a model that relates a working memory to the kinds of associations people try to think about and why they remember them at particular times. The overall theory is complex; the computer program provides a practical means of testing the coherency and completeness of the theory.*

Methodology

We began with an extensive review of the medical problem-solving literature (e.g., see Elstein, Shulman, & Sprafka, 1978; Feltovich, Johnson, Moller, & Swanson, 1980; Miller, 1975; Pauker & Szolovits, 1977; Rubin, 1975; Swanson, Feltovich, & Johnson, 1977). We returned to this previous work to augment and refine the NEOMYCIN model of diagnostic strategy, after the study described here was complete.

From the period February 1 through December 1, 1980, we met regularly with a physician consultant with the purpose of revising MYCIN's rules to make the teaching points clear. Protocol analysis (using cases MYCIN had previously solved) was the chief method. We also attended classes taught by this physician and compared them to another physician's handling of the same course. In addition, we presented several cases to our physician's best student to compare his reasoning and explanations to his teacher's.

Our physician's approach was logical and easy to emulate. After listening to several other physicians and sitting in on other classes, we decided that we had found an unusually good teacher, someone who was consistent from case to case, and moreover did what he told students to do. Other teachers we observed were not able to articulate their approach as clearly and seemed to be less sure of what students were thinking. There were common strategic

---

* See (Kosslyn, 1980) for further discussion of the relation of theories to programs as models.

concepts, however, that our experts all used to explain their reasoning ("hit the high points," "consider risk factors"). In our opinion, the reason our physician was a good teacher was because his explanations were not as "flat" as other physicians'. Rather than saying, "Well, the patient hasn't traveled, so it isn't Valley fever," he would say "Well, travel would have widened the spectrum of possibilities, so we can rule out things like TB picked up in Mexico." That is, he supplied abstractions that said *what he was trying to do,* how his thinking was oriented.

Our framework of structural, support, and strategic knowledge for organizing, justifying, and controlling the use of heuristic rules served well in knowledge acquisition dialogues. We would always ask ourselves, "What kind of explanation is he giving us? A data/hypothesis rule? Why he believes a rule? Why he thought to consider that association (the indexing, the approach)?" We organized these kinds of knowledge around each rule we discussed (Fig. 9.9), and directed the conversation appropriately. In contrast, several years ago, before deriving this framework, our interviews tended to take a depth-first plunge into pathophysiological details (we always asked, "And what causes that?"), which did not shed much light on the physician's strategies and organization of data/hypothesis relations.

We tape-recorded sessions whenever a case was presented to the physician. A note file was maintained in which we recorded what we learned from each meeting. A summary of the kinds of interactions is given below (in the order they occurred).

A. *Informal discussion of a case previously diagnosed by MYCIN.* The experimenter presents data and asks how it is useful. Among the points of discussion: how the expert cuts up the problem (for example, acute vs. chronic), how he remembers data/hypothesis relations (diagnostic values are related to a mnemonic story), the significance of frequently-mentioned problem features ("predisposition," "compromised host"), how urgency and faulty data factor into reasoning. Later comparison of the expert's terms and rules to MYCIN's suggest questions for subsequent meetings.

B. *The expert solves a case, while the experimenter actively questions his reasoning throughout.* Initial data is presented, the expert must then request information in any order he desires, and make a diagnosis. Among the items we record: the differential (hypotheses under consideration); strategy (either a domain-specific goal, such as "look for evidence of a focal lesion," or a domain-independent goal, such as "pursue most likely causes first"*); rule-like associations ("diplopia suggests increased brain pressure"); and meta-statements about strategy ("think before the lab results,

---

* These are often stated aphoristically as well: "When you hear hoof beats, think of horses, not zebras."

not from the results"; "make reliability checks of data"). NEOMYCIN's strategy rules were first derived from analysis of one of these protocols.

Designing a general program from a single, typical interaction is a common method in AI. The knowledge base designer idealizes the interaction, specifying knowledge (frames, rules, etc.) and processing (general procedures, strategy rules) that will bring about the desired program behavior in the particular case. GUIDON's tutorial procedures were first sketched out in this way by proceeding from a sample interaction in which we played both the part of the student and teacher (generating realistic student input and then looking in the rule base to find what response would be satisfying). The program is generalized and debugged by testing it on many other cases afterwards. For example, single statements might become separate procedures as the complexity of problem situations becomes better understood. This method presupposes that the general framework of the system (or meta-strategy in the case of NEOMYCIN) can be induced, at least in preliminary form, from any particular problem solution.

C. *The expert is asked to describe a typical case for each of the main diagnoses.* The expert finds this easy to do. This method brings out the diagnostic or invariant associations, as well as what evidence is required to rule out competing hypotheses. For comparison, the expert is asked to describe atypical presentations of the same disorders. (In these cases, the expert gives the impression that he is telling a joke.) From these analyses, we developed a theory of what makes a case easy or difficult.*

D. *The expert is asked to present a case to the experimenter, reversing the roles of method B.* This helps the experimenter determine whether he has formalized an "executable procedure." This method quickly reveals any gaps in knowledge or approach that have not been extracted from the expert. The expert is asked to present both easy and difficult cases so the evolving model can be more fairly evaluated.

E. *The same cases discussed in B and D are presented to different experts.* Because we already understand the significance of the data (the data/ hypothesis rules) we are especially interested in comparing strategies that bring the data to mind.

F. *The developed strategy model is presented to the original expert for his evaluation.* What resonates with his thinking? What does he care to elaborate upon? Where do students have problems? (The expert says things like,

---

* *Diagnosticity* (sharpness of measurements [classicality]; presence of important factors [but not necessary]; presence of invariant factors [sufficient]); *dissonance* (absence of extraneous, unexplained factors) and inconsistencies (unexpected factors); *the a priori likelihood of the problem* (expert has less confidence in unlikely diagnoses); and *multiplicity of cause* (before reaching a diagnosis, the expert will struggle to find a simpler, single explanation).

"Most students encounter roadblocks—they're not sure what to do next. They focus too narrowly and specifically on details of the case.")

G. *The same cases discussed previously are presented to the expert's best student.* We find which phrases have been picked up ("establish a database") and how the student carries out the strategies he has learned. For example, a student might verbalize his reasoning more slowly and carefully, providing some details that the expert skips over.

H. *We discuss each rule with the expert, grouping them according to the hypotheses they support* (e.g., rules that conclude "bacterial meningitis"). From this analysis, we fill in the structure of data and the hypothesis space (e.g., we find out about different kinds of compromised hosts) and acquire a support story for each rule (why it is believed to be correct).* By asking "when would you think about requesting this datum," we are able to cross check our strategic concepts and rules.

In summary, the methodology used to develop NEOMYCIN was task-oriented, namely to acquire the knowledge to place MYCIN's rules in order so they were more useful for teaching. We originally intended to simply "clean up" the rules, but decided that a more radical change in MYCIN's control structure was called for (use predominantly forward-directed reasoning instead of backward chaining).

To implement the expert's strategy, we had to translate his task statements ("establish the etiology") into more procedural terms ("establish a grouping of possibilities by confirming a path upwards in the hierarchy"). The idea that the initial problem formulation takes the expert into the middle of an etiological hierarchy was not stated by the expert. In fact, the concept of "initial problem formulation" came from previous work in problem solving.†

The general methodology that we are following is summarized by this next list. (NEOMYCIN development is now iterating in Steps 4 to 6):

1. Formulate design guidelines (This is the task orientation: What should the system do? Who will use it? This conception may change over time.)
2. Model system on paper (hand simulations) (Steps 4–6) (This may take several months or more than a year, including the experiments described in this section.)
3. Code/modify program (including simplifications for elegance)
4. Experiment with program
   ■ observe behavior on test cases

---

* We discovered that some rules were redundant or simply encoded incorrectly; some problem situations were not considered; some rules were "folklore" and not worth teaching.

† Significantly, the expert did tell students "you have to search the tree of possibilities," so he knew something about how he organized his knowledge.

5. Analyze program behavior (to determine shortcomings)
- determine appropriateness (expert perspective)
- assign credit and blame to code sections, determining if there is a programming error or shortcoming in the general theory or domain specific knowledge

6. Theorize/reformulate model (to eliminate shortcomings)
- restate theory principles and/or collect domain knowledge through reading and dialogue with expert
- use, modify, and develop programming technology

7. Go to Step 3.

Testing NEOMYCIN will cover both its performance (comparing it to MYCIN) and use for teaching (incorporating it in GUIDON Version 2): We expect that our experience with students using GUIDON2 will enable us to refine the expert model and to construct, perhaps as a variation of NEOMYCIN, a preliminary model of novice diagnostic thinking.

Methodological Pitfalls

In the course of developing a program like NEOMYCIN, it is possible to lose the way temporarily. The pitfalls of an AI orientation to Cognitive Science include the problems of introspection, non-empiricism, and over-formalization.

Introspection and Representation

In order to understand what the expert was teaching us, we drew diagrams of the hierarchies of data, hypotheses, and rule generalizations. Then, in trying to understand the expert's strategies, we found ourselves remembering these diagrams, so we were unable to separate our interpretation of the expert's behavior from our evolving representation of his knowledge. In particular, we came to realize that the structures we had drawn could account for the expert's reasoning in multiple ways, and we had been mistaken to think that we were capturing structures that were isomorphic to something that was "in his brain."

Some examples of this phenomenon might be useful. When the expert learns that the patient has a fever, he frequently will ask for details (severity, periodicity, etc.). This is modeled in NEOMYCIN as "process" questions that are directly associated with the concept of "fever." Yet, one could also say that the expert is thinking about a particular cause of fever, so asks about severity, for example, to see if the fever confirms his guess. This is in fact how Ann D. Rubin (Rubin, 1975) interpreted this kind of question, and it is consistent with her general model of hypothesis formation. However, we found no reason to postulate the intermediate steps of reasoning (setting up a hypothesis), even though the follow-up question is relevant because it is potentially useful.

The point is that in interpreting expert behavior we can easily crank through the reasoning processes and knowledge structures we have already formalized, producing system performance that matches the expert's but which does not simulate his reasoning steps (associations). The cause of this problem is that people's associations can be ad hoc, made efficient through rote, and are not restricted to the principled structures of subtype, causality, process, and so on that we postulate in a system like NEOMYCIN. This is the idea that knowledge can be "procedurally attached" and doesn't need to be stepped through in declarative form (Winograd, 1975). (Anderson's program for modeling learning is based on proceduralization of this form [Anderson, Greeno, Kline, & Neves, 1980].)

In NEOMYCIN, we have attempted to capture the "compiled associations" of the expert, while labeling them to record their principled basis. Thus "acute and chronic," process terms, are placed in what should be a strictly causal network (the etiological taxonomy, Fig. 9.9). Similarly, the expert doesn't always clearly distinguish between the concepts of "subtype" and "cause," so a principled representation that does make this distinction must be interpreted by procedures that blur the difference.

Our investigation indicates that people form associations on any useful basis, and it is not trivial to find principled theories for the basis of these associations. For example, Pople is trying to account for how classificational and causal knowledge are combined. Pople's concept of "bridge concepts" provides a first order theory of how "trigger associations" evolve by combining the two kinds of associations through a form of transitive closure (Pople, 1982). However, this model predicts far more trigger associations than expert behavior demonstrates. We will need to refine this theory by appealing to notions of complexity and usefulness of triggers.

Similarly, we can find "proceduralized associations" which have been learned by rote instead of the kind of composition that Anderson's model describes. For example, an expert considering fungal meningitis tends to ask about travel first; considering virus, he asks about absenteeism in the schools (for a child); considering TB he asks about crowded conditions and previous illnesses. We can explain these questions in terms of the principle "try to confirm the enabling step of a causal process first." Thus, in infectious disease diagnosis one first tries to establish exposure to the causative agent. But this is a rationalization, for neither we nor the expert learned what questions to ask in this way.

In conclusion, one pitfall of modeling using the AI-oriented approach we describe is the tendency to be satisfied with a consistent, coherent model (a knowledge representation and model of reasoning for diagnosis, learning, explanation, etc.) that produces the same behavior as the expert. Because we can learn by rote and we are able to compose factual knowledge with procedure, an expert's associations may be more complex, and not fit the formal elegance of the program. But relying only on introspection, and introspectively observing that we can reach the same results as the expert by reasoning like the program, we can be misled into thinking we have modeled his reasoning. More precise experimentation is necessary if we hanker after psychological validity.

Empiricism and Technology

In developing the first version of GUIDON, we were dangerously close to saying that because we could relate a student's partial solutions to MYCIN's rules, we had an explanation of his reasoning—as if just because a model could be constructed by a program, it was accurate. Similarly, it is easy to suppose that when a program is able to parse a user's English sentence (as in MYCIN's question/ answer module), it has determined what the user is trying to say. One never considers that the next question could be a restatement or request for clarification—it is just the "next input." In a variant of the introspective pitfall, the programmer is now thinking like his model of the machine. Rather than thinking in terms of what he can do with his representation (what is suggested by the technology), the AI-oriented cognitive scientist must be oriented to the phenomenon he is trying to emulate. Simulating the program in the problem-solving environment is a valuable approach.

The technological pitfall is exacerbated by those who never get their program working, so they don't get the hard shock of empirical test. In short, a program isn't a "functional model" (Pylyshyn, 1978) if it isn't functional.

Validity and Elegance

As in the hard sciences and mathematics, it is important that a computational model be formally simple and elegant. However, programming provides special opportunities for reframing and reorganization that add nothing to the theory being programmed, and tend to even obscure its implementation. On the other hand, a theory sometimes profits from reorganization of the code that implements it, in the same way a physicist can find formal clarity by manipulating his equations, looking for symmetry and the like.

One measure of improvement is the perspicuity of the code. If the new rules or frames make it easier for a colleague to understand the theory (to see the theory in the code), the representation (and accompanying interpretation) has probably been improved. For example, a programmer may rerepresent a single rule with multiple steps in its action as a set of ordered rules with identical premises, producing what he takes to be a more elegant representation with only single steps in each rule. But this obscures the simple idea of a procedure being a block of steps. More effort is required to interpret the code to see the procedure within it, just as the problem solver would need to exert more effort to carry out the procedure. Requiring a rule for each step of the procedure therefore violates our understanding of the theory we are implementing, so we say that the representation is not improved.

Areas for Collaboration

We now list some research problems that have been suggested by our work. In doing this, we have two purposes: first, to demonstrate that a computational model like NEOMYCIN can suggest new areas for psychological research; and second, to encourage non-AI cognitive scientists to contribute methodological assistance for attacking these problems. The list of research problems follows:

1. *The structure of working memory.* Is the differential a simple list? A hierarchy? Does it include a stack of goals? For example, when refining a hypothesis, moving down a hierarchy, how is each child visited in turn? By a strategy that iteratively focuses on siblings, as in NEOMYCIN, or by a separate, "saved" list of waiting hypotheses to consider?

2. *Identifying lines of reasoning.* The expert stated a rule generalization (Fig. 9.9) that might be used in multiple ways. One could think in terms of "differential broadening factors," leading to consideration of "compromised host risk factors" (data orientation). Or one could think in terms of "unusual causes," leading to consideration of "gram-negative organisms" (hypothesis orientation). Is it possible to say that the expert is following one line of reasoning and not the other? Could he in some sense be doing one thing that combines the goal and method, namely "trying to broaden the differential by considering compromised host risk factors"? Is it possible to get at the expert's line of reasoning without being misled by his rationalization? Or is it wrong to say that there is some explicit, conscious line of reasoning that we can discover?

3. *The effect of problem context.* Our expert supplied details to make the cases presented to him seem more realistic ("I'm at the patient's bedside" or "I'm in the emergency room and this patient comes up to me, accompanied by her mother"). Presenting a case twice, separated by many months, we saw that this story can change the expert's approach, even leading him to explore completely different hypotheses. How does the expert's imagination of the situation affect his reasoning? What variables must be specified to control for this effect?

4. *Clustering of hypotheses for manageability.* One diagnostic task is to refine a category by considering what causes it. Thus, the physician considers the types of chronic meningitis. However, a physician does not run through the several dozen organisms that might be causing bacterial meningitis. He thinks in terms of common and unusual causes to make the set more manageable. What happens when there are too many common causes to entertain? What other kinds of groupings are useful?

5. *Experimentally verifying diagnostic strategy.* How can we test NEOMYCIN's diagnostic strategy? For example, how do we confirm that focusing on a hypothesis and asking a question to confirm it are best described as two separate decisions, made independently? Or that an expert requests details before following-up on the implications of data (process-oriented questions before making associations with hypotheses)? How can we test the control structure of strategies: a pure production system at the task level, tasks arranged hierarchically, and inherited "abort conditions"?

6. *Explanatory theory of strategy.* Can we construct a principled, explanatory theory that could in some sense generate the diagnostic meta-strategy? Viewing the processor ideas as constraints—a differential (working memory), focused activation, hierarchical problem space and problem features, trigger associations, and strategic control—how do we derive a diagnostic procedure? For example, "reviewing the differential" is not motivated by computational needs, but is a reflection of human forgetting. Rather than viewing this as a "forced imperfection" in the system, the review process (and indeed, the structure of the differential) might follow from a deeper model for retrieval of disease knowledge, along the lines of Lehnert's model of question answering (Lehnert, 1984).

7. *Modeling belief.* What makes an expert believe that a hypothesis is confirmed or unlikely? Are there general principles for dealing with missing data, for knowing when to drop a losing line of inquiry, or to return to a previously discarded hypothesis?

8. *Shifts of attention and noticing subproblems.* When the problem solver gets more data, he may be receiving information that supports a hypothesis he is not currently considering. What determines whether he does/can shift attention temporarily? The NEOMYCIN model allows for focused associations to other hypotheses, but does not allow for "filing a reminder" to take something up later or noticing that a hypothesis is ruled out, so it is not considered later. What does the problem solver notice about other parts of the problem as he moves along and what kinds of notes does/can he make to himself to affect his performance later? What kinds of errors might shifts of attention cause? How does the problem solver avoid retracing his steps? If the current differential is poorly grouped, circumstantial evidence might support widely different hypotheses. Might this ambiguity be a likely point of error, in which one of the interpretations is missed? Are there meta-cognitive strategies for checking these errors?

9. *Effect of level of abstraction on problem formulation.* In discussing the same case separated by the period of months, the expert stated his initial differential (guess) differently. In one case he said "mass lesion." In the other case he broke this down into subtypes. Very clearly, stating the subtypes brought other associations to mind, leading to a quite different explo-

ration (using the same strategies). How can we account for this choice in level of abstraction? There is a clear trade-off, for the expert forgot to consider a traumatic problem when he was so busy reciting and considering the subtypes of mass lesion. What reasoning strategies do people use to maintain a manageable level of abstraction in working memory? What errors occur?

10. *Observation strategies.* We need to deal with the richness of the data collection procedure: partial stories are corrected later, making backtracking necessary; data must be verified; questions must be asked so they are understandable to the layman; therapeutic benefit, urgency, and availability of medical equipment must be factored in. Expertise surely requires a good deal of common sense. Just how the two are cross-related and build upon one another are difficult questions.

The Prospects for Collaboration

In carrying out the NEOMYCIN research, we have not had as many collaborative discussions as might have been useful. Few computer science graduate students, the most likely collaborators, have the necessary LISP programming experience, a background in AI techniques, a willingness to learn medical technology, and an inclination to do psychological research. Therefore, the most immediate methodological problem we face is superficial: a lack of trained people to share in the research. But what kind of collaboration is possible? Should we think of cognitive scientists as hybrids, or as specialists sharing in a common project?

Looking at the fields of cognitive psychology and AI today we find a wide spectrum of interests and methods, particularly along the dimensions of experimentation and programming. In cognitive psychology, we find, for example, Bower at one end, doing traditional psychology experiments and no programming, but making some use of AI concepts (Bower, 1981). In the middle, we find someone like Feltovich, doing traditional experiments, but whose analyses and questions tend to be based in information-processing terminology. At the other end, John Anderson is experimenting and writing programs, to the extent that people in computer science might think of him as being in AI.

In AI we find the same kind of spectrum. On the one hand, we find researchers with a psychological bent whose main goal is to build a working program, but who periodically say "It would be interesting to find out if people work this way" (e.g., Fahlman, 1980; Friedland, 1979). This group includes the "knowledge engineers" (Feigenbaum, 1977): who have practical objectives; have fears about "listening to experts too closely" ("experts can't really explain how they reason"); and avoid the "paper modeling" of the psychologists. They want to build useful tools, therefore they are concerned with difficult, realistic problems (and never toy blocks). They want programs to be better than people, involving formalization of computational methods that perhaps people don't and can't use. Experimentation, to determine "what anybody's grandmother could have said" (as Gordon Bower puts it), is unnecessary. Talk to an expert and incorporate his heuristics. Test the program by asking the expert to point out shortcomings.

Finally, we find AI researchers using the behavioral studies of the cognitive psychologists to build a complex system for doing some real task (e.g., NEO-MYCIN, Lehnert, 1980). These researchers are output-oriented like the first group, but their task involves human interaction in such a way that the program's reasoning should model human performance. This group also includes researchers who believe that the performance of AI programs can be enhanced if we better understand how people solve problems. When they listen to an expert, they are oriented to understanding how he is reasoning, not simply filling in their representation of slots, rules, and so on. Potentially, this group could include any researcher in AI; work in learning, natural language understanding, and intelligent tutoring systems seems especially likely to benefit from cognitive studies.

In considering collaboration between AI and other fields in cognitive science, we should consider that people differ along these dimensions of interest and methodology. It is not at all clear that only people doing both experimentation and programming should be called cognitive scientists. It seems more likely that cognitive science will be made of people using interdisciplinary analogies and sharing research results.

The easiest form of collaboration is by evolution of common interests. We may not talk to each other directly very often, but we will communicate in the literature, translating ideas to our own application. For example, this is the way in which GUIDON research benefits from the work of Tversky concerning biases in human judgment (Tversky & Kahneman, 1977).

A second possibility is "mission-based" collaboration, in which we work together on a single project, sharing tasks according to our expertise. We might work in parallel—we might work with someone to precisely define a problem and months later he would return with experimental results.

It is important to remember the dialectic power of a program. The strength of cognitive science is surely in the way theories are changed and suggested by the very process of building computational models. Besides worrying that perhaps not enough formal experimentation is being done, we should be concerned that not enough cognitive scientists are writing programs, or helping to write programs. Too often experimental analysis seems to fall short by not being precise enough to be programmable. Or the simplifications to make an experiment tenable eliminate the very points that we need to build a working system (as fixed-order experiments in medical diagnosis eliminate focusing and data selection strategies).

Within the GUIDON/NEOMYCIN project, the experimentation that we do in the future, outside of continuing to interview experts, will consist of having students use GUIDON2. In many respects, these trials will resemble the experiments carried on by Feltovich, and others. (As his experiments have prepared us for the kinds of diagnostic errors students make.) Our theory of knowledge representation and strategies, and our lower-level concepts of the working memory and control structure will evolve as we change the program to meet the needs of the task. It is an open question just how detailed an "explanatory theory" is needed to build a reasonably effective intelligent tutoring system. In our collective work on diagnostic tasks, "bugs" and epistemology, we are already going beyond what the average teacher knows about reasoning. As the knowledge engineers, we reach for computational methods that surpass human expertise. However, in building an intelligent tutoring system, it is not sufficient to seek improvements in formal efficiency and elegance alone; we must also ask why people fail.

Acknowledgments

The members of this project at the time of this writing (1981) include the author, Research Associate in Computer Science at Stanford University; Bruce Buchanan, Adjunct Professor of Computer Science; two Research Assistants, Reed Letsinger (MS candidate in AI program) and Bob London (PhD candidate in the Department of Education); and Dr. Timothy Beckett, Research Fellow at Stanford University Medical Center. Funding has been provided in part by ARPA and ONR Contract N00014-79C-0302. Computing resources are provided by the SUMEX-AIM facility (NIH Grant RR00785).

Glossary

An attempt is made here to generalize terminology beyond the medical application, though the reader should realize that some definitions are peculiar to our research project and others have a slightly different meaning in other areas of AI.

causal rules: productions of the form, "if A then B" with the interpretation that "A is caused by B."

compiled association: composition of a chain of productions into a single production, e.g., "if A then B" and "if B & C then D" might be compiled to "if A & C then D."

compromised host: in medicine, a patient in a weakened condition that increases susceptibility to disease.

data: facts about a problem in the form of direct measurements or circumstantial evidence.

differential: a list of hypotheses that the problem solver is considering as possible solutions to the diagnostic problem.

diagnostic problem: a situation, entity, or event that the problem solver attempts to explain (characterize its nature) by observing its appearance and behavior over time.

disease: in general, some underlying condition or process in a system that has an undesirable effect on the system.

disease process knowledge: descriptive facts about diseases that have been previously observed in a system along the lines of how the disease is caused and how it affects the system over time.

domain-dependent knowledge: with respect to a given kind of diagnostic problem (e.g., electronic troubleshooting) and a given problem being diagnosed (e.g., a Zenith computer terminal), those facts about the design of the system and its functionality, as well as of scientific theories pertaining to its operation, that are useful for explaining how the system operates.

domain-independent knowledge: facts and reasoning procedures brought to bear in problem solving that are not domain-dependent.

etiological taxonomy: a hierarchy of diseases or possible causes of a diagnostic problem, in which the leaf nodes of the hierarchy are well-defined specific causes and intervening nodes are abstract categories of diseases.

expert: a problem solver with sufficient knowledge to make correct diagnoses a high percentage of the time and to know when a problem cannot be confidently solved using the knowledge available to him.

expert system: an AI computer program that is designed to solve problems at the expert level in some scientific, mathematical, or medical domain.

forward-directed inferences: associations between data and hypotheses that are made by the problem solver at the time new data comes to his attention.

group and differentiate: a diagnostic strategy that attempts to compact the differential so the hypotheses under consideration fall under a single node in the etiological taxonomy, generally by ruling out alternatives through discriminating data collection.

hypothesis: a disease or more general causal category that the problem solver is considering as a solution of the diagnostic problem.

intelligent tutoring system: an expert system whose domain of expertise is teaching, containing an expert system within it relevant to the area the tutoring system is teaching about.

interpreter: a program that generally follows a simple control policy for applying knowledge to the problem at hand. The interpreter for disease knowledge determines how new problem data leads to inferences being made to augment working memory. The interpreter for strategical knowledge determines how planning knowledge is used for collecting new data or changing the phase of problem solving.

knowledge base: domain-dependent knowledge represented in various AI formalisms.

knowledge engineering: the art of building expert systems by working with experts to codify their knowledge.

meta-strategy: a hierarchy of general tasks related by meta-rules, by which a problem solver directs his attention during diagnosis.

problem formulation: the task of characterizing a diagnostic problem so that the correct etiological category is brought into the differential.

procedurally embedded: knowledge that is implicit in the design of a program; for example, the rationale for ordering a sequence of steps in a particular way. A procedure is represented *declaratively* if the knowledge behind its design is explicitly represented in the system so that an interpreter can be applied to the design and domain knowledge to execute the procedure.

production rule: an association of the form, "if A then B," whose interpretation is such that when A is considered, believed, or accomplished by the problem solver, it is valid (according to some unspecified justification) to consider, believe, or achieve B.

screening relation: an association between data of the form, "A screens (for) B," with the interpretation that A should be considered before B with the justification that B might be derived from knowledge of A. For example, the sex of a patient screens for whether or not the patient is pregnant.

structural knowledge: any organizational constructs based on domain-independent relations ("sibling of," "location," "process question follow-up," "screening question"), used by a meta-strategy to index domain-dependent knowledge.

subgoal: in MYCIN, a reasoning step that appears as a clause in the premise of some production rule; for example in the rule "if A & B then C," A and B are subgoals.

subtype: a relation between disease categories, synonymous with "kind of."

top-down refinement: the diagnostic strategy of searching the etiological taxonomy in breadth-first manner starting at some node of the tree; called "refinement" because each level of the tree specifies a finer or more precise diagnosis.

triggers: production rules of the form, "if A then B" where A is a conjunction mentioning problem data which are said to "trigger" or "suggest directly" the hypothesis B, that appears in the etiological taxonomy.

References

Anderson, J. R., Greeno, J. G., Kline, P. J., & Neves, D. M. (1981). Acquisition of problem-solving skills. In J. R. Anderson (Ed.), *Cognitive skills and their acquisition*. Hillsdale, NJ: Lawrence Erlbaum Associates.

Boden, M. A. (1977). *Artificial intelligence and natural man*. New York: Basic Books.

Bower, G. H. (1981). Mood and memory. *American Psychologist, 36,* 129–148.

Brown, J. S., Burton, R. R., & Bell, A. G. (1974). *Sophie: A sophisticated instructional environment for teaching electronic troubleshooting*. BBN Report No. 2790.

Brown, J. S., & Burton, R. R. (1978). Diagnostic models for procedural bugs in basic mathematical skills. *Cognitive Science, 2,* 155–192.

Burton, R. R., & Brown, J. S. (1979). An investigation of computer coaching for informal learning activities. *International Journal of Man-Machine Studies, 11,* 5–24.

Clancey, W. J. (1979a, August). *Transfer of rule-based expertise through a tutorial dialogue*. Computer Science Doctoral Dissertation, Stanford University, STAN-CS-769.

Clancey, W. J. (1979b). Tutoring rules for guiding a case method dialogue. *International Journal of Man-Machine Studies, 11,* 25–49.

Clancey, W. J., & Letsinger, R. (1981). NEOMYCIN: Reconfiguring a rule-based expert system for application to teaching. *Proceedings of the Seventh IJCAI.*

Clancey, W. J. (1983). The epistemology of a rule-based expert system. *Journal of Artificial Intelligence, 20*(3), 215–251.

Collins, A. (1976). Processes in acquiring knowledge. In R. C. Anderson, R. J. Spiro, & W. E. Montague (Eds.), *Schooling and the acquisition of knowledge*. Hillsdale, NJ: Lawrence Erlbaum Associates.

Davis, R. (1976, July). Applications of meta-level knowledge to the construction, maintenance, and use of large knowledge bases. STAN-CS-76-552, HPP-76-7, Stanford University.

Davis, R. (1979). Interactive transfer of expertise: Acquisition of new inference rules. *Journal of Artificial Intelligence, 12,* 121–157.

Elstein, A. S., Shulman, L. S., & Sprafka, S. A. (1978). *Medical problem-solving: An analysis of clinical reasoning*. Cambridge, MA: Harvard University Press.

Fahlman, S. E. (1980, August). Design sketch for a million-element NETL machine. *Proceedings of the First Annual National Conference on Artificial Intelligence,* Stanford, CA.

Feigenbaum, E. A. (1977, August). The art of artificial intelligence: I. Themes and case studies of knowledge engineering. *Proceedings of the Fifth IJCAI,* Cambridge, MA: MIT.

Feltovich, P. J., Johnson, P. E., Moller, J. H., & Swanson, D. B. (1980, April). *The role and development of medical knowledge in diagnostic expertise*. Presented at the Annual meeting of the American Educational Research Association, San Francisco.

Friedland, P. (1979, August). Knowledge-based experiment design in molecular genetics. *Proceedings of the Sixth IJCAI,* Tokyo.

Kosslyn, S. M. (1980). *Image and mind.* Cambridge, MA: Harvard University Press.

Lehnert, W. (1980). Narrative text summarization. *Proceedings of the First Annual National Conference on Artificial Intelligence,* Stanford, CA.

Lehnert, W. G. (1984). Paradigmatic issues in cognitive science. In W. Kintsch, J. R. Miller, & P. G. Polson (Eds.), *Methods and tactics in cognitive science.* Hillsdale, NJ: Lawrence Erlbaum Associates.

McDermott, J. (1980, April). *R1: A rule-based configurer of computer systems.* Department of Computer Science, Carnegie-Mellon University, CMU-CS-80-119.

Miller, J. R., Polson, P. G., & Kintsch, W. (1984). Problems of methodology in cognitive science. In W. Kintsch, J. R. Miller, & P. G. Polson (Eds.), *Methods and tactics in cognitive science.* Hillsdale, NJ: Lawrence Erlbaum Associates.

Miller, P. B. (1975, September). *Strategy selection in medical diagnosis.* Project MAC, Massachusetts Institute of Technology, MAC TR-153.

Nii, H. P., & Feigenbaum, E. A. (1978). Rule-based understanding of signals. In D. A. Waterman & F. Hayes-Roth (Eds.), *Pattern-directed inference systems,* New York: Academic Press.

Pauker, S. G., & Szolovits, P. (1977) Analyzing and simulating taking the history of the present illness: Context Formation. In Schneider/Segvall Hein (Eds.), *Computational linguistics in medicine.* North-Holland Publishing Company.

Pople, H. E. (1982). Heuristic methods for imposing structure on ill-structured problems: The structuring of medical diagnostics. In P. Szolovits (Ed.), *Artificial intelligence in medicine.* Boulder, CO: Westview Press.

Pylyshyn, Z. W. (1978). Computational models and empirical constraints. *The Behavioral and Brain Sciences, 1,* 93–127.

Rubin, A. D. (1975, January). Hypothesis formation and evaluation in medical diagnosis. Artificial Intelligence Laboratory, MIT, Technical Report A1-TR-316.

Scott, A. C., Clancey, W. J., Davis, R., & Shortliffe, E. H. (1977). Explanation capabilities of production-based consultation systems. *American Journal of Computational Linguistics.* Microfiche 62.

Shortliffe, E. H. (1976). *Computer-based medical consultations: MYCIN.* New York: Elsevier.

Sleeman, D., & Brown, J. S. (1981). *Intelligent tutoring systems.* London: Academic Press.

Stevens, A. L., Collins, A., & Goldin, S. (1978). *Diagnosing student's misconceptions in causal models.* BBN Report No. 3786.

Swanson, D. B., Feltovich, P. J., & Johnson, P. E. (1977). Psychological analysis of physician expertise: Implications for design of decision support systems. MEDINFO77, 161–164.

Tversky, A., & Kahneman, D. (1977). Judgment under uncertainty: Heuristics and biases. In P. N. Johnson-Laird & P. C. Wason (Eds.), *Thinking: Readings in cognitive science.* Cambridge University Press.

van Lehn, K., Brown, J. S., & Greeno, J. (1984). Competitive argumentation in computational theories of cognition. In W. Kintsch, J. R. Miller, & P. G. Polson (Eds.), *Methods and tactics in cognitive science.* Hillsdale, NJ: Lawrence Erlbaum Associates.

van Melle, W. (1980). *A domain-independent production-rule system for consultation programs.* Computer Science Doctoral Dissertation, Stanford University.

Winograd, T. (1975). Frame representations and the declarative/procedural controversy. In D. G. Bobrow & A. Collins (Eds.), *Representation and understanding.* New York: Academic Press.

Yu, V. L., Buchanan, B. G., Shortliffe, E. H., Wraith, S. M., Davis, R., Scott, A. C., & Cohen, S. N. (1979). Evaluating the performance of a computer-based consultant. *Computer Programs in Bio-medicine, 9,* 95–102.

Yu, V. L., Fagan, L. M., Wraith, S. M., Clancey, W. J., Scott, A. C., Hannigan, J. F., Blum, R. L., Buchanan, B. G., & Cohen, S. N. (1979). Antimicrobial selection by a computer —A blinded evaluation by infectious disease experts. *Journal of the American Medical Association, 242,* 1279–1282.

10/ Theoretical Frontiers in Building a Machine Tutor

BEVERLY P. WOOLF

Introduction

We are on the frontier of developing substantially more powerful intelligent tutoring systems. By more powerful systems, we mean systems that reason about a student's knowledge, monitor a student's solutions, and custom-tailor their teaching strategy to a student's individual learning pattern. We also mean systems that enable a student to simulate "worlds" (e.g., the ocean, atmosphere, power plants, ecosystems, etc.) in a visually rich and informationally dense way that is not currently possible. Natural language interfaces that will enable a student who has little or no knowledge of programming to communicate freely to such a system will make these tutors educationally and visually intriguing to any student.

Obviously, we are not yet capable of building these systems; formidable barriers, both hardware and software, stand between us and full realization of the potential. However, many of these barriers involve theory rather than engineering; that is, they depend on providing new abilities or new results to the computer. In this chapter we discuss some theoretical barriers in knowledge that fall under the general rubric of "knowledge engineering," that is, analyzing the knowledge of a domain, of discourse, or of the student's knowledge, and transmitting that knowledge to a machine.

The very fact that knowledge representation issues remain as barriers to successful development of intelligent tutors underscores the difference between intelligent teaching systems and traditional computer-aided instruction (CAI). The objective of an intelligent tutor is to enable a machine to understand both the concept to be taught and how the student can learn that concept. Intelligent tutors differ from pre-AI systems in that they distinguish among the components

---

This work was supported in part by the Air Force Systems Command, Rome Air Development Center, Griffiss AFB, New York 13441 and the Air Force Office of Scientific Research, Bowling AFB, D.C. 20332 under contract no. F30602-85-C-0008. This grant supports the Northeast Artificial Intelligence Consortium (NAIC).

of the teaching process itself, separating knowledge of the student (Miller, 1979) from knowledge of the domain (Brown & Bell, 1977; Stevens, Collins, & Goldin, 1978) and both these kinds of knowledge from strategies about how and what to teach (Clancey, 1982; Woolf & McDonald, 1984). Given this wealth of knowledge, often coded in the form of hundreds of "if-then" rules, such systems can perform fine-grained reasoning about a student and his progress.

Building an intelligent tutor requires that we analyze and codify the tacit knowledge of the domain and of teaching in that domain. Dozens of major intelligent tutoring projects have been completed in the past decade (see Sleeman & Brown, 1982). While most have been research projects and not used extensively in classrooms, their goal has distinguished them from conventional CAI programs—they reason about the student, the domain, the tutoring discourse, or all three. By virtue of student models (Bonar & Soloway, 1985; Johnson & Soloway, 1984) and diagnostic routines (Miller, 1979), intelligent tutoring programs have represented what the student does and does not know about the subject matter and have provided guidance in the form of a coach or tutor while keeping the student in control of the interaction.

In this chapter, we identify several knowledge theoretic issues that are central to the representation of knowledge in an intelligent tutor, including:

1. domain—concepts and processes of the domain;
2. teaching—teaching strategies for the domain;
3. discourse—discourse conventions implicit in tutoring; and
4. authoring—interface for teachers to input knowledge into the teaching system.

We also discuss how to scale up existent intelligent tutoring technology to practical levels so we can bring tutoring systems into the real world.

Though we focus on knowledge engineering issues, other issues, such as development of hardware and multi-media facility, obviously require research and development. Artificial intelligence (AI) based workstations with memories equal to a few thousand contemporary IBM AT's and available below a thousand dollars, along with high-resolution graphics, mouse sensitivity, sound, and videodisc are a few of the hardware advances that we expect will be available within five years to complement the research into knowledge representation described in this chapter.

Knowledge of the Domain

Historically, the first knowledge frontier to be conquered in the development of intelligent tutors was knowledge of the domain. Knowledge of the topics in a domain had to be analyzed and represented in early tutors in order to translate the student's input into a usable form to be evaluated against the expert's knowledge. In some cases, domain knowledge provided problems to solve or topics to discuss (Brown & Bell, 1977; Clancey, 1982). Earlier tutoring systems could not solve the problem presented to the student, though they could often recognize an incorrect solution. When domain knowledge began to be analyzed and intelligent reasoning included, the tutors began to respond to a broader range of input and, in some cases, to understand the nontraditional student (i.e., the student who has the correct answer but expresses it in a fundamentally different way). Intelligent reasoning in this module enhanced the system's ability to express its own knowledge, for example, and enabled it to explain its reasoning in problem solving.

However, the more powerful tutoring systems contained more sophisticated knowledge of the domain (see, for example, Woolf et al., 1986). In particular, lists of concepts and rules, such as found in textbooks, were not sufficient. Domain knowledge required an investigation into an expert's understanding of the laws of the domain broken into at least four kinds of knowledge: declarative (data), procedural (rules and processes by which the data is used), heuristics (rules of thumb that guide use of the rules), and simulation (rules needed to graphically implement the data and rules). In this section, we explain how such knowledge can be represented in a computer tutor.

An intelligent tutoring system must solve the problem it presents to the student. To do so, it must identify the *tacit* knowledge needed to learn or teach the problem. As an example of such knowledge, we describe a tutor being developed to help a student study the crane boom (see Fig. 10.1).* The tutor will present the student with a variety of activities, shown schematically in Fig. 10.2, from which either the student or the system can select the next interaction. The structure of the system is represented in Fig. 10.3; the modules labeled *Pedagogical Approach* and *Decider* contain rules to enable the system to reason about the pedagogical strategy used with the student. This reasoning is described in the section "Knowledge of Teaching," later in this chapter. Activities are presented to students to allow them to build up their own intuitions about the problem and to test hypotheses. Examples of these activities include canned problems, interactive simulations, and an erector set for designing their own problems. Each activity uses sophisticated interactive graphics and a frame-based language to enable the system to reason about its graphic interface.

For instance, if students select the erector set activity they are provided with elements from which they can build a crane boom problem (see Fig. 10.4). Knowledge built into the graphics will enable the elements to be simulated to "work" or "fail" according to the laws of physics. The goal is to aid students in developing their own problem-solving skills and to help them acquire intuitions about designing systems that will work.

In another activity, the tutor will present examples to the student in increasing complexity (see Fig. 10.5) and will intentionally select problems that illus-

---

* The crane boom tutor is one of several statics and dynamics physics tutors being developed as a part of the Exploring System Earth Consortium, which includes San Francisco State University, the University of Hawaii, the University of Wisconsin, and the University of Massachusetts.

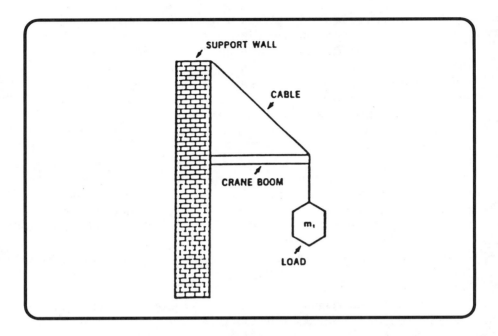

Figure 10.1 A Typical Crane Boom Setup. A typical crane boom setup
includes a beam (the boom) attached to a wall or center post
and supported at the other end by a cable also attached to the
same wall or post. The load on the crane system is usually hung
from the end of the boom. The boom end attached to the wall
must be supported vertically as well as horizontally. The support
force of the wall on the boom is typically unknown and the
unknown horizontal and vertical components are to be found
by the student.

trate similarities among related phenomena. Students will be tested to predict
their ability to transfer knowledge about a prototypical situation to similar situations; ultimately they will be questioned about anomalous examples. Advanced
students could be given problems that asked for parametric relationships between components of the crane or they could draw graphs of the relationships
on the screen or insert measuring devices that dynamically show such parameters as tension, relative velocities, or location of a center of mass as a function
of changing density. The student could also work on less structured design
problems where there might be many possible solutions. The program might
not be able to tell if a particular solution is the "best," but it should be able to
say if the student's solution is valid.

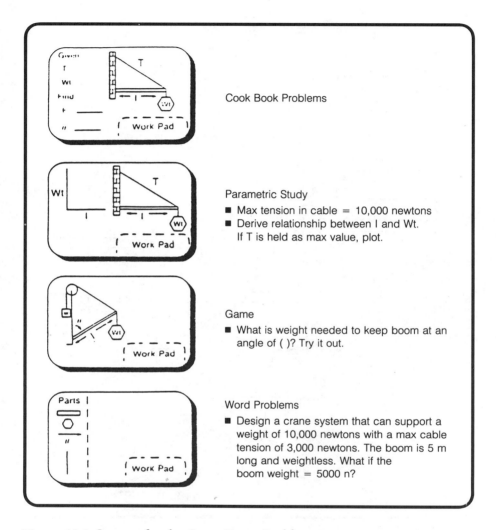

Cook Book Problems

Parametric Study
- Max tension in cable = 10,000 newtons
- Derive relationship between I and Wt.
  If T is held as max value, plot.

Game
- What is weight needed to keep boom at an
  angle of ( )? Try it out.

Word Problems
- Design a crane system that can support a
  weight of 10,000 newtons with a max cable
  tension of 3,000 newtons. The boom is 5 m
  long and weightless. What if the
  boom weight = 5000 n?

Figure 10.2 Screens for the Crane Boom Problem

In order to build such a tutor, we need to represent knowledge of concepts, rules, and learning in the domain. These rules, assumptions, and concepts are described below in terms of the crane boom problem. They are outlined in Fig. 10.6 and must be specified in excruciating detail before the tutor is built. For the physics tutor, we have broken this knowledge into three classifications: declarative, procedural, and heuristic knowledge.

Declarative knowledge includes concepts in the domain and their relation to each other. This knowledge has traditionally provided a tutor with its primary

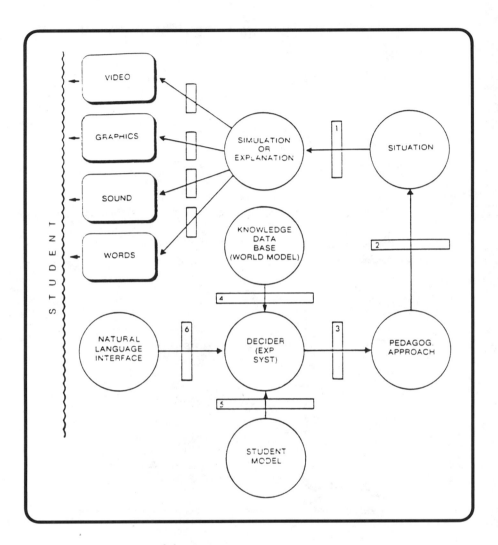

Figure 10.3 Structure of the System

source of knowledge about the domain. Concepts are typically represented by a frame or other data structure that encodes default values within an explicit set of attributes for each concept. The data structure generally expresses information in two ways: it records attributes of a concept and then relates concepts to each other. An example of the concept **negative x-component** of force for the physics tutor is given in a frame notation:

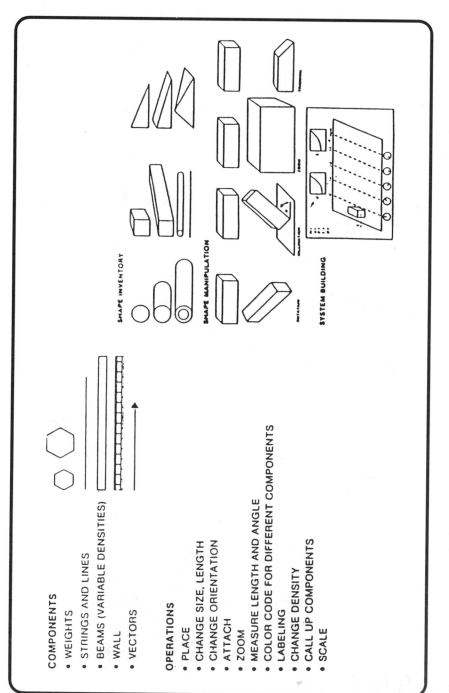

Figure 10.4 Erector Set for the Crane Boom Problem

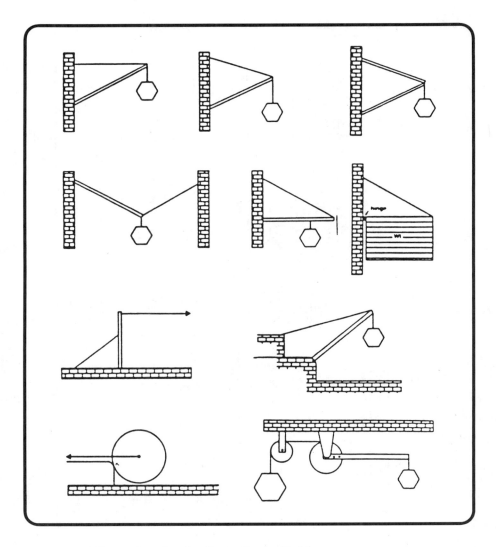

Figure 10.5 Exemplars for the Crane Boom Problem

English: The negative **x**-component of force is a portion of the
                  x-component of force that points to the left.

Physics tutor: (deframe **x-neg-force**
                      (element-of **x-force**)
                      (line-of-action **to-the-left**))

Frames have inheritance and so can relate concepts to each other and can
be defined in terms of other more general concepts. Defining inheritance re-

- **Physical Assumptions and Assertions**
  A. Force of tension in a cable always lies along the direction of the cable, as does the line of action of that force.
  B. Force of tension or compression on a boom with weight does not usually lie along the direction of the boom. This force can be represented by its horizontal and vertical components.
  C. The center of mass of a uniform body is located at the geometric center of the body. Nonuniform bodies require calculus to locate the center of mass.
  D. The weight force vector is always pointed downward.
  E. Etc.

- **Basic Concepts Needed for This Module Segment**
  A. Force
  B. Components of force
  C. Direction and line of action for forces
  D. Mass, weight, density
  E. Tension and compression
  F. Torque and direction of a torque
  G. Moment arms and axis of rotation

- **Typical Problems with Graphic Displays**

  Typical problems could be solved and explained in detail and then manipulated to resemble student-generated problems.

Figure 10.6 Assumptions, Assertions, and Concepts in the Crane Boom Problem

lationship eliminates the need to enter redundant information in the database. For instance, **x-force** can be defined as:

English: The x-component of force is along the **x**-axis and it has a quantitative measurement.

Physics tutor: (deframe **x-force**
                     (element-of **force**)
                     (direction-of **x-axis**)
                     (measurement **nil**))

The attributes of **x-force**, including element-of **force**, direction-of **x-axis**, and measurement **nil**, will be inherited by all frames that represent forces in the **x** direction, such as **x-neg-force** given above. Consequently, when the tutor examines a frame called **x-neg-force** it automatically finds that the direction of the **x-neg-force** is along the **x-axis** since it is an element of **x-force**, which has a direction along the **x-axis**. There is no need to explicitly state this information within the **x-neg-force** frame.

Procedural knowledge includes the reasoning used by the system to solve problems in the domain. This knowledge has traditionally been included in teaching systems that reason about procedural tasks, such as programs for solving arithmetic problems (Brown & Burton, 1978) or for simulating the operations of a steam engine (Forbus & Stevens, 1981). Figure 10.7 gives an important rule for a system in equilibrium. The rule is stated in three ways: in traditional physics notation, in English, and in the tutor's internal frame-based representation. The tutor will represent this rule and all other procedural knowledge through either forward or backward chaining rules.

Heuristic knowledge describes actions taken by an expert to make measurements or to perform transformations in the domain. This knowledge has rarely been included in teaching systems, but will be required if a tutor is to monitor the student's problem-solving activities. Heuristic knowledge defines the operations performed to solve problems in the field and the actions that are a part of an expert's experiential knowledge about how to realize solutions in the domain. This knowledge (illustrated by Fig. 10.8) is distinguished from procedural knowledge, shown in Fig. 10.7, in that it does not describe concepts

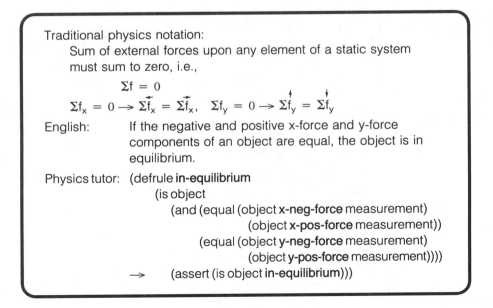

Figure 10.7 caption content:

Traditional physics notation:
Sum of external forces upon any element of a static system must sum to zero, i.e.,

$$\Sigma f = 0$$

$$\Sigma f_x = 0 \rightarrow \Sigma \vec{f_x} = \Sigma \vec{f_x}, \quad \Sigma f_y = 0 \rightarrow \Sigma \vec{f_y} = \Sigma \vec{f_y}$$

English: If the negative and positive x-force and y-force components of an object are equal, the object is in equilibrium.

Physics tutor: (defrule **in-equilibrium**
                (is object
                   (and (equal (object **x-neg-force** measurement)
                               (object **x-pos-force** measurement))
                        (equal (object **y-neg-force** measurement)
                               (object **y-pos-force** measurement))))
            →   (assert (is object **in-equilibrium**)))

Figure 10.7 Procedural Knowledge for the Rule Equilibrium

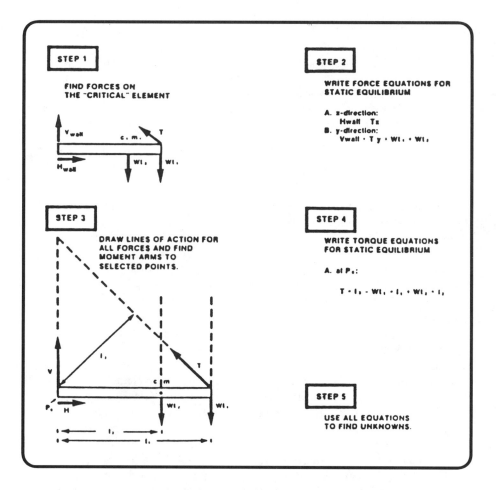

Figure 10.8 Heuristic Knowledge for Solving for Equilibrium

that are part of the domain; rather it adds knowledge of how we solve problems in the domain.

Philosophers of science believe that heuristic knowledge about natural phenomena is best acquired by experience and through working examples illustrating aspects of the phenomenon. Educators and cognitive scientists also have observed that students benefit from numerous hours solving problems. Yet there is nearly a total absence of information about which strategies and heuristics really work, about how a student learns from the doing of homework, or what precisely is being learned from doing homework (see Larkin, 1982, for some innovative studies here).

In his remarkable text *The Structure of Scientific Revolutions,* Kuhn (1970) states:

> A student cannot, it is said, solve problems at all unless he has first learned the theory and some rules for applying it. Scientific knowledge [it is said] is embedded in *theory* and *rules; problems* are supplied to gain facility in their application. I have tried to argue, however, that this localization of the cognitive content of science is wrong. After the student has done many problems, he may gain only added facility by solving more. But at the start and for some time after, *doing problems is learning consequential things about nature.* In the absence of such exemplars, the laws and theories he has previously learned would have little empirical content. [Emphasis added]

We intend to use the computer as a major aid to help students *learn how to learn* from what they do, that is, to learn from the false paths taken while trying to solve the problem. Using a variety of problems, we can explore the space of problem-solving activities chosen by students and compile their path through the available strategies. Identifying heuristic knowledge and recording the tasks used by learners as they solve the problem allows us to study the particulars of rule-of-thumb knowledge a student uses to solve the problem. We intend to derive some of the properties of the cognitive process underlying heuristic knowledge and to elucidate the operations used by both the expert and the student to solve the problem.

Heuristic knowledge will have to be analyzed from procedural knowledge and its rules identified as something distinct from the laws and formulas of the domain. Procedural knowledge describes the operant laws and formulas of nature or science as we know it; heuristic knowledge is derived from specifications of the problem solution, as shown in Fig. 10.8. Because heuristic knowledge is involved with strategies for solving a problem, it must also point to the prerequisite knowledge that a student should have before he can solve the problem. Prerequisite knowledge for learning concepts, procedures, and heuristics, and the way the machine can investigate each, is discussed in the following two sections.

Knowledge of Teaching

The second theoretical frontier to overcome if we are to build sophisticated teaching systems is the representation of knowledge of teaching. In addition to building an expert system to solve a problem such as the crane boom problem, we must develop a system that can *teach* a student how to solve the same problem.* It must monitor the student's actions, advise the student about obvi-

---

* Because teaching a topic is often more difficult than "knowing" the same topic, a teaching system is more complex than an expert system. Therefore, development of tutoring systems will either *precede* or *follow* development of expert systems (see Clancey, preceding chapter), and neither position. relative to an expert system, is enviable.

ous errors, and anticipate future actions based on inferences about the student's current activities. In this interaction the tutor must respond sensitively to the student, must know which activity to suggest (see Fig. 10.2), and know how to monitor the student's answers or questions.

Building knowledge into the *teaching* component of a tutor is critical to development of the tutor. By knowledge of teaching we mean the machine should know how to *ask* the right questions and how to *focus* on the appropriate issue. The system should act as a partner, not as a disinterested, uncommitted, or uncooperative speaker. Effective communication with a student does *not* mean natural language understanding or generation; this has been achieved to some degree in some systems such as WHY (Stevens, Collins, & Goldin, 1978), SOPHIE (Brown & Bell, 1977), and SCHOLAR (Carbonell, 1970). Rather, effective communication requires looking beyond the words that are spoken and determining what the tutor and student *should* be communicating about. This problem becomes acute when the student organizes and talks about knowledge in a way that is different from the way the expert organizes and presents it.

Few systems have been effective in the way that they communicate with the student. GUIDON (Clancey, 1982) is an exception. It can carry on a flexible dialogue with the student based on inferences made about the student's knowledge and can select among alternative dialogues the one which is most appropriate based on the tutor's ability to make inferences about the student's previous interactions and the student's current information. GUIDON can switch its discussion to any topic listed on an AND/OR graph, representing the rules of the expert system, and can respond to a student's hypothesis using a variety of techniques, such as "entrapment," which forces the student to make a choice leading to incorrect conclusions, as a means of revealing some aspect of the student's understanding or misunderstanding.

Teaching Strategies in Meno-tutor

As an example of a system that reasons about the *way* it communicates with the student and the *topics* that it discusses, we describe Meno-tutor (Woolf, 1984; Woolf & McDonald, 1984a, 1984b). Meno-tutor structures its response to the student based on a model of the student's goals, the domain complexity, and the current discourse history. It uses a student model, an annotated domain, and a representation of tutorial planning to custom-tailor its response to the student, both in content and in form.

Figure 10.9 presents two discourses produced by Meno-tutor. The tutor produced the high-level transitions in these two discourses. These discourses and twelve others were used to "reverse engineer" the Meno-tutor. Common transitions and speech patterns in the discourses were used to abstract the structures and knowledge necessary for a machine tutor to have a model of the student that we conjectured the human tutor had and to make the same transi-

Tutor: Do you know what the climate is like in Washington and Oregon?

Student: Is it cold?

Tutor: No, it is rather mild. Can you guess about the rainfall there?

Student: Normal, I guess.

Tutor: Well, the Japan current, which starts in the southeastern Pacific, goes along the coast of Japan and across the North Pacific ending up off the coast of Washington and Oregon. How do you think that current affects the climate there?

Student: It's probably rainy.

Tutor: It is indeed very wet, there are rain forests in both Washington and Oregon. What does that tell you about the temperature of the Japan current?

Student: It's warm.

Tutor: Do you think it rains much in Oregon?

Student: No.

Tutor: Why do you think it doesn't rain much in Oregon?

Student: Because the neighboring states are dry.

Tutor: The neighboring states are dry, but you cannot generalize from that. In fact, it does rain a lot in Oregon. Can you guess what causes the rain there?

Student: Well, there are high mountains in the region and the state borders the Pacific Ocean.

Tutor: Yes. The Pacific borders Oregon. How do you think it is involved in the heavy rainfall there?

Student: Ocean air rises and cools upon reaching the land.

Tutor: That is right.

Figure 10.9 Two Discourses Produced by Meno-tutor

tions. For instance, in the first discourse, the tutoring system "recognized" that the student made two wrong answers and inferred that the student had limited knowledge.* The tutor judged that the question-answer approach, which had been used until then, was ineffective and should be changed and that a new topic, the "Japan Current," should be discussed because it is a dominant influence behind the region's climate. The system decided to supply the additional data in a descriptive rather than an interrogative style, because the student seemed confused and might profit from the addition of supplemental data. This first discourse was generated by Meno-tutor in such a way that all the decisions, topics, and tutoring styles available to the system were not only explicit to the programmers, but were modifiable by them. Modifying these decisions allowed us to generate additional discourses.

The Discourse Management Network (DMN)

The responses of Meno-tutor are dynamically generated by passage of control through an augmented transition network (ATN)–like mechanism, called a discourse management network, DMN (see Fig. 10.10). The DMN allows both default and exceptional behavior; default behavior is preconfigured in the states of the DMN and exceptional behavior is determined by meta-rules that define opportunistic deviations from the controller's path through the ATN.

The control structure contains 40 hierarchical states broken into three levels that divide the system's reasoning into three levels: pedagogic, strategic, and tactical. Decision-units organized into three planning levels successively refine the actions of the tutor. The refinement at each level maintains the constraints dictated by the previous level and further elaborates the possibilities for the system's response.

Figure 10.11 provides two representations of the meta-rules that define exceptional behavior: Fig. 10.11(a) is an informal representation of two meta-rules and Fig. 10.11(b) is a representation of the actions of two meta-rules. For instance, the tutor's default response to a wrong answer might be defined as a sequence through two states, listed as **explicitly acknowledge incorrect answer** and **teach topic attribute**. However, this default sequence can be abandoned if a meta-rule fires and replaces the default sequence with a sequence such as **provide example** and **question topic**. Exceptional behavior, triggered through meta-rules, is based on predicates about the student model, discourse model, discourse history, and domain complexity and can examine such data structures as the student model (e.g., Does the student know a given topic?), the discourse model (e.g., Have enough questions been asked on a given topic to assess

---

* It's not that those answers were simply "wrong," rather that they reflect reasonable default assumptions about the weather in "northern states." An attempt to probe the student's default assumptions is made in the second discourse.

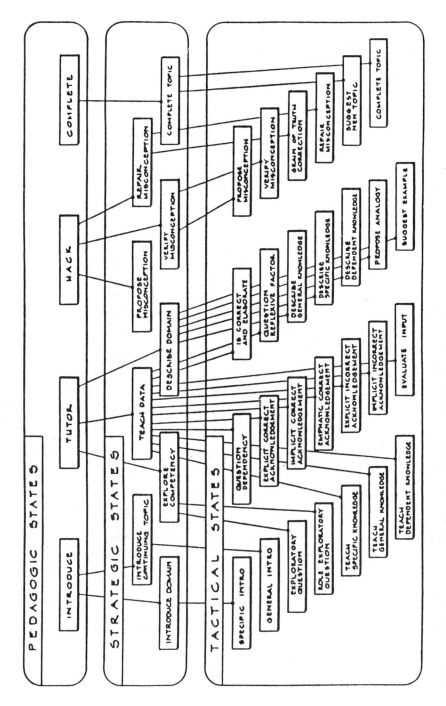

Figure 10.10 Discourse Management Network (DMN) for Meno-tutor

S1-EXPLORE—a Strategic Meta-rule
    From: **teach-data**
    To: **explore-competency**
Description: Moves the tutor to question the student about a variety
    of topics.
Activation: The present topic is complete, but the tutor has little
    confidence in its assessment of the student's knowledge.
Behavior: Generates an expository shift from detailed examination of
    a single topic, to a shallow examination of a number of topics.

T6-A.IMPLICITLY—a Tactical Meta-rule
    From: **explicit-incorrect-acknowledgment**
    To: **implicit-incorrect-acknowledgment**
Description: Moves the tutor to utter a brief acknowledgment of an
    incorrect answer.
Activation: The wrong answer threshold has been reached and the
    student seems confused.
Behavior: Shifts the discourse from an explicit correction and expla-
    nation of an incorrect answer to a simple response that recog-
    nizes, but does not dwell on, the incorrect answer.

(a)

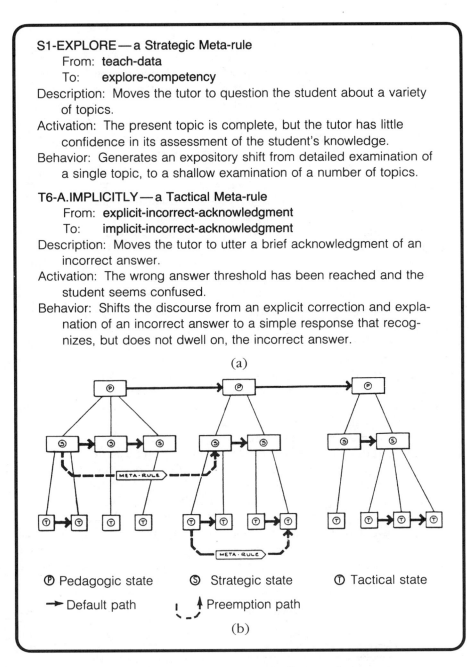

Ⓟ Pedagogic state   Ⓢ Strategic state   Ⓣ Tactical state

➤ Default path   Preemption path

(b)

Figure 10.11 Meta-rules to Determine Transitions in the Discourse
          Control Mechanism

whether the student knows it?), and the domain model (e.g., Do related topics exist?).

Meno-tutor separates planning and generation of a tutorial discourse into two distinct components: the tutoring component based on the DMN and the surface language generator. The tutoring component makes decisions about what discourse transitions to make and what information to convey or query; the surface language generator takes conceptual specifications from the tutoring component and produces the natural language output. These two components interface at the third level of the tutoring component.

At the highest level, the discourse is constrained to a specific tutoring approach that determines, for instance, how often the system will interrupt the student or how often it will probe the student about misconceptions. At this level a choice is made between approaches that would diagnose the student's knowledge (**tutor-student**), or introduce a new topic (**introduce-topic**). At the second level, the pedagogy is refined into a strategy, specifying the approach to be used. The choice here might be between exploring the student's competence by questioning, or by describing the facts of the topic without any interaction. At the lowest level, a tactic is selected to implement the strategy. For instance, if the strategy involves questioning the student, the system can choose from a half-dozen alternatives. For example, it can question the student about a specific topic, the dependency between topics, or the role of a subtopic. Again, after the student has given an answer, the system can choose from among eight ways to respond. For example, it can correct the student, elaborate on his or her answer, or, alternatively, barely acknowledge the answer.

Each state in the DMN is organized as a LISP structure with slots for functions that run when the state is evaluated. The slots define such things as the specifications of the text to be uttered, the next state to go to, or how to update the student and discourse model. The DMN is traversed by an iterative routine that stays within a predetermined space of paths from node to node.

Meno-tutor provides a general framework within which tutoring rules can be defined and tested. It is not a fully capable tutor for any one subject but rather a vehicle for experimenting with tutoring in several domains. At this point, its knowledge of the two domains on which it has been defined is shallow.* However, the mechanism for managing student-tutor interactions is generalizable and applicable to new domains; that is, tutoring rules and strategies can be held constant while the knowledge base is altered to effect a

---

* Meno-tutor had been developed without a full-scale natural language understander or generator. The conceptual equivalent of a student's input is fed by hand to the tutor (i.e., what would have been the output of a natural language comprehension system) and the output is produced by standard incremental replacement techniques. We have not yet worked with MUMBLE, a surface language generator, because we haven't yet invested in building a large enough knowledge base which would then be translated into portions of MUMBLE's dictionary. Our intent is to develop a complex knowledge base, possibly in the domain of Pascal, to extend the surface language generator to deal with the domain, and to build a simple natural language parser to interface with the student.

change in domain of discourse. Meno-tutor is thus a "generic" tutor, one not committed by design to a single subject.

Student Model

The student model is discussed only briefly here, although it is an essential component of the knowledge of teaching. The student model contains the system's knowledge of the student and it must be represented in excruciating detail and updated dynamically during the course of the tutoring discourse. Figure 10.12 presents a first tabulation of this prerequisite knowledge for the crane boom and an indication of the pointers to remedial work.

The student model cannot be a simple subset of domain knowledge; it should contain common errors and misconceptions compiled by classroom teachers and cognitive scientists. In the rainfall domain, we made use of earlier cognitive studies about student misconceptions in causal reasoning about rainfall (Stevens, Collins, & Goldin, 1978). In the Pascal tutor (see the "Knowledge of Discourse" section) we used a group of errors developed empirically. In the latter domain, extensive testing and videotaped interviews of correct and incorrect programming strategies yielded a set of high-level procedural plans that are said to be used by experts to transform problem descriptions into programs (Bonar, 1982a).

Summary of Knowledge of Teaching

This brief description of discourse management in Meno-tutor has illustrated the kind of knowledge a tutoring system must have to make inferences about how to teach, independent of the content of the domain. It provides a view of the tutoring space available to the system and demonstrates the effect of analyzing knowledge apart from domain knowledge. By changing tutoring topics and the particulars of the tutoring rules, we were able to plan and generate responsive tutoring discourse independent of the domain. The key point about the discourse manager is its flexibility; it receives its motivation, justification, and guidance from inferences made by the system about the student's knowledge and the ongoing discourse.

Knowledge of Discourse*

The third knowledge barrier to overcome, and one of the largest theoretical stumbling blocks in the design of effective machine discourse systems, is a lack of adequate representation of discourse conventions. We do not understand enough about the conventions employed by speakers and the structural aids

* Portions of this section appeared in an article entitled "Understanding Discourse Conventions in Tutoring," published in IEEE *Expert Systems in Government,* co-authored by David D. McDonald, 1985.

- Algebraic logic
- Simple simultaneous linear equations
- Locating vectors—directions
- Lines of action
- Finding moment arms
- Simple trig functions
- Properties of right triangles
- Sign conventions for forces and torques

(a)

- Placement of vectors (direction, magnitude, location)
- Proper angle and distance calculations
- Location of line action
- Selection of "good" axis to calculate torques
- Correct selection of all vectors acting on system element
- Use of trig to find vector components
- Correct force and torque equations for a system element
- Calculation of mass to weight
- Location of center of mass when needed
- Evidence of system manipulation—did student vary parameters?
- Proper abstracting of real-life example—knowing what to ignore
- Correct solution to equilibrium equations

(b)

Figure 10.12 Prerequisite Knowledge and Checklist for the Crane Boom

used by humans to make inferences and to set up expectations in conversation. *Human* speakers employ subtle linguistic cues to shift topics or provide supplementary knowledge; *human* listeners use these cues to set up expectations about the underlying structure of the discourse and to relate current utterances to preceding ones. The expectations set up by listeners are what the speaker tries to anticipate and to deliberately control for.

We have been working to represent such discourse conventions in a machine speaker. We want the system to respond to a user based on its inferences about the user's knowledge, model of the domain, or the discourse history. Early computer discourse systems produced canned text that were typically the same regardless of the user's knowledge or the discourse history (Mann, Moore, & Levin, 1977; McKeown, 1980). More recent interface systems have begun to tailor their responses to the user and to discourse context (Finin, 1983; Wilensky, 1982). The basic problem in designing responsive machine discourse is how to make inferences about the user and how to have these inferences govern the form of the text produced. We are studying how discourse expectations can be used to anticipate a student's *choice* of responses. This section describes a way to formalize such expectations and how to use them to transform interpretation and speech act knowledge into computational elements, such as plans and rules.

Inferences and conversational moves are powerful forces in any human conversation; they are especially powerful in tutoring. A tutor might choose conversational moves based on the responses of the student. For instance, a tutor might interpret what a student says and "read into" the answer additional material in order to fill in his or her understanding of the student's knowledge. The tutor might also make assumptions about the student's lack of knowledge, as in the case when a sequence of wrong responses is interpreted to mean the student doesn't understand the topic. Such tutoring process models must be represented in a machine tutor.*

The adjustments that a *computer tutor* should make are dependent upon its specific experience with a student and a variety of experiences that lead to a variety of responses. We want a computer tutor to interact with a knowledgeable student in a way that is fundamentally different, both in style and content, from the way it engages a confused one. It is not intended that the computer simply produce correct answers in response to a student's wrong answers; rather before responding to a wrong answer, the machine should resolve issues such as:

- When and how to stop to explain a wrong answer
- Whether it is preferable to explain an error or to start a lengthy exploration of the student's knowledge
- Whether to allow uncertainty about the student's knowledge to persist temporarily while it explores a potential misconception
- How hard the machine should work to understand why a student answered a question incorrectly or how much effort should be exerted to resolve questions about the student's presumed knowledge or misconceptions

Though many areas of research on understanding discourse conventions are interesting and several problems are ripe for a solution, we have focused on the role of the speaker because we are studying discourse in the context of tutoring. Tutoring is a rich, well-contained field in which to study discourse conventions from a speaker's point of view. There is a wealth of research on language and tutoring at the University of Massachusetts. One research effort has focused on natural language comprehension (Lehnert et al., 1983), genera-

---

* We recognize that a machine cannot know with certainty what a listener knows; neither can a listener know what a machine knows; a machine cannot be omniscient or clairvoyant. However, the machine can deduce, on the basis of evidence, something about what the listener assumes. These assumptions can be used to govern the form of the text generated.

tion (McDonald, 1983), discourse control (Woolf, 1984), and legal reasoning (Ashley & Rissland, 1985). Another effort has focused on tutoring discourse (Woolf & McDonald, 1984) and a related effort at Yale has focused on student errors (Johnson & Soloway, 1984) and the learning and teaching of Pascal looping constructs (Bonar & Soloway, 1985).

Qualitative Reasoning about Discourse

Discourse is often described in qualitative terms along with the *effect* of the utterance on the listener. For instance, in analyzing a discourse a person might say:

"The example was [useless/illuminating]."

"The argument was [powerful/unsubstantiated]."

"The speaker was [angry/abrupt]."

"The student was [confused/unprepared]."

"The topic was [understood/trivial]."

Figure 10.13 contains further analyses from three researchers: a psychologist, a computational linguist, and a psychiatrist. In each case, the researcher has analyzed implicit rules of discourse that suggest how a speaker should interpret a listener's level of knowledge or understanding. In these analyses qualitative inferences have been made about:

"What the student already knows"

"A deeper level of analysis"

"A shared focus of attention"

The inferences about qualitative entities are not defined or explained in the analyses. Neither are metrics provided to help the reader understand such processes as:

"*Building* on what a student knows"

"*Raising* issues"

"*Establishing* a shared focus of attention"

In fact, such casual use of these qualitative measurements suggests a degree of subjectivity about discourse conventions that is shared by humans. Also implicit in the analysis is the impact of such inferences and the rules implicit in them; the suggestion being made is that people would be better speakers or tutors if they followed the rules implicit in the analyses. We need to represent such rules in a machine tutor and to enable it to demonstrate the same aspects of good discourse conventions alluded to in the analyses. Toward this end, we have begun to capture several of the features we recognized in the analyses of Fig.

From *Analysis and Synthesis of Tutoring Discourse* (Collins et al., 1975):

> [A tutor] builds on what *the student already knows* [and] can question him about *his previous knowledge*. Then he can teach new material by relating it to that *previous knowledge* [p. 50].
>
> [A tutor] can respond directly to student errors, . . . question him to *diagnose the confusion* and can provide *relevant information* to *straighten him out* [p. 50].
>
> The question *raised the issue* of . . . moving [the discourse] to a *deeper level of analysis* than made so far [p. 67].

From *Plain Speaking: A Theory and Grammar of Spontaneous Discourse* (Reichman, 1981):

> Much of the implicit *knowledge speakers and listeners share* is knowledge of the particular components of various conversational moves—what kinds of utterances must be made in order to fulfill various discourse functions [chap. 3, p. 1].

From *Parental Communication Deviance and Schizophrenia: A Cognitive-Developmental Analysis* (Sass, 1984):

> A failure on the part of the speaker to *establish and maintain a shared focus of attention* with one's listener [p. 68].
>
> A tendency to *equivocate concerning one's commitment* to one's statements and a tendency to *vacillate concerning the content* of one's statements [p. 68].
>
> A *lack of specificity* with regard to the referent, *unexplained contradictions* . . . inappropriate responses suggestive of a failure to grasp the *intent of a question by the interlocutor* [p. 62].
>
> [A failure] to take into account the *cognitive needs* of the listener [p. 62].

Figure 10.13 Analyses of Discourse Conventions from the Literature

10.13. For example, we are learning to recognize qualitative states, such as when a *topic is generally known, when a *student has background information, or when a *student is confused.

We are beginning to use qualitative expressions of knowledge to represent complex discourse conventions and metrics. The difficulties are enormous; tracing qualitative inferences in discourse is relatively intractable, compared with, for example, tracing speech acts. Qualitative inferences will be multiplexed between and within other streams of inferences, some being initiated or continued while others are simultaneously being started. The result is that the intent of a particular stream of inferences can become confounded. Yet, we suggest that it is worth the effort to make such qualitative inferences and expect them to provide a powerful representation of the intention of the speaker. There is evidence from other fields that qualitative reasoning and representations are useful: examples include teaching (Larkin et al., 1980), artificial intelligence (Forbus & Stevens, 1981), and the domain of physics (de Kleer & Brown, 1981). We will be tracing implications as a way to evaluate the effect of a discourse.

We speak of implications in the same sense as did Grice (1975), but in reference to sequences of words perceived as a single conversational move. Grice's implications originally referred to inferences made over single words. For example, the italicized words in Fig. 10.14 have explicit implications. The word *and* in the first sentence carries an implication that the activity of going to jail preceded and possibly caused the second activity, that George became a criminal. The use of the word *tried* in the second sentence carries with it an entailment that Millie failed to swim the English Channel, and the use of the phrase *one leg* in the third sentence implies that the speaker *does not* in fact have two legs.

Implications, as we use them, define each participant's common-sense reasoning about a conversational move. They include the desiderata normally accepted by a rational discourser in his or her interactions in the discourse. We would like to think that implications embody a speaker's motivation, intention, and involvement in the discourse.

Maxims of Tutoring

We suggest that tutoring consists of following certain maxims of discourse conventions (in the same sense used by Grice) and we analyzed research such as that in Fig. 10.13 to identify these maxims. We expect to be able to evaluate the reasonableness of the tutoring discourse we produce by recognizing whether

1. George went to jail *and* became a criminal.
2. Millie *tried* to swim the English Channel.
3. I have *one* leg.

Figure 10.14 Implications in Text

the maxims are satisfied. In this section we define some tutoring maxims and outline how we intend to monitor discourse based on a notion of maxim satisfaction.

In order to model the qualitative effect of utterances we first define conversational *move-classes* as groups of utterances that have the same rhetorical effect, such as **question topic, summarize topic, acknowledge correct answer,** and **provide example.** We suggest that a tutor's choice of conversational move indicates its "intention" in the sense that a move sets up expectations in a listener. For instance, a conversational move such as **make accusation** typically would elicit negative responses from a listener. Consider some queries a tutor might pose to a student about loop execution in a Pascal program, as suggested in Fig. 10.15. Each sentence has a similar locutionary force, yet each conveys a different intention on the part of the speaker. Further, there is a continuum such that a tutor may couch its statements at any place along the higher end. The implication drawn would be of close attention, even commitment, to the student. On the other hand, a statement at the lower end would imply noncommitment, noninvolvement, and possibly antagonism. Relative to the four utterances above, we say that use of a phrase representing a certain point on the scale implies that the tutor chose *not* to phrase the utterance by another expression lower on the list. This reasoning on the part of the listener is licensed by the Gricean maxim of manner. Grice has defined very general maxims for discourse that are evocative, yet not detailed enough to provide a basis for a computational theory of discourse by themselves.

Our goal is to propose a computational model of tutoring discourse that elucidates and refines these maxims and links them with specific conversation moves. Ultimately inferences about conversational moves will be used to guide the system's choice of utterances. The tutoring maxims that we propose are

---

(*provide-example*)
(*question-hypo*)
    If the input is 10, how many times would your loop execute?

(*question-topic-value*)
    Do you know how many times your loop would execute?

(*make-a-claim*)
    I bet you don't know how many times your loop will iterate.

(*make-an-accusation*)
    You couldn't possibly understand loop execution.

Figure 10.15 Reading Implications from Utterances

derived from Gricean maxims for discourse and are tailored for tutoring. They include:

Quality: be committed and interested in the student's knowledge;
            be supportive and cooperative;
            do not take the role of "antagonist"

Quantity: be specific and perspicuous;
            use a minimum of attributes to describe a known concept;

Relation: be relevant;
            find a student's threshold of knowledge;
            bring up new topics and viewpoints as appropriate

Manner: be in control;
            allow a student to determine a new topic;
            allow context to determine a new topic.

Figure 10.16 further discriminates these maxims in terms of move-classes that support each one. Maxims are listed on the left and the sequence of move-classes that supports them on the right. By being attentive to moves during discourse, a system can monitor its own behavior and guide subsequent moves so as to be consistent with the maxims of good tutoring. The system can identify maxims on the left, and invoke the move-classes on the right that are associated with them. For instance, if the system plans to be more organized, it can **outline topics, introduce topics, terminate topics**, and then **review topics**. Alternatively, if the system needs to record the "effect" of its actions on the listener, it can list the actions taken by the tutor and determine if its own actions are consistent with certain maxims. For instance, if the interaction with the student could be described as an ordered set of utterances, such as **question student, acknowledge answer, propose misconception**, and **provide example**, the overall effect of the actions could be to determine the student's threshold of knowledge. Whether or not that threshold was determined is a nontrivial, and as yet unanswerable, question.

The table in Fig. 10.16 can be read in two directions: from left to right it allows the system to select a maxim and plan subsequent tutoring discourse by invoking the associated sequence of move-class; from right to left it provides an abstraction of the system's activities so that the effect of the system, in terms of the expectation of the listener and the maxims of good tutoring, can be expressed.

Maxims and Move-classes

In order to computationally associate maxims with sequences of move-class, we need to make inferences about the qualitative effect of each move-class on the discourse. To do this, we suggest the effect that each move-class has on dis-

Maxims	Conversational Move-classes
Be cooperative:	
—work with student	explain topics
	summarize topics
	clearly terminate topics
	review or repeat topics
	release control of dialogue
Be committed:	
—show interest	acknowledge answer
	explain topics
—support student	outline topics
	introduce topics
Be relevant:	
—find student's threshold	question student
	evaluate student hypotheses
	propose and verify misconceptions
—teach at threshold	provide analogy example
	summarize topic
Be organized:	
—structure domain	outline topics
	introduce topics
	terminate topics
	review topics
—complete information	clearly terminate topics
	teach subtopics after topic
	teach attributes after topic
	teach subgoals after goal
Be in control:	
—strictly guide discourse	introduce topic
	describe topic
	question student

Figure 10.16 Tutoring Maxims Supported by Move-classes

course entities, such as topics or a student's knowledge. Each conversational move is defined as a data structure and two inferences are made from it. The first inference or *implication* is linked *directly* to a move-class. It represents an assessment made about the move-class itself and is fixed and nonnegotiable. The second kind of inference or *global implication* is linked indirectly to sequences of move-classes. It represents an inference made about the effect of several move-classes and is volatile over the life of the dialogue. Global inferences are dynamically modified by the sequence of move-classes. Each inference type is discussed below.

Implications

Implications are bound to the move-class itself. They exist independent of the "truth" or "meaning" of the utterance and define what the listener receives in addition to the spoken words. In our model, a qualitative implication bound to the move-class is placed on a stack whenever its move-class is invoked. Figure 10.17 lists the implications bound to two move-classes, **question topic** and **present topic**. For instance, if a tutor questions a student about a topic, the implications of this are that the tutor (1) knows (or is trying to learn) the student's threshold of knowledge, (2) assumes the student can answer the question, and (3) thinks the topic is important or is learnable through the discourse. These implications can be assumed by a listener independent of the content of the query.

Additional global inferences that we expect the machine to make are presented in Fig. 10.18, in which global implications are listed on the left and the assessments of which they are a "gloss" on the right.

Global implications are based on extended reasoning about sequences of move-classes. They include assessments such as ***student is confused, *topic is known**, or ***misconception is resolved** and are modified with each new tutor/student interaction. Global implications are uncertain and represent the system's best estimate about the state of affairs of knowledge of the student or topic at the current time. Whereas implications were known with certainty at the time a move-class was invoked, global implications require reasoning under uncertainty to deduce which one of a number of competing global implications might take effect. Reasoning with uncertainty must allow for the accumulation of support for or against a number of global implications.

Summary of Knowledge of Discourse

We have shown how discourse conventions can be included in the knowledge of an intelligent computer. Our focus has not been on the generation of syntactically correct natural language output, but rather on the deep-level planning required to motivate and plan that language generation. We have looked at a way to dynamically record and update inferences made by the tutor about the student or topic based on its knowledge of discourse.

We have suggested that reasoning about discourse requires codification of discourse elements that are qualitative, not quantitative. Tracing implicit qualitative assessments made by the machine is more intractable than tracing actual

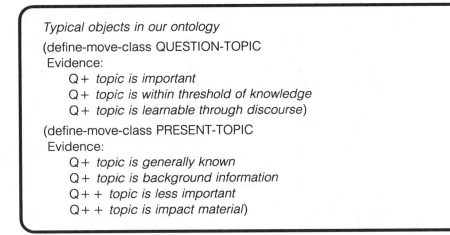

Figure 10.17 Implications Bound to Move-classes

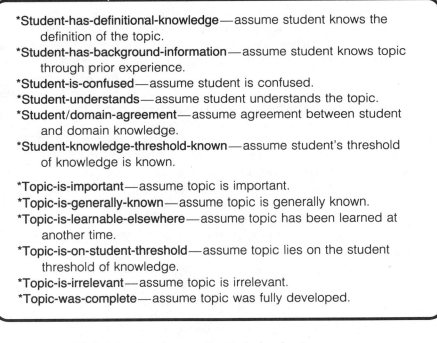

Figure 10.18 Global Implications to Be Made by the System

utterances; yet we posit that qualitative inferencing provides us with a more powerful representation of students' intentions than simply tracking their verbal answers. Qualitative inferences will also be used to generate new problems and examples to be presented to students. It will be used to evaluate and possibly redirect the progress of the discourse. Our intent is to use qualitative reasoning to improve the flexibility and reasonableness of the discourse.

Knowledge of Authoring

The fourth theoretical barrier that must be addressed before we can build intelligent tutoring systems is knowledge of authoring, or knowledge of non-programming natural interfaces through which a user can modify the concepts or rules of a computer system. "Real-time" development of intelligent tutoring systems requires contributions by many people from many disciplines. Class-room teachers, psychologists, domain specialists, and cognitive scientists all have valuable expertise, examples, analogies, and strategies to contribute to an emerging teaching system. To speed up the entry of such experiential data into an intelligent tutoring system requires that we develop *education-specific* AI tools that would allow curriculum designers and others to represent their own knowledge within a developing tutoring system.

Yet teachers and other experts are not able to work with intelligent tutoring systems; the systems are too complicated and typically require expertise in both LISP and AI before the educators can make a notable contribution. For instance, a teacher working to change the contents of an in-class tutoring system would have to work in LISP or an AI programming language such as Prolog. Such languages are not useful to a teacher either for programming or for modifying concepts. They are difficult to use, not merely because they require knowledge of another programming language, but also because they require the teacher to understand techniques for representing knowledge, drawing inferences, conducting dialogues, and other features assumed in an AI language. A teacher who does not know an AI language (and hence the associated AI concepts) cannot construct intelligent tutoring programs. Presumably, this obstacle could be at least partially overcome by teaching everyone how to program in LISP or Prolog. There would still remain, however, the task of teaching AI knowledge-representation methods. Obviously, this is not a satisfactory solution for teachers who want to develop intelligent tutoring programs without becoming AI programmers.

Given this start-up constraint, several years are required to analyze, design, implement, and evaluate an intelligent tutoring system. Such a tremendous investment in time, specialized training, and high-level funding limits teacher involvement. Another limitation is the work required to represent the knowledge of each domain (see "Knowledge of Domain") and of teaching strategies (see "Knowledge of Teaching"). Building a system in a new domain potentially requires access to all the problem-solving knowledge in the domain and then requires indexing in precise rules, such as was done in West (Burton & Brown, 1982) to teach each concept. This is very difficult. Building a precise indexing scheme is potentially tractable for the concepts and procedures of a domain. It is less clear how to enumerate the rules for heuristics and simulations. In addition, the indexing scheme for each piece of knowledge must be available to the program so it can articulate how the knowledge interacts and what assumptions have been made.

Progress toward development of intelligent authoring systems that reduce such limitation has been slow, specifically because of the knowledge representation issue. The focus of this knowledge frontier is to discover a knowledge representation that the teacher can work with. This does not mean that we seek the "best" knowledge representation for each domain to be taught (see, for instance, Clancey, Chapter 9; Johnson & Soloway, 1984; or Sleeman, 1983). Rather, we have selected a pragmatic approach: we are exploring a number of representations that teachers can work with. The representation language we might use will have the advantage of being tested with teachers; it may not prove more expressive or complete than a more formal language, but it will have been found useful in facilitating communication of science concepts between teachers and the system. The intent is to make concepts and rules in the domain available to the teacher.

Authoring System Example

As an illustration of the components required in an authoring system, we return to the crane boom problem (see "Knowledge of Domain") and describe a system we are building to allow a teacher to modify domain and teaching knowledge of the crane boom. The teacher will be able to view concepts in the domain, such as the concept **force** shown in Fig. 10.19.

In using the physics tutor, we know the teacher will want to express the physics knowledge in a fairly natural way and to represent general concepts, such as **force**, as well as specific ones such as the **positive x-component of force** with equal ease. In order to make knowledge about the crane boom available, the interface allows a teacher to view and modify internal knowledge about physics, such as force and mass, along with rules and strategies to solve and teach the problem.

Each screen is designed so that a teacher, using mouse-sensitive tools, will be able to edit or order concepts, to adjust the application of rules, or simply to scan the set of concepts used by the tutor. The authoring interface includes a *browser,* a graphic display that shows concepts and rules and allows the user to move through the knowledge base looking at concepts in succession. The browser allows the teacher to visualize the structure and inheritance of concepts and to see the relationship of concepts and rules to each other.

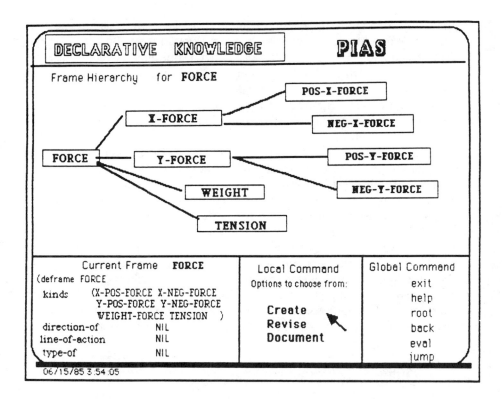

Figure 10.19 Procedural Knowledge for Force

For instance, procedural knowledge, or the rules and laws of physics, must be represented to the teacher. Since the system represents procedural knowledge through forward or backward chaining rules, we need to show these rules to the teacher. We expect to deduce this representation automatically from the English definition of the rule by using a limited predictive parser, similar to the one recently built at the University of Massachusetts (Lehnert, 1984). An early prototype of a semantic parser to comprehend a student's input to a teaching system was used in the SOPHIE system (Brown & Bell, 1977).

An alternative way to represent procedural rules is given in Fig. 10.20. Here the rule is displayed as a network that illustrates a relationship between tension in a crane boom and the direction of the cable. Translations such as this one, moving from a rule stated in English to a network representation, will be more difficult, as the object display is not a simple tree as was the case for the concept **force**. Again, we intend to use a limited predictive parser to comprehend the input, but the graphic realization will provide more in the way of a research problem.

English: The force of tension in a cable always lies along the direction of the cable, as does the line of action of that force.

Physics tutor:

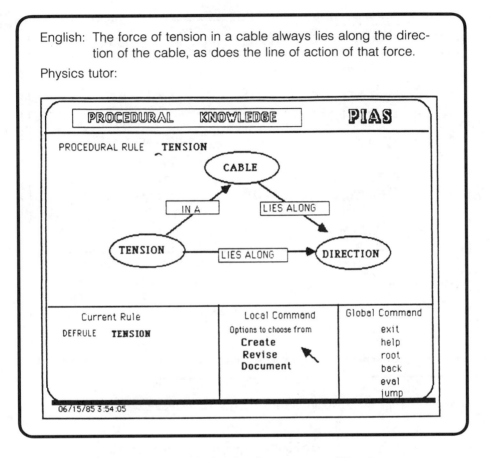

Figure 10.20 Procedural Knowledge for the Concept of Tension

The authoring system must also articulate the heuristic knowledge or detailed operant knowledge used by the machine to solve the crane boom problem (see Fig. 10.21). Such data can be used by the teacher to see which rules guide the system's solution of problems and which rules the student is using. A set of heuristic rules is used by the machine to order every problem the machine can work on and to guide the system's transformation of one physical situation into another.

The browser representation for heuristic knowledge is derived from detailed specifications of the problem solution, as shown in Fig. 10.8. Again, the rules can be derived from the English language statement by using a predictive parser based on a limited set of physics-specific English words. Thus, for a

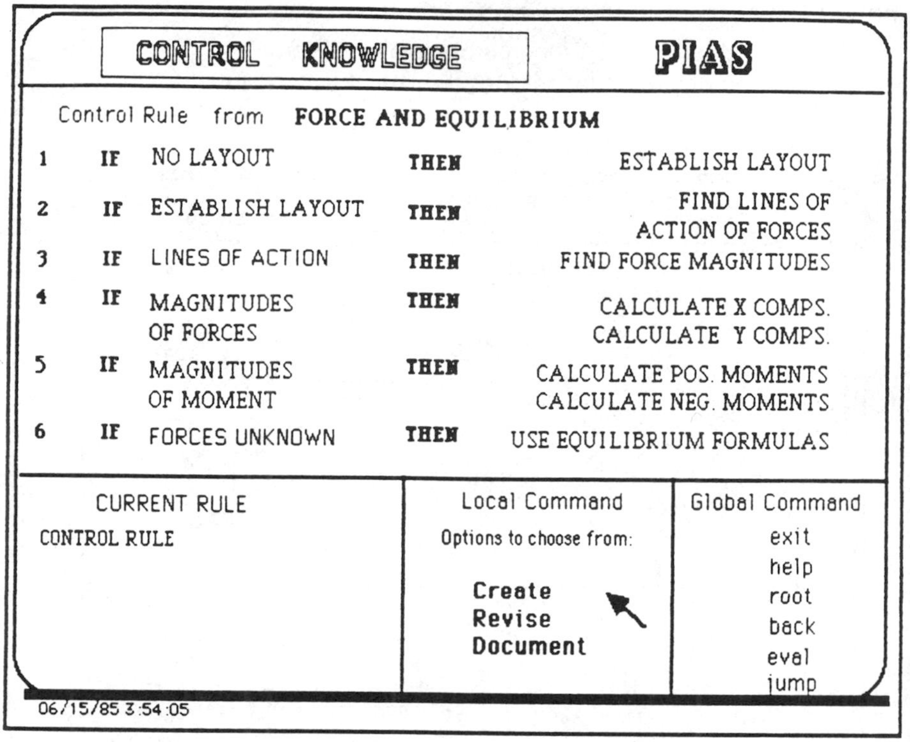

```
┌─────────────────────────────────────────────────────────────────┐
│  ┌──────────────────────────────┐                                │
│  │   CONTROL   KNOWLEDGE         │            PIAS                │
│  └──────────────────────────────┘                                │
│ ─────────────────────────────────────────────────────────────── │
│   Control Rule  from   FORCE AND EQUILIBRIUM                      │
│   1   IF   NO LAYOUT           THEN          ESTABLISH LAYOUT     │
│                                                                   │
│   2   IF   ESTABLISH LAYOUT    THEN             FIND LINES OF     │
│                                              ACTION OF FORCES     │
│   3   IF   LINES OF ACTION     THEN     FIND FORCE MAGNITUDES     │
│                                                                   │
│   4   IF   MAGNITUDES          THEN        CALCULATE X COMPS.     │
│            OF FORCES                        CALCULATE Y COMPS.     │
│                                                                   │
│   5   IF   MAGNITUDES          THEN     CALCULATE POS. MOMENTS    │
│            OF MOMENT                     CALCULATE NEG. MOMENTS    │
│                                                                   │
│   6   IF   FORCES UNKNOWN      THEN     USE EQUILIBRIUM FORMULAS  │
│ ─────────────────────────────────────────────────────────────── │
│       CURRENT RULE          │  Local Command   │ Global Command  │
│   CONTROL RULE              │ Options to choose│     exit        │
│                             │      from:       │     help        │
│                             │   Create         │     root        │
│                             │   Revise    ↖    │     back        │
│                             │   Document       │     eval        │
│                             │                  │     jump        │
│ ─────────────────────────────────────────────────────────────── │
│  06/15/85 3:54:05                                                 │
└─────────────────────────────────────────────────────────────────┘
```

Figure 10.21 Browser Notation for Heuristic Knowledge

rough goal such as "solve for equilibrium," the system will follow a plan, such as suggested in Fig. 10.21, passing through each state indicated.

Teaching knowledge, too, has to be made explicit for the teacher. Figure 10.22 suggests a way to do this. Figure 10.22(a) displays the states of the discourse manager (see the section on DMN), makes them available to the teacher, and suggests those parts of the strategic, pedagogic, or tactic strategies that the teacher can modify. Figure 10.22(b) lists the options available to the teacher for modifying a student's interactions with a simulation. The system screen will allow the teacher to instruct the machine as to the number of parameters the student might change, how often, and through which intervals of change.

For instance, if the teacher wants the parameters of distance and mass to be modifiable by the student, but not the parameter of time, the teacher would delete the line "time" from the list of allowable parameters in the second line of Fig. 10.22(b).

The domain and teaching screens will allow a teacher to manage the machine's interaction with the student. Using the browser, the teacher can ob-

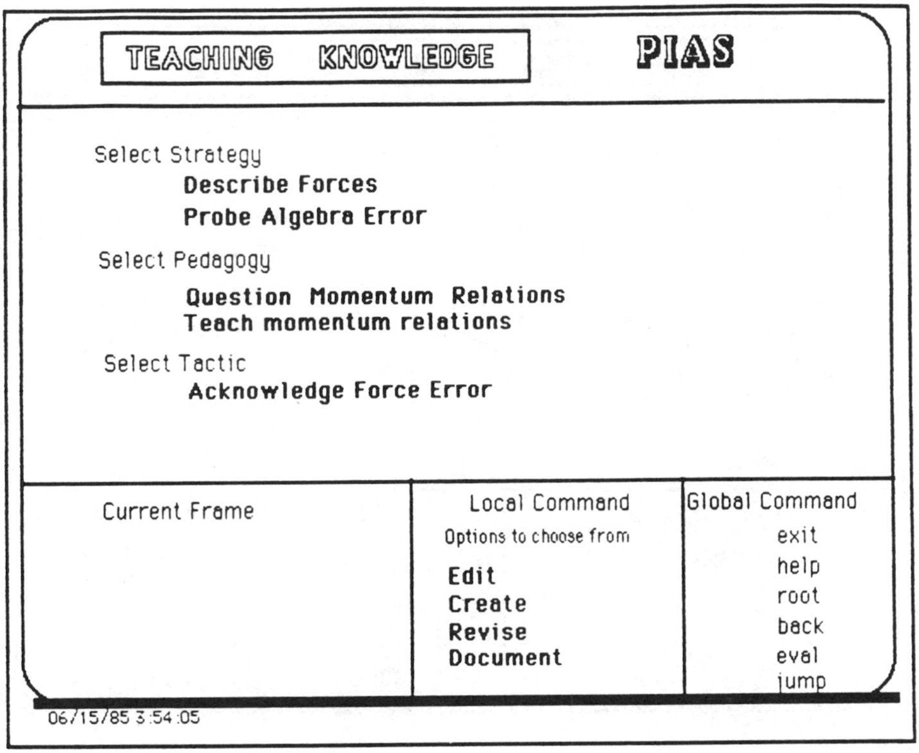

```
┌──────────────────────────────────────────────────────────────────┐
│ ┌─────────────────────────────────────┐                          │
│ │  TEACHING    KNOWLEDGE  │      PIAS                           │
│ └─────────────────────────────────────┘                          │
│ ───────────────────────────────────────────────────────────────  │
│                                                                    │
│    Select Strategy                                                │
│         Describe Forces                                           │
│         Probe Algebra Error                                       │
│                                                                    │
│    Select Pedagogy                                                │
│         Question Momentum Relations                               │
│         Teach momentum relations                                  │
│                                                                    │
│    Select Tactic                                                  │
│         Acknowledge Force Error                                   │
│                                                                    │
│ ──────────────────────────┬─────────────────────┬──────────────  │
│                           │  Local Command      │Global Command   │
│     Current Frame         │ Options to choose from │    exit       │
│                           │                     │   help          │
│                           │    Edit             │   root          │
│                           │    Create           │   back          │
│                           │    Revise           │   eval          │
│                           │    Document         │   jump          │
│ ──────────────────────────┴─────────────────────┴──────────────  │
│  06/15/85 3:54:05                                                 │
└──────────────────────────────────────────────────────────────────┘
```

Figure 10.22(a) Browser Screen for Accessing Teaching Knowledge

serve the conditions under which the tutor makes its decision about teaching, and how it updates its model of the student's knowledge. The teacher can adjust the way the system made those decisions, or the laws of nature as encoded in the machine, and test the machine with the new concepts or rules to see how it interacts with the student.

As an example of the advantages of an authoring system for enhancing teacher participation in the development of machine tutors, we describe an event that occurred recently while we developed our planetary motion tutor. An astronomer[*] was watching a simulation of planets revolving around the sun. He suggested a unique modification to the traditional exemplar of the two-body problem. The astronomer could see that changes made by the programmer in either the size of the planets or their position could lead to dependent changes in the angular momentum of the planets.

[*] Harold Weaver, Department of Astronomy, University of California at Berkeley, and member of the Exploring System Earth consortium, San Francisco, California.

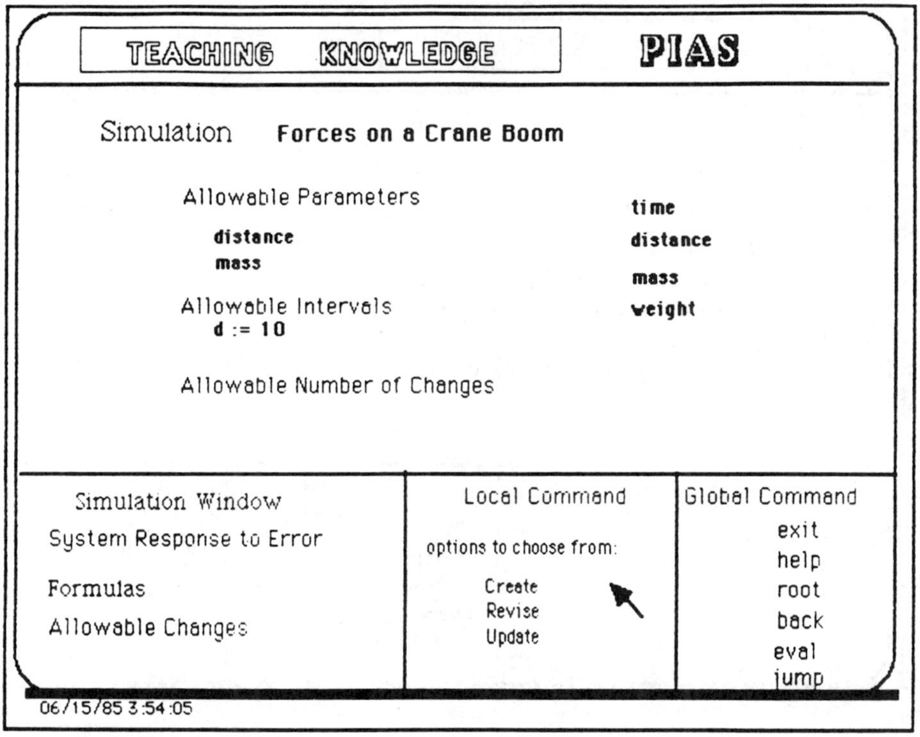

Figure 10.22b   Browser Screen for Accessing Teaching Knowledge

The astronomer/teacher suggested that a person should be shown standing on the planet earth and should drop an apple to the ground. Rather than let the apple hit the earth, at the moment that it would reach the ground, the planet should be shrunk and the apple shown to revolve around the earth. Such a simulation would provide a graphic example of the relation of mass to gravitation and an anomalous example of the two-body problem.

Generating and including such powerful examples in a machine tutor is critical to its effectiveness. Only a teacher trained both in the domain and in working with students could create such a rich and exciting example. One of the clearest ways to include these people in the process of building intelligent tutoring systems is to build intelligent authoring systems.

Conclusion

Technological advances, such as affordable AI-based work stations and expert systems tools, will allow us to build powerful computers for education. These computers should be able to reason about the domain, the student, and the discourse, and to teach in a sensitive one-on-one dialogue with a student. Such a machine will·customize its responses to the complexity of the domain, to the specific event, and to the idiosyncracies of the student. To do this, the tutoring system must have knowledge of the domain, of the student, of tutoring, and of discourse.

The knowledge that will enable us to build such intelligent tutors is not yet fully understood by cognitive or computer scientists. Further research into each area and exploration of knowledge engineering issues is required. In this chapter we have suggested a variety of ways that knowledge representations and control structures can be built to encode the missing knowledge areas. We suggest that sophisticated AI techniques, excruciating attention to detail, and intuitions about teaching and learning must each be analyzed and represented if we are to overcome knowledge theoretic frontiers that stand in the way of realizing sophisticated machine tutors.

References

Ashley, A., & Rissland, E. (1985). Toward modelling legal arguments, *Proceedings of the Second International Congress, Logica, Informatica, Diritto, Automated Analysis of Legal Texts,* Florence, Italy.

Bonar, J. (1982a). Collecting and analyzing on-line protocols from novice programmers. *Behavioral Research Methods and Instrumentation.*

Bonar, J. (1982b). Natural problem solving strategies and programming language constructs. *Proceedings of the Fourth Annual Conference of the Cognitive Science Society.*

Bonar, J., & Soloway, E. (1985, Sept.). Models of novice programmer constructs. *Human Computer Interactions, 1* (3).

Brown, J. S., & Bell, A. (1977). SOPHIE: A sophisticated instructional environment for teaching electronic troubleshooting (an example of A.I. in C.A.I.). *International Journal of Man-Machine Studies,* (7).

Brown, J. S., & Burton, B. (1978). Diagnostic models for procedural bugs in basic mathematical skills. *Cognitive Sciences, 2,* 155–192.

Burton, R., & Brown, J. S. (1982). An investigation of computer coaching for informal learning activities. In D. Sleeman & J. S. Brown (Eds.), *Intelligent tutoring systems.* New York: Academic Press.

Carbonell, J. R. (1970, June). *Mixed-initiative man-computer instructional dialogues.* Technical Report 1971. Cambridge, MA: Bolt, Beranek and Newman.

Clancey, W. (1979a). *Transfer of rule-based expertise through tutorial dialogue.* Ph.D. dissertation, Department of Computer Science, Stanford University, Stanford, CA.

Clancey, W. (1979b). Dialogue management for rule-based tutorials. *Proceedings of the International Joint Conference on Artificial Intelligence,* Tokyo, Japan.

Clancey, W. (1982). Tutoring rules for guiding a case method dialogue. In D. Sleeman & J. S. Brown (Eds.), *Intelligent tutoring systems.* New York: Academic Press.

Clancey, W. (1984). Classification problem solving. *Proceedings of the National Conference on Artificial Intelligence* (AAAI-84), Austin, TX.

Collins, A., Warnock, E., & Passafiume, J. (1975). Analysis and synthesis of tutorial dialogues. In *Psychology of learning and motivation* (Vol. 9). New York: Academic Press.

de Kleer, J., & Brown, J. S. (1981). Foundations of envisioning. *Proceedings of the Eighth International Joint Conference on Artificial Intelligence,* Vancouver, Canada.

Finin, T. (1983). Providing help and advice in task-oriented systems. *Proceedings of the International Joint Conference on Artificial Intelligence,* Karlsruhe, West Germany.

Forbus, K., & Stevens, A. (1981). Using qualitative simulation to generate explanations. Report 4480. Cambridge, MA: Bolt, Beranek and Newman.

Grice, H. (1975). Logic and conversation. In P. Cole & J. Morgan (Eds.), *Syntax and semantics* (pp. 41–58). New York: Academic Press.

Johnson, L., & Soloway, E. M. (1984, March). PROUST: Knowledge-based program debugging. *Proceedings Eighth International Software Engineering Conference,* Orlando, FL.

Kuhn, T. S. (1970). *The structure of scientific revolutions.* International Encyclopedia of Unified Science, University of Chicago Press.

Larkin, J. H. (1982). Enriching formal knowledge: A model for learning to solve textbook physics problems. In J. R. Anderson (Ed.), *Cognitive skills and their acquisition* (pp. 311–344). Hillsdale, NJ: Lawrence Erlbaum Associates.

Larkin, J., McDermot, J., Simon, D. P., & Simon, H. (1980). Expert and novice performance in solving physics problems. *Science, 208,* 20.

Lehnert, W. (1984). Plum: A limited predictive parser. Counselor Project Paper, University of Massachusetts.

Lehnert, W., Dyer, P., Johnson, P., Yang, C., & Harley, S. (1983). Boris—An experiment in in-depth understanding of narratives. *Artificial Intelligence, 20,* 15–62.

Lehnert, W., & Loiselle, C. (1984). *An introduction to plot units.* COINS Technical Report 84-13, Computer and Information Sciences, University of Massachusetts, Amherst.

Mann, W., Moore, J., & Levin, J. (1977). A comprehension model for human dialogue. *International Joint Conference on Artificial Intelligence.*

McDonald, D. (1983). Natural language generation as a computational problem: an introduction. In M. Brady & R. Berwick (Eds.), *Computational models of discourse.* Cambridge, MA: MIT Press.

McKeown, K. (1980). Generating relevant explanations: Natural language responses to questions about data base structure. *National Proceedings of the Association of Artificial Intelligence* (AAAI-80), Stanford, CA.

Miller, M. (1979). A structured planning environment. *International Journal of Man-Machine Studies, 11.*

Reichman, R. (1981). Plain speaking: A theory and grammar of spontaneous discourse. Ph.D. thesis, Harvard University, Department of Mathematics. Also Technical Report 4681. Cambridge, MA: Bolt, Beranek and Newman.

Rissland, E. (1978). Understanding mathematics. *Cognitive Science, 2*(4).

Rissland, E., & Soloway, E. (1981). Constrained example generation: A testbed for studying learning. *Proceedings of the Eighth International Joint Conference on Artificial Intelligence,* Vancouver, Canada.

Sass, L. (1984). Parental communication deviance and schizophrenia: A cognitive-developmental analysis. In L. Vaina & H. Hintikka (Eds.), *Cognitive constraints on communication.*

Sleeman, D. (1983). Basic algebra revisited. Heuristic Programming Project Report, No. HPP-83-9, Stanford University.

Sleeman, D., & Brown, J. S. (1982). *Intelligent tutoring systems.* New York: Academic Press.

Soloway, E., Bonar, J., Woolf, B., Barth, P., Rubin, E., & Erlich, K. (1981). Cognition and programming: Why your students write those crazy programs. *Proceedings of the National Educational Computing Conference* (NECC), Denton, TX.

Stevens, A., Collins, A., & Goldin, S. (1978). Diagnosing student's misconceptions in causal models. *International Journal of Man-Machine Studies, 11.*

Sullivan, M., & Cohen, P. (1985). An endorsement-based plan recognition program. *International Joint Conference on Artificial Intelligence,* Los Angeles, CA.

Wilensky, R. (1982, Aug.). Talking to UNIX in English: An overview of UC. *Proceedings AAAI-82,* Pittsburgh, PA.

Woolf, B. (1984). *Context-dependent planning in a machine tutor.* Ph.D. Dissertation, Computer and Information Sciences, University of Massachusetts, Amherst, MA.

Woolf, B., Blegen, D., Verloop, A., and Jensen, J. (1986). Tutoring the complex industrial process. *Proceedings of the National Conference on Artificial Intelligence (AAAI-86),* Philadelphia, PA.

Woolf, B., & McDonald, D. (1984a). Context-dependent transitions in tutoring discourse. *Proceedings of the National Conference on Artificial Intelligence (AAAI-84),* Austin, TX.

Woolf, B., & McDonald, D. (1984b, Sept.). Design issues in building a computer tutor. *IEEE Computer,* special issue on Artificial Intelligence for Human-Machine Interaction.

11 / The TEACHER'S APPRENTICE: Designing an Intelligent Authoring System for High School Mathematics

MATTHEW W. LEWIS,
ROBERT MILSON, and
JOHN R. ANDERSON

Introduction

The goals of the TEACHER'S APPRENTICE project overlap with the goals of other authors appearing in this collection: Improve education by making intelligent computer-assisted instruction more effective, available, and realistically usable. At the same time that we are developing tutoring software, we, like others, are also deliberately exploring the epistemological issues about the nature of the knowledge that is being tutored and how that knowledge can be learned. In our project, the design of tutoring software and the refinement of cognitive theory go hand in hand and affect one another (Anderson, 1985). The constraint that an operational tutoring system must, by definition, be well defined presents the opportunity to examine the system's successes and failures in terms of the underlying epistemological and pedagogical decisions made during its design and implementation.

This work is supported by grant MDR 8470337 from the Science and Engineering Education division of the National Science Foundation. The ideas in this chapter owe a great deal to interactions and research done with James Greeno of the University of California, Berkeley. Many thanks go to Ms. Margaret Shields, Dr. John R. Young, and Dr. Paul G. LeMahieu of the Pittsburgh city schools for their generosity and cooperation. We feel that comments made by Patrick Thompson, Bret Wallach, and Derek Sleeman on an earlier draft have substantially improved this chapter. This work also benefited from fruitful interactions with Frank Boyle and with members of the algebra research group: Julie Epelboim, Steve Garlick, Kate McGilly, Kevin Singley, Joe Thompson, and Ik Yoo.

The TEACHER'S APPRENTICE project is so named because the goal of our research is to produce a system that has many of the attributes of a human TEACHER'S APPRENTICE, or student teacher. This system has knowledge of the domain (it can solve all the problems it teaches), it has knowledge about patterns of errors that occur in its domain of expertise, it has knowledge about teaching strategies, and it has the intelligence to emulate a human teacher's language and tutoring strategies.

The first domain for which the TEACHER'S APPRENTICE is being developed is a first-year course in high school algebra. Basic algebra was chosen because there has been other relevant research in the areas of algebra problem solving (Davis, 1975; Davis, Jockusch, & McKnight, 1978; Lewis, 1981; Wagner, Rachlin, & Jensen, 1984), errors (Matz, 1982; Sleeman, 1982; Sleeman, 1984), simulation (Bundy, 1983; Bundy & Welham, 1981), and tutoring (Brown, 1983; McArthur, 1985; Sleeman, 1982). In addition, basic algebra is fundamental to later work in much of mathematics and in most technical fields.

Relative to the other intelligent tutoring research in progress at Carnegie-Mellon University, the TEACHER'S APPRENTICE project is still in its early stages. Other local projects have had the goals of constructing intelligent tutoring systems for LISP (Anderson & Reiser, 1985) and for high school geometry (Anderson, Boyle, & Yost, 1985). These systems, while successful, have led us to investigate the domain-independent parts of tutoring and how to speed up the task of building such systems. The TEACHER'S APPRENTICE project is an exploration of these questions.

The TEACHER'S APPRENTICE project has aspects which are aimed at each of three general goals:

- *Make intelligent tutors "effective": design, implement, and evaluate an intelligent tutor that emulates effective human tutoring and is based on specific predictions of a learning theory.* The goal of making intelligent tutors "effective" translates into having them emulate what good human tutors do when tutoring. The teaching effectiveness of individual tutoring over standard classroom instruction has been documented (Bloom, 1984) and has been referred to as the "two-sigma" effect: children being tutored perform two standard deviations above children learning the same materials in a standard classroom setting. This size of an effect is quite impressive in the world of instructional interventions. We also wish to keep as many of the pedagogical decisions as possible grounded predictions of a learning theory.

- *Make intelligent tutoring systems "available": cut development time and cost through design modularity and get intelligent tutors to run in real time.* To make intelligent tutoring software available means being able to produce it at a reasonable cost. Producing an intelligent authoring system as a tutoring architecture for a domain like high school mathematics would greatly reduce the time needed to bring up lesson materials in similar subdomains. If a tutoring component could be designed that was relatively independent of the exact expertise it was teaching, then the possibility of using a single architecture across the subdomains of Algebra I, Algebra II, and high school calculus becomes possible. There are also the important issues of how to make the software run in real time on machines that will be affordable to schools five years from now.

■ *Make intelligent tutors "usable": design systems which will be amenable to different problem solving and teaching styles and fit into the culture of classrooms.* The reality of teachers and students in a dynamic classroom environment presents another goal for our project: Make this system usable for real teachers in real classrooms. Different teachers might teach subtly different algorithms and use different language for math entities and concepts. We are pursuing the development of a system that tailors its tutorial style to the style of the individual teacher using it. Individual teaching style is one part of a larger "culture of the classroom" into which this teaching aid must be integrated. The tutor's design might capitalize on features of the culture to maximize the probability of the tutor's eventual acceptance and effective use.

It is appropriate to also state what is *not* one of our goals; It is *not* our goal to replace high school mathematics teachers. Mathematics teachers have other roles besides transmitting skills. There are many activities that are part of a well-rounded mathematics education that teachers often complain they never get a chance to do: they are too busy teaching the required skills to get into activities often put under the title of "enrichment and motivation." This is where the "art" of mathematics can be conveyed as well as conveying a broader appreciation for the structure and functionality of mathematics. Motivating algebra learners seems to be a large part of the battle in the "normal level" classrooms we've observed. High school students want better answers to such questions as "Why are we learning to factor?" than the standard responses of "You'll need it later" or "It will be on the SATs." These terse answers are necessitated by the constraints of have 30 students in a classroom and not being able to digress to answer such questions. By giving teachers intelligent teaching tools that are more effective at transmitting problem-solving skills than a normal classroom environment we may be able to restructure classrooms into groups that effectively reduce the student-teacher ratio. This allows more opportunities for teachers to provide enrichment and motivation as well as supplying time to attend to the needs of individual learners.

We do foresee situations where the tutor might be practical without the aid of a human teacher. These are settings with adults involved in remedial mathematics or settings where human teachers are not available. These cases are discussed at the end of the chapter.

We will first briefly describe the theoretical foundations of the project and how those theoretical foundations translate into the design of intelligent tutoring systems. We then describe the components of the system and their interactions. Following this description of the system we discuss some possible interesting side effects of developing intelligent authoring systems for ICAI and how it might affect teacher training and teacher participation in learning research. We also address how the system differs from quality CAI: how the surface similarity of the system's output to the output of CAI belies the flexibility of the underlying mechanisms in the TEACHER'S APPRENTICE that generate that output. We close with a summary of how the TEACHER'S APPRENTICE project attempts to achieve the general goals stated above. Our experiences with pilot studies and preliminary results with algebra-naive learners are interspersed throughout the sections.

Theoretical Foundations of the TEACHER'S APPRENTICE Project

Fundamental to our tutoring work is the claim that we can construct models of how students actually perform the skills that are to be tutored and how these skills are acquired. Our cognitive model of performance and learning is the ACT* model (Anderson, 1983) of cognition. Skills are represented as sets of productions which must be acquired through practice. Learning in ACT* is strongly a learning-by-doing model of skill acquisition with a clear distinction between declarative and procedural knowledge. Students can encode (often incorrectly or incompletely) the description of a skill from a text or from examples into some declarative form. The declarative encoding is then run interpretively by general productions in the system. As the set of declaratively represented productions are applied in the service of problem solving they are automatically compiled into a set of faster, more smoothly operating problem-solving actions through the mechanisms of composition and pro-ceduralization: problem-solving steps are collapsed and the productions are generalized (Anderson, 1982). Strengthening and tuning of productions takes place through repeated application, with the end product being the automatic application of problem-solving skill.

Components of the TEACHER'S APPRENTICE System

A theory of instruction should be maximally effective when it is based on a theory of learning. Based on the ACT* theory of problem-solving performance and skill acquisition, a set of design principles for intelligent tutoring systems has been enumerated and the connections between the principles and the learning theory have been argued (Anderson, Boyle, Farrell, & Reiser, in press). These principles, presented in Fig. 11.1, have driven the design decisions of the TEACHER'S APPRENTICE. What follows is a description of the components of the TEACHER'S APPRENTICE system: the student model, consisting of the "ideal"

1. Represent the student as a set of productions.
2. Communicate the goal structure underlying problem solving.
3. Provide instruction in the problem-solving context.
4. Promote an abstract understanding of the problem-solving knowledge.
5. Minimize working memory load.
6. Provide immediate feedback on errors.
7. Adjust the grain size of instruction with learning.
8. Facilitate successive approximations to the target skill.

Figure 11.1 Design Principles for Intelligent Tutoring Systems, Based on Predictions of the ACT* Model of Cognition (from Anderson, Boyle, Farrell, & Reiser, in press)

and errorful or "buggy" models of student performance (Brown & Burton, 1978; Sleeman, 1982), the interface, the tutorial component, and the rule induction component for learning tutoring rules.

The Ideal Model of the Student

Having a simulation of the ideal performance of a student is required for the "model tracing" methodology of tutoring (Reiser, Anderson, & Farrell, 1985). The human learner's problem-solving behavior is compared with the performance of the ideal model. The instruction provided to the learner at each point is a function of our interpretation of the learner's internal state in the problem solving. This can be inferred by matching the learner's output to problem states generated by various ideal and "buggy" rules. Creating sets of production rules that simulate the problem-solving processes of an ideal student is a sizable but largely achievable task. As in the other tutoring projects at Carnegie-Mellon University, this is accomplished through iterations of writing rules followed by observation of student performance. The observation allows assessment of the completeness of the rule set, relative to productions inherent in the performance of human learners.

Figure 11.2 contains an example of one possible set of productions from an ideal model for doing distribution. These rules would be invoked if an expression such as $3(7x + 5)$ appeared somewhere in the equation being simplified. The first rule recognizes that distribution is applicable to this equation and sets the subgoal to distribute (strategic knowledge). The second rule

P1: IF   the equation to be solved contains a subexpression of
             the form num(term1 + term2)
     THEN   set as a subgoal to distribute num over term1 and term2

P2: IF   the goal is to distribute num over term1 and term2
     THEN   set the subgoal to multiply num times term1
     AND   set the subgoal to multiply num times term 2
     AND set the subgoal to combine the previous results with +

P3: IF   the goal is to multiply num times term
     THEN   write the product of num and term

P4: IF   the goal is to combine term1 and term2 with a +
     THEN   write term1 + term2

Figure 11.2 Examples of Ideal Model Rules for Doing Distribution

sets up three subgoals: to multiply $7x$ by 3, to multiply 5 by 3, and to add these intermediate results together. The third rule evaluates multiplication subgoals. The fourth rule evaluates add-together subgoals. Rules 2, 3, and 4 are instances of axiomatic knowledge in this rule set.

These rules highlight two features that are critical in generating rule sets for the student model:

1. The grain size of rules is critical when simulating students.

2. Both the strategic and axiomatic knowledge must be simulated.

If the ideal model does not contain rules for a problem-solving action, then that action cannot be independently recognized or tutored by the system. If strategic knowledge is represented independently from the axiomatic knowledge of a domain, this leaves the opportunity to tutor each independently. Having the ability to focus a student's attention solely on strategic decision making at some points and solely on axiomatic knowledge application at other points is a tutoring strategy we have observed some teachers using. The load on working memory can be lightened by varying this division of knowledge between student and tutor during a tutorial session. Results of some informal studies of novices learning to apply the transformations of algebra imply that simply learning how the axioms manipulate symbols may be easier than learning when to apply that axiom in service of problem solving. These strategic and axiomatic components of a skill must both be well learned if the skill is to be applied successfully in problem solving.

But what lower bound do we set on simulating the ideal student? Do we simulate the addition of positive integers as a set of productions that simulate counting on fingers? The answer is no, but how does one make decisions about grain size of ideal model rules in a principled way? There seems to be no clear-cut answer, but the general heuristic is that if you don't *ever* want to tutor a subskill, then represent it as a function call to LISP instead of an ideal model rule that has to fire. This saves time because you don't have to write the rule originally nor does the rule need to be matched during the ideal model's problem solving.

Simulation of Errorful or "Buggy" Problem Solving   When a student makes a problem-solving action that is nonoptimal (perhaps a legal but strategically nonuseful transformation) or incorrect (the application of the axiom is carried out incorrectly in some way), a good human tutor would have some idea of the underlying cognitive cause of the problem. Error-recognition productions of this sort were hand-coded into the LISP tutoring system (Reiser, Anderson, & Farrell, 1985). A goal for the TEACHER'S APPRENTICE is to simulate and recognize these errors on line, in the manner of Brown and van Lehn (1980). Very nice work on the processes underlying algebra errors has been done by Matz (1982). However, from observing classrooms and test performance, there appear to be other classes of errors not covered in the set of generative bugs mapped out by Matz. Errors in factoring that we have observed provide an illustration of these classes.

An amazing variety of errors occurred when an Algebra I class that had studied factoring of both two- and three-term expressions was asked to factor an expression such as $3x + 6y + 12$. Some consistent errors fit into classes covered by Matz, for example, $3(x + 2y) + 12$. This is the failure to repeat the application of an iterative procedure. It is possible that the student is still using a nongeneral, two-term form of the factoring procedure. Also note that this is not a "true error" (a transformation that does not preserve equivalence), but an incomplete application of a transformation.*

However, there seem to be other classes of errors that appear to be amenable to simulation. An example is what we call "form errors." Students gave answers to factoring problems that had the proper form (they looked like an answer to a factoring problem) but had none of the operations of factoring. Examples we saw included $3x(6y + 12)$ and $3(x + 6y + 12)$. Both responses conform to the informal rule that you "pull something out of the terms and leave something in parentheses." Both answers have the *form*

---

* Indeed, there are times when you need to refrain from applying the distributive property to an entire expression in an equation to solve that equation in a simple manner. However, there is also the ability to correctly factor out the greatest common factor from all terms of an isolated expression.

of a correct solution. The latter is different from a "failure-to-iterate" error in that the terms that have not been factored are included in the parentheses. This is a "true error," unlike the incomplete iteration bug above.

In work done with James Greeno, we interviewed students who make such form errors to acquire data regarding how they are misparsing transformations. An example is the student who applied the associative law—presented as $A + (B + C) = (A + B) + C$ to the student—to the arithmetic expression $3 + (4 + 5)$ and got the expression $(4 + 5) + 3$. This is a legal application of the commutative law, but not a legal application of the associative law. When asked how she did this she responded, "You take the part that is sticking out and flip it around to the other side of the parentheses." This response shows no encoding of the fact that the variables have to have the same bindings (i.e., A has to keep the value of 3) or the goal of the application of the associative law: change the grouping of terms. However, the form of the answer was correct. We are working on algorithms that will relax the conditions of some productions to generate buggy rules, as in the work of Brown and Burton (1978). At the same time, we are investigating procedures that will wrongly induce the transformation action embodied in a correct algebra transformation rule.

A study of errors in factoring (Seigler & McGilly, in preparation) is being carried out in parallel with our research. This study investigates the performance of students on factoring problems given different amounts of partial solutions. One of the goals of the pencil-and-paper tests is to decompose the skill of factoring into psychologically meaningful subprocedures. The classroom of study was a nonaccelerated Algebra I class who had not restudied factoring for several weeks, and the problems were presented in the context of a normal class examination. For the problem of factoring $3x + 6y + 12$, students received one of the following frames to fill in answers:

_____   (write out the answer)

___(___ + ___ + ___)   (fill in the blanks)

3(___ + ___ + ___)   (fill in the blanks)

___(x + 2y + 4)   (fill in the blank)

The first is the standard, unaided answer, the second provides the form of the answer and prompts for at least three terms inside the parentheses, the third has the greatest common factor already factored out, and the fourth has the terms with factors removed, leaving only the identification of the greatest common factor. The general result to date is that the more of the subprocedures that were done for the student, the better the performance. Correct responses were most prevalent in the third (88%) and fourth (100%) cases and least prevalent in the first case (58%). Correct performance with the second case was intermediate (71%). Interestingly, there were significantly more correct answers in the second case than the first. Prompting with the form of the answer provided greater support for the correct procedure than no prompt at all. This result fits in with an observation of Matz's (1982) that the first hurdle of the student is knowing what the goal is, that is, inferring the features of the desired result from the instruction. Apparently once the goal is clear, performance improves significantly. This result also corroborates the reports of teachers who identify a class of students who are able to solve sets of problems they are competent to solve only after an example is done for them. This worked example apparently provides the form or goal of the problem, and the students can then apply their skill.

There are also special cases where students with generally correct procedures make errors. An example is the case of factoring an expression where the greatest common factor is an integer term in the expression, for example, $24x + 12$. Some students we observed will not write out 1 as a term in the factored expression. Erroneous responses to the expression given by such students include $12(2x + 12)$ or $12(x)$. These errors might be manifestations of an operator like:

$$X/X \rightarrow X$$

or

$$X/X \rightarrow 0$$

An alternative explanation, offered by a reviewer, is that many students think they are acting *on the symbols per se.* When they are factoring the expression $24x + 12$, they "take the twelve out," leaving a blank space, not zero. This would produce answers like $12(x)$ or $12(2x)$.

These special-case errors can be simulated explicitly and can be candidates for matching buggy responses in situations other than the context of factoring problems. If the error occurred in a division problem, for example, $12/12 = X$, then possible simulated buggy responses from the erroneous rules above would be $0 = X$ and $12 = X$. Siegler and McGilly plan on varying this special case of errors within the factoring experiment mentioned above.

The Interface

Previous experience with developing intelligent tutors has shown that the design of the interface can make or break the effectiveness of a tutor, regardless of the clever design that went into the guts of the underlying system. Our experience points to five critical features of an effective interface for tutoring. It should:

1. Be as easy to use as possible. This means it should minimize the number of actions (e.g., keystrokes, mouse-clicks) needed to communicate with the tutor.

2. Have a structure or representation that is as congruent as possible to the underlying structure of the problems to be solved.

3. Be highly interactive and provide as much information about intermediate problem-solving states of the learner as possible. Given that the feedback received by the student is meaningful, Malone (1981) has pointed to interaction as a motivator in computer-based activities.

4. Have the ability to notice low-level errors as they occur; that is, it should continuously monitor the student's input.

5. Have the ability to vary working memory load. This can be accomplished by giving the student ready access to problem-relevant information and minimizing the number of parts of the screen that have to be attended to and integrated.

A sample of the current interface screen, in reduced form, is presented in Fig. 11.3. Our development machine is the Xerox 1109 DandeTiger.

The TEACHER'S APPRENTICE interface component is a software module that gives both the teacher/curriculum designer and learner access to the input/output facilities of the underlying hardware. It turns the computer's high-resolution display into a combination notebook, scratch pad, and blackboard that is used to echo tutoring interactions and store a record of the student's intermediate work. This design allows the mouse to be used as the primary input device: students can select parts of expressions or menu options with the mouse.

At the current time we have the following windows:

- The Tutoring Window (made to resemble a blackboard), where tutorial interactions are printed.
- The Scratch Pad, which has keypads for generating algebraic expressions needed for responses to the tutoring interactions.
- The Current Equation Window, which displays the current state of the student's equation transformation process.
- The History Window (made to resemble a notebook), where a trace of the problem-solving interaction is recorded for on-line review and later printing by the student.

Our goal was to make the interactions with the interface as easy as using pencil and paper. When generating responses to the tutorial dialogue, students need not type anything on the keyboard. In fact, in most cases, a response can be generated by pointing to parts of the existing expressions in the current

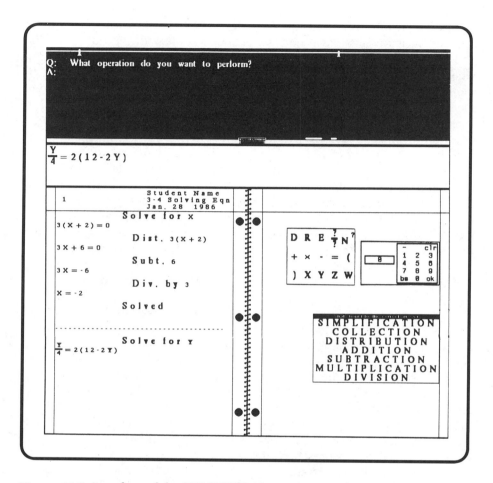

Figure 11.3 Interface of the TEACHER'S APPRENTICE with a Problem Trace
and Prompt for Initial Strategic Decision for a New Problem

equation window. By using pointing instead of requiring students to regenerate
complete expressions when only part might be changed, we may eliminate the
majority of simple slips we've seen in the early stages of learning algebra.
Accidentally dropping a negative sign or forgetting to bring down a term are
common errors when moving from one equation to the newly transformed
equation. By having students point to expressions and having the system bring
down the untransformed parts of the equation intact, we can minimize the
chance that these low-level errors would interfere with the goal of the lesson,
for example, practicing the distributive law in equation solving.

However, this also raises the "training-wheels" issue: what happens when the student leaves this environment that supports his or her problem solving and has to face the realities of pencil and paper? The purpose of training wheels in this context is to unburden working memory with extra tasks until the subskill can be refined and strengthened. Then the burden of working memory required by an unsupported environment can be added in. For example, after bringing down all the untransformed terms and symbols in an equation the system could require the student to bring down individual terms and then eventually end with having the learner enter the entire expression, just as in pencil-and-paper work. We have experience with a PC-based version of a tutor for solving linear equations* that at one point required students to type in entire expressions. Observing high school algebra novices interact with this system made it clear that even the action of typing was, for many students, a large burden. Many errors occurred due to slips and mis-strikes of keys. Often the cause of the system's responses to a simple low-level typing error was misattributed by the learners to a misunderstanding on their part. We want to reduce these often nonconstructive or counterproductive errors in the early stages of skill acquisition.

The interface also has the capability to represent some of the structure of the nested-goal nature of the domain. Figure 11.4 shows a trace of a fine-grained tutorial interaction for factoring. The subskills involved in factoring include the ability to find the greatest common factor of a set of terms. This subgoal must be set at some point, either explicitly or implicitly, depending on the grain size of your rule system at the time of tutoring. Since these are subgoals to the top goal of factoring an expression (which in itself might be in service of some higher-level goal of isolating a variable), we represent the setting of this subgoal as an indented expression in the history window. As subgoals are stacked, the indentation increases, representing the nested structure of the problem solving.

One area where we currently do not represent the structure of the domain with our interface is the idea of search during algebra problem solving. In the geometry tutor (Anderson, Boyle, & Yost, 1985), the search of applying inference rules to generate parts of a proof is represented graphically. The to-be-proven statement is at the top of the screen and the givens of the problem are along the bottom. As the search proceeds, a tree structure is drawn on the screen connecting the entities used in the inferences and generated by the inferences. A claim of the geometry tutoring project is that this graphic representation of the proof-solving process as a tree provides the students with an understanding of what it means to "prove" something in a formal system. A similar tack is being taken in algebra tutoring work by Brown (1983) and McArthur (1985). They represent the search of applying algebraic transformations to expressions as a

---

* This system currently runs on an IBM PC in under 192K of memory, contains an expert system for solving linear equations, and allows multiple solution paths.

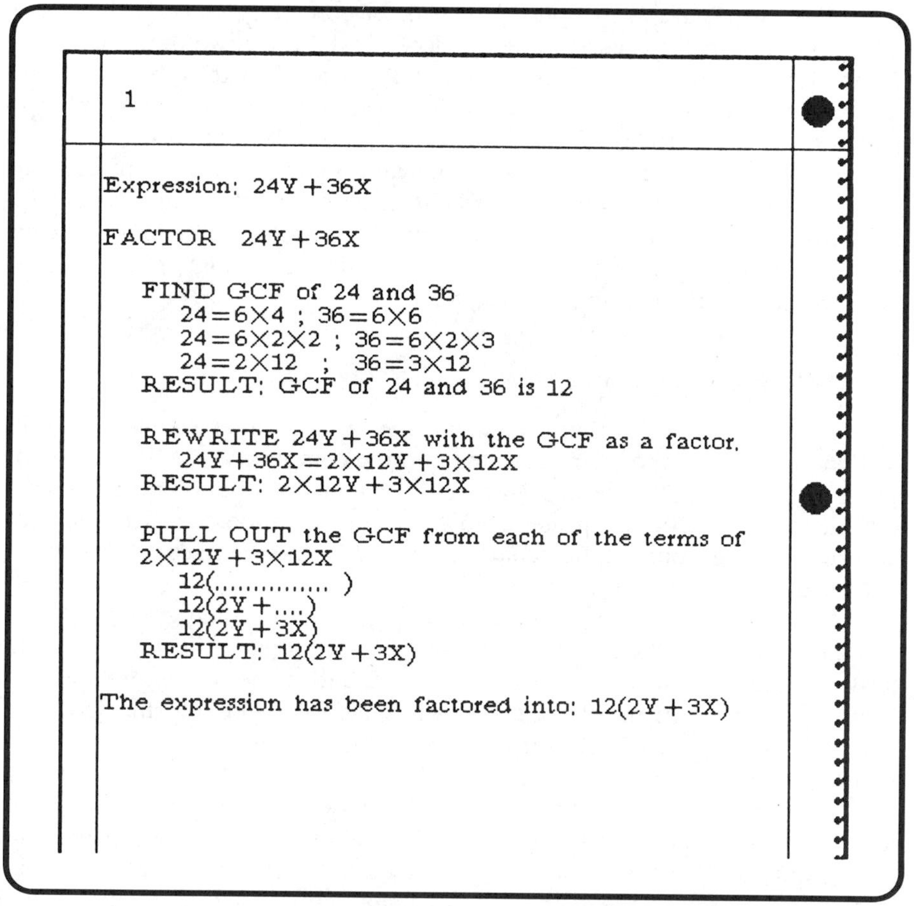

```
1                                                          ●

Expression: 24Y+36X

FACTOR   24Y+36X

    FIND GCF of 24 and 36
        24=6×4 ; 36=6×6
        24=6×2×2 ; 36=6×2×3
        24=2×12  ;   36=3×12
    RESULT: GCF of 24 and 36 is 12

    REWRITE 24Y+36X with the GCF as a factor.
        24Y+36X=2×12Y+3×12X
    RESULT: 2×12Y+3×12X

    PULL OUT the GCF from each of the terms of
    2×12Y+3×12X
        12(............... )
        12(2Y+....)
        12(2Y+3X)
    RESULT: 12(2Y+3X)

The expression has been factored into: 12(2Y+3X)
```

Figure 11.4 An example of the problem-solving trace which appears in the history window during the course of factoring an expression. This trace shows the use of indention to represent subgoals.

tree structure. The reason that this has not been incorporated into the TEACHER'S APPRENTICE project is that the model-tracing methodology currently keeps the learner on one of the correct solution paths in the problem. The possibility of going off one of the correct solution paths is not currently allowed. When an attempt is made at a strategically nonoptimal move the student is told that it is nonoptimal, given a justification in terms of reducing differences in the expression, and prompted to choose again. The efficacy of letting students search off of correct or optimal problem-solving paths is very much an open question that invites some incisive research.

Although the graphic displays of tutors have been explored, a dimension of an interface that we have not yet explored is the use of synthesized speech for the tutorial dialogues. Use of speech would embody part of the fourth goal of effective interface design enumerated above: try to reduce the number of parts of the screen to be attended to and integrated. The interactions of good human tutors with students of algebra contain a great deal of pointing while talking. In most cases students never take their eyes off of the expressions being manipulated as the tutor points to parts of that expression. We feel that extra pedagogical leverage might be gained through the use of highlighting expressions while presenting synthesized speech.

The Tutoring Component

The third component of the system, and the one that interacts with both the student models and the interface, is the tutoring component. The tutoring component determines the exact nature of the interactions between the tutoring system and student by taking cues from the state of the student model simulation and by utilizing input/output facilities provided by the interface so that appropriate advice and feedback can be given to the learner.

The tutoring component implements a specific tutoring strategy that is, roughly speaking, a set of rules describing the sort of questions to present, the answers to expect, and the nature of feedback during the student interactions. Thus the same problem-solving task is amenable to several tutoring strategies. For instance, if the tutoring domain is the solution of linear equations in one variable, two strategies are conceivable.

The first possible strategy is to guide the student through the solution path a step at a time and be very explicit regarding the nature of responses when asking questions of the student. Thus, for the example $3(x + 2) = 14$, the system might provide the very simple dialogue given in Fig. 11.5. The tutorial interactions we present are intentionally impoverished and simplified due to space constraints and belie the flexibility of the system. As mentioned earlier, students can solve a single problem in a variety of ways, and errors can be detected and handled intelligently. The goal of presenting examples of interactions is simply to illustrate the operation of the system. The richness of the tutorial interaction is in the hands of the implementor.

The dialogue in Fig. 11.5:

■ Presents the student with a menu of possible operations that can be performed on the equation, accepting only DISTRIBUTION as a correct choice.

■ Makes the student indicate the term to be distributed (3) and the expression over which to distribute it.

■ Guides the student through the distribution process one term at a time (3 over $x \rightarrow 3x$ and then 3 over 2 $\rightarrow$ 6).

CURRENT EXPRESSION: $3(x + 2) = 14$

Q: What operation do you want to perform?

> *Operations*
> COLLECT LIKE TERMS   SUBTRACT FROM BOTH SIDES
> DISTRIBUTE   MULTIPLY BOTH SIDES
> ADD TO BOTH SIDES   DIVIDE BOTH SIDES

A: DISTRIBUTE   [student moused the DISTRIBUTE menu option]
→ Correct

Q: To what expression do you want to apply the distributive law?
A: $3(x + 2)$ [student has boxed this expression with the mouse]
→ Correct

Q: What term do you want to distribute?
A: 3   [boxed in the current expression]
→ Correct

Q: What expression do you want to distribute 3 over?
A: $(x + 2)$ [boxed in the current expression]
→ Correct

Q: What part of the expression of $x + 2$ do you want to distribute over?
A: x   [boxed in the current expression]
→ Correct

Q: What is $3 * x$?
A: 3x   [boxed in the current expression, as two
                   individual entities]
→ Correct

Q: What part of the expression of $+ 2$ do you want to distribute over?
A: 2   [boxed in the current expression]
→ Correct

Q: What is $3 * 2$?
A: 6   [generated from a keypad menu on the screen]
→ Correct

Q: What is the new expression after distribution?
A: 3x + 6   [generated from the current expression and the
                   keypad menu]
→ Correct

CURRENT EXPRESSION: $3x + 6 = 14$

Figure 11.5 An Example of an Extended Tutorial Dialogue for the Application
of the Distributive Law in the Service of Simplifying an Equation

■ Requires the student to assemble the new expression and then rewrites the rest of the equation.

A second possible tutoring strategy would be to allow the student to reach the solution as independently as possible. This strategy would be implemented by allowing the student to type in any equation that is closer to the final solution than the equation considered previously. Feedback is given when the student enters an equation that is not closer to the final solution. The exact content of the feedback depends on the problem-solving context and the student's actual error. For example, the erroneous transformation:

$$3(x + 2) = 14 \quad \rightarrow \quad 3x + 2 = 14$$

generates feedback such as "You only distributed the 3 over the x and not over the 2. When distributing, the distributing term has to multiply each term in the distributed expression." Students are then allowed to correct the mistake once; if they fail, they are simply given the next equation on the solution path and allowed to continue independently.

The two tutoring strategies outlined above have very different consequences in regard to the problem-solving processes. The first strategy will greatly restrict the kinds of errors that the student may make by taking a very strong-handed or structured approach to the tutoring process. The second strategy is much less restricted, allowing more freedom for learners to collapse steps. We are working towards a general and tailorable tutoring component to allow precisely this sort of difference: both of the strategies may be implemented on a system with the same student model of equation solving and the same interface capabilities. The issue of the tutoring strategy is thus separable from the specific nature of the student model and the tutoring interface. In other words, it should be possible to design the student model and the tutoring interface without an exact specification of the tutoring strategy.

The Operation of the Tutoring Component   The control of the tutoring component is determined by a production systemlike construct called the tutoring rule (Clancey, 1982) controller. The basic unit of the controller is the tutoring rule (t-rule) whose execution determines the exact behavior of the system. The selection of which t-rule will fire is a consequence of:

1. The state of the ideal model as it computes a solution to the given problem.

2. The content of the "active set" of t-rules that restricts the full set of t-rules known to the system down to the few that are applicable to the given state of the ideal model's execution.

Assuming, for the simple case, that the solution path of the given problem is strictly linear (i.e., at each production firing there is only one production that will be appropriate), the action of the student model will be a sequence of production firings. Each t-rule specifies a single student model production that will trigger it. The t-rule controller will start from the current point on the solution path and scan downward until the first occurrence of a student model production that is specified by one of the t-rules in the active set. This allows the instructional designer to exclude any number of intermediate problem-solving steps from the tutorial dialogue. Subsequent cycles of the controller will then proceed from that production.

The execution of a t-rule has the effect of:

1. Formatting and sending output or soliciting input via the interface.

2. Determining the active set of t-rules for the next system cycle.

In the case of an output t-rule, the active set is specified unconditionally while an input t-rule determines the active set based on the nature of the learner's response. When the input t-rule fires, the input from the student is fitted into any of several t-rule categories. Each category has a set of t-rules associated with it and that set becomes the active set for the following cycle of the t-rule controller. Typically, one of these categories will correspond to correct inputs, another to requests for help from the student, and the rest to the various kinds of errors that are predicted by the student model at that particular point on the solution path. As an example of this process, take the current equation to be $3(X + 2) = 14$. If the ideal model productions are the four productions in Fig. 11.2, then the following sequence of firings will result:

Working memory: $3(X + 2) = 14$
    P1: num binds to 3, term1 binds to X, term2 binds to 2

Working memory: Distribute 3 over X and 2
    P2: bindings stay the same

Working memory: Multiply X by 3
    P3: num binds to 3, term binds to X

Working memory: Multiply 2 by 3
    P3: num binds to 3, term binds to 2

Working memory: Combine 3X and 6 with a +
    P4: term1 binds to 3X, term2 binds to 6

Working memory: $3X + 6 = 14$

The t-rules in Fig. 11.6 specify a possible tutoring strategy for distribution, working with the ideal model productions in Fig. 11.2. To start this example, the active set of t-rules must be initialized as {T1}. Given the current expression, the current ideal model production to apply is P1. (This simple example contains only one solution path and no buggy rules. Only a single ideal model rule is in the conflict set at any point.) The tutor will go through the following states:

```
Name:  T1
Production:  P1
Action Type:  Output
Action Body:  Print "What operation do you want to perform?"
Active Set Transition:  {T2}
```

```
Name:  T2
Production:  P1
Action Type:  Input
Action Body:  Bring up a menu of choices.
Active Set Transition:  if student input is
                            DISTRIBUTION → {T3}
                            anything else   → {T4}
```

```
Name:  T3
Production:  P2
Action Type:  Output
Action Body:  Print "Correct."
Active Set Transition:  {T5}
```

```
Name:  T4
Production:  P1
Action Type:  Output
Action Body:  Print "Wrong. The right answer was DISTRIBUTION."
Active Set Transition:  {T5}
```

Figure 11.6 T-rules to Be Used with the Ideal Model Rules in Fig. 11.2

Since the current production is P1 and the active set includes T1, and T1 is associated with P1, T1 will fire:

The tutor types "What operation do you want to perform?"

Active Set becomes {T2}, T2 is associated with P1, so now T2 fires.

The tutor brings up a menu of choices and waits for the student to select one of them. Assume that the student chooses DISTRIBUTION.

Active Set becomes {T3}. P1 finishes firing and P2 becomes the current production. Then T3 is selected as the next tutoring rule, and fires.

Name: T5
Production: P2
Action Type: Output
Action Body: Print "What is the result of distributing "num" over
    "term1 + term 2"?"
Active Set Transition: {T6}

Name: T6
Production: P4
Action Type: Input
Action Body: Make the student enter an algebraic expression.
Active Set Transition: if student input is
                        term1 + term2 $\rightarrow$ {T7}
                        anything else $\rightarrow$ {T8}

Name: T7
Production: P4
Action Type: Output
Action Body: Print "Correct."
Active Set Transition: Empty set (End tutoring session)

Name: T8
Production: P4
Action Type: Output
Action Body: Print "Wrong. The correct answer was" term1 + term2
Active Set Transition: Empty set (End tutoring session)

Figure 11.6 T-rules to Be Used with the Ideal Model Rules in Fig. 11.2 (cont.)

The tutor types "Correct."

Active Set becomes {T5}, T5 is associated with P2, so the tutor will fire ideal model productions until the current production is P2 and then T5 will fire.

The tutor types "What is the result of distributing 3 over X + 2?"

Active Set becomes {T6}, T6 is associated with P4 which is now the current ideal model production so that T6 fires.

The tutor brings up the scratch pad and lets the student enter an algebraic expression.

Suppose the student enters 3X + 2 (an error). Active Set becomes {T8}. Since T8 (the "catchall" specified in T6) is associated with P4, T8 will now fire.

The tutor types "Wrong. The correct answer was 3X + 6."

Active Set is now empty and the tutoring interaction concludes.

What happens when more than one ideal model rule applies at the same time? What sort of tutoring strategies are possible in such a case? How must the t-rule controller be configured to implement them? Assume that we have the equation 3(X + 2) = −2(4 − 2X). The student model may allow either of the two distributions to be performed first. A function of any tutor must be to find out which operation the student wants to perform first. One can accomplish this goal by posing the appropriate question to the student and using the student's response to specify the branching in the ideal model production solution path. Before the exact path determination is made, the controller has to execute a parallel sequence of t-rule firings for each branch in the solution path. Moreover, the output produced by each parallel sequence of t-rules has to be the same, or the tutor would be faced with a dilemma: which of the t-rules being executed in parallel should determine the behavior of the system?

Here is what would happen if we used the ideal model and the t-rules of the previous example on an equation with two places to perform distribution:

Current equation is 3(X + 2) = 2(4X + 2).

BRANCH-1:   distribute 3(X + 2)

    The tutor types "What operation do you want to perform?"

    The tutor brings up a menu of choices and waits for the student to select one of them. Assume that the student chooses DISTRIBUTION.

    The tutor types "Correct."

    The tutor types "What is the result of distributing 3 over X + 2?"

    The tutor brings up the scratch pad and lets the student enter an algebraic expression. Suppose the student enters 3X + 2 (an error).

    The tutor types "Wrong. The correct answer was 3X + 6."

BRANCH-2:   distribute 2(4X + 2)

    The tutor types "What operation do you want to perform?"

    The tutor brings up a menu of choices and waits for the student to select one of them. Assume that the student chooses DISTRIBUTION.

    The tutor types "Correct."

    The tutor types "What is the result of distributing 2 over 4X + 2?"

The tutor brings up the scratch pad and lets the student enter an algebraic expression. Suppose the student enters 4X + 2 (an error).

The tutor types "Wrong. The correct answer was 8X + 4."

Note that the first three t-rule firings result in identical tutor behavior, so that it is impossible to distinguish which path the student is currently pursuing. At the fourth t-rule firing the tutor is faced with a dilemma: it is not clear which ideal model production path to follow and the tutoring strategy is giving ambiguous instructions. This means that the tutoring strategy outlined above is somehow deficient, that is, it won't handle a multiple distributions situation. One could enrich it by adding the t-rules shown in Fig. 11.7 that make the student specify the part of the equation that should be distributed. With the addition of such t-rules the tutoring interaction would be:

The tutor types "What operation do you want to perform?"

The tutor brings up a menu of choices and waits for the student to select one of them. Assume that the student chooses DISTRIBUTION.

The tutor types "Correct."

The tutor types "What part of the equation do you want to distribute?"

The tutor brings up the scratch pad and lets the student enter an algebraic expression. Suppose the student enters 2(4X + 2).

At this point the tutor knows that the student is pursuing branch 2 of the solution path and no subsequent ambiguity will arise.

The tutor types "Correct."

The tutor types "What is the result of distributing 2 over 4X + 2?"

The tutor brings up the scratch pad and lets the student enter an algebraic expression. Suppose the student enters 4X + 2 (an error).

The tutor types "Wrong. The correct answer was 8X + 4."

So, all in all, the t-rule controller has the flavor of a very simple programming language that has input and output capabilities but no ability to manipulate data. It has access to the information generated by the student model in the form of the specific production firings and the information gained by the binding of student model production system variables during the execution of the production system. However, it cannot do things like bind new variables, increment counters, and so forth. Thus control of flow is similar to the control execution for a finite state automaton where there are a finite number of transitions from any particular state of the system. The equivalent of "state" for the t-rule Controller is each t-rule which is capable of transitioning to certain other t-rules, the exact successor being determined by the productions fired by the student model and the behavior of the tutored student.

```
Name:  T4-A
Production:  P1
Action Type:  Output
Action Body:  Print "What part of the equation do you want to distribute?"
Active Set Transition:  {T4-B}
```

```
Name:  T4-B
Production:  P1
Action Type:  Input
Action Body:  Make the student enter an algebraic expression.
Active Set Transition:  if student input is
                    num (term1 + term2) → {T5}
                    anything else          → {T4-C}
```

```
Name:  T4-C
Production:  P1
Action Type:  Output
Action Body:  Print "Wrong. " num(term1 + term2) " is the expression
        to apply distribution to."
Active Set Transition:  {T5}
```

Figure 11.7 Additional t-rules to those in Fig. 11.6 which would have the student specify the part of the equation that should be distributed. These t-rules would be inserted by changing the active set transition pointer in T3 and T4 from T5 to T4-A. These are to be used with the ideal model rules in Fig. 11.2.

We have not yet considered the exact method for entering t-rules into the system. The system modularity/efficiency constraint requires that the t-rule controller, the interface, and the student model be specified independently from any given tutoring strategy and be able to implement a large number of different strategies. It is also important to have the t-rule entry process be as simple as possible. To avoid the necessity of a special syntax and editor for entering tutoring rules, we have taken a "learning-by-example" approach: The human instructional designer/teacher determines the tutoring interactions by specifying concrete examples in the act of tutoring simulated students on the system. This is detailed in the next section.

The Rule Induction Component: Induction of Tutoring Strategy by Example

The goal of being able to implement new tutoring strategies for a skill quickly and simply is best met when you minimize the diversity and specificity of the knowledge needed by the instructional designer or teacher (referred to hereafter as the implementor) who is implementing that strategy. This means that programming skills should not be requisite, nor should the implementor have to be familiar with the syntax and the internal details of the production system that underlies the student model. Another feature that should speed up the implementation process is an interface that programs the tutoring component interactively rather than via an indirect process such as the edit/compile/execute cycle that one finds in more conventional programming. These two goals may be achieved by making a graphics-based authoring system available to the implementor that, in an uncomplicated and straightforward manner, allows the implementor to determine the tutor's action at any specific instant in the tutoring process.

Our attempt at reducing the load on the implementor involves building an authoring system that depends on having the implementor play out the roles of the tutor and an ideal student (one that gets every answer correct) within the context of a particular problem. The authoring system translates the implementor's surface behavior into a set of general tutoring rules that will serve to specify a tutoring strategy for all problems utilizing the same student model productions as the original problem. The induced t-rules should faithfully reproduce the behavior that the implementor gave as an example.

Tutoring behavior can be divided into the categories of output and input. An output t-rule must specify the content of the output as well as its destination (prompt window or history window) and its form (font, background shade, and other appearance features). Input of arbitrary algebraic expressions and equations occurs via the scratch pad. Multiple choice decisions can be presented and choices input via menus. The content of a particular tutoring interaction can be further subdivided into the problem-independent and problem-dependent categories. If the system is tutoring on the solution of $2(X + 1) = 4$ and the tutor prints the question: "What is 2 distributed over $X + 1$?" the "2" and the "$X + 1$" are problem dependent, while the form of the question (the exact wording used) is problem independent; that is, it will be the same for any tutored problem solved in the same way as the "$2(X + 1) = 4$" problem.

Since the tutor deals with algebraic problems, the problem-dependent components will be algebraic expressions (algebraic fields of t-rules). In specifying these algebraic fields the t-rule controller utilizes the names of production system variables that are bound during the student model's solution of the problem. The implementor has access to the ideal student model and its variable bindings via a set of protocols/comments that the system generates as it runs the production system simulation. These protocols contain an English explanation of what each production firing accomplished and lists the algebraic fields that the production utilized. The implementor must choose the ideal model rule that corresponds to that particular interaction before specifying any sample behavior. The implementor does this by indicating to the authoring system one of the protocol steps that narrate the problem solution. For instance, if the implementor wants the tutor to ask the question "What is the result of multiplying 1 by 2?" he or she should associate that question with a protocol that describes a production that instantiates this operation. When the time comes to give the actual content of a tutoring interaction, the algebraic fields detailed in the selected protocol can be used by the implementor to specify algebraic expressions to include in the tutoring interaction. Thus, in the example above, "2" and "1" would be expressions that the implementor could select from the body of the protocol rather than specifying them arbitrarily. Such a selection indicates to the authoring system that these expressions are problem dependent and should be simulated by production system variables bound during the execution of the ideal model.

Another feature of this process of associating tutoring interactions with ideal model rules is that not every ideal model rule has to be tutored. In fact, by skipping intermediate steps the implementor has control over the grain size of the tutoring strategy that is being implemented.

If there are multiple solution paths for the given problem, then there will be multiple protocol traces of these production firings. Implementors can specify the path that they want to follow as they detail the tutoring strategy for the current problem. In particular, this means that if there are multiple algorithms for solving a problem, implementors have to indicate to the system which of these algorithms they are assuming to underly the current tutoring strategy.

The following is an example of the induction process operating on a portion of one set of ideal student productions that deal with solution of linear equations. N and N1 are variables that match any positive integer. V is a variable that matches any algebraic variable. T1 and T2 match to any term, and SIGN matches either + or −.

P1: N (T1 SIGN T2) → COMBINE {+ DISTRIBUTE {N , T1} ,
$\qquad$ SIGN DISTRIBUTE {N T2}
$\qquad$ }

P2: N (− T1 SIGN T2) → COMBINE {− DISTRIBUTE {N , T1} ,
$\qquad$ SIGN DISTRIBUTE {N T2}
$\qquad$ }

P3: DISTRIBUTE {N , N1} → (TIMES N N1)

P4: DISTRIBUTE {N , V} → N V

P5: DISTRIBUTE {N , N1 V} $\twoheadrightarrow$ (TIMES N N1) V
P6: DISTRIBUTE {N , $-$ N1} $\twoheadrightarrow$ $-$ (TIMES N N1)
P7: DISTRIBUTE {N , $-$ V} $\twoheadrightarrow$ $-$ N V
P8: DISTRIBUTE {N , $-$ N1 V} $\twoheadrightarrow$ $-$ (TIMES N N1) V
P9: COMBINE {+ T1 , + T2} $\twoheadrightarrow$ T1 + T2
P10: COMBINE {+ T1 , $-$ T2} $\twoheadrightarrow$ T1 $-$ T2
P11: COMBINE {$-$ T1 , + T2} $\twoheadrightarrow$ $-$ T1 + T2
P12: COMBINE {$-$ T1 , $-$ T2} $\twoheadrightarrow$ $-$ T1 $-$ T2

The current problem is $2(X + 1) = 4$, and it is up to the implementor to demonstrate a strategy for distributing a positive number over a two-term expression. What follows is the sequence of ideal model firings and the resultant modifications to working memory.

Equation 0: $2 (X + 1) = 4$

P1 fires   N (T1 SIGN T2) $\twoheadrightarrow$ COMBINE { + DISTRIBUTE {N , T1} ,
                                           SIGN DISTRIBUTE {N , T2}}

   Bindings: N = 2, T1 = X, SIGN = +, T2 = 1

Equation 1:   COMBINE { + DISTRIBUTE {2 , X} , +
                 DISTRIBUTE {2 , 1}} = 4

P3 fires   DISTRIBUTE {N , V} $\twoheadrightarrow$ N V
   Bindings: N = 2, V = X

Equation 2:   COMBINE { + 2 X , DISTRIBUTE {2 , 1} } = 4

P4 fires   DISTRIBUTE {N , N1} $\twoheadrightarrow$ (TIMES N N1)
   Bindings: N = 2, N1 = 1

Equation 3:   COMBINE { + 2 X , + 2} = 4

P9 fires   COMBINE { + T1 , + T2} $\twoheadrightarrow$ T1 + T2
   Bindings: T1 = 2 X, T2 = 2

Equation 4:   2 X + 2 = 4

Below are samples of the protocols for these productions that the system would present to the implementor.

P1 Fires: (Annotation)
    Solving $2(X + 1) = 4$ necessitates a distribution operation.
    Set the goal to distribute 2 over X.
    Set the goal to distribute 2 over 1.
    Combine the resulting terms, both of which will be positive.
    Algebraic fields available: 2 , X , 1 , +.

P2 Fires: (Annotation)
       Distributing 2 over X.
       The result is 2 X.
       Algebraic fields available: 2, X.

P3 Fires: (Annotation)
       Distributing 2 over 1.
       The result is 2.
       Algebraic fields available: 2, 1, 2.

       (Note: the second "2" is specified as the result of the multiplication.
       N * N1 will not always equal N, so this apparent redundancy is no
       redundancy at all.)

P9 Fires: (Annotation)
       Combining + 2 X and + 2
       The result is 2 X + 2
       The equation is now 2 X + 2 = 4.
       Algebraic fields available: 2 X, 2.

Let us assume that the implementor wishes to specify a strategy that forces
the student to take three steps in three interactions:

1. Establish the operation to be performed.

2. Specify the multiplier and the two terms.

3. Specify the answer.

For the first of these interactions the implementor would indicate the first
protocol, since it is at that point that the distribution operation is selected. The
implementor would then have the tutor print the question "What operation
should you perform now?" on the blackboard and then specify a menu that
contained the label "DISTRIBUTION" along with several erroneous distractor
menu items. The implementor would indicate that the answer "DISTRIBUTION"
was the correct one.

The tutoring interactions that asked for the two terms would also be associated with the first production. The answer to "What are the terms of the
expression?" would be answered by X and 1. The implementor could specify
the "X" and the "1" by selecting appropriately from the list of algebraic fields
available in the protocol of the first production.

The last production would be chosen to correspond to the third interaction.
In response to the question (which the implementor specifies to appear on the
blackboard) "What is the overall result of the distribution?" the tutor will expect
the correct answer 2X + 2. The implementor could indicate "2X + 2" to the
tutor by using the algebraic fields of the fourth protocol (they are 2X and 2)
and one plus sign, which is actually invariant because the production, COMBINE
$\{+T1 , +T2\} \rightarrow T1 + T2$, fires only when positive terms are combined.

After entering the strategy for the ideal case, the implementor has to indicate the tutoring behavior for the case of incorrect student responses. This is done in much the same way as the specification for the correct strategy. For each production in the solution path there may be several bugs known to the system (each of these buggy productions is available as an improper variant of the correct production) that may fire at that point. The buggy productions would have a protocol associated with them. The role of the implementor would be to select the buggy production's protocol, to indicate the response made by a buggy student, and to specify the tutoring strategy to remediate such an error.

The following is an example of a buggy production that is a variant of P1 from the immediately previous set of ideal model productions.

P1* (buggy version)
$$N \ (T1 \ \text{SIGN} \ T2) \rightarrow \text{COMBINE} \ \{ + \ \text{DISTRIBUTE} \ \{N \ , \ T1\} \ , \ \text{SIGN} \ T2\}$$

The buggy production simulates a student who fails to distribute the multiplier over the second term (the failure-to-iterate bug, Matz, 1982). In the context of our previous example—solving $2 \ (X + 1) = 4$—the student would derive $2X + 1 = 4$. A student who followed the bug would behave exactly as an ideal student in the example interactions outlined above, except for the final question ("What is the final result of this distribution operation?") to which the student would respond with "$2X + 1$." The implementor would simulate the bug for the system by selecting the protocol that corresponds to the buggy production, and then enter a desired remediation strategy after the student errorfully enters "$2X + 1$" in response to the last question of the distribution interaction.

The implementor also has to indicate the tutor's strategy for the case when the student makes an error that is not predicted by the error model, or the case when the student asks for help. There are several such strategies: give the right answer and go on, give a couple of hints before continuing, loop N times and then continue, and so on. This is left to the implementor's choice.

A working induction system promises to be a real boon to developers of tutors. Once the cognitive skills and their attendant errors have been simulated via a student model, building a tutor becomes the simple task of giving example interactions for a set of problems (in the case of our work the size of this set is on the order of 100 problems).† This is a process of days and not months, the time previously required to implement an intelligent tutor. The process by which the savings are gained is analogous to the savings granted by a state-of-the-art authoring system to the designer of CAI curricula: much of the work is done for the implementor. The induction component of the TEACHER'S APPRENTICE is an authoring system for intelligent tutors.

---

† We foresee such a system being delivered to the teacher or district with complete set of tutoring strategies encoded. These would then be amenable to change and refinement as the district or teacher saw fit.

The Pragmatics of Integrating ICAI into the Classroom

Our regular observations of an algebra class coupled with interviews of both geometry and algebra teachers have provided valuable data regarding the pragmatics of integrating intelligent tutoring systems into public school classrooms. A brief account of the insights gained by Frank Boyle and the geometry tutoring project as they took the final steps of getting the geometry tutoring system out of the lab and into the classroom is illustrative of this point.*

A tutoring system for geometry proofs has been developed in the lab and has been both piloted (Anderson, Boyle, & Yost, 1985) and used in a controlled study. The results were very encouraging: high school students were learning not only how to solve proofs but also what it means to prove a statement. They also felt positively about the experience of learning with the tutoring system. The next step was to put the tutors into a classroom. What was learned about how geometry is taught in the classroom is that proofs are very rarely assigned as classwork! Proof problems are assigned as homework. Enter the pragmatics of the classroom: If students in a standard class are given the task of solving some proof problems, there will be some fairly large proportion who will get stuck very early in the problem. These students, being stuck and frustrated, will be likely to disturb others and generally get into trouble. Hence teachers solve examples on the board and lecture in class but reportedly seldom assign proof problems.

In order for the geometry system to be useful as a tutor of problem-solving skills, teachers must change their style of teaching and assign problems during class. We hope the pedagogical effectiveness and motivational aspects of quality intelligent tutoring systems outweigh the cost to the teachers involved in changing their teaching style. This is also a nice illustration of how interactive teaching systems can accomplish multiple goals of tutoring problem-solving skill on line in the classroom and reducing the effective student/teacher ratio. If the systems can engage the students and keep them working productively (as would a good human tutor) then teachers have more options for alternative classroom structures. They would have to spend less time policing behavior.

However, the idea of changing the structure of a high school algebra or geometry class is a radical change to the normal culture of mathematics classes. A case in point is that the algebra class we have been observing contains a commercial CAI system that can accommodate eight students at a time. How is such a limited resource to be used? Should teachers rotate students through the system in three groups? What happens to the time it takes to switch students in and out of the work stations? And if you have students grouped, how do you take best advantage of the reduced student/teacher ratio? Many high school teachers apparently are not specifically trained in techniques of creating and

---

* The geometry tutoring system went into a classroom in the Pittsburgh public schools in January 1986 and is currently under evaluation.

using groups in classrooms or in techniques of using centers and minimizing transition time. However, many elementary school teachers are trained in such techniques. With the advent of intelligent tutors in the classroom there may need to be additional training of existing teachers and possibly additions or changes to the skills taught in high school teacher education programs.

We currently envision that a one-to-one ratio of machines to students will be necessary in classrooms. This is the ratio at the current site of the geometry tutor test classroom. However, use of intelligent tutors may fit more effectively into a "learning laboratory" type setting. Students have time allotted to go to the room where the machines are and use them at their own pace as an activity separate from the classroom. There is a precedent for this type of structure in existing reading and language laboratories in high schools.

Interesting Possible Side Effects from Developing ICAI

Possible interesting side effects of developing ICAI for mathematics may come in the area of educating teachers. A system that can emulate a teacher's style allows the possibility for a teacher to watch this emulation teach either simulated or real students and reflect on their personal pedagogical decisions and strategies. Observation and reflection is different from watching a videotape of oneself teaching. Although observing oneself teaching can be quite informative and constructive, it is difficult to step out of the context one was in when the taped events were taking place. This biases the actors' observations. It is often necessary to have another person watch the tape and make observations or ask questions to get other perspectives on the interaction.

Being able to step back and watch one's personal strategies being applied faithfully to new examples might allow the distance necessary to see incongruities in one's style, such as treating certain cases of problem solving differently than other equivalent cases. A simple example is how distribution might be handled. It is possible that some teachers might want to teach separate rules for how to do distribution of a negative sign over a parenthesized expression, $-(x + 3)$, and for how to do distribution of an integer over a parenthesized expression, $-2(x + 3)$. Because teachers might want these as separate cases, we can put in separate rules for these cases. The first case might be tutored as "change the signs of all the terms inside the parentheses" and the second case might be tutored with the iterative procedure for doing distribution. It is possible that a teacher might observe these two cases being tutored differently and decide that they might be more effectively tutored as cases of the same iterative algorithm.

This is also a nonthreatening way to observe another teacher's teaching style and possibly gain some insights, language, strategies, or tricks. One could imagine groups of teachers cooperating to build different tutoring models that could then be tested on students in their classrooms. In this way teachers could be included in the loop of instructional research: their classroom-earned expertise could be collected and shared with other teachers and researchers. An interesting research question involves the possibility of collecting sets of tutoring rules that have been developed by teachers and have proved effective in classrooms. These sets could be the object of research to deduce why such sets are effective. There is clearly more potential for ICAI than just the benefits to end-user learners in the classroom.

Settings Where Math ICAI Might Be Effective outside the Standard High School Environment

Remedial math students are another potentially large population for whom mathematics ICAI might be useful. A local university reports that 40% of the incoming first-year students take some course in remedial algebra. The military also has an extensive need to do rapid remedial math training for incoming recruits. This older population may have different motivations for pursuing mathematics, and the interaction with a human teacher may be less critical than we perceive it to be in a standard high school class. Our experiences with a population of adults taking remedial algebra at a local junior college suggest that there is a fairly large subset of these students that don't want to have humans around to tutor them. They would rather, in many cases, keep their mistakes to themselves. The other population where intelligent tutors might be recommended for use without a human teacher in attendance would be children in isolated environments due either to health or to geographical constraints.

How the TEACHER'S APPRENTICE Differs from Traditional CAI

It is important to ask the question of how various ICAI systems differ from or improve upon the technology of quality computer-assisted instruction; that is, to perform a rational comparison, free of "straw men." Where is the "intelligence"? We acknowledge the observation that the surface output of the TEACHER'S APPRENTICE strongly resembles that of standard CAI: prompts, responses that are matched, and branching to new prompts. What this surface similarity does not reveal is the major difference that underlies the surface behavior: generative ability. In fact, it is possible to hand-program CAI that would exactly match any behavior of the TEACHER'S APPRENTICE. However, it would take huge amounts of programming time to map out the problem-solving path in any detail and specify the responses at each point for every problem in a reasonably large problem library. In the TEACHER'S APPRENTICE, the ideal model's trace and a tutorial interaction can be generated on-line for arbitrary problems: there is not a library of problems, but a library of knowledge. In addition, the ability to generate errors relieves the need to pre-establish all specific errors and all the contexts in which they will occur. So, if there is "intelligence" in the system, it lies in the ability to generate tutorial instruction.

Conclusions

This chapter began with a set of very general goals for ICAI in general, and for the TEACHER'S APPRENTICE project specifically. After describing the various components of our system and their interaction, it is now time to recap how the system attempts to fulfill the goals laid out initially.

Goal 1: Make Intelligent Tutors Effective

We have designed and are implementing an intelligent tutor based on a learning theory: ACT*. Based on the learning theory, certain principles for how to do effective tutoring have been enumerated. These principles are embodied in the design of the interface, the construction of the ideal and buggy models of the skill, and in both the timing and content of feedback students receive when errors are made.

Goal 2: Make Intelligent Tutoring Systems Available

We have attempted to cut the development time and cost of bringing up new tutors by attempting to keep the components of the system modular and independent. By maintaining modularity, it should be possible to create new tutors for related domains of mathematics such as Algebra II and calculus with reduced effort. A new student model and set of tutoring rules would need to be developed, but the tutoring control, induction, and interface components would theoretically not need to be altered a great deal.

We are also experimenting with techniques to speed up the execution of the ideal model. Letting the ideal model solve the problems before the tutorial interaction begins allows the generation of a search space for the correct solutions of the problem which can then be quickly searched "on-line" during the interactions. The only rules that would have to run in real-time would be the buggy rules.

One counterpoint to the "availability" issue is that the system currently runs on a class of very powerful and very expensive machines. We are targeting this system for the machines of the early 1990s. Reports from hardware companies and the general trend of the hardware industry support the belief that machines capable of running our software will be in the affordable range for schools by the early 1990s.

Goal 3: Make Intelligent Tutors Usable

We are building a system that will be amenable to different problem-solving and teaching styles by emulating individual teachers' language and grain size of instruction. We have taken the position that we cannot second-guess what teachers currently want, nor what they will want in the near future. We also do not want to dictate how tutoring interactions should take place: different teachers might teach subtly different algorithms and use different language for math entities and concepts because of regional differences or differences in training. By giving teachers a flexible tool we hope to maximize the probability that this new technology ends up being integrated into the teaching style of the individual teachers and hence better fits into the culture of the classroom.

References

Anderson, J. R. (1982). Acquisition of cognitive skill. *Psychological Review, 89,* 369–403.

Anderson, J. R. (1983). *The architecture of cognition.* Cambridge, MA: Harvard University Press.

Anderson, J. R. (1985). Production systems, learning, and tutoring. In D. K. Klahr, P. W. Langley, & R. Neches (Eds.), *Self-modifying production systems: Models of learning and development.* Cambridge, MA: Bradfor Books/MIT.

Anderson, J. R., Boyle, C. F., Farrell, R. G., & Reiser, B. J. (in press). Cognitive principles in the design of computer tutors. In P. Morris (Ed.), *Modelling cognition.* New York: Wiley.

Anderson, J. R., Boyle, C. F., & Yost, G. (1985). The geometry tutor. *Proceedings of the International Joint Conference on Artificial Intelligence* (pp. 1–7). Los Angeles, CA.

Anderson, J. R., & Reiser, B. J. (1985). The LISP Tutor. *Byte,* 159–175.

Bloom, B. S. (1984). The 2 sigma problem: The search for methods of group instruction as effective as one-to-one tutoring. *Educational Researcher, 13,* 3–16.

Brown, J. S. (1983). Process versus product: A perspective on tools from communal and informal electronic learning. In *Report from the Learning Lab: Education in the Electronic Age.* New York: WNET Educational Broadcasting Corporation.

Brown, J. S., & Burton, R. R. (1978). Diagnostic models for procedural bugs in basic mathematical skills. *Cognitive Science, 2,* 155–192.

Brown, J. S., & van Lehn, K. (1980). Repair theory: A generative theory of bugs in procedural skills. *Cognitive Science, 4,* 379–426.

Bundy, A. (1983). *The computer modelling of mathematical reasoning.* London: Academic Press.

Bundy, A., & Welham, B. (1981). Using meta-level inference for selective application of multiple rewrite rule sets in algebraic manipulation. *Artificial Intelligence, 16,* 189–212.

Clancey, W. J. (1982). Tutoring rules for guiding a case method dialogue. In D. Sleeman & J. S. Brown (Eds.), *Intelligent tutoring systems* (pp. 201–225). New York: Academic Press.

Davis, R. B. (1975). Cognitive processes involved in solving simple algebraic equations. *Journal of Children's Mathematical Behaviour, 1*(3), 7–35.

Davis, R. B., Jockusch, E., & McKnight, C. (1978). Cognitive processes in learning algebra. *Journal of Children's Mathematical Behaviour, 2*(1), 10–20.

Lewis, C. (1981). Skill in algebra. In J. R. Anderson (Ed.), *Cognitive skills and their acquisition* (pp. 85–110). Hillsdale, NJ: Lawrence Erlbaum Associates.

Malone, T. W. (1981). Toward a theory of intrinsically motivating instruction. *Cognitive Science, 4,* 333–369.

Matz, M. (1982). Towards a process model for high school algebra errors. In D. Sleeman & J. S. Brown (Eds.), *Intelligent tutoring systems* (pp. 25–50). New York: Academic Press.

McArthur, D. (1985). Developing computer tools to support performing and learning complex cognitive skills. In D. Berger, K. Pedzek, & W. Bankes (Eds.), *Applications of cognitive psychology: Computing and education.* Hillsdale, NJ: Lawrence Erlbaum Associates.

Reiser, B. J., Anderson, J. R., & Farrell, R. G. (1985). Dynamic student modelling in an intelligent tutor for LISP programming. *Proceedings of the International Joint Conference on Artificial Intelligence* (pp. 8–14). Los Angeles, CA.

Siegler, R. S., & McGilly, K. (in preparation). Cognitive processes in factoring algebraic expressions. Carnegie-Mellon University.

Sleeman, D. (1982). Assessing aspects of competence in basic algebra. In D. Sleeman & J. S. Brown (Eds.), *Intelligent tutoring systems* (pp. 185–199). New York: Academic Press.

Sleeman, D. (1984). An attempt to understand students' understanding of basic algebra. *Cognitive Science, 8,* 387–412.

Wagner, S., Rachlin, S. L., & Jensen, R. J. (1984). *Algebra learning project final report.* Athens, GA: Department of Mathematics, University of Georgia.

Part 5 Implementing ICAI Systems

Just as there are many design considerations in the development of an ICAI system, there are also many implementation issues, including choice of programming language, performance optimization, and minimizing development time and costs. However these issues become important only when systems are put into actual use. The two chapters in Part 5 deal with some of these issues.

Chapter 12, by Wallach, discusses development strategies for implementing ICAI programs on the current generation of personal computers based on experience with programs such as Micro-PROUST and Micro-SEARCH. The choice of a programming language for ICAI development is affected by a number of factors, including performance, transportability, licensing, costs, and availability of programming tools. Wallach reaches an interesting conclusion about a general development strategy for ICAI: develop prototypes first using an AI language or programming environment and then rewrite the run-time programs in a general-purpose language (such as Pascal) to achieve optimal performance, transportability, and distribution costs.

Chapter 13, by Begg and Hogg, describes a prototype intelligent authoring system implemented on a personal computer system. The system consists of a series of editors (e.g., discourse, knowledge network, error rules) and a set of objects that these editors can create and modify. The system generates run-time programs in Prolog. The system does not contain a user interface, however. This means that the author using the system must already know how to formulate ICAI programs. Indeed, such an interface would amount to a tutor or expert system on ICAI.

Begg and Hogg reach insightful conclusions regarding the development of ICAI systems. They suggest that the resulting ICAI program generated by an intelligent authoring system is highly dependent on the completeness of the knowledge network provided by the author. If the knowledge network is not sufficiently detailed, the student model produced will not allow much precision in terms of representing student understanding. In other words, if the knowledge representation is inadequate, the ICAI program may work poorly.

This kind of information on the implementation of ICAI systems will ultimately help us develop cost-effective applications of AI in education and training. At the present time, we have very little data upon which to base ICAI implementation decisions. Consequently, implementations of ICAI systems in the near term are likely to be expensive, inefficient, and time-consuming. We have spent 15 years learning how to build intelligent tutors; nobody knows how many years it will take to make them work in the classroom.

12 / Development Strategies for ICAI on Small Computers

BRET WALLACH

Introduction

One of the major goals of ICAI is to improve the quality of education and training. For this to happen, intelligent tutoring paradigms that have been adequately researched and are known to be educationally effective must be made commercially available to those that can benefit from them. To become commercially available to end users, ICAI programs must run on inexpensive computers and development costs must be minimized so that the programs are affordable.

Even though significant effort has been devoted to ICAI research for only the past decade, enough information and insight have been gathered about ICAI program design and its impact on student learning to build effective ICAI systems. Paradigms that have received significant research attention and success include mixed initiative tutors such as WHY (Stevens, Collins, & Goldin, 1976) and SOPHIE (Brown, Burton, & de Kleer, 1981), diagnostic tutors such as SEARCH (see Chapter 4), and ACT* (Anderson, Boyle, & Reiser, 1985), and coaches such as PROUST (see Chapter 3) and WEST (Burton & Brown, 1979). A large number of variations within each type of paradigm are possible, though a given ICAI program can be used for many applications. Although none of these programs are commercially available, it must be noted that commercial success was not a goal of these applications. Instead, they were created to explore the possibilities of ICAI.

Although most ICAI applications have been developed for LISP machines and mainframe computers, smaller, inexpensive computers now have the power required for some ICAI applications. As processing power and memory capacity costs continue to drop, inexpensive machines will be capable of supporting significant ICAI systems. An IBM PC (Intel 8088 based), with 512 kilobytes of memory, supports versions of PROUST and SEARCH, as can the Burroughs Canada ICON (Intel 186 based). The Motorola 68000–based MAC (Apple Macintosh™ with 512 kilobytes memory) is significantly faster and has graphics and windowing capabilities to augment the ICAI component of a tutoring system. Newer machines, such as the Commodore Amiga and the Atari 520ST, have as much power as the Macintosh at a considerably lower price, which is important for bringing ICAI to the financially restricted classroom. Even smaller machines can support some limited types of ICAI, as shown by the implementation of BUGGY (Brown & Burton, 1978) in BASIC to run on a 64K Apple II. An ICAI application may require significant optimization when ported to a small machine, but a well-planned development can minimize the optimization effort.

The final key to widespread distribution of ICAI and achieving the goal of improving the quality of education is to lower the development cost so that the programs themselves become affordable. The development time associated with many of the current ICAI programs is thousands of hours for each hour of instruction created. However, this large ratio of development effort per instruction hour occurred because these programs were pioneer explorations of ICAI, not because ICAI programs require inherently larger development efforts. In fact, because ICAI programs contain intelligence about what they teach and how they teach it, domain knowledge and tutoring rules can be entered quickly in a highly concentrated form. This knowledge can then be used to generate large amounts of highly effective tutoring. This contrasts with conventional CAI, where every interaction with the student must be specified by the author.

In this chapter, strategies for cost-effective development of ICAI programs for small computers are described. These strategies include choosing a language and an environment for developing the ICAI application's executing code based on transportability requirements, language costs, development costs, and performance requirements; and developing authoring tools for the rapid, cost-effective development of the domain and tutoring knowledge bases that are accessed by the executing code.

The recommendations and information presented here are based on the implementation of several ICAI programs and authoring systems on small computers. Versions of PROUST in LISP and BUGGY in BASIC were implemented on the IBM PC. SEARCH has been implemented in LISP, C, and Pascal on the IBM PC and in LISP and Pascal on the Apple Macintosh. In addition, authoring environments for the Burroughs Canada ICON have been prototyped for mixed initiative and diagnostic tutors.

The Generalized ICAI Program

A typical ICAI program contains most or all of the following: a domain expert, a teaching expert, a diagnostic expert, and a student model. In addition, it may contain a gaming environment or simulation. A high-quality student interface is needed, usually containing graphics or natural language. The functional components of this generalized ICAI program are shown in Fig. 12.1.

The domain expert contains the knowledge (procedural and factual) that the student needs to learn. This knowledge is used to answer student questions

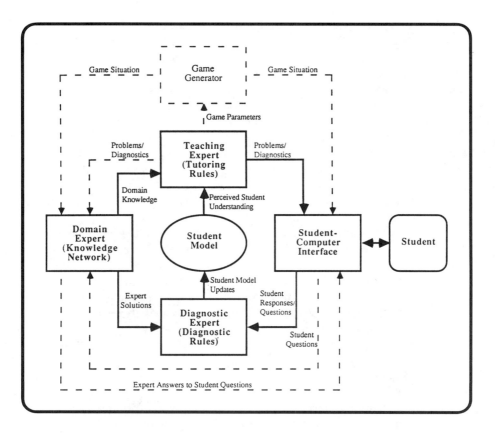

Figure 12.1 Major Components of Typical ICAI Programs

in a mixed initiative tutor or to solve problems generated by the teaching expert or game generator in order to provide a basis for comparison by the diagnostic expert.

The diagnostic expert uses rules to analyze student responses. Based on those responses, it makes hypotheses about what knowledge the student has acquired or what misconceptions the student may have. These hypotheses are reflected in the current state of the student model. The student model is the model of the student's understanding of the domain knowledge as perceived by the ICAI system.

The job of the teaching expert is to choose the next strategy for teaching the student based on the current state of the student model. This includes providing diagnostics, presenting new information, and posing questions or problems to the student.

Each expert consists of knowledge bases and an executable program called the inference engine that uses the information in the knowledge bases to search through the solution space and arrive at conclusions based on the current set of inputs. Knowledge can be represented in many ways, ranging from simple if-then statements to sophisticated knowledge networks consisting of objects, actions, and relationships between the objects and actions. Representations that are tailored for a specific domain are often inadequate for other domains. Generalized knowledge representations designed for a wide range of applications may not closely fit any given specific application. As a result, different knowledge representations may be required for each expert within an ICAI program (at least the internal representation), especially when considering optimal performance and efficiency that are often required for implementations on small computers.

There are a variety of methods for searching through the knowledge bases, depending on the knowledge representation and the purpose of the expert. Two common techniques are backward chaining and forward chaining. Backward chaining begins with a hypothesis or goal that is to be proven or disproven. It then works backward through the knowledge base, looking for rules that can prove the goal. Other rules to prove the premises of those rules are then sought. If there is no information contained in the knowledge base regarding a premise, the user is asked a question. The process continues until the goal is either proven or disproven. The backward chaining technique often matches the requirements of the teaching expert, which has the specific goal of deciding what to do next.

Forward chaining is just the opposite. All rules whose premises are satisfied by the current inputs fire. These rules in turn satisfy the premises for and trigger other rules. This continues until one or more goals are satisfied or no more rules can be triggered. This technique is useful for the diagnostic expert, which uses the current student response to the last stimulus to derive all student model updates.

Simulations as in STEAMER (see Chapter 6) and games such as the one in WEST (Burton & Brown, 1979) are also important. Simulations provide feedback to student responses based on real-life situations. Games provide an informal learning environment, allowing students to freely explore the underlying game structure and to develop strategies to increase their performance. The ICAI coach associated with a game provides an example strategy (the domain expert plays the game), competition (games with novice students can be kept close by rigging the chance aspects of the game), and advice and direction (with minimal interruption so the game remains spontaneous and fun) for the student. For both simulations and games, the student computer interface should support graphics, multiple fonts, and multiple windows for segmenting information displayed to the student.

This generalized ICAI model does not match all ICAI programs, but it does describe several key functional components that are either present or similar to other components in all ICAI systems. As a result, this model is used as a basis to consider development strategies.

While the overall system, including knowledge representations, inferencing strategies, simulations and games, and interfaces should be designed together, the actual implementation can be broken down into two phases: the development of the executable code and the development of the knowledge and other databases. Environments for developing the executable code are considered first.

Programming Languages

Any language can be used to develop the executable code for ICAI programs. An AI language is not required. However, some languages and their associated development and run-time environments on small computers provide faster and easier development for ICAI, while others provide better performance. Some languages are standardized and available on many different computers, small as well as large. Some languages require run-time environments to be licensed, while others are compiled into object code and can run on their own.

Programming languages fall into two categories, which are denoted here as AI and non-AI languages. AI languages are generally used for symbolic and object-oriented processing, and non-AI languages are generally used for business and scientific numerical and control processing. Differences between the two categories are shown in Table 12.1.

The major difference between AI and non-AI languages is that the basic atomic data type for an AI language is an object, whereas for a non-AI language

	AI Languages	**Non-AI Languages**
Examples	LISP, Prolog	C, Pascal, BASIC
Primary atomic data types	Object	Number
Primary composite data types	Lists, trees	Arrays, records
Code and data treated the same?	Yes	No
Memory management	Implicit	Explicit
Primary method of repetition	Recursion	Iteration
Development and run-time environment	Primarily interpreted	Interpreted, compiled

Table 12.1 Differences between AI Languages and Non-AI Languages

it is a number. The built-in functions in AI languages operate on the objects by building them into lists and other structures, extracting the objects from lists, changing the order of the objects, and making decisions based on the value of the objects. The built-in functions of non-AI languages are arithmetic and operate on numerical arguments.

In AI languages, code is treated the same as data and programs can modify themselves. This is generally not true in non-AI languages. Memory management is automatic in AI languages, while memory management functions generally need to be explicitly called in non-AI languages. Recursion is the easiest way to cause repetition in AI languages, whereas iteration is preferred in non-AI languages.

The effect of each aspect of AI and non-AI languages on transportability, licensing, performance, and development costs requires careful consideration before a development strategy is chosen.

Transportability

One way to increase the number of possible end users for any software program is to make it available for many different computers. This makes it much more likely that a potential user owns or has access to at least one of the machines the program runs on.

To be transportable, a program must ultimately be developed in a language that is available on all targeted machines with very little translation required between machines. The language should also have a compiler available and should interface easily to external routines. Table 12.2 rates the capabilities of several common languages to satisfy these requirements.

The most important attribute of a language is its availability. If the language chosen is not available on the computers for which the application is to be implemented, then it is a poor choice. It is often important that the language has adequate popularity so that it becomes quickly available when new machines are developed. For example, Pascal, BASIC, and assembler were the first available languages for the Commodore Amiga when it came out, while LISP and Prolog are still not available. In general, LISP and Prolog are not very widely available for small machines and are rarely the first languages available.

Compiler availability can also be very important. A compiler will make the program run several times faster and usually fit into a considerably smaller space. This consideration favors C and Pascal.

Transportability with little required translation is another major advantage of C and standard Pascal. Prolog, when available, usually requires little translation since many implementations follow the specification described by Clocksin and Mellish (1984).

BASIC is not very transportable, as demonstrated by a translation of BUGGY from AppleSoft BASIC to IBM BASICA. More than 50% of the code had to be

	Availability on Small Computers	Compiler Availability	Interfacing to External Routines	Transportable with Little Translation
LISP	Fair	Fair	Fair	Fair
C	Very good	Very good	Excellent	Very good
Pascal	Very good	Good	Very good	Good
Prolog	Fair	Fair	Fair	Good
LOGO	Good	Poor	Poor	Good
BASIC	Excellent	Fair	Fair	Fair
Ada	Poor	Poor	Good	Excellent
Assembler	Excellent	NA	Excellent	None

Table 12.2 Transportability of Common Languages

modified. The IF and WHILE program structures had to be changed, random numbers were handled differently, and string manipulation functions also had to be translated.

Ease of access to the outside world is important when special user interfaces such as windows, menus, or graphics are used. This is also important from a translation standpoint. It is usually necessary to translate only the graphics and other machine-specific routines when moving the application from one computer to another and leave the majority of the code intact. The compilable, linkable languages such as C and Pascal have the clear advantage here, since any object code can be linked in and executed under the control of the main program.

C and Pascal are currently the best languages to use if implementing the application on several different machines is required. These may lose some of their advantages to Ada if the current U.S. Department of Defense push succeeds, or possibly to Common LISP if it should gain popularity. However, C and Pascal are likely to remain the most portable languages on small machines for several years.

Language Costs

Special run-time environments (i.e., programs used only to run a developed program) are required by most interpreters and some compilers. The cost of licensing the run-time environment could add significantly to the cost of the product. For example, if a software developer were required to buy at retail price the full Golden Common LISP environment (a product of Gold Hill

Computer) each time for a potential market of 10,000 copies of an ICAI program, it would theoretically cost $5 million in addition to development costs.*

However, most language developers have or are developing run-time only systems that sell for a small fraction of the price of the full development environment. The run-time system price is usually very negotiable, and often a suitable agreement can be reached. The ICAI developers have the advantage in negotiation because they can choose either a different development language or to reimplement the distribution version in a different run-time language.

The cost of purchasing a language's development environment for a small machine is a minor factor. Few languages for small computers sport a price tag of more than $1000, and this is insignificant when compared with the cost of just a few months of programmer time.

Once again, C and Pascal are currently the best languages to use if licensing costs are a factor, as well they might be depending on royalty agreements with the software publisher. This is true especially considering the low price tag of most educational programs.

Performance

Performance can be a very important issue in choosing a development language, especially on a small machine where computing power is limited. The first two columns of Table 12.3 summarize the differences in performance and development effort between LISP, Pascal, and C implementations of the SEARCH problem solver for the IBM PC and Apple Macintosh. Both the PC and the Macintosh had 512K of memory.

The SEARCH problem solver applies transformations such as

$$\tan x \rightarrow 1/\cot x$$

to the left side of an identity such as

$$\tan x + 1/\cot x = 2 \sin x \sec x$$

to generate the entire search tree to a specified depth using breadth first search. All branches that do not eventually transform the left side of the equation to the right side are pruned. The SEARCH problem solver is a good example of the processing required for ICAI, because it requires a substantial amount of symbolic computation such as pattern matching and a large search space.

For the PC, the Pascal version runs between 15 and 20 times as fast as the LISP version. The C version runs even faster. What takes five seconds in C or Pascal will take over a minute in LISP. Memory capacity, measured in maximum number of equations in the solution tree before memory error occurs, is much better for both the Pascal and C versions. These versions can either handle

---

* At the time this chapter went to press, Gold Hill had announced a run-time environment for GC LISP, but no pricing information was available.

	Relative Execution Time	Tree Capacity (nodes)	Relative Development Time	Relative Lines of Code
IBM PC				
Golden[a] Common LISP	1.000	538	1.0[b]	1
Microsoft Pascal	0.063	2146	1.8	3
Lattice C	0.055	963	8.5	6
Apple Macintosh™				
Lisa Pascal	0.014	769	.05	1
ExperTelligence ExperLISP	0.092	234	.05	3

[a] Interpreter
[b] Translated from working prototype

Table 12.3 Performance and Development Effort Comparisons

larger problems or run with less memory. There are several reasons for the performance increase.

First, Gold Hill LISP is interpreted, while MicroSoft Pascal and Lattice C are both compiled. Gold Hill Computer has recently released a compiler for their LISP environment. They estimate the compiled code is two to four times as fast as the interpreter. Even with this improvement, the Pascal and C versions are still several times as fast. Also, since the new compiler still uses the same data structures as the interpreter, memory usage will not change significantly. While Golden Common LISP is not the fastest or most efficient LISP interpreter for the PC, it does perform fairly well (Kenyon, 1985). In fact, Gold Hill claims that its Golden Common LISP system for the IBM AT runs slightly faster than some dedicated AI machines or a VAX 750.

Second, the data structures for the Pascal and C versions contain only necessary information, allowing for better performance and considerably more efficient memory utilization. For example, LISP allows atom names to be any length and provides a flexible addressing scheme to access atoms. The atoms can also have properties. In SEARCH this is unnecessary since the longest atom names are three-letter operators such as *sin* or *cos,* there are very few different atoms, and all atoms are values and need no other property designators. The Pascal version takes advantage of this by assigning one-byte integer values to each atom. This simplifies accessing the atoms and saves memory. In the C version, since pointers are four bytes and the longest operator is only three characters (or bytes), the pointers to the atoms are also eliminated.

Also, memory management (often referred to as garbage collection) is greatly simplified in the C and Pascal versions. The LISP interpreter needs to provide a flexible memory reutilization scheme that is efficient for a wide variety of applications. The general scheme calls for allocating memory until free memory is exhausted, marking all atoms and list elements that are referenced and returning (sweeping) the unmarked ones back to free memory. For a specific application such as SEARCH, where it is always known exactly what memory is being used and not being used, it is not necessary to have a central memory collection routine. Memory is returned to the free queue as soon as it becomes unused.

This also accounts for the difference in memory capacities for the C and Pascal versions. The C version uses the built-in system library allocation and deallocation routines. These routines allow for allocation of blocks of memory of different sizes. This is unnecessary because all list elements are the same length. The Pascal version does all of its own memory management after allocating all of free memory at start-up.

It is important to explicitly call the garbage-collection routine when a break in processing is anticipated for ICAI applications written in LISP. Otherwise, the garbage-collection routine is invoked any time the free memory is exhausted. This often happens at inopportune times and causes erratic response times to student input.

The Macintosh, with its 68000 microprocessor, is several times faster than the PC for applications similar to SEARCH. The major factors are larger data buses, a larger directly accessible data space (i.e., 24 address bits instead of 16 with page or segment registers), faster clock speed, and a somewhat more powerful and efficient instruction set. The Lisa Pascal Workshop version for the Macintosh is nearly five times as fast as the MicroSoft Pascal version for the PC and nearly twice as fast as the IBM AT.

ExperLISP is an incrementally compiled LISP and is the fastest LISP available for the Macintosh (Kenyon, 1985) at this time. Yet it is still roughly six times slower than the Lisa Pascal Workshop version. A great deal of work is left to be done regarding optimizing LISP compilers for small machines.

If performance is an important factor, the final program almost certainly needs to be written in Pascal or C instead of LISP, unless new LISP compilers with far better performance appear for small computers. The resulting ICAI program will likely be several times as fast and able to handle considerably more data.

Development Costs

Development costs are generally related to the cost of equipment and the cost of labor. However, considering the cost of software engineers, the cost of equipment plays a secondary role in ICAI development. The primary attention for reducing development costs should be focused on labor hours. The last two columns of Table 12.3 summarize the difference in development time for the different versions of SEARCH.

Parallel efforts were begun in implementing the C and LISP versions of the SEARCH solver. The two versions were done by different programmers of approximately equal skill and experience who did not interact at all after the preliminary design was discussed. The C version took nearly ten times as long to develop as the LISP version. This ratio may even be somewhat low considering the LISP version is slightly more flexible.

Based on the LISP version, the MicroSoft Pascal version took less than twice as long to develop. This ratio would be reduced even further in future developments because many of the functions written for the Pascal version can be used again. These include a read function to input lists and dynamically build internal list structures, a print function to print lists, an equal function to determine equality of lists and atoms, and an association function to retrieve the bindings of dynamically allocated variables. In addition, cons and other data structures are specified and garbage-collection strategies defined. In fact, many common LISP functions were implemented in Pascal and can be reused after slight or no modification. The reusable work required about one-third of the Pascal development effort.

Using LISP or other AI languages rather than Pascal or C for developing ICAI is faster for several reasons:

- *The AI language environments are interactive.* Functions and data can be added directly to the environment and tested both individually and together.

- *Memory management is handled automatically.* The AI languages automatically allocate memory as needed.

- *Symbolic structures are more easily referenced.* Pointers are implicitly handled in AI languages. For example, the second element in a list named 1 is (cadr 1) in LISP and 1^.cdr^.car in Pascal. Note that the structure for 1 needs to be explicitly defined in Pascal.

In addition, type checking is automatic and trace and debug functions are generally more powerful and easier to use in AI languages.

The main reason the Pascal version required less development time than the C version was that it had the advantage of a working prototype. Since the problem was not well defined initially, the interactive LISP environment was much more conducive to rapid experimentation. However, once the program was written in LISP, it was relatively simple to convert it to Pascal. Some of the LISP functions were translated directly to Pascal, line by line, and some were functionally converted. Procedures that were functionally converted were usually easily rewritten using an iterative structure.

Pascal is also easier to use for developing this type of application than C. The C design makes it extremely useful for developing operating-system functions and other low-level programs because it allows the programmer to access most of the machine's functions directly and efficiently. However, C is fairly tedious when used for high-level applications such as SEARCH, since most variable references need to be explicitly defined. The lack of implicit return variable parameters for procedures is one example of this. This is further supported by the fact that the C development required twice as many lines of code as Pascal and six times as many as LISP. A line of code is defined to contain one major function call or variable assignment.

The Pascal and LISP versions were ported to the Macintosh. Even though ExperLISP is significantly different from Golden Common LISP and Lisa Pascal is nonstandard, the translation effort went very smoothly. It took less than two hours for each translation.

Developing ICAI functions from scratch in ExperLISP (version 1.0) is relatively difficult. Programmer errors, especially those accessing the graphics and other built-in Macintosh functions, often result in system crashes from which recovery includes the long, tedious Macintosh and ExperLISP start-up. In addition, the trace function only traps the first entrance to a function and does not catch direct recursive entries, making it difficult to pinpoint errors.

However, the use of LISP and other AI development languages will significantly reduce the development time for ICAI programs. When a prototype is available this factor is reduced significantly. It is faster to develop the ICAI application in an AI language and then translate it to a non-AI language than to implement it from scratch in a non-AI language.

Expert System Generators

At first glance, it may seem that a rule- or frame-based expert system generator would be an ideal environment for ICAI development because ICAI applications involve multiple interacting expert systems with domain knowledge and rules. There are many existing expert system generators for the PC, and new ones are constantly being developed. A version of OPS5 is available for the Macintosh from ExperTelligence, and several other expert systems are available for this machine.

Any of the expert system generators that do not have access to outside routines are of limited use in ICAI development because none of them have built-in functions for graphics, screen layout, font control, and multiple windows. They don't support flexible natural language capabilities. Most do not allow flexible keyboard monitoring or programming to allow intelligent use of the function keys. Their interfaces are too sterile for instruction and they must rely on external routines to alleviate this limitation. Outside routines must also provide games or simulations that may be required for a given ICAI application.

Direct coding of games and simulations using expert systems is extremely cumbersome. Even if outside routines are accessible, constant external access slows the system down considerably. Communication is often via files. More memory and disk space is required and a hard disk may be necessary.

The knowledge bases and inference engines of the expert systems tend not to fit the domain, teaching, and diagnostic experts very well, because each of the experts needs its own type of expert system generator. The domain expert, which contains the domain knowledge and the structure of that knowledge, may be best fit by a frame-based system. The teaching expert, which is goal driven, may require a backward-chaining-rule-based system. The diagnostic expert, which derives all the hypotheses it can about the current state of student understanding, may map most efficiently on a forward-chaining-rule-based system. Few of the expert system generators currently available for small computers allow for this kind of flexibility, and it is still difficult to implement ICAI with those that are because they are not designed for ICAI.

Representing the student model can be difficult using an expert system generator. The student model is often conveniently represented as a vector or matrix, yet such data structures are rarely available in expert system generators for small computers.

Porting applications implemented using an expert system generator from one small computer to another is extremely difficult. Only the PC and Macintosh have expert system generators available, and none are available for both machines.

Language and licensing costs are a major factor if an expert system generator is used. Both the development and run-time systems are significantly more expensive than standard development languages.

The performance of applications created by expert system generators tends to be slow. The expert system run-time environment is usually interpreted, and the added flexibility of the environment is coupled with an added layer of inefficiency. Programs resulting from expert system generators may be considerably slower than the same application developed in LISP. Because of the nonoptimal fit between the ICAI experts' structure and the expert system's structure, development time is increased.

While it is straightforward to translate a working LISP program to Pascal, translating a program built by an expert system generator is considerably more difficult. The built-in inferencing mechanism is not explicitly available to the developer as it is in LISP, and this highly recursive part of the system needs to be developed without the advantage of a working prototype. If the application needs to be translated to another language for any reason, this is a significant consideration.

Note that many of these drawbacks are being alleviated, especially where performance is concerned. Many run-time environments are being recoded in C and Pascal. Easy access to external programs and other resources is another common upgrade. Also, some expert system development environments for large machines, such as KEE from IntelliCorp, are flexible and powerful enough to be used for ICAI development. Both ExperTelligence and Gold Hill provide network links to Symbolics AI machines for their LISP systems.

Choosing the Development Environment

Now that the pros and cons of several types of development environments have been examined, a general strategy can be created for choosing the development tools for ICAI on small machines. The sequence of decisions required is illustrated in Fig. 12.2. All paths lead to building a prototype in an AI language (e.g., LISP or Prolog) development environment. Even if the distribution version is ultimately written in a non-AI language, it is faster to write an AI language–based prototype first and convert it than to write the final version directly in a non-AI language. This is based on the assumption that all serious developers can at least afford to invest in an IBM PC (or compatible) with one of the LISP packages (e.g., Golden Common LISP). This provides a fine environment for prototyping ICAI applications. Note that the development environment (DE) and run-time environment (RE) are the same for some packages.

The first step, as in all product development, is to define the problem. What aspect of learning can be assisted by ICAI? If one or more of the known paradigms do not apply to this problem, a new one must be developed. Interfaces to the student must be specified and shown to be effective. Small prototypes should be built to test ideas and answer questions until the problem is defined and a plan for an effective solution is identified.

The next step is to identify the target computers. This step involves characterizing the end users and determining what types of computers they have (or will have) access to. If they use several different types of machines and most of them do not have access to a single type, then it is wise to develop a final prototype in the best AI language development environment available to those developing the code and translate it to a non-AI language (i.e., Pascal or C) for the distribution version. Note that the development environment for the prototype need not reside on any of the target machines. LISP machines or a mainframe may provide the best development environment. It is important to provide a common input/output interface across all targeted computers. That is, the I/O routines in the final non-AI language version should be isolated from the rest of the code. These will need translation (assuming different interfaces), but the majority of the code should not.

If the ICAI application needs to be developed for only one computer, the effort is simplified. If there is no AI language development environment for that computer, the performance of the application in the AI language is most likely too slow anyway, or the cost of licensing available AI language run-time environments is too high, then the final prototype should be developed in the best

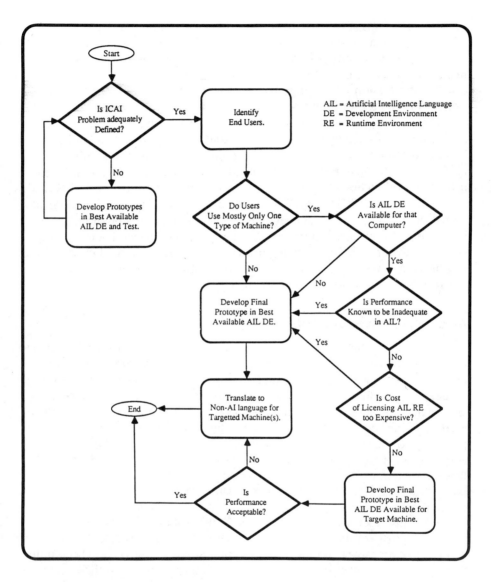

Figure 12.2 Flow Chart to Minimize Development Cost

available AI language development environment and then translated to a non-AI language for that machine for the distribution version. Otherwise, the best AI development environment available for that machine should be used. If performance turns out to be adequate, the final prototype can be updated to be the distribution version. If not, the program can be translated to Pascal or C for a significant increase in speed.

Maintenance and upgrades are somewhat more complicated when translation from an AI language to a non-AI language is required. This problem can be minimized by stressing modular programming, which allows only the modified parts of the system to be retranslated, and by insisting that the AI language prototype be functionally complete and robust before the translation is made.

In summary, it is important to perform software engineering and develop a final prototype in an AI language development environment and translate to Pascal or C if transportability, licensing cost, or performance issues are important. Note that this strategy is being used by Teknowledge and other knowledge engineering firms in the translation of some of their knowledge engineering environments into C for small computers.

Authoring Environments

Up to this point, the discussion has focused on development environments to be used by programmers and software designers for ICAI. However, authoring environments to be used by courseware developers are also needed for ICAI. While it is possible that a single environment could be used by both programmers and courseware developers, this seems unlikely, because the requirements and interests of the two groups are different. Courseware developers are primarily concerned with tools that allow them to create and modify the major components of ICAI programs (e.g., knowledge networks and student models). Programmers, on the other hand, are primarily interested in the issues previously discussed (i.e., optimizing performance, portability, etc.). Furthermore, development environments must be more powerful than authoring environments because they are used to create the authoring environments.

Even with an optimized development strategy for the executable code, ICAI is still very expensive in terms of development hour per instruction hour unless many knowledge bases can be effectively added and used with the executable code for a variety of domains. Courseware authors, domain experts, and teachers should all be able to add knowledge bases, rather than just the original ICAI developer. This allows the developed executable code for the ICAI paradigm to have wider use.

For example, the code for the SEARCH program could be used in domains such as trigonometry, algebra, integration, differentiation, predicate calculus, and chemical synthesis in organic chemistry by developing sets of transformations (domain knowledge), diagnostic rules, and rules about how to generate problems (tutoring rules). Code for the PROUST paradigm could be extended for any computer language, including standard languages such as C, Pascal, and Ada, expert system languages such as M1, and database query and report-generation languages such as FRED (Ashton Tate Frameword Editor Language) by developing goal lists, plan templates, and bug catalogs. PROUST could even be used to provide training diagnostics to courseware authors on developing these databases.

Most of the knowledge bases can be developed and entered into the target machine using standard editors. If the layouts of the knowledge bases are simple enough for the courseware developers, standard editors may be adequate. The knowledge can be translated into a more efficient internal format if necessary. Programs are needed to check the syntax, consistency, and completeness of the knowledge bases before they are used. Otherwise, situations may arise where the ICAI program gets stuck. This might happen, for example, if a specific problem is added to SEARCH that cannot be solved with the available transformations.

If the knowledge bases are complex or the courseware authors are less sophisticated, specialized editors can be developed to guide the author through the development of the knowledge bases. Different parts of the knowledge-base items can be separated visually and hence modularized by using special screen formats. Different levels of guidance should be available to provide adequate support for a novice author but not impede a sophisticated one with unnecessary details. Syntax can be checked as things are entered. Facilities to allow the author to add notes and comments to different objects can be added.

Another aspect of the authoring environment to consider is the course-development process. This involves linking databases developed for specific lessons together in a meaningful sequence as a curriculum is developed or for a specific textbook. Sequential ordering may suffice, or a more complex scheme can be created to allow branching to one of several lessons based on the student's overall performance in the current lesson.

Ultimately, the authoring environment would package all the tools together with as much automatic checking and flexible guidance provided to the author as possible. With the courseware-development environment in place, many effective hours of instruction can be efficiently developed, spreading out the development cost of the executable code.

Summary

ICAI can now be made commercially feasible. The recent developments making this possible are research and development of several ICAI paradigms and the increase in processing power of small, inexpensive computers accessible by nearly everyone. To reduce the cost of the software, the strategy for developing an ICAI system needs to be carefully considered.

Choosing a development environment for the executable code should be based on transportability, licensing, performance, and labor cost issues. Expert system generation environments available for small machines are not currently applicable to ICAI. AI languages such as LISP minimize development effort, while non-AI languages such as C and Pascal favor transportability, licensing, and performance. A good strategy is to develop a detailed prototype in an AI language and then translate to a non-AI language if any of the cost issues other than labor become important.

Entering the knowledge bases for ICAI applications could be made easier by the development of authoring tools. Depending on the complexity of the knowledge representation and the sophistication of the courseware authors, such an authoring tool would require simple syntax, consistency, and completeness checkers to specialized editors integrated into a complete authoring environment.

References

Anderson, J. R., Boyle, C. F., & Reiser, B. J. (1985). Intelligent tutoring systems. *Science, 228,* 456–462.

Brown, J. S., & Burton, R. (1978). Diagnostic models for procedural bugs in basic mathematical skills. *Cognitive Science,* 155–192.

Brown, J. S., Burton, R., & de Kleer, J. (1982). Pedagogical, natural language, and knowledge engineering techniques in SOPHIE I, II, and III. In D. Sleeman & J. S. Brown (Eds.), *Intelligent tutoring systems.* New York: Academic Press.

Burton, R., & Brown, J. S. (1979). An investigation of computer coaching for informal learning activities. *International Journal of Man-Machine Studies, 11,* 5–24.

Clocksin, W. F., & Mellish, C. S. (1984). *Programming in Prolog* (2nd ed.). New York: Springer-Verlag.

Kenyon, T. (1985). Shopping for a LISP. *Computer Language, 1,* 85–92.

Stevens, A., Collins, A., & Goldin, S. E. (1979). Misconceptions in student's understanding. *International Journal of Man-Machine Studies, 11,* 145–156.

13/ Authoring Systems for ICAI

IAIN M. BEGG and IAN HOGG

Introduction

The existence of intelligent computer-aided instruction (ICAI) programs has opened up new avenues for the use of computers in education. These programs are able to tackle difficult instructional problems and, in so doing, expand the usefulness of the computer as an instructional tool.

ICAI involves the application of artificial intelligence principles to the development of computer-assisted instruction (CAI) programs. ICAI programs differ from conventional CAI programs in a number of ways, as shown in Table 13.1. A key point is that the ICAI author need only provide a knowledge network and a set of inference rules without specifying the exact instructional sequence. This may well be the single major characteristic of ICAI programs. These differences will be addressed in more detail below.

Approximately 20 to 30 major ICAI projects have been conducted in the past 10 years. Many of these have been described in Sleeman and Brown (1982). Even though each ICAI program has been developed to study a specific instructional problem, there are some common features in their design and implementation. These commonalities allow for the possibility of developing some general guidelines for the creation of ICAI programs.

Two major obstacles to the wider use of ICAI programs are the significant time required for their development and the scarcity of ICAI development expertise. At the moment, ICAI programs are written in AI languages, such as LISP or Prolog. To construct an ICAI program, a great deal of knowledge of AI methodologies and programming techniques is needed. Another constraint is the delivery system hardware.

To increase the availability of ICAI programs, it is necessary to make substantial reductions in this development time and in the heavy reliance on AI knowledge. This can be achieved through the development of an intelligent authoring system (IAS), that is, a program generator for ICAI programs (Bork, 1985). A wide range of authoring systems exists for conventional CAI (Kearsley, 1982, 1984). Similarly, many program generators now exist for expert systems (e.g., M1 and Rulemaster). There is no reason why authoring tools should not be developed for ICAI. The development of a prototype IAS on a microcomputer was the goal of our project.

1. The author defines the knowledge network and inference rules but not the detailed instructional sequence.
2. A model of student performance is maintained dynamically and used to drive the instructional sequence.
3. Students can ask sophisticated questions or pose problems (characteristic of "mixed-initiative tutors").
4. The tutor provides detailed diagnostics of student errors (characteristic of "coaches").

Table 13.1 Major Differences between ICAI and CAI Programs

A major issue in developing an IAS is the question of whether a single authoring framework would be suitable for the development of different types of ICAI programs. For example, are authoring processes for a game like WEST (Burton & Brown, 1979) similar to those involved in the development of a procedural simulation such as SOPHIE (Brown, Burton, & de Kleer, 1982) or STEAMER (see Chapter 6), or in causal reasoning programs such as WHY (Stevens & Collins, 1980)? It is difficult to use an authoring system designed primarily for drills to develop procedural simulations or games; hence the generality of an IAS across different authoring approaches is a question critical to this work.

A related issue has to do with the generality of the knowledge representations, tutoring rules, and diagnostic (debugging) strategies that have been described and used by ICAI researchers. It is not clear that such structures apply across different kinds of instructional settings (even at meta-levels). In fact, it is not even obvious for programs that tackle the same task domains; for example, in programming, compare BIP (Barr, Beard, & Atkinson, 1976), FLOW (Gentner, 1979), and SPADE (Miller, 1979).

Research into intelligent authoring systems should shed some light on the instructional development process in the same way that ICAI projects have resulted in advances in our understanding of teaching/learning and cognitive processes. Despite a great deal of research in instructional system development (e.g., O'Neil, 1979a, 1979b), we still do not understand much about the process of creating materials for interactive instruction.

We decided to examine the question of whether it was possible to design an IAS capable of creating intelligent CAI programs. In this, our approach has been toward pragmatic, top-down design rather than toward taking existing software and grafting authoring capabilities onto them. There seems little doubt that this latter approach can pay dividends, but our desire has been to try to search out some generality in the production process and thus we favored the former approach.

Elements of ICAI

As mentioned in the Introduction, each ICAI program (or "tutor") created to date has been unique. However, basic components are present in some, if not all, ICAI programs. These components, depicted in Fig. 13.1, are a knowledge network, a student model, error/diagnostic rules, teaching rules, and a student-tutor interface. The knowledge network represents the content to be taught in terms of concepts, rules, and examples and their interrelationships. It can be thought of as more than just a network of facts; it could be coupled to a domain expert or could be a collection of procedures. The student model is the representation of what the student has learned and currently knows. Error/diagnostic rules are used to identify student misunderstandings and update the student model. Teaching rules determine what should be taught to the student given the current state of the student model.

Current ICAI programs can be seen to emphasize different elements. For example, Micro-PROUST (described in Chapter 3) performs diagnostic analysis on Pascal programs through the use of a knowledge network consisting of a procedural bug catalog and a complex series of error/diagnostic rules defining the intention-based diagnosis. The implementation of Micro-SEARCH (described in Chapter 4) relies on a full knowledge tree and a set of teaching rules (or heuristics) to control the instruction. The mixed-initiative tutor we shall describe attempts to utilize all components equally.

The basic operation of the ICAI program is as follows: the student model is continuously compared with the knowledge network to determine what the student does and does not know. This comparison generates discrepancies that are analyzed by the teaching rules. The teaching rules identify what components of the knowledge network should be presented next. The error/diagnostic rules identify misconceptions and mistakes in the responses or questions produced by the student, provide appropriate feedback, and update the student model accordingly. The teaching process continues until there is no identifiable discrepancy between the student model and the knowledge network. The student is buffered from the tutor by the student-tutor interface, which formats the tutor's output and handles the student's input. Games and simulations can play an important instructional role and are provided via a games expert, providing input to the teaching rules via the knowledge network.

It is important to realize that most ICAI programs do not contain all of these components but focus on one or two of them. In addition, past ICAI programs have implemented the four major components in different ways. The challenge in constructing an IAS is to establish a generic form of the four basic components and inferencing mechanisms that can be used across different instructional applications and problems.

Let us now consider how the characteristics and the basic structure of ICAI programs compare with their conventional CAI counterparts. A CAI program could respond to simple questions through effective use of a help facility. Pro-

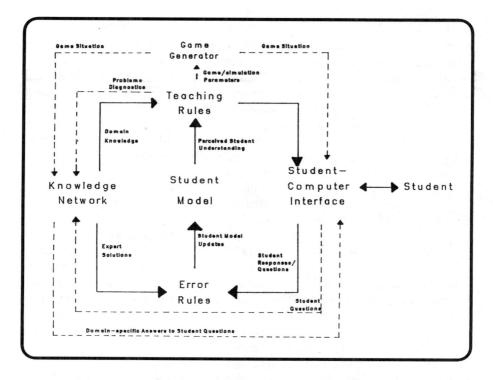

Figure 13.1 Model of ICAI Environment

vided all possible branches have been built in, the student's level of understanding could indeed drive the instructional sequence. With sufficient effort on the part of the author much diagnosis can be provided to the student, although such diagnosis is unlikely to be inductive (e.g., Micro-PROUST). With reference to Fig. 13.1, the knowledge network is implemented as text display instructions (facts) or equations (procedures). The student model is some sort of counter or buffer that accumulates student performance data. The teaching rules and error/diagnostic rules are embedded in the branching instructions used to control the sequence of presentation or to generate feedback messages. In terms of the structure described above, all of the components of an ICAI program exist in conventional CAI in a rudimentary form. The key point, however, is that these components are neither explicit nor distinct in conventional CAI programs.

The fact that ICAI programs can take these elements and a set of inferencing rules to produce a detailed instructional sequence is a qualitative, and not a mere quantitative, difference. Although all programming/authoring languages provide capabilities to parse input, match strings, and generate output, only a crude level of inferencing is available (e.g., downshifting, spelling tolerances, variable substitutions). Since it is primarily the inferencing capability that provides the intelligence in ICAI programs, it is no surprise that this aspect would largely be absent from conventional CAI programs. ICAI techniques are especially appropriate for instructional problems that involve a larger number of possible responses or alternatives (i.e., a large search space).

The implications of these differences for authoring systems are as follows. Traditional authoring tools have allowed people to create courseware in which the content and logic are intermixed. Flow of control is determined by prespecified branching. Teaching rules and error/diagnostic rules are embedded in these branching instructions and cannot be made explicit. Also, there is no facility for building an explicit student model other than in terms of counters and buffers.

Thus we find that an IAS must allow the author to access the elements of the ICAI program and perform the functions shown in Table 13.2. Similarly, the ICAI program created by the authoring system must be able to function in the ways described in Table 13.3.

Like an authoring system for conventional CAI, an IAS requires a specification of content, instructional strategies, and response feedback. However, this information is provided in a considerably different form. In addition, an IAS does a considerable amount of "housekeeping" (e.g., generation of inferencing rules, modification of property lists, student model creation, etc.) in the process of creating an ICAI lesson.

Fundamentally, there are four components to an IAS: (1) a user interface through which the user formulates an ICAI program; (2) an editor, or perhaps a set of editors, with which the user can create and modify the underlying databases (knowledge network, error/diagnostic rules, and the teaching rules); (3) a set of utilities to assemble the student model and link it to the databases, and a set of inferencing routines to check the completeness and consistency of

---

- Create and modify a knowledge network consisting of either facts/concepts or procedures/functions.
- Specify and modify error/diagnostic rules and teaching rules linked to the information in the knowledge network.
- Specify and modify the format of user input, program output, and screen displays.
- Identify inconsistencies and incompleteness in the knowledge network, error/diagnostic rules, and teaching rules.

Table 13.2 Major Functions Performed by an IAS

- Create a student model and continuously modify the student model based on actions of the error/diagnostic rules and teaching rules.
- Compare the student model and knowledge network identifying differences (perhaps as part of the teaching rules).
- Apply the error/diagnostic rules and the teaching rules to the difference between the student model and the knowledge network to generate output (in the form of error diagnostics or tutoring/coaching).
- Parse and match all input.
- Derive all inferences for the basic components.

Table 13.3 Major Functions Performed by Generated ICAI Programs

all the data; and (4) a code generator that will produce the executable ICAI program. Figure 13.2 depicts these four elements and describes some of their functions. We shall discuss each in turn, looking at the general requirements and then following them through the design of an IAS prototype.

This prototype had two purposes: to examine the possibility of creating an IAS and to explore, by extension, the generality between types of ICAI programs. We designed a prototype system using the ICON, an educational microcomputer designed exclusively for the educational market by CEMCORP and marketed by Burroughs Canada. This distributed computer system is based around the Intel iAPX186 processor and makes use of an iconic interface to the user. Given this strategy, we elected to follow a pragmatic, top-down design approach.

The User Interface

The primary user of an IAS is the course author or developer. The user interface performs three main functions: to provide the user with uniform access to the components of the system, to give guidance to the user in the construction of courseware, and finally, to help the user conceptualize a problem or instructional domain in a form amenable to treatment by ICAI. Currently, ICAI programs are constructed by ICAI experts who have a good knowledge of AI principles and techniques and who have, typically, become experts in the subject domain. This expertise allows them to decide how to represent or select an instructional problem that is suitable for ICAI.

However, the idea behind a fully functional IAS is that the user does not need to have AI expertise to be able to construct an ICAI program. Further, the user is expected neither to be an expert in instructional theory nor to have a profound knowledge of the techniques of ICAI production. Thus the user interface component can be seen to contain an expert system, able to provide help in:

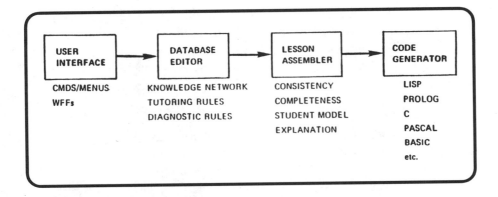

Figure 13.2 Elements of an IAS

1. The formulation of the problem in an ICAI format

2. Advice on the best method for its production

3. The selection of the appropriate instructional strategies and heuristics to be used by the courseware

To put these ideas into perspective, the reader can consider the construction of Micro-PROUST (see Chapter 3), Micro-SEARCH (see Chapter 4), and the French tutor described below. The user interface should, ideally, be able to formulate the problem in some type of "ICAI format" that would allow the user interface expert to deduce the optimal ICAI method; in the above cases, tutor, coach, heuristic, and mixed-initiative tutors, respectively. The expert would then provide assistance on the best pedagogy for the program. It is obvious that the production of such an expert system is a large task.

Furthermore, it is far from clear whether the elements in the creation of ICAI can be generalized sufficiently to allow a general interface of this type to be provided. Domain selection and production selection are currently done by ICAI experts. Similarly, the formulation of the problem in ICAI terms suffers from the same lack of generality. The learning theory strategies and heuristics are currently coded into the ICAI program, although they may be the easiest to abstract into an expert interface.

Nonetheless, we envisage three main approaches to providing a user interface: system probing, a storyboard, and menus.

For the user naive in AI, it would be necessary to extract information by probing to form the basis of the ICAI program. As an example, Table 13.4 shows a possible sequence that might be used to elicit a lesson to teach correct French grammar. As we said, this would result in a preliminary form of the databases that would then be manipulated using the database editors.

* What is the next concept the student should learn?
– Forming the past participle.
* To what previous concepts does forming the past participle relate?
– Verb root and infinitive.
* Any others?
– Gender and number.
* How do you decide the students have learned this concept?
– When they can handle the regular verbs and the main irregular ones.
* What difficulties do people have learning this concept?
– Forming the wrong root, mixing gender, and mixing number.
* What specific errors do students make when they form the wrong root?

    .
    .
    .

Table 13.4 Sample User-Interface Interaction

A somewhat less demanding alternative for the user interface is a type of on-line storyboard function. In the production of conventional CAI, a storyboard is used to specify the screen display, answer analysis, feedback, and branching logic. Although in the ICAI case we do not wish to specify the exact logic, we can split the sequence into smaller pieces for which we could determine the beginning and ending states for different levels of the problem and the way these parts connect. At each step the necessary concepts and procedures can be identified from which error and teaching rules can be devised. The system would then be able to compose a knowledge network diagram that would help the user to decide which aspects of the knowledge network, error rules, and teaching rules exist or are needed.

The simplest form of a user interface is a menu or fixed prompting structure that provides the same set of questions about every instructional sequence being analyzed. The interface is not context-sensitive and relies on the user answering all the questions. The onus is on the user to select the right functions at the right time, since there is no inherent guiding or sequencing.

Regardless of what level of interface is designed, a considerable knowledge of the appropriate questions to ask in the formulation of the problem for ICAI must be built into the interface. Given the complexity of this task, we decided to avoid this component in our first attempt at building an IAS. However, the difficulty in creating ICAI without some form of interface taught us that authors need some form of interface to simplify and structure the input. It also revealed that there was not always a clean division between the elements and that the absence of a proper user interface could be alleviated by the introduction of helpful editors.

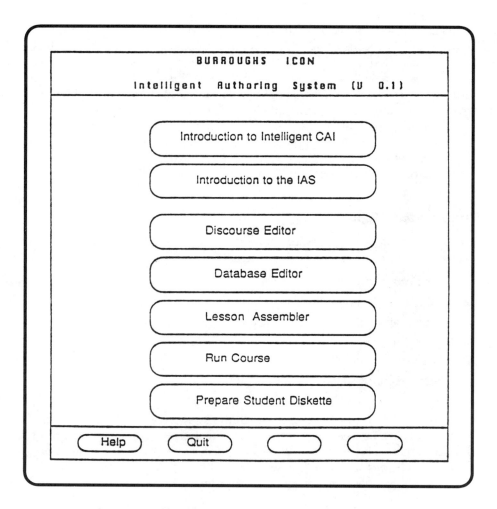

Figure 13.3 System Manager Menu

The resulting functional structure is shown by the introductory screen in Fig. 13.3. The final courseware can consist of a number of lessons, each of which has been related via the discourse editor. The individual lessons are formed by the lesson assembler from the IAS database, this database being created by the knowledge editor. Code generation is provided as part of the lesson assembler creating Prolog code and a course interpreter (the student-tutor interface).

The discourse editor provides a reasonable method of structuring the IAS input in logical lessons. It is, in fact, quite general and can be used to link quite different lessons together.

As can be seen in Fig. 13.4, the iconic approach provides a consistent look to the editor. The icons along the bottom line represent the operations of link, specify connection, specify name, replicate, undo, and delete ("trash"). The connections can be made under several types of constraint. In most cases, a particular state of the student model will be sufficient to define the link, but error-driven traps like a maximum time limit or number of errors can be pedagogically important.

Despite the limits of this approach, it was found to be a manageable solution to one part of our problem to create an IAS. Obviously, a more satisfactory solution would have to be found for future versions.

The Database Editors

The creation of the knowledge network, teaching rules, and error rules databases requires a similar set of functions:

- ADD a concept, procedure, or rule
- MODIFY an existing item
- REMOVE an item from the database
- REPLACE an item
- DISPLAY full or partial contents of an item
- FIND an item or string in the database

Although these functions will work the same way in all three databases, there are differences for each database. In the knowledge network, the author must distinguish between assertions (concepts, facts), theorems (procedures, processes) that act on assertions, and literals that simply print values (questions, menus). Assertions are stated as associative lists, while theorems would be stated as conditionals or actions. For instance, extending the French example:

> KN29:   (past participle X) (verb root) (ending)
>
> KN43:   TO CHANGE (past participle) USE (verb root)
>
> KN78:   WRITE "What is the root of the above verb?"

The contents of the knowledge network are not restricted to text. They could be graphics, sound, or video.

All entries in the error rules and teaching rules databases are stated as conditionals. Both may have associated messages. For example, error rules would provide some feedback:

> ER19:   IF (wrong gender) THEN SET SN10 = 5 AND WRITE "Your gender is wrong; look at the subject."

Teaching rules could provide some further direction or guidance; for example:

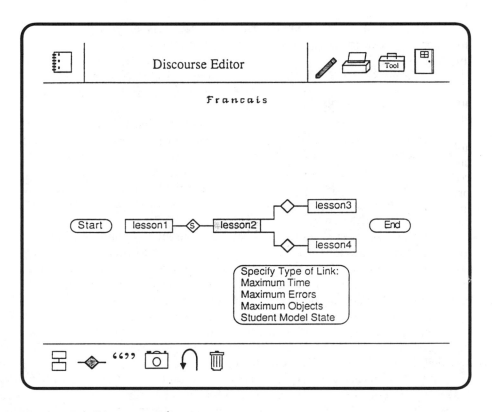

Figure 13.4 Discourse Editor

TR05:   IF ER19 and ER32 THEN USE KN85

KN85:   WRITE "Do you understand when you make agreement with the subject?"

To achieve maximum flexibility and usability, the user would not be required to get the exact syntax right for the database. This would be handled by some form of menu or command interface within the editor and would provide the user with quick access to the editing functions. However, this does not mean that the user will need to be aware of the appropriate semantics for each database and be guided in the creation of well-formed expressions.

In the IAS, the constraints over the user interface mean that the heart of the system is the knowledge editor. This helps users to structure their input and relieves them of the responsibility to produce correct syntax, a tiresome element of our earlier version. By so structuring the input, the system can reduce its need for syntax checking and provide a measure of completeness checking. Indeed, as items are added and referenced within the database, they are checked or flagged for later verification. The lesson is built up from a number of items or objects, each of which corresponds in some way to the elements of Fig. 13.1.

The database consists of 11 types of objects: topic, concept, dictionary, answer, question, window, picture, text, state, exit, and entry. The mapping from Fig. 13.1, shown in Table 13.5, is as follows.

The knowledge editor operates on three related objects: topics, concepts, and dictionary objects that compose a knowledge network. Topics are essentially larger concepts; that is, a topic describes the general idea covered by several concepts. We found this to be a useful pedagogical distinction as it helped to organize the lesson and to reduce the interaction between database objects. An important property of topics is that they can be used to separate background knowledge from the new ideas being taught.

Concepts are used to represent what the program is trying to teach and to respond to user questions. They are a Prolog representation of the facts or rules the program will use. The concept contains two further pieces of information: an initial level of the student understanding for the object, and a list of questions that will be presented to the student to invoke a response from which a more accurate picture of the student's understanding can be made.

Dictionary objects describe words pertinent to the lesson that the parser will need to know in order to understand the questions posed by the user and to be able to generate correct responses.

The error rules are provided by answer objects that analyze and acknowledge the student's response together with making any appropriate changes to the student model. The object contains a set of conditions under which it will be applied (or the conditions under which the rule will "fire"); the answer to be matched; descriptions of what and where to respond to the student; and a set of actions to update the student model.

The teaching rules are provided by window, picture, question, and text objects. Although it is basically questions that drive the instructional sequence, all can be referenced by knowledge and answer objects. Windows define the output screen area and would be used with the other objects. Pictures are graphic objects defined using the NAPLPS standard (NAPLPS, 1983). This approach is convenient because it provides a compact, machine-independent, standard representation of graphic images within the ASCII character set. Pictures can be viewed as possessing some intelligence in the sense that they have pre- and corequisite fields that define other objects which must be shown prior to or concurrently with other objects. The requisite fields also contain information about what state the student model should be in to display the object or fire the rule.

Text and question objects have a similar syntax. Although both can contain text and font control information, they are used slightly differently. Text objects can provide feedback and information, while questions drive the instructional

Editor	Objects
Knowledge network	Topic
	Concept
	Dictionary
Error rules	Answer
Teaching rules	Question
	Display — Picture
	Text
	Window
Student model	Overlay model
	Exit
	Entry
Simulator	State

Table 13.5 Mapping of ICAI Elements

sequence. This distinction was made on pragmatic grounds since it provided us with more structure in the design of courseware.

The student model itself is an overlay representation of the knowledge network in which we assign integer values to each concept. A maximum value of an element, say 10, indicates that the concept has been learned correctly. Finally, exit and entry objects provide the connection between lessons and are used by the course interpreter to change lessons.

State objects provide a dynamic view of the "state of the world" within the teaching sequence. If we were using simulations, then this object might reflect the various parameters of the simulation. In a mixed-initiative dialogue, it could represent the current subject. Thus they represent not only part of a game/simulation component but also part of the knowledge network, since they can describe dynamic properties of knowledge objects.

Given the complexity of the interrelations between objects, it is important to be able to obtain an uncluttered view of the objects. This is the significance of the knowledge editor. Each object has a name and the editor makes the manipulation of these items a simple matter. Figures 13.5 and 13.6 show examples of editor screens. In particular, Fig. 13.5 shows how the user can examine and manipulate the related objects. In this case, the structure helps to simplify the interaction.

The database editor that we are using has to satisfy two needs. First, it must provide editing functions for the whole knowledge base, and second, it must reduce the impact of limited user interface capabilities. Careful orthogonal design of the first function can help to resolve the second.

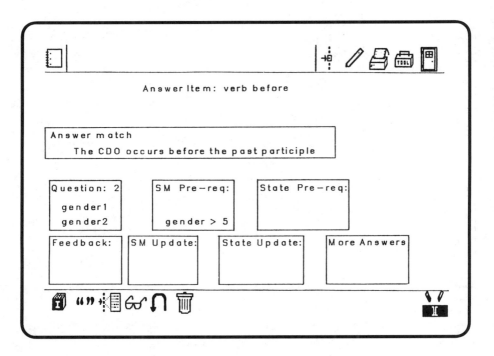

Figure 13.5 Editor-Answer Item Entry

In keeping with an iconic design philosophy, the editor provides access to functions through pop-up menus and meaningful icons. For instance, the "tool-box" icon will let the author access other parts of the IAS, for example, the lesson assembler. Typically, system-level icons are on top and internal editing function icons are on the bottom. Each database item can be selected through the "item" icon, which will cause an appropriate descriptive screen to be displayed. Figure 13.5 shows a typical answer item. The screen is structured to follow the exact syntax of the database item. In this way, the field structure itself constrains data entry to syntactically correct forms. A pleasant side effect is that the author is relieved of the responsibility of learning an abstruse syntax. A certain amount of consistency checking can obviously be performed at this stage.

Given the complex interitem relations, it is important to provide a substantial capacity to cross-reference. This is shown in Fig. 13.6. While editing a concept item, it was necessary to view some associated text items. These are displayed, viewed, and manipulated in a constraining, secondary window. The user can thus have a clear idea of which items to use. This mechanism is

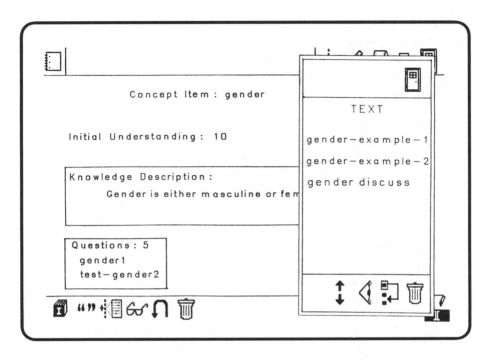

Figure 13.6 Editor-Index Mechanism

quite general and is used either to index different item lists or to examine related items. In this way, the structure can be used to simplify the interaction.

The Lesson Assembler

The function of the lesson assembler is to assemble the elements stored in the other databases into a program. This includes the construction of the student model and any inference mechanisms needed. It also includes the capability to check the completeness and consistency of the databases.

The creation of the student model does not involve the user, although functions should be provided to allow the user to inspect the model and modify values at run-time.

As the user edits the knowledge network, a second representation of the network must be constructed for the student model. Since a duplicate copy of this network is not likely to be feasible (unless the network is very small), the student model must index the network in some fashion. There are several different approaches to user/student modeling (Sleeman, 1984). Overlay models provide a useful middle ground between scalar modeling, or keeping a single scalar value to represent understanding, and comprehensive predictive models. Two simple examples involve setting flags or switches on each component of the network to indicate its status or creating a vector or array whose elements correspond to the components of the network.

The student model is generated the first time the program is run. As an element of the knowledge network is presented or an error rule is invoked, the student model is updated. For example, if a concept is presented to the student, this concept could be flagged as now being known by the student. Associated with this concept (or a superordinate concept) are one or more error diagnostics. Should the student provide a response that triggers these error messages, the status of the associated concept(s) in the student model is altered to reflect misunderstanding. The nature of the misunderstanding is a function of the pattern of errors diagnosed. Clearly, the more precise the error diagnostics, the more precise the representation of student understanding in the student model.

After the student model has been updated, the teaching rules are matched against the model and all matches are identified. The topmost teaching rule is used to decide what component of the knowledge network should be presented to the student next. The selection of exactly which rule to select is one of the thorny problems of developing an ICAI program. Unless the priority scheme is carefully specified, the tutoring effectiveness of the program will be poor. A great deal of tryout and "tuning" of these rules is necessary. At this stage, there seems to be little option but to do this by hand.

The completeness checker attempts to identify missing rules or information in the databases. For example, using the knowledge network, it would identify missing error rules and using the student model it could identify missing teaching rules. Note that the completeness checker is the key to making an ICAI program adaptive (i.e., self-modifying). The capability to detect "holes" in the knowledge network and error/teaching rules is the first step in developing a self-modifying program. With this capability, the program can help the author to add needed rules and concepts.

The Code Generator

Often classed as part of the lesson assembler, the code generator has the function of producing executable code from the assembled lesson. Essentially, the code generator consists of a set of translation rules written for a specific output language, such as LISP, Prolog, Pascal, or C. These rules translate the internal representation of the assembled lesson into code. In theory, a set of translation rules could be written for a number of languages and the author could specify the output language(s) desired for his or her ICAI program. The selection of which language to generate is an interesting problem, covering important questions such as ease of programming, efficiency of the final courseware, and availability of compilers. It has been well-discussed elsewhere (see Chapter 12) and will not be elaborated further here.

Our lesson assembler provides utility functions. It will translate the database specifications into executable Prolog code and include a course interpreter. We chose Prolog for two reasons. First, its operation was well suited to the particular problem we were using; and second, we had access to a good development system. The course interpreter provides the student-tutor interface of Fig. 13.1 and can be either a standard or debugging version so that the creator can step through his courseware. The lesson can be checked for completeness and consistency, although an exhaustive analysis of all possible states of the program is not performed. Finally, users can test their courseware within the system.

Properties of IAS Courseware

Within IAS an attempt has been made to highlight the instructional and learning goals for the creator of the courseware. This can be viewed as a first step toward the creation of the sort of intelligent user interface we described above. Additionally, it means that it is that much easier to switch strategies when another would be more effective.

The main learning strategy used in IAS is mastery learning. Users are deemed to have learned all the material in the lesson when they have mastered all the concepts. However, given the flexibility of the tutoring, this does not mean that they are forced to go through the course by rote.

There are two elements to the main teaching strategy. First, IAS courseware has a built-in bias toward the least-well-learned concept. Second, the initial organization and ordering of concepts is important to the efficacy of the courseware, and this is ultimately in the hands of the courseware creator. The strategy of the "least-well-learned concept" should overcome a poor ordering, but it is unlikely to overcome poor management of the values of the student model. Obviously, choosing another heuristic could be a generation option in future versions.

An ICAI program generated by IAS on the basis of these database objects works as follows. The tutor will look for the first topic containing concepts whose student understanding value is unsatisfied (for example, less than 10). If no such object can be found, that is, all the student understanding values have been satisfied, then the program will stop, on the assumption that the student has learned all the program has to teach, and give a concluding message to the student.

It is important to realize that the next topic to be presented to the student need not be the next in the ordered list of topics. Background knowledge will always be skipped until student responses trigger their action. Once a topic has been selected, all unsatisfied concepts are taught. The objects associated with the concept are first checked for presentability. That is, the object that is present-able and has been presented the least times is used. This notion of presentability is important as it ensures that no object is used before the student is ready to interact with it.

To determine if an object is presentable, the student model prerequisites are checked. If these do not match the current values of the student model, then the next-least-used object is tried. If none match the value of the model object, then the next concept is checked. If none of the concepts and, hence, the topics have presentable objects, the program cannot proceed and will exit with a statement of the state of the student model. Despite completeness checking by the lesson assembler, it is hoped that the database does not cause the program to get stuck in states from which it cannot proceed and eventually a presentable object will be found satisfying the student model prerequisites.

The remaining requisites will be textual or graphical and the program will attempt to present them as we have already described. The presentation of questions will elicit a response from the student that will then be matched against an answer object. Both the student model and the simulation state may be altered as a result. Once a correct match has been found, the loop continues to the next presentable object.

The strategy outlined above can be changed dynamically by the student through question-and-answer sequences. The student is free, at any point in the lesson, to pose questions to the tutor. After interpreting the question, the tutor will scan its knowledge base and generate a response. If the question was relevant to the current concept, the tutor will continue from where it was. However, it will permit digressions to other concepts by the student. In these cases, a number of options are possible. The tutor can handle the di-gression but return to its current concept if the student has digressed too much. It can change its teaching topic to reflect the new wishes of the user. Control on the amount of digression is another heuristic over which the au-thor has some control.

Properties of the User Questioning Mechanism

It is worth expanding on the way in which the student's responses are handled by the course interpreter. Prolog is a language well suited to manipulating language (Clocksin & Mellish, 1981), and considerable work has been done on the provision of natural language interpreters. A promising avenue is the defini-tive clause grammars (DFCs) described by Pereira and Warren (1981). In this approach, the inferencing and matching properties of Prolog are used to trans-late natural language into predicate logic. Indeed, Warren and Pereira (1981) have provided an intelligent database query interface capable of handling and optimizing complex inquiries.

We were interested primarily in the handling of English questions and imperatives. It was simple to extend the standard translation into predicate logic to handle the action rules and the verb *to be*. Given this translation, we initially reduced our concepts to predicate logic and matched the student's question to them. This was adequate but did mean that the student had to phrase a question in such a way that it would translate into exactly the same form as we used to create the concepts. We also had to write our own matcher.

To make more use of the inferencing facilities of Prolog and reduce the work that had to be done to answer questions, we decided to go fully into Prolog. That is, we decided to translate not only the student's question but also the concepts themselves into Prolog. We could then use Prolog to resolve the questions and generate the response. This necessitated adding a small indexing mechanism to control the Prolog search, but the resulting mechanism is far more resilient than it would be otherwise.

Obviously, we wish to improve the natural language comprehension to handle more complex and less specific input. The work on definite clause translation grammars (Abramson, 1984) looks promising in this respect. On this note, our current natural language interface is not used to generate question and text displays, since the author can, at this stage of development, produce them more efficiently by hand.

An Example of an ICAI

As a suitable example of an ICAI to try out the prototype IAS, teaching a French grammar rule was chosen. The rule, the agreement of the past participle with the preceding direct object, was chosen to provide a tractable teaching problem with sufficient complexity for the ICAI to behave in interesting ways.

The grammar rule, for those not proficient in French grammar, is as follows. The past participle of a verb conjugated with the auxiliary verb *avoir* agrees with the direct object in gender and number. Consider this example:

"Les personnes que tu as **rencontrées** travaillent avec moi."
(The people that you met work with me.)

The root form of the past participle, *rencontré,* has *es* appended to make it agree with the direct object *que,* which refers to the feminine plural noun *personnes.*

It can be seen that the understanding of several concepts such as auxiliary verb, direct object, and agreement in number and gender is prerequisite to learning the rule. In turn, these concepts may be decomposed to an understanding of direct object, complementary pronoun, agreement in number, agreement in gender, and so on.

With the IAS, this decomposition of the direct-object rule is implemented directly as a topic with associated concepts in the knowledge network. The prerequisite knowledge is implemented as topics and associated basic concepts.

The design of the courseware followed the principles of mastery learning. The initial state of the student model assumes an understanding of the intermediate topics and basic concepts. The inferencing provided by the teaching rules and the error/diagnostic rules updates the student model to reflect the student's actual understanding or misunderstanding in the course of execution. Thus it is not necessary to burden the student with extensive diagnostic pretests.

An example of a question probing the student's understanding of the direct-object rule is:

What is the correct form of the past participle in this sentence?

"Les durs efforts que nous avons (**fournir**) étaient vains."

(The equivalent sentence in English would be, "The great efforts that we have made were in vain.") In this case, the correct form of the past participle is *fournis*. The direct object, *que,* refers to the masculine plural *efforts* and precedes the verb, so the root form of the past participle *fourni* will be changed to *fournis* to agree with the gender and number of *efforts.*

The answer matching items implement the error/diagnostic rules. For example, if the student answered *fournies,* the feminine plural form of the past participle, it can be assumed that the student (1) mistook *efforts* for a feminine noun, (2) does not understand agreement with gender, (3) made an unfortunate slip, or (4) made a wild guess, in that order of likelihood. Student model values associated with the relevant concepts are decremented by an amount proportional to the likelihood of the error. Similarly, for correct answers associated student values are incremented.

After several questions and the application of the error/diagnostic rules associated with the answers given, the student model reflects the student's understanding or misunderstanding of the component concepts. The least-understood concept will fire questions that are appropriate to the student's learning requirements.

In the description above, the instruction is initiated by the tutor. It is also possible for the student to control the learning path. The concepts are encoded as English statements. Questions of the form "What is ... ?" are answered by matching the parsed query with the knowledge network. After a question response, a student is asked whether he or she would like to know more about the topic containing the concept matched. If the student says yes, a topic shift will occur—that is, the tutor will be recursively invoked for the given topic. The student may also force a topic shift by entering an imperative of the form "Tell me about ..." Once the concepts of the new topic have been fully explored, the lesson will resume where the topic shift was made—with, however, the updated student model reflecting the fact that the student now understands the concepts of the digression topic.

Coding the ICAI involved entering the components of an instructional design into a database of topics concepts, questions, displays, and answers. The lists of indices that associate concepts with topics, questions with concepts, and displays and answers with questions were added to the database. Finally, the results of the instructional analysis were encoded with the answers—incrementing, decrementing, or otherwise updating the student model values of the associated concepts. Testing indicated where fine tuning was required to improve the courseware.

The resulting courseware was highly adaptive. The student who knew the direct-object rule or apprehended the rule almost immediately could finish the lesson after only five or six questions. Students missing one or more prerequisite concepts had the opportunity to learn these before going on to mastering the direct-object rule. Students displaying serious gaps in understanding over basic concepts such as gender or the past tense could be routed to other lessons dealing with these topics. Finally, students could query the knowledge network and shift to several subtopics, establishing their own path to learning the direct-object rule.

A sample interaction with the French tutor is shown in Table 13.6. The student has already answered several questions, some correctly and some incorrectly. The tutor is making the inference that the student does not clearly understand how to make the past participle agree. The student's responses in Table 13.6 are typed in capital letters.

Conclusion

This chapter has discussed the design considerations for the creation of an intelligent authoring system (IAS). One of the observations about the use of an IAS relative to a conventional CAI authoring tool is that the effectiveness of the resulting ICAI lesson is much more dependent on the completeness of the teaching model as represented in the knowledge network, teaching rule, and error rule components. In particular, if the knowledge network is not sufficiently detailed, then the student model generated will not allow much precision in terms of representing student understanding. Also, if the teaching rules are not very elaborate or detailed, the resulting instruction is very simpleminded. In a conventional CAI program, only the fragments of a teaching model needed for specific branches is revealed; in an ICAI program, the entire model is required.

We had two reasons for attempting the implementation of an IAS: first, to examine the feasibility of its construction, and second, to see whether some generality existed in the formulation of different types of ICAI. We conclude that the construction of an IAS is indeed feasible and that we can use such a system to create ICAI programs. In particular, we have successfully generated a mixed-initiative tutor. The system consisted of three major components: database editors, a lesson assembler, and a course interpreter. The missing component is the user interface. Given the complexity of this interface, we

---

"Les personnes que tu as (**rencontrer**) travaillent avec moi."

What is the correct form of the past participle?   RENCONTRES

Not quite. "Les personnes" is feminine plural so we must add "es" to make the correct agreement, i.e., "**rencontrées**."

"Elles avaient fait des progres enormes."

In this sentence, does the Direct Object come before the past participle?   NO

That's right. There is no Direct Object in this sentence. Will we make an agreement on the past participle?   NO

That's correct.

"La pomme qui etait sur la table, Louise l'a-elle (**manger**)?"

Is there a CDO in this sentence?   YES

What is the gender and number of the noun to which it refers?
FEMININE SINGULAR

Right. What will we add to the past participle "**mangé**" to make the agreement?   E

So the correctly agreed form of the past participle in our example will be "**mangée**." What will be the correct form of the past participle in this sentence:

Les crayons que tu as (**acheter**) etaient de qualite.   ACHETES

Right. Let's try some other examples.

Table 13.6 Sample Student Interaction with the French Tutor

recommend that work on it be delayed until considerable experience has been accumulated in the ICAI authoring process and in the formulation of pedagogical strategy. In lieu of a user interface, the IAS would be better used by authors with ICAI experience.

Our research with the IAS prototype has shown that there are a number of important functions needed in an IAS. One of these is the capability to help the author keep track of the relationships between the different database objects. Another critical function is the capability to identify potential "holes" in the database that might cause the program to get stuck. A third essential function is the capability to identify additional error and teaching rules needed based on the current state of the student model.

The extent to which we have been able to answer the question of generality within ICAI programs is at best moot. Naturally, the user interface would play a key role in the selection of the best strategy and ICAI implementation to follow. However, the lesson assembler and discourse editor components seem to be general. The use of the discourse editor in splitting up courses into smaller lessons does seem a nontrivial step forward.

Many issues have not been addressed in this chapter. The importance of the hardware configuration and capabilities (e.g., memory and display characteristics) was assumed but not discussed. The relationship between an IAS and expert system builders, as between ICAI programs and expert systems, is an interesting area that has also not been discussed. Finally, the issue of how to select instructional problems that are best suited to ICAI programs was ignored. It is not clear that ICAI programs are applicable to all types of instructional domain. This question can be answered only in practice, by the creation of more ICAI programs, and by the examination of other intelligent authoring systems.

Acknowledgments

The authors wish to thank Greg Kearsley and Bret Wallach for their contributions to the design of the IAS prototype. Robert Jean Denault implemented the knowledge editor and gave much help in the provision of Prolog on the ICON.

References

Abramson, H. (1984, Feb.). Definite clause translation grammars. *Proc. Intl. Sym. on Logic Programming.* Atlantic City, NJ.

Barr, A., Beard, M., & Atkinson, R. C. (1976). The computer as a tutorial laboratory: The Stanford BIP project. *International Journal of Man-Machine Studies, 13,* 567–596.

Bork, A. (1985, Sept.). Computer based development of scientific reasoning. *Proc. COMPINT85.* Montreal.

Brown, J. S., Burton, R. R., & de Kleer, J. (1982). Pedagogical, natural language, and knowledge engineering techniques in SOPHIE I, II, and III. In D. Sleeman and J. S. Brown (Eds.), *Intelligent tutoring systems.* New York: Academic Press.

Burton, R. R., & Brown, J. S. (1979). An investigation of computer coaching for informal learning activities. *International Journal of Man-Machine Studies, 11,* 5–24.

Clocksin, W. F., & Mellish, C. S. (1981). *Programming in Prolog.* New York: Springer-Verlag.

Gentner, D. R. (1979). Toward an intelligent computer tutor. In H. O'Neil (Ed.), *Procedures for ISD.* New York: Academic Press.

Kearsley, G. (1982). Authoring systems in computer-based education. *Communications of the ACM, 25*(7), 429–437.

Kearsley, G. (1984). Authoring tools: An introduction. *Journal of Computer Based Instruction, 11*(3), 67.

Miller, M. L. (1979). A structured planning and debugging environment for elementary programming. *International Journal of Man-Machine Studies, 11,* 79–95.

NAPLPS (1983). *Videotex/teletext presentation level protocol syntax (North American PLPS).* Canadian Standards Association T500-1983, ANSI X3.110-1983.

O'Neil, H. F. (1979a). *Issues in instructional systems development.* New York: Academic Press.

O'Neil, H. F. (1979b). *Procedures for instructional systems development.* New York: Academic Press.

Pereira, F. C. N., & Warren, D. H. D. (1980). Definite clause grammars for language analysis—A survey of the formalism and a comparison with augmented transition networks. *Artificial Intelligence, 13,* 231–278.

Sleeman, D. (1984). *UMFE: A user modelling front end subsystem.* Heuristic Programming Project HPP-84-12, Department of Computer Science, Stanford University, Stanford, CA.

Sleeman, D., & Brown, J. S. (1982). *Intelligent tutoring systems.* New York: Academic Press.

Stevens, A. L., & Collins, A. (1980). Multiple conceptual models of a complex system. In R. E. Snow, P. Federico, & W. E. Montague (Eds.), *Aptitude, learning and instruction.* Hillsdale, NJ: Lawrence Erlbaum Associates.

Warren, D. H. D., & Pereira, F. C. N. (1981). *An efficient, easily adaptable system for interpreting natural language queries.* IJCAI-81, Vancouver.

Index